WIN-
01/16

Measuring National Well-being 2015

In replacement of 'Social Trends'

The data displayed in this document was correct at the time of downloading 12/01/16

Source: Office of National Statistics reproduced under the Open Government Licence V3.0

Measuring National Well-being 2015

CD containing supplementary articles and reference tables relating to:

Office for
National Statistics

Measuring National Well-being - An Analysis of Social Capital in the UK

Author Name(s): **Veronique Siegler, Office for National Statistics**

Abstract

This article provides a baseline analysis of social capital in the UK, using the latest available data. The data are based on 25 headline measures proposed by ONS, which cover four key aspects of social capital: personal relationships, social network support, civic engagement and trust and cooperative norms.

Introduction

This article gives a baseline assessment of social capital in the UK using the latest data available. The data are based on the draft headline measures proposed by ONS in July 2014, and further developed following user consultation (ONSb, November 2014). The 25 measures have been developed using a framework that covers four key aspects of social capital: personal relationships, social network support, civic engagement and trust and cooperative norms.

In general terms, social capital represents social connections and all the benefits they generate. Social capital is also associated with civic participation, civic-minded attitudes and values which are important for people to cooperate, such as tolerance or trust. "Social capital is the glue that holds societies together and without which there can be no economic growth or human well-being" (Grootaert, 1998). Without the social connections that link people to each other and lead them to exchange resources, without trust and other cooperative norms of behaviours, society could not function. The networks of individual relationships with family and friends, local community and through civic engagement, form the fabric of a cohesive society.

Recent government evidence, submitted by the Cabinet Office to the UK Parliament's Environmental Audit Committee as part of their inquiry on well-being, recognised that social capital is one of the three pillars of sustainable development to be considered together with natural capital and human capital. It highlighted the need for better evidence and further in-depth research to better understand social capital. The current ONS work, as part of the Measuring National Well-being Programme, is helping to build the evidence-base to better understand social capital, using data from existing sources.

ONS will continue to develop and refine its measures on social capital based on feedback from users and plan to carry out further analysis, in particular to highlight inequalities in social capital.

Key Points

- Around 1 in 10 people (11%) in the UK reported feeling lonely all, most, or more than half of the time in 2011/12.
- Just over a third of people in the UK reported that they wish they could spend more time with their family (36%) and have more social contacts (36%) in 2011/12.
- Nearly 1 in 5 people (19%) in the UK reported looking after or giving special help to someone sick, disabled or elderly inside their household (7%), outside their own household (10%) or both (1%) in 2012/13.
- Nearly a fifth (19%) of people in the UK had given unpaid help or worked as a volunteer in a local, national or international organisation or charity in the last 12 months in 2012/13.
- Half of people (49%) in the UK reported being very or quite interested in politics in 2012/13.
- Around two-thirds (65%) of people in the UK thought people in their neighbourhood could be trusted in 2011/12. Nearly three-quarters of people in the UK felt people in their neighbourhood get along with each other (72%) and are willing to help each other (71%) in 2011/12.

Personal relationships

Table 1: Headline measures for Personal Relationships

United Kingdom

Measure	Geographical coverage	Source	Latest year	Latest data
Proportion of people who have at least one close friend	United Kingdom	Understanding Society	2011/12	95%
Proportion of people who meet socially with friends, relatives or work colleagues at least once a week	United Kingdom	European Social Survey	2012/13	63%
Proportion of people who have felt lonely all, most or more than half of the time (over previous two weeks)	United Kingdom	Eurofound, European Quality of Life survey	2011/12	11%
Proportion of people who belong to a social network website	United Kingdom	Understanding Society	2011/12	46%
Average rating of satisfaction with family life	United Kingdom	Eurofound, European Quality of Life survey	2011/12	8.2 out of 10
Average rating of satisfaction with social life	United Kingdom	Eurofound, European Quality of Life survey	2011/12	7.1 out of 10
Proportion of people who regularly stop and talk with people in neighbourhood	United Kingdom	Understanding Society	2011/12	66%

Download table

This aspect of social capital aims to measure characteristics of personal relationships, such as the composition and the size of people's networks, or people's satisfaction with their relationships. The relationships an individual has with relatives and friends (described as 'strong ties' or 'bonding ties'), work colleagues or neighbours (described as 'weak ties' or 'bridging ties') are all important for personal well-being.

'People who have close friends and confidants, friendly neighbours and supportive co-workers are less likely to experience sadness, loneliness, low self-esteem and problems with eating and sleeping... Subjective well-being is best predicted by the breadth and depth of one's social connections' (Helliwell and Putnam, 2004).

Friends and relatives

One important aspect of personal relationships is the size of people's networks such as the number of close friends. Most people (95%) reported having at least one close friend, with a majority (68%) having between 2 and 6 close friends (Source: Understanding Society, 2011/12). The proportion of people reporting being dissatisfied with their life increases as the number of close friends decreases.
  A quarter (26%) of people with no close friends reported being mostly, somewhat or completely dissatisfied about their life compared to 21% of those having 1 close friend, 17% of those having 2-6 close friends and 14% of those having more than 10 close friends (Figure 1).

Figure 1: Overall life satisfaction by number of close friends, 2011/12

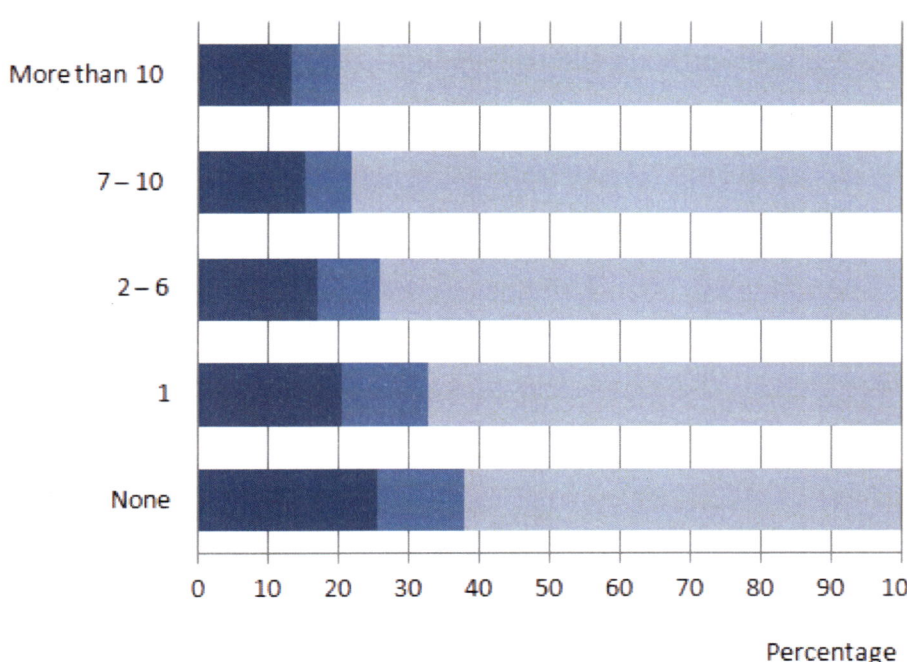

United Kingdom

- Completely, somewhat, mostly dissatisfied about life
- Neither satisfied, nor dissatisfied about life
- Somewhat, mostly or completely satisfied about life

Number of close friends

Percentage

Notes:

1.   Source: Understanding Society

Download chart

XLS XLS format
(26.5 Kb)

The frequency of contact with others has been highlighted as an important indicator of people's well-being (The Organisation for Economic Co-operation and Development (OECD), 2013b and 2011). Just over a third of people reported that they wish they could spend more time with their family (36%) and have more social contacts (36%) (Source: European Quality of Life Survey, 2011/12).

 A large majority reported being in touch (by visiting, telephoning or any other mode of contact) with their closest friend very regularly, either on most days (34%), or at least once a week (38%) (Source: Understanding Society, 2011/12).

According to the European Social Survey 2012/13, 63% of people met socially with friends, relatives or colleagues at least once a week, but 13% of people did so less than once a month or never. The main reasons for not going out socially or visiting friends were: the lack of time (as mentioned by 31% of those who did not go out socially), a health condition, illness or impairment or disability

(26%), financial reasons (19%) and caring responsibilities (18%), or no one to go with (9%) (Source: Understanding Society, 2011/12).

Loneliness

Social exclusion is a growing concern across Europe (Eurofound, 2012), with new policy measures required to tackle its causes and effects. Around 1 in 10 people (11%) reported feeling lonely all, most, or more than half of the time (Source: European Quality of Life Survey, 2011/12). There was a strong relationship between loneliness and other negative experiences, such as feeling left out of society, feeling that things done in life are not worthwhile and feeling a lack of recognition by others (Figure 2).

Among those reporting feeling lonely all of the time, nearly half (48%) also reported feeling left out of society, while 4 out of 10 (41%) reported feeling that what they do is not recognised by others and 3 out of 10 (32%) feeling things they do in their life are not worthwhile. In comparison, among those reporting never feeling lonely, 7% reported feeling left out of society, 17% feeling that what they do is not recognised by others and 5% feeling that what they do in their life is not worthwhile.

Figure 2: People's negative personal well-being by feeling of loneliness, 2011/12

United Kingdom

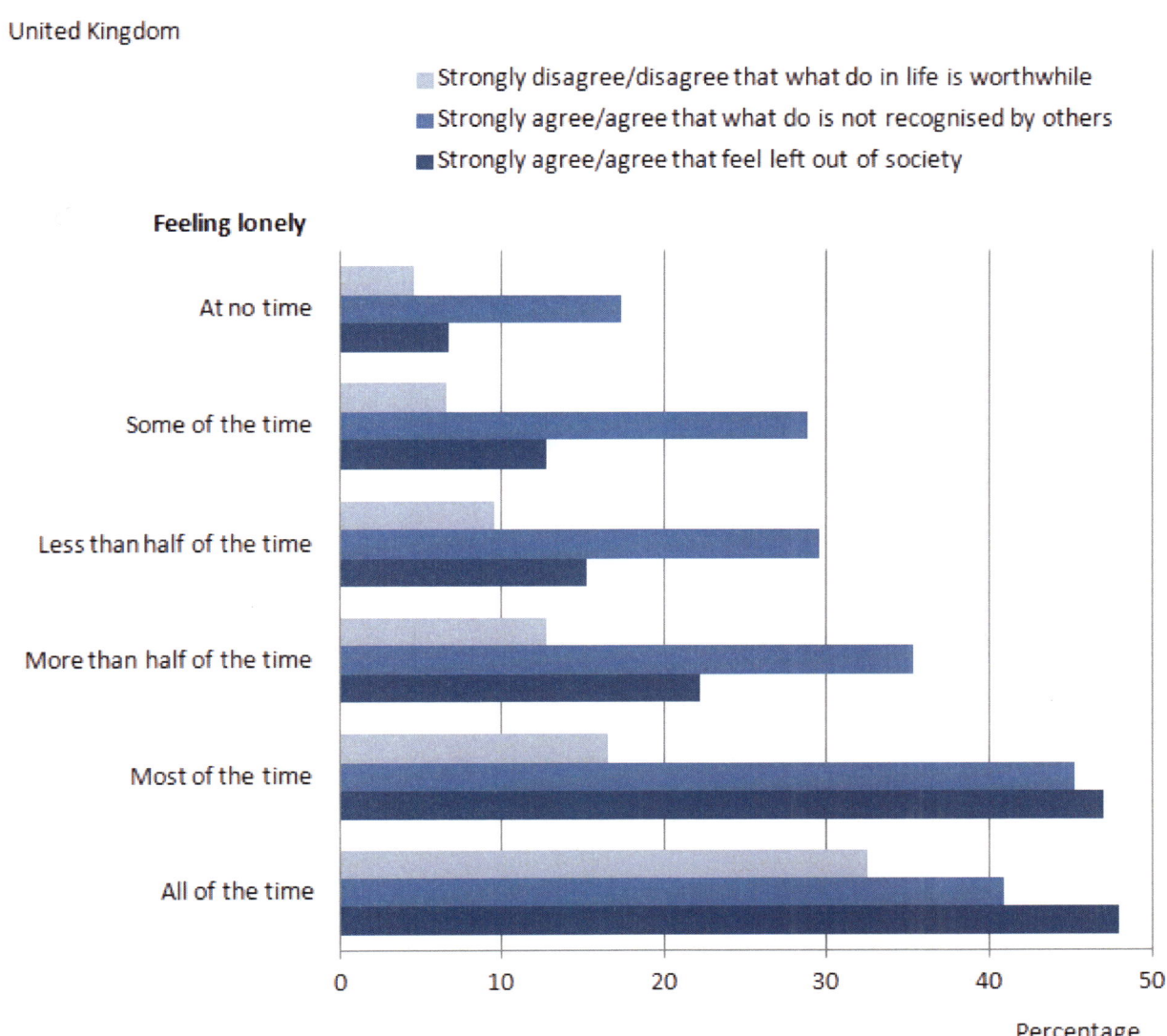

Notes:
1.   Source: European Quality of Life Survey

Download chart

XLS   XLS format
(26 Kb)

Social Networking

Belonging to a social network website could help build social capital, by maintaining links with family and friends and widening existing social networks. Half of people (46%) reported belonging to a social website (Source: Understanding Society, 2011/12). Among those who belonged to a social website, half of people (53%) spent less than an hour per day on week days interacting with friends through social websites, while a quarter (24%) spent between 1-3 hours per day interacting with friends through social websites on week days.

Quality of relationships

Subjective measures of satisfaction could reflect the quality of relationships an individual has with family and friends. Satisfaction with both family life and social life has been shown to have a positive correlation with life satisfaction and happiness (Eurofound, 2012). The average ratings for satisfaction with family life and social life (as published in the National Well-being Wheel of Measures) were 8.2 and 7.1, respectively, out of 10 (Source: European Quality of Life Survey, 2011/12). Figure 3 shows the distribution of ratings for satisfaction with family life and with social life. A higher proportion of people (53%) rated their satisfaction with family life as very high (rating of 9 or 10 out of 10), compared to their satisfaction with social life (30%). A higher proportion of people (15%) rated their satisfaction with their social life as low (rating of 1 to 4 out of 10), compared to their satisfaction with family life (6%).

Figure 3: Distribution of satisfaction with family life and satisfaction with social life ratings, 2011/12

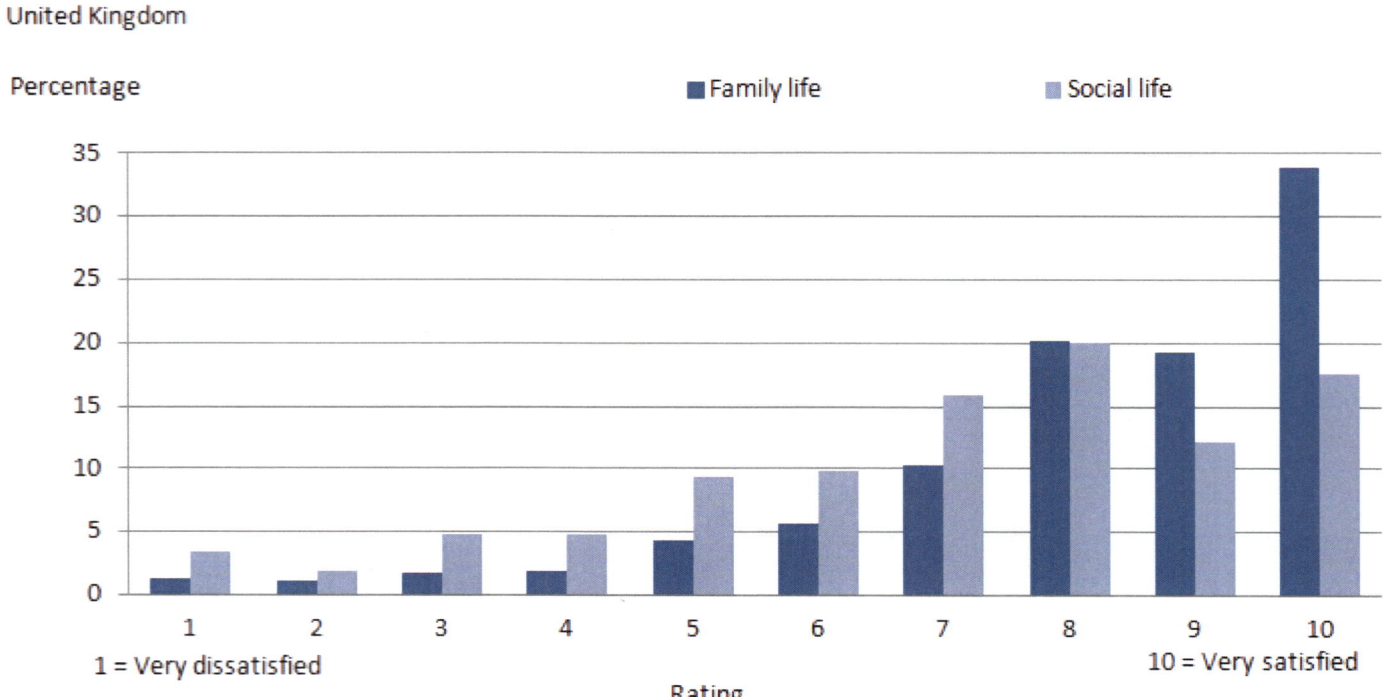

Notes:
1.   Source: European Quality of Life Survey

Download chart

 XLS format
(25.5 Kb)

Talking to neighbours

Around 2 out of 3 people (66%) reported that they regularly stop and talk with people in their neighbourhood (Source: Understanding Society, 2011/12). A large proportion (85%) of those for whom having a local friend is important, reported stopping and talking regularly with people in their neighbourhood. In comparison, only 24% of those for whom having local friends is not important reported stopping and talking regularly with people in their neighbourhood (Figure 4).

It has been highlighted before that for people to form interconnected social networks in their local area, residential stability is very important (Buke and Rabe, 2011). Data from Understanding Society 2011/12 suggest that most people (94%) liked their present neighbourhood and 67% of people planned to stay in their neighbourhood.

Figure 4: Talk regularly with people in neighbourhood by local friends mean a lot, 2011/12

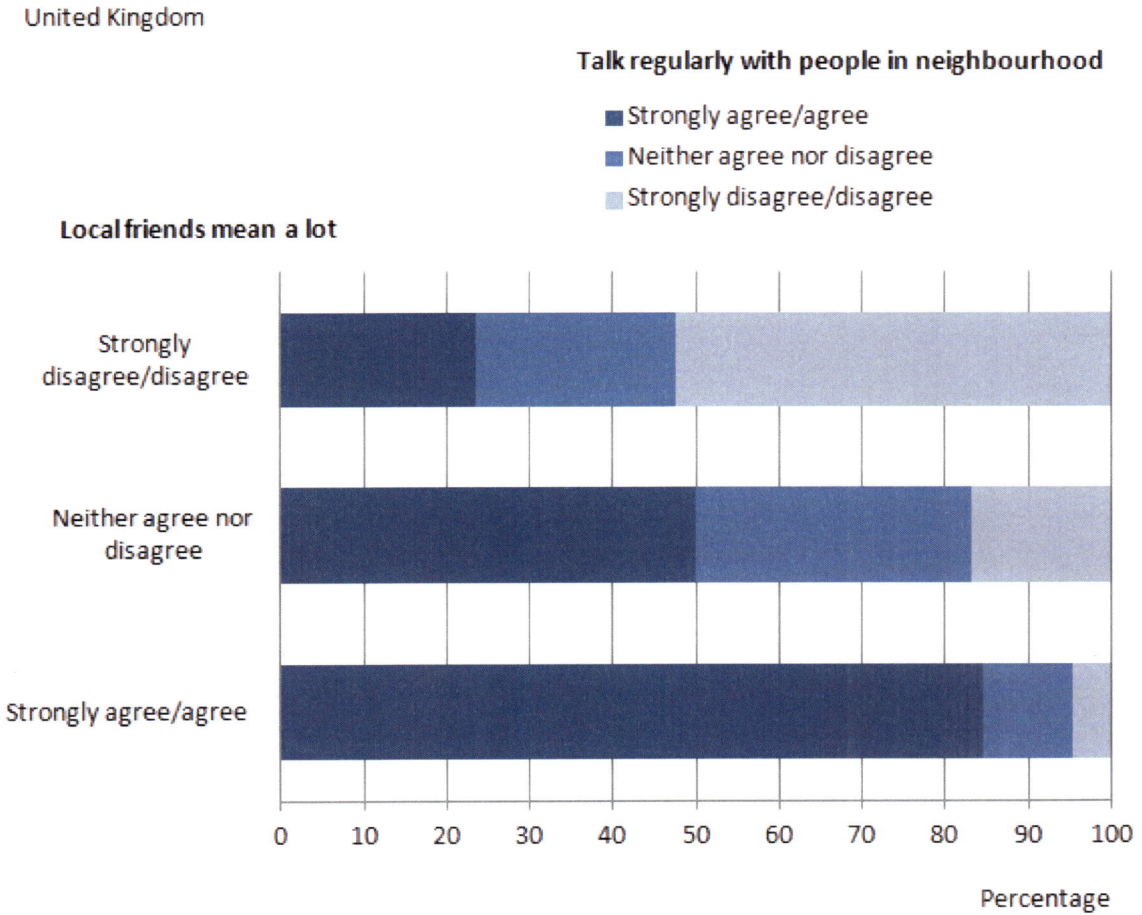

Notes:

1.   Source: Understanding Society

Download chart

XLS XLS format
(26.5 Kb)

Social Network Support

Table 2: Headline measures for Social Network Support

United Kingdom

Measure	Geographical coverage	Source	Latest year	Latest data
Proportion of people who have a spouse, family member or friend to rely on if they have a serious problem	United Kingdom	Understanding Society	2010/11	87%
Proportion of people who give special help to at least one sick, disabled or elderly person living or not living with them	United Kingdom	Understanding Society	2012/13	19%
Proportion of parents who regularly receive or give practical or financial help from/to a child aged 16 or over not living with them	United Kingdom	Understanding Society	2011/12	Receive:42% Give: 63%
Proportion of people who borrow things and exchange favours with their neighbours	United Kingdom	Understanding Society	2011/12	41%

Download table

XLS XLS format
(26.5 Kb)

Social network support is both about the perceived and the actual support that people give to and receive from others. Support can be derived from many different sources, such as family, friends and neighbours (but also more formally, from organisations). A strong support network can reflect the extent to which an individual has strong ties within his own social network of family, friends, and neighbours. There are different types of social support an individual can give or receive, such as emotional support, practical or financial support, but also advice or guidance.

Social support has been shown to be associated with better physical health (Uchino, 2009 and Uchino, 2004). People with higher social support have a lower risk of death (Uchino, 2004) and an increased likelihood of survival (Holt-Lunstad et al., 2010). Social support is also associated with better mental health (Taylor, 2011). People with higher social support cope better with stressful times and are less likely to suffer from anxiety or depression (Taylor, 2011). The support provided by family, friends or neighbours has also an important economic value (ONS, 2013a; Understanding Society Insights, 2014).

Someone to rely on

Family and friends are important because of the support they can provide, either in times of need (because of a serious problem occurring), or on a more regular basis. It has been shown that perceived support is consistently linked to better mental health, independently from the actual support received (Uchino, 2009).

Most people (87%) reported feeling being able to rely a little, somewhat or a lot on their partner, family or friends in case of a serious problem (Source: Understanding Society, 2010/11). People reported being able to rely a lot on their partner (83%) and on their family (62%), but less than half of people (45%) felt they could also rely a lot on their friends (Figure 5).

Figure 5: People's feeling of being able to rely on their partner, family or friends in case of a serious problem, 2010/11

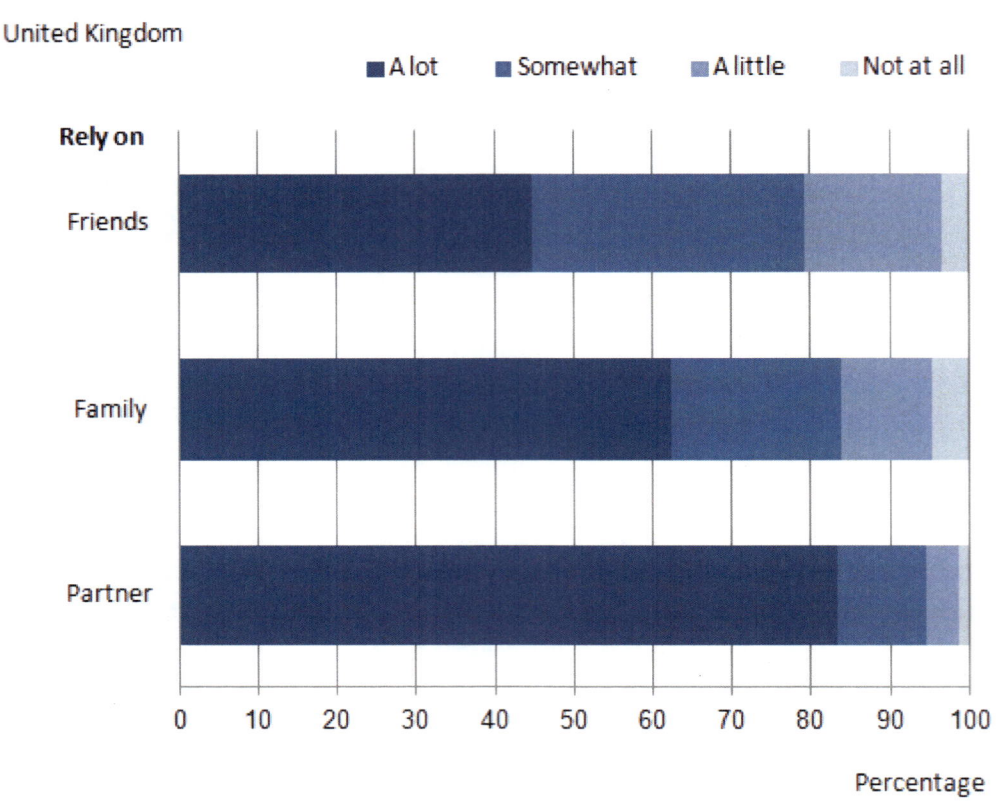

Notes:

1. Source: Understanding Society

Download chart

XLS XLS format
(27 Kb)

Caring and family support

The UK care system is currently heavily dependent on the informal care provided by family and friends (Pickard, 2013), particularly in the context of an ageing population.

Nearly 1 in 5 people (19%) reported looking after, or giving special help, to someone sick, disabled or elderly inside their household (7%), outside their own household (10%) or both (1%). (Source: Understanding Society, 2012/13). Around 7 in 10 carers spent up to 19 hours a week caring, 1 out of 10 carers between 20 and 99 hours, and 1 out of 10 carers reported giving continuous care (100 hours or more per week) (Table 3).

Among those giving help to people outside their household, 3 out of 4 people (76%) gave help to one person only, usually a relative (78%), a friend or neighbour (19 %) or someone else through voluntary organisations and others (3%).

Table 3: Number of hours per week spent by informal carers (providing help to someone sick, disabled or elderly), 2012/13

United Kingdom

Percentage

Number of hours per week	Informal carers
0 – 4	38
5 – 9	19
10 – 19	13
20 – 34	7
35 – 49	3
50 – 99	2
More hours per week/continuous care	9
Variable number of hours per week	9

Table notes:
1. Source: Understanding Society

Download table

 XLS format
(26 Kb)

The different generations within a family can support each other by exchanging regular practical and/or financial help. This can be especially important in difficult economic times; it has been shown that the number of grandparent childcare hours have risen by nearly 35% between the recession years 2009-10 and 2010-11, for example (Understanding Society Insights, 2014).

Table 4 shows that a third of parents (32%) who had children over 16 living outside the household reported exchanging help (both giving and receiving help) with at least one of their children (Source: Understanding Society, 2011/12). Parents were more likely to give help to their children than receive help (63 % compared to 42%).

Table 4: Proportion of parents reporting giving help to at least one of their children and/ or receiving help from at least one of their children over 16 living outside the household, 2011/12

United Kingdom

Percentage

		Parents receiving help from at least one of their children[1]		Total
		YES	NONE	
Parents **giving help** to at least one of their children[1]	YES	32	31	63
	NONE	10	27	37
Total		42	58	100

Table notes:

1. Children over 16 living outside the household
2. Source: Understanding Society

Download table

 XLS format
(27 Kb)

Table 5 gives details of the type of help given and received by parents. The most common type of help given to children was financial help (as reported by 31%) and looking after grand children (31%). It has been previously reported that 63% of all grandparents with a grandchild under 16 look after their grandchildren (Understanding Society Insights, 2014).

The most common type of help received from children was giving lifts in cars (24%) and shopping for them (19%) (Table 5). As many parents reported receiving help than giving help with decorating, gardening or house repairs (13%).

Table 5: Most common types of help parents receive from or give to children over 16, living outside the household, 2011/12

United Kingdom

Help received from children [1]			Help given to children [1]		
Rank	**Type**	**Percentage**	**Rank**	**Type**	**Percentage**
1	Lifts in your car	24	1	Financial help	31
2	Shopping for them	19	2	Looking after grand-children	31
3	Providing/ cooking meals	14	3	Providing/ cooking meals	20
4	Decorating, gardening or house repairs	13	4	Lifts in your car	19
5	Dealing with personal affairs (eg. paying bills, writing letter)	6	5	Shopping for them	14

Table notes:
1. Children over 16 living outside the household
2. Source: Understanding Society

Download table

XLS XLS format
(28 Kb)

Support from neighbours

Aside from family and friends, neighbours can provide support, by looking after the house while away on holidays or lending things, for example. Around 4 out of 10 people (41%) strongly agreed or agreed that they borrow things and exchange favours with their neighbours (Source: Understanding Society, 2011/12). People were more likely to borrow things and exchange favours with their neighbours if they also reported regularly stopping and talking to their neighbours.

Half of those (52%) who reported regularly stopping and talking to their neighbours also borrowed things and exchanged favours with their neighbours. In comparison, only 1 in 10 people (12%) of those who did not regularly stop and talk with neighbours borrowed things and exchanged favours with their neighbours (Figure 6).

Figure 6: Borrow things and exchange favours with neighbours by talk regularly with people in neighbourhood, 2011/12

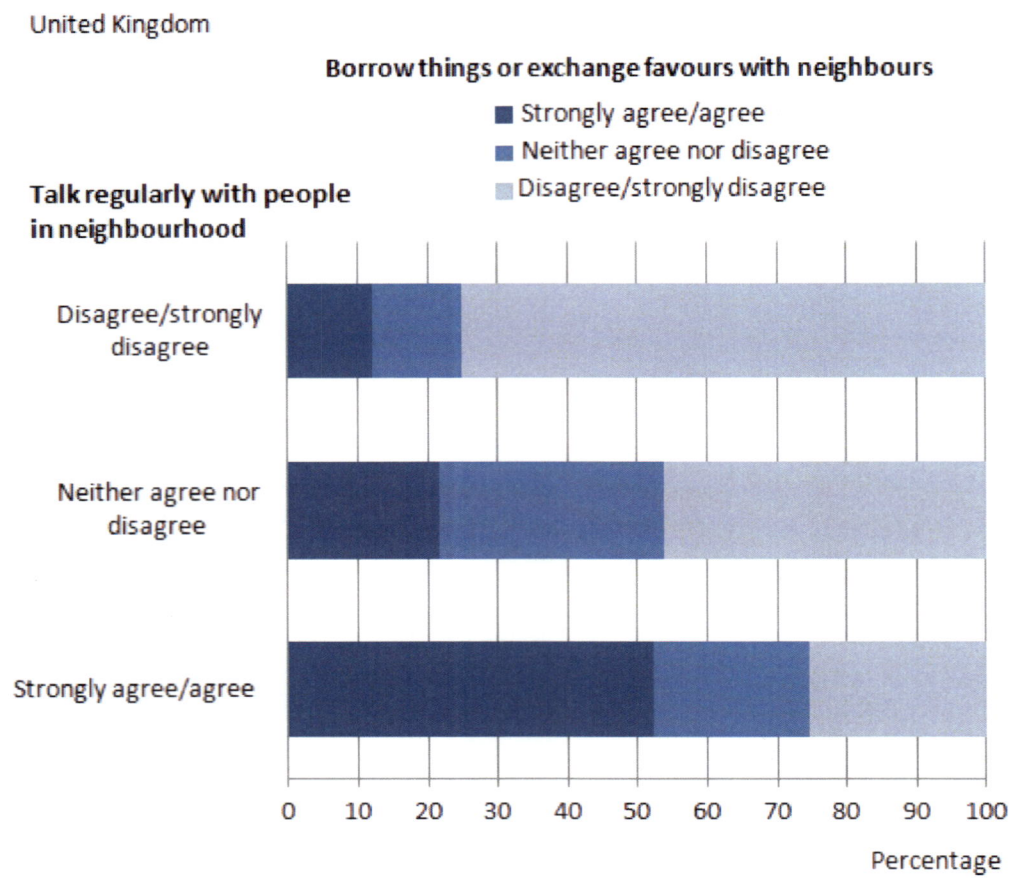

United Kingdom

Borrow things or exchange favours with neighbours
■ Strongly agree/agree
■ Neither agree nor disagree
■ Disagree/strongly disagree

Talk regularly with people in neighbourhood

Percentage

Notes:

1.   Source: Understanding Society

Download chart

XLS XLS format
(26.5 Kb)

Civic Engagement

Table 6: Headline measures for civic engagement

Measure	Geographical coverage	Source	Latest year	Latest data
Proportion of people who volunteered in the last 12 months	United Kingdom	Understanding Society	2012/13	19%
Proportion of people who are members of organisations, whether political, voluntary, professional or recreational	United Kingdom	Understanding Society	2011/12	52%
Proportion of people who have been involved in at least one social action project in their local area in the previous 12 months	England	Community Life Survey	2013/14	18%
Proportion of people who definitely agree or tend to agree that they can influence decisions affecting their local area	England	Community Life Survey	2013/14	34%
Proportion of people who voted in the UK General Elections	England	The International Institute for Democracy and Electoral Assistance	2010	61%
Proportion of people who have been involved in at least one political action in	United Kingdom	Eurofound, European Quality of Life Survey	2011/12	34%

Measure	Geographical coverage	Source	Latest year	Latest data
the previous 12 months				
Proportion of people who are very or quite interested in politics	United Kingdom	European Social Survey	2012/13	49%

Download table

XLS XLS format
(27.5 Kb)

Civic engagement refers to "the actions and behaviours that can be seen as contributing positively to the collective life of a community or society" (Organisation for Economic Co-operation and Development (OECD), 2013a). Civic engagement includes activities such as volunteering, political participation and other forms of community actions. Such activities are important for democratic and cohesive societies, and also have an important role in preventing social exclusion (Eurofound, 2012).

It has been suggested that high levels of civic engagement encourage more efficient and less corrupt public governance institutions (Putnam, 1993) and help individuals to develop their skills and social values (Putnam, 1993). As reported by the OECD (2011), 'civically engaged people tend to be happier (Morrow-Howell et al., 2003), report better health status (Borgovoni, 2008) and have a greater sense of purpose in life (Greenfield and Marks, 2004)'.

The data provided in this article gives more detail about the types and levels of civic engagement in the UK.

Volunteering

This aspect of social capital has been set out as a government priority by the Giving Green and White papers (Cabinet Office, 2011). Volunteering is important for personal well-being and benefits the society as a whole, by improving the lives of others, the community or the environment. Volunteering is an opportunity for people with very different backgrounds to work together. Volunteering is also important for the economy: the value of voluntary activity in the UK for 2012 has been estimated to be £23.9 billion, approximately 1.5% of GDP (ONS, 2013b).

In 2012/13, around one in five (19%) of people had given unpaid help or worked as a volunteer in a local, national or international organisation or charity in the last 12 months (Source: Understanding Society, 2012/13). This compares to 17% of people who reported volunteering in 2010/11.

Half (49%) of the volunteers reported doing something to help local, national or international organisations or charities at least once a week or more.

Around two-thirds (67%) of all people reported having donated money to charities or other organisations in the last 12 months (Source: Understanding Society, 2012/13). Half of those donating money to charities or other organisations (52%) did so at least monthly.

Membership of organisations

Organisations (whether political, voluntary, professional or recreational) are the social fabric that can create bonds between people who have common interests (for example, sport) and bring together people who have very different backgrounds. They play a very important role for democracy.

Half of people (52%) reported being members of organisations among those listed in Table 7 (Source: Understanding Society, 2011/12). Sports clubs were most popular (33%) followed by religious groups or church organisation, trade unions and professional organisations (all 21%). Only 4% of people reported being members of a political party.

Table 7: Proportion of people who are members of organisations by type of organisations (political, voluntary, professional or recreational), 2011/12

United Kingdom

Percentage

Organisations	Members
Sports club	33
Religious group or church organisation	21
Trade Unions	21
Professional organisation	21
Other	17
Social club/working men's club	12
Voluntary services group	11
Tenants/residents group or neighbourhood watch	8
Other community or civic group	6
Parents/school association	5
Environmental group	5
Pensioners group/organisation	4
Political party	4
Women's institute/townswomen guild	2
Women's group/feminist organisation	2

Table notes:
1. Source: Understanding Society

Download table

XLS XLS format
(27 Kb)

Social action and community engagement

The Community Life Survey Statistical Bulletin 2013-14 (Cabinet Office, 2014) describes social action as "people getting together to cover a community project in their local area", such as:

- Trying to set up a new service or amenity to help local residents
- Trying to stop the closure of local service or amenity
- Trying to stop something happening in the local area
- Running local services on a voluntary basis (e.g. childcare, youth services, parks and community centres)
- Organising a community event such as a street party.

Just under a fifth of people (18%) were involved in at least one social action project in their local area in England in 2013/14. This was a significant decrease compared to 2012/13, where 23% of people were involved in at least one social action project in their local area (Cabinet Office, 2014).

If individuals within a local area feel they can influence decisions in their local area, local community empowerment is more likely. This is where community empowerment refers to the process of local communities taking ownership and action for shaping the services and the environment in the area where they live.

In 2013/14, 34% of people felt they could influence decisions affecting their local area in England (Source: Community Life Survey). This is a significant decrease compared to all years since 2011 (Cabinet Office, 2014).

Political engagement

The proportion of people voting in UK General Elections as a proportion of those registered to vote, represents an important indicator of the vitality of a democracy and the degree of civic engagement. Voter turnout is part of the National Well-being Wheel of measures. 61% of people voted in the UK General Elections 2010 compared to 58% in 2005.

Around one-third of people (34%) reported having been involved in at least one political action in the previous 12 months (Source: European Quality of Life Survey, 2011/12). The most common type of political action, in which people got involved, was signing a petition, including an email or an online petition (29%), and contacting a politician or public official, other than routine contact, arising from use of public services (11%) (Table 8).

According to the European Social Survey 2012/13, 19% of people also reported having boycotted certain products in the previous 12 months. The boycott for political, ethical or environmental reasons is regularly characterised as an example of new political engagement (Yates, 2011).

Table 8: Proportion of people who have been involved in at least one political action in the previous 12 months, by type of political action, 2011/12

United Kingdom

	Percentage
Type of political action	
Attended a meeting of a trade union, a political party or a political action	7
Attended a protest or demonstration	4
Signed a petition, including an email or an online petition	29
Contacted a politician or public official (other than routine contact arising from use of public services)	11
Any of above	34

Table notes:
1.   Source: European Quality of Life Survey

Download table

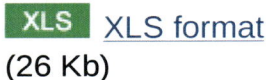 XLS format
(26 Kb)

Interest in politics is a subjective measure, which indicates how much people are engaged with the democratic system. Half of people (49%) reported being very or quite interested in politics, while a quarter (23%) reported not being interested at all (Source: European Social Survey, 2012/13).

There is a weak relationship between interest in politics and trust in politicians. Among those who rated their trust in politicians as low (ratings 0 to 4 out of 10), 46% were very or quite interested in politics. For those who rated their trust in politicians as medium (ratings 5 and 6 out of 10), 56% were very or quite interested in politics and for those who rated their trust in politicians as high or very high (ratings 7 to 10 out of 10), 57% were very or quite interested in politics (Source: European Social Survey, 2012/13).

However, there was a strong relationship between interest in politics and voting in the last national elections (Figure 7). 88% of those who said they were very interested in politics also reported voting in the last national elections, compared to only 43% of those who said they were not at all interested by politics (Source: European Social Survey, 2012/13).

Figure 7: Voted in last national elections by interested in politics, 2012/13

United Kingdom

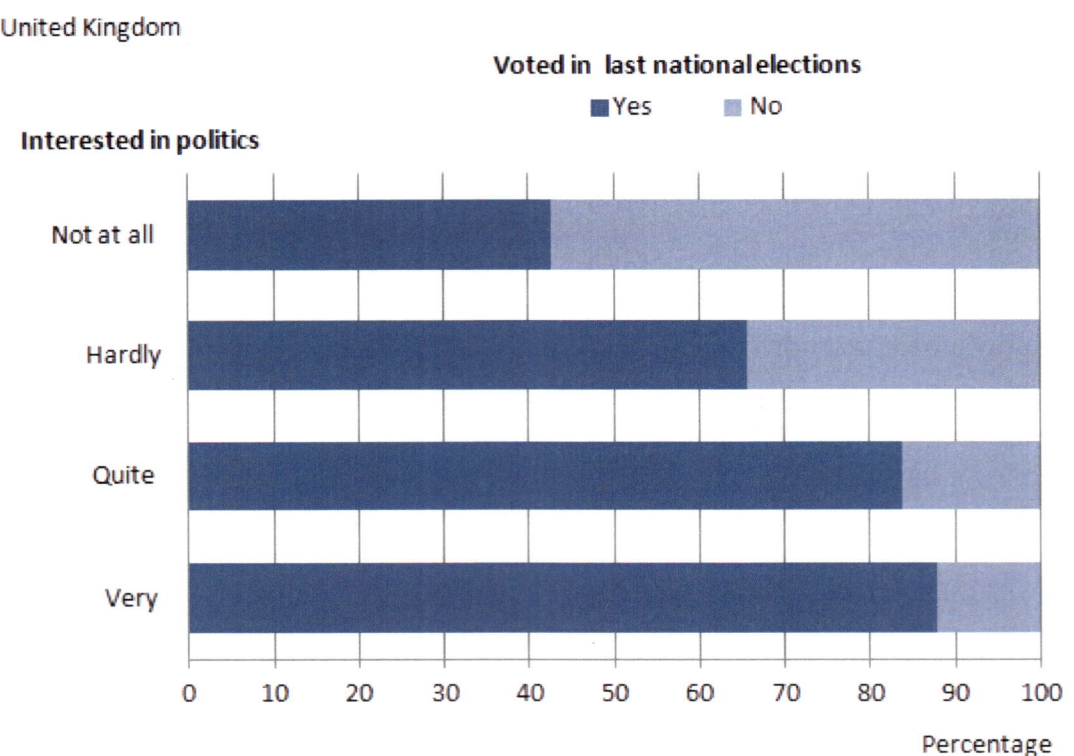

Notes:

1.   Source: European Social Survey

Download chart

XLS   XLS format
(26.5 Kb)

Trust and Cooperative Norms

Table 9: Headline measures for Trust and Cooperative Norms

Measure	Geographical coverage	Source	Latest year	Latest data
Proportion of people who have trust in national government	United Kingdom	Eurobarometer	November 2014	31%
Proportion of people who would say that most people can be trusted	United Kingdom	Understanding Society	2009/10	35%
Proportion of people who would say that most people in their neighbourhood can be trusted	United Kingdom	Understanding Society	2011/12	65%
Proportion of people who definitely agree or tend to agree that their local area is a place where people from different backgrounds get on well together	England	Community Life Survey	2013/14	85%
Proportion of people who feel very or fairly walking alone at night in their local area	England and Wales	The Crime Survey for England and Wales (CSEW)	2013/14	M:85% F: 58%
Proportion of people who agree or strongly agree that people around whether they	United Kingdom	Understanding Society	2011/12	71%

Measure	Geographical coverage	Source	Latest year	Latest data
live are willing to help their neighbours				
Proportion of people who agree or strongly agree that they feel they belong to their local area	United Kingdom	Understanding Society	2011/12	63%

Download table

XLS XLS format
(28 Kb)

This aspect of social capital encompasses trust and cooperative norms, such as willingness to help each other, reciprocity, tolerance or respect. It has been shown that people living in places characterised by higher levels of institutional trust or trust in others have higher levels of personal well-being (Hudson, 2006; Helliwell and Putnam, 2004).

Trust and other cooperative norms are important for the functioning of the society at all levels. Trust in national government and trust in other institutions are key to credible, healthy governance and to the effective running of a country. Trust is fundamental to any economy involving transactions, in particular in a globalised world where transactions occur within a range of different countries with different institutions and cultures.

Trust in Government

Only a third (31%) people reported that they "tended to trust" national government in November 2014 (Eurobarometer).This compares to 24% of people who "tended to trust national government" in November 2013. There is a concern in the UK and across Europe that trust in politicians and governments has been declining since 2002, as reported by several international surveys (ONS, 2014c; NatCen report, 2013; Organisation for Economic Co-operation and Development (OECD) report, 2013c).

 With a low trust in national government, effective public policies and regulations might be more difficult to implement, consumers and businesses might be more reluctant to invest and take risks, and economic activities might slow down. The OECD has proposed a framework of 6 areas for government to win back trust. A report ('Stemming the trend of declining trust') published by Eurofound in 2014 suggested that key determinants in trust in institutions are:

- people's levels of satisfaction with the quality of public services
- how people perceive the economic situation in their country
- a perceived absence of corruption in public life.

Figure 8 shows that the proportion of people who rated their trust in government as low (ratings 1-4 out of 10) was higher among those who were dissatisfied (ratings 1-4 out of 10) with their standard of living (74%) and the economic situation of the country (63%). Only 1 in 10 (9%) of those who were dissatisfied with their standard of living and 14% of those who were dissatisfied with the economic situation of the country rated their trust in national government as high (ratings 7-10 out of 10).

However, 34% of those who were satisfied (ratings 7-10 out of 10) with the economic situation and 46% of those who were satisfied with their standard of living rated their trust in national government as low (ratings 1-4 out of 10).

Figure 8: Trust in national government by satisfaction with standard of living and economic situation, 2011/12

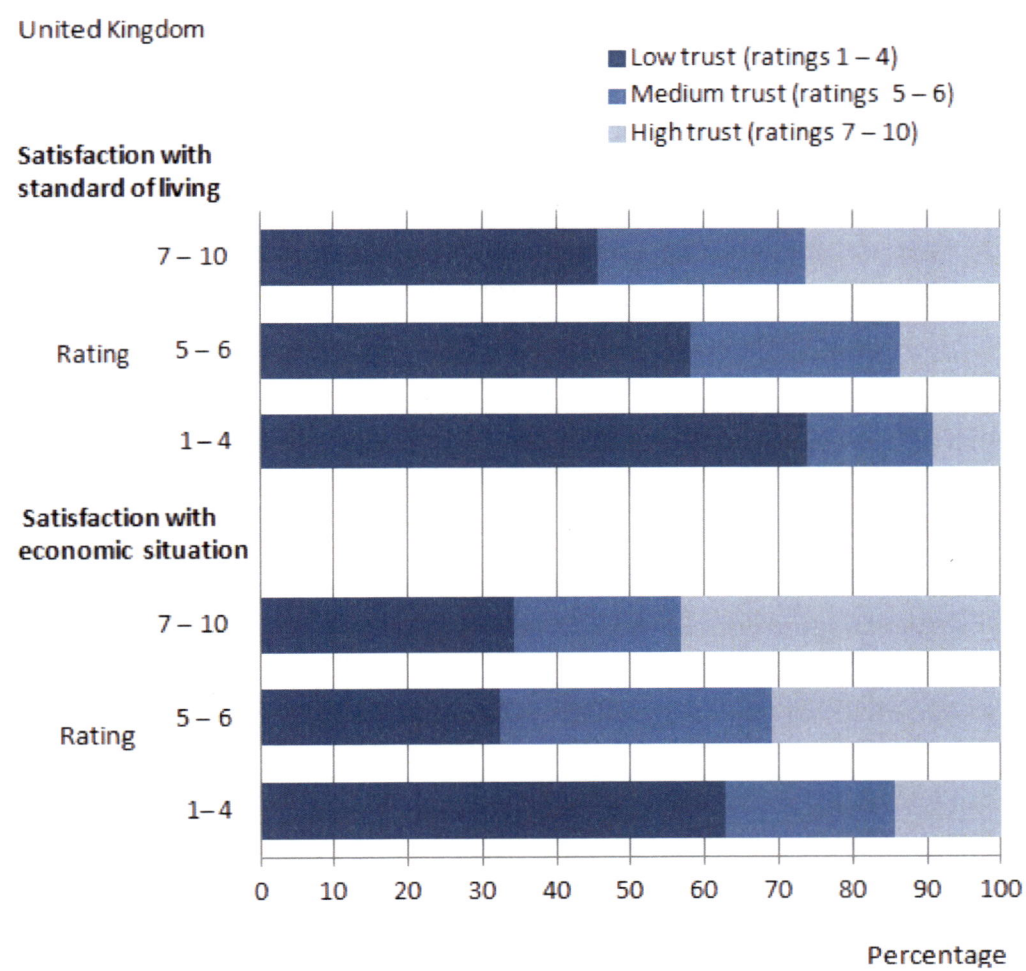

Notes:

1. Respondents are asked to give their answers on satisfaction on a scale of 1 to 10, where 1 is 'very dissatisfied' and 10 is 'very satisfied'. Respondents are asked to give their answers on trust on a scale of 1 to 10, where 1 is 'do not trust at all' and 10 is 'trust completely'.
2. Source: European Quality of Life Survey

Download chart

XLS XLS format
(28.5 Kb)

Trust in people

Generalised trust refers to trust in all other people, including strangers. It usually reflects people's perception of how much others share values and norms of behaviour or are reliable. If people trust each other, they are more likely to interact and to cooperate with each other.

Trust in others, for example in their personal commitment, their knowledge and their integrity, play a fundamental role in the workplace when people have to work together to complete projects or provide services. Trust in others increases the capacity for collective action, for example, through voluntary organisations in the community. At an individual level, trust in others is important to build strong, lasting and supportive relationships.

Research has also shown that people who trust others also have the highest levels of confidence in public institutions, such as the police, the legal system, parliament and politicians (ESS findings).

Just over a third (35%) of people reported that they would say that most people can be trusted (Source: Understanding Society, 2009/10). Around 4 in 10 people (42%) reported that they would say "you can't be too careful" and another 23 % reported that "it depends".

Data from the European Social Survey (2012/13) shows that the proportion of people who rated as high or very high (7 or more out of 10), on a scale of 0 to 10, was: 34% for trust in others, 38% for thinking that most people try to be helpful and 40% for thinking that most people try to be fair.

Neighbourhood

At a neighbourhood level, trust is important for people to live together harmoniously in local communities. People can have different backgrounds in terms of age, sex, socio-economic group, ethnicity, nationality or beliefs. If people of different backgrounds get on well together in a local area, one can reasonably assume more social contact between people of different backgrounds in the local area, and some shared social values of trust, tolerance and respect within the community.

Around 65% of people felt people in their neighbourhood can be trusted (Source: Understanding Society, 2011/12). A majority of people (85%) in England also thought that their local area is a place where people from different backgrounds get on well together (Source: Community Life Survey, 2013/14). Nearly three-quarters (72%) of people in the UK felt that people in their neighbourhood get along with each other (Source: Understanding Society, 2011/12). Around 7 in 10 people (71%) reported strongly agreeing or agreeing that people in their local area are willing to help their neighbours (Source: Understanding Society, 2011/12).

Measures of regularly stopping and talking to neighbours and trust in others in the local area were related. Three quarters (74 %) of those who regularly stopped and talked to neighbours reported trusting others in their local area, compared to 39% of those who did not regularly stop and talk to neighbours.

Measures of whether people are getting on well with others in local area were related to both trust in others in the local area and the feeling that people are willing to help their neighbours.

Data from Understanding Society, 2012/13 suggest that among those feeling that people in their neighbourhood get along with each other, three-quarters (77%) reported trusting others in their local area, and only 3% not trusting others in their local area. On the other hand, among those who reported feeling that people in their neighbourhood do not get along with each other, 42% did not trust others in their local area (Figure 9).

Similarly, among those feeling that people in their neighbourhood get along with each other, 8 out of 10 (82%) reported that people in their local area were willing to help their neighbours. Among those who reported feeling that people in their neighbourhood did not get along with other, only 4 people out of 10 (42%) reported that people in their local area were willing help their neighbours.

Figure 9: Feeling that people in this neighbourhood can be trusted by feeling people in this neighbourhood do not get along with each other, 2011/12

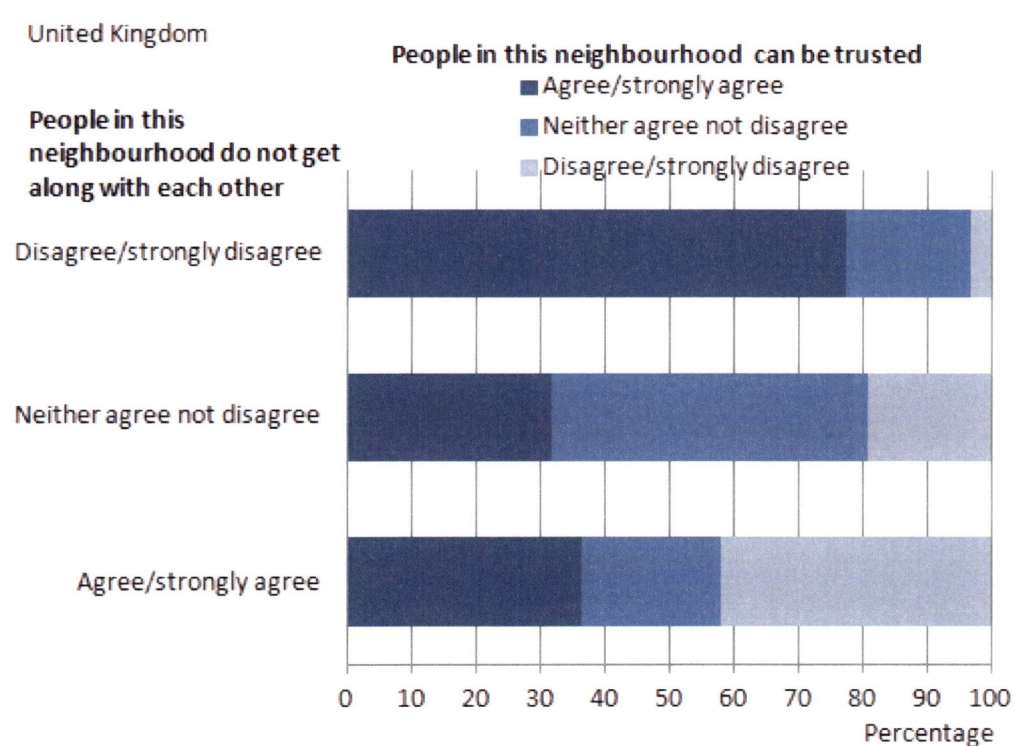

Notes:

1. Source: Understanding Society

Download chart

XLS XLS format
(26.5 Kb)

Feeling safe walking alone after dark and fear of crime can be very important factors in determining people's quality of life. The perception of safety is not necessarily directly correlated to crime rates.

According to the Crime Survey for England and Wales 2013/14, 85% of men and 58% of women felt very or fairly safe walking alone in their local area after dark.

Feeling safe walking alone after dark and fear of crime are both linked to trust. Previous analyses, using European Social Survey data (2010/11), have shown that people who reported that fear of crime reduces their quality of have life, also had less trust in the police, and were less likely to think that the police are doing a good job.

Data from Understanding Society 2011/12 (Figure 10) suggest that people (in particular women) reporting trusting others in their local area were more likely to feel very or fairly safe walking alone after dark in their local area, than those who did not. Around 7 out of 10 women (68%) who reported trusting others in their local area also felt very or fairly safe walking alone in their local area after dark, compared to 4 out of 10 women (40%) who reported not trusting others in their local area.

However, 40% of women and 71% of men who reported not trusting others in their local area nevertheless felt very or fairly safe walking alone in their local area. Similarly, 46% of women who felt that people in their local area did not get on reported feeling very or fairly safe walking alone after dark in their local area (Source: Understanding Society, 2011/12). Similar trends can be observed for the measure on feeling that the local area is a close-knit community; these findings suggest that although trust in others, feelings that people get on in their local area and forming a close-knit community are important, they are not enough to explain why people feel safe walking alone in their local area after dark.

Figure 10: Feeling safe walking alone at night in local area by people in this neighbourhood can be trusted, 2011/12

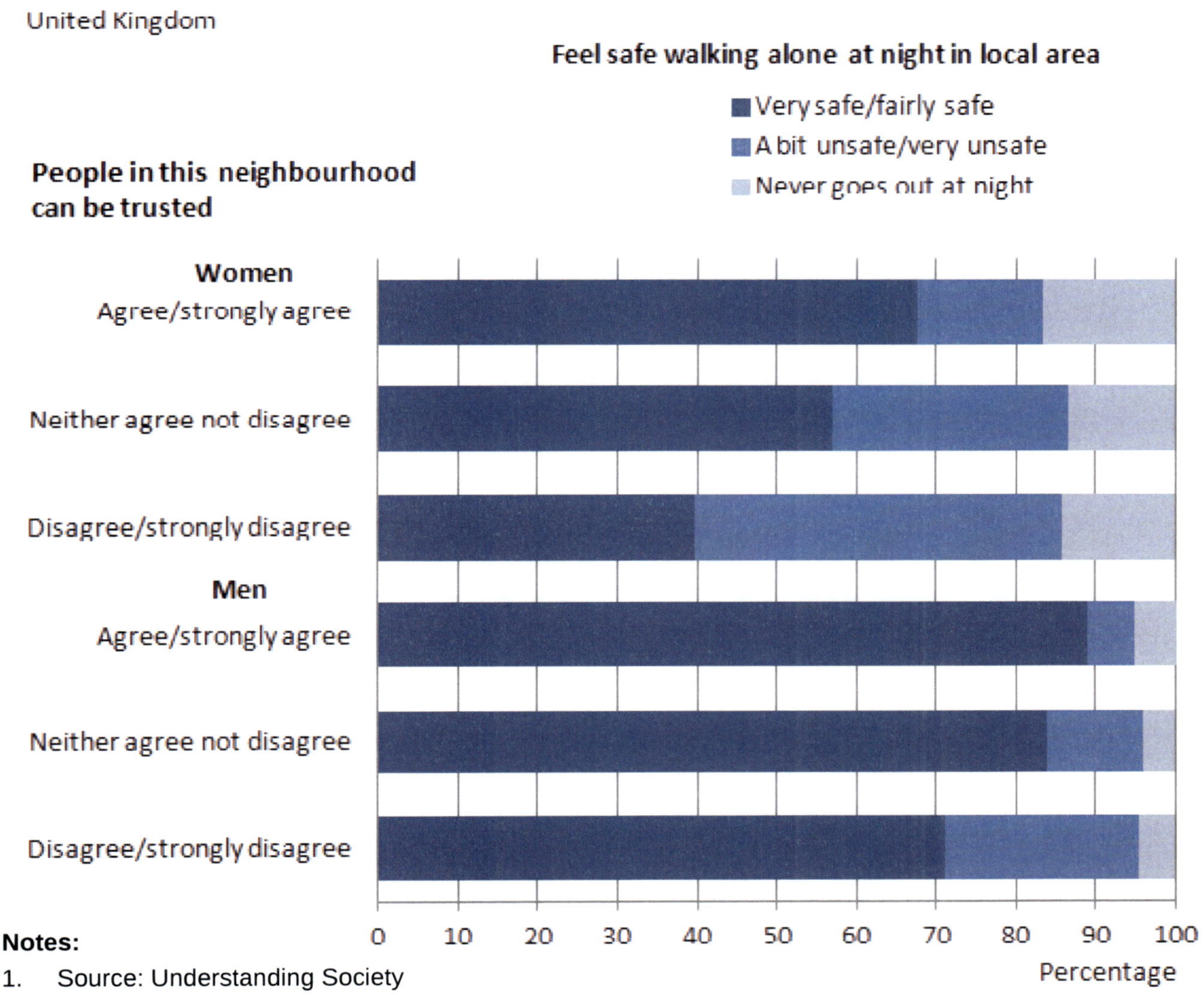

United Kingdom

Feel safe walking alone at night in local area
- Very safe/fairly safe
- A bit unsafe/very unsafe
- Never goes out at night

People in this neighbourhood can be trusted

[Bar chart showing percentages for Women and Men groups across Agree/strongly agree, Neither agree nor disagree, and Disagree/strongly disagree categories. X-axis: Percentage 0 to 100.]

Notes:

1. Source: Understanding Society

Download chart

 XLS format
(46 Kb)

A sense of belonging to the local area indicates a feeling of connection and acceptance within the local community. People who feel they belong to their local area are likely to have established a social network within their neighbourhood.

Data from Understanding Society 2011/12 indicate that nearly 2 out of 3 people (63%) feel they belong to their neighbourhood. There was an association between the feeling of belonging and feeling similar to others in the neighbourhood (Figure 11). Nearly 8 out of 10 (79%) of those who felt that they were similar to others in their neighbourhood also felt strongly that they belonged to their local area, compared to just under 3 out of 10 (27%) who did not feel similar to others in their neighbourhood.

Figure 11: Feel like belong to neighbourhood by feel similar to others in neighbourhood, 2011/12

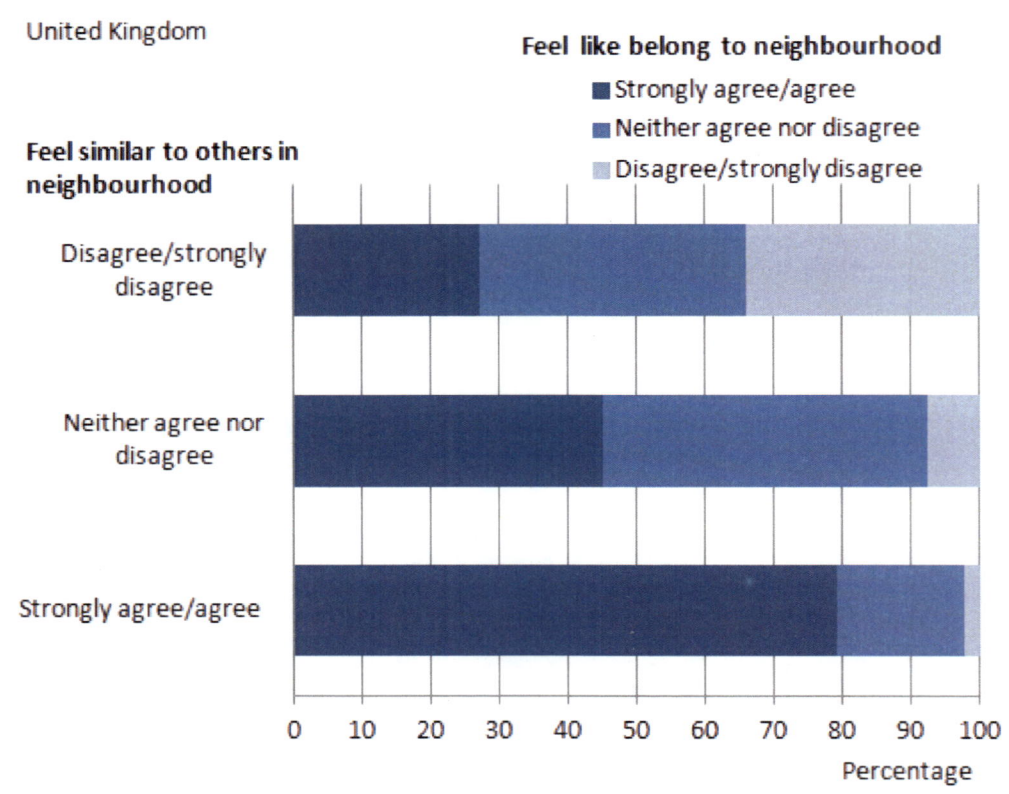

Notes:
1. Source: Understanding Society

Download chart

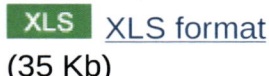 XLS format
(35 Kb)

Uses of social capital data

Why social capital is important

Social capital is important for individuals. Several studies have shown that people who have a wide range of connections, hence access to greater resources, have a better personal well-being (Halpern, 2005; Helliwell and Putnam, 2004; Helliwell, 2003) and are healthier (Veenstra, 2002 and 2000). Civic participation can also help to prevent people from becoming socially isolated, improve the diversity of people's social connections (Putnam, 2000) and improve people's skills (Musick and Wilson, 2003).

The support provided by family, friends or neighbours also has an important economic value. For example, it has been estimated that the total value of informal adult care[1] in the UK has almost tripled in 15 years, from £21.5 billion in 1995, to £61.7 billion in 2010 (ONS, 2013a). The latest value of childcare provided by grand-parents is estimated to be £7.3bn (Understanding Society Insights, 2014).

Social capital is important for communities. The attitudes that people have towards each other, towards institutions, towards contributing to the "common good" through volunteering or political activities are all crucial for communities. Communities where people are integrated, feel more connected to each other, to their local area and its institutions can better shape their local environment (Cabinet Office , 2013). This in turn can have a positive impact on individuals who generate a network of friends for themselves.

Social capital is important for the nation and its economy. The norms and values which are important for individuals are also important for the effective running of institutions in a democracy (Eurofound, 2014a; The Organisation for Economic Co-operation and Development (OECD) report, 2013c). Social interactions based on trust lead to transactions, hence having an impact on the economy (Putnam, 2000 and Putnam, 1993).

A nation with a high national well-being, made-up of people with high personal well-being, is a society where social capital stocks are high: where people are connected, tolerant, help each other, trust others and institutions, and are empowered to shape the society they live in.

Social capital and policy making

A 2014 report on social cohesion and well-being in the EU (Eurofound, 2014b) has suggested that social capital is linked to inequalities: inequalities weaken social capital, which in turn decrease some aspects of well-being. Social capital and its concerns with social inequalities are embedded in the Europe 2020 strategy that defines social and economic policies in Europe.

Social capital is relevant across a range of possible social and welfare policies. Many area based interventions promote aspects of social capital and deal with inequalities. Examples of such government projects include:

- The Community First Neighbourhood Match Fund, a neighbourhood funding programme in which neighbourhood panels make decisions to fund local projects. For the programme as a whole, as of May 2014, panels had made 14,996 project recommendations, totalling £22,603,795 in funding. Many projects have focused on connecting local people together and encouraging people to get involved and volunteer. Some 4.7 million volunteering hours had been generated by May 2014.
- The Big Lunch, a one day get-together for neighbours.
- Our Place! Programme (formerly 'neighbourhood community budgets'), which give communities the opportunity to take control of dealing with local issues in their area.
- Neighbourhood Planning, which give communities more power in planning local development.

Examples of non-government projects include:

- Timebanking, in which for every hour participants 'deposit' in a timebank (by giving practical help and support to others), they are able to 'withdraw' equivalent support in time when they themselves are in need.

- Spice Time Credits, in which people are thanked with time credits for contributing time to their community. People use credits to access events, training and leisure services, or to trade time with neighbours.
- Neighbourhood Watch, a voluntary network of schemes where neighbours come together, along with the police and local partners, to build safe and friendly communities.
- The Social Integration Commission, which has been set up to explore key questions related to the UK's increasing diversity. The commission is also seeking to understand the financial and social benefits or costs associated with different levels of social integration.

Social capital can also be used to assess the policy implications of interventions such as understanding the impacts of policy on civic attitudes and trust. For example, policy makers can consider how their policies affect the four dimensions of social capital, with a view to minimise negative impact and, if possible, delivering policies in a way that will enhance the dimensions of social capital. Where policies are deemed to deplete social capital, mitigating actions can be taken to reinvest in and replenish stocks.

Notes

1. The help provided by people to family members, friends or neighbours in need of help because of a long-term physical or mental ill health, disability or problems related to old age.

References

Borgonovi F (2008), 'Doing well by doing good: The relationship between formal volunteering and self-reported health and happiness', Social Science & Medicine 66(11), pp.2321-2334

Buke N and Rabe B (2011), 'Local environments', Early Findings from the First Wave of the UK's Household Longitudinal Study

Cabinet Office (2013), 'Giving of time and money. Findings from the 2012-13 Community Life Survey'

Cabinet Office (2011), 'Giving White and Green Paper', TSO (The Stationery Office)

Cabinet Office (2014), 'Community Life Survey Statistical Bulletin 2013-14'

European Social Survey (2002-2012), ESS findings, European Social Survey Publications

Eurofound (2012), 'Quality of Life in Europe: Impacts of the crisis', 3rd European Quality of Life Survey

Eurofound (2014a), 'Stemming the trend of declining trust', Spotlight theme: Quality of life

Eurofund (2014b), 'Social Cohesion and Well-being in the EU'

Greenfield E A and Marks N F (2004), 'Formal Volunteering as a Protective Factor for Older Adults' Psychological Well-Being', Journal of Gerontology: Social Sciences 59B (5), pp 258-264

Grootaert (1998), 'Social Capital: the Missing Link', Social Capital Initiative Working Paper Number 3, Social Development Department Publications

Halpern D (2005), 'Social Capital', published by Polity Press: Cambridge

Helliwell J F and Putnam R (2004), 'The social context of well-being', Philosophical transactions, Royal Society of London series B Biological Sciences, pp: 1435-1446

Helliwell JF (2003), 'How's life? Combining individual and national variables to explain subjective well-being', Economic Modelling, 20(2), pp: 331-360, Elsevier

Holt-Lunstad J, Smith TB, Layton JB (2010), 'Social Relationships and Mortality Risk: A Meta-analytic Review'. PloS Med 7(7):e1000316

Hudson J (2006), 'Institutional Trust and Subjective Well-Being across the EU', Kyklos, 59:1, pp.43-62

Morrow-Howell N, Hinterlong J, Rozario P and Tang F (2003), 'Effects of Volunteering on the Well-Being of Older Adults', Journals of Gerontology: Series B: Psychological Sciences and Social Sciences 58:3, pp: 137-145

Musick M and Wilson J (2003), 'Volunteering and depression: the role of psychological and social resources in different age groups', Social Science and Medicine, 56, pp: 259-269

NatCen (2013), 'Political Disengagement and Trust in Europe'

OECD (2011), 'How's Life? Measuring well-being', OECD Publishing

OECD (2013a), Scrivens, K. and Smith C. (2013a) 'Four Interpretations of Social Capital: An Agenda for Measurement', OECD Statistics Working Papers, 2013/06, OECD

OECD (2013b), 'How's Life? 2013: Measuring well-being', OECD Publishing

OECD (2013c), Government at a Glance, OECD Publishing

Office for National Statistics, Foster R and Fender V (2013), 'Household Satellite Accounts -Valuing Informal Adultcare in the UK'

Office for National Statistics, Foster R (2013), 'Household Satellite Accounts – Valuing Voluntary Activity in the UK''

Office for National Statistics, Siegler V (2014a), 'Measuring Social Capital, 2014'

Office for National Statistics (2014b), 'Measuring Social Capital Consultation Response'

Office for National Statistics, Randall C, Corp A and Self A. (2014c), 'Measuring National Well-being: Life in the UK, 2014'

Pickard L (2013), 'A growing care gap? The supply of unpaid care for older people by their adult children in England to 2032'. Ageing and Society, pp.1-28

Putnam R (1993), 'Making Democracy Work: Civic Traditions in Modern Italy', Princeton University Press: New Jersey

Putnam R (2000), 'Bowling Alone: The Collapse and Revival of American Community', Simon and Schuster: New York

Taylor S E (2011), 'Social support: A Review'. In M.S. Friedman. The Handbook of Health Psychology. New York, NY: Oxford University Press, pp.189-214

Uchino B (2009), 'Understanding the links between social support and physical health: A life-span perspective with emphasis on the separability of perceived and received support'. Perspectives on Psychological Science 4: 236-255.

Uchino B (2004), 'Social Support and Physical Health: Understanding the Health Consequences of Relationships', New Haven, CT: Yale University Press, p.17

UK Parliament's Environmental Audit Committee – Fifteenth Report; Well-being inquiry (2014)

Understanding Society Insights 2014 (2014), 'Grandma & Grandpa-the unsung heroes of modern UK childcare ' in Chapter 3 'Family Ties& Social Connections', Understanding Society publications

Veenstra G (2002), 'Social capital and health (plus wealth, income inequality and regional health governance)', Social Science and Medicine 54(6), pp: 849-68

Veenstra G (2000), 'Social capital, SES and health: an individual level analysis', Social Science and Medicine 50:5, pp.619-29

Yates L (2011), 'Critical Consumption: Boycotting and Buycotting in Europe', European Societies, 13:2, pp.191-217

Background notes

1. If you have any comments on the ONS approach to measuring social capital and /or the presentation of the social capital data, please email us at: nationalwell-being@ons.gsi.gov.uk

2. The data analysed in this report were from collected from a variety of different sources: The UK Longitudinal Survey (UKHLS, also referred as Understanding Society); the European Quality

of Life Survey (Eurofound, EQLS); the European Social Survey (ESS); the Crime Survey for England and Wales (CSEW); the Community Life Survey (CLS).

3.   The UK Longitudinal Household Survey (UKHLS) also referred to as Understanding Society study began in 2009, as a successor to the British Panel Survey (BHPS). It is conducted by the Institute for Social and Economic Research (ISER) at the University of Essex and captures important information about the socio-economic circumstances, well-being and attitudes of people living in 40, 000 households. It is an annual survey of a nationally representative sample of individuals. Each person aged 16 or older answers the individual adult interview and self-completion questionnaire. Young people aged 10-15 years old are asked to respond to a paper self-completion questionnaire. Information from the longitudinal survey is primarily used by academics, researchers and policymakers in their work, but the findings are of interest to a much wider group of people. These include those working in the third sector, health practitioners, business, the media and the general public. More information can be found on the Understanding Society webpage.

4.   The European Quality of Life Survey (Eurofound, EQLS) is carried out every 4 years since 2003. The survey in 2012 covered individuals aged 18 or older from 27 EU Member States and 7 non-EU countries. Questionnaires-based with interviews are conducted face-to-face in people's households in the national language(s) of the country. Data are collected on a range of subjects, such as employment and work-life balance, income and deprivation, education, housing and local environment, family and social contacts, perceived quality of society (such as trust in institutions), perceived quality of public services, social exclusion, health and mental well-being, personal well-being (eg. happiness and life satisfaction). More information can be found on the EQLS 2012 webpage.

5.   The European Social Survey (ESS) is a survey jointly funded by the European Commission and the European Science Foundation, covering 35 nations and carried out every 2 years since 2002. Individuals aged 15 years and over and resident within private homes are interviewed face-to-face The questionnaire include a core module which remain constant from round to round and some rotating modules repeated at intervals. The module captures a wide range of demographic and socio-economic information, including personal and social well-being, health, work, family, social exclusion, trust, political interest and participation, media use, governance and efficacy, citizenship and democracy. More information can be found on the European Social Survey webpage.

6.   The Crime Survey for England and Wales (CSEW), previously known as the British Crime Survey (BCS) started in 1981. Up to 2001, the survey was conducted biennially and from April 2001, interviewing was carried out continually and reported on in financial year cycles. The

survey covers a wide range of information covering demographics, crime, and crime-related subjects such as attitudes to the police and to the criminal justice system and perceptions of crime and anti-social behaviours. Questionnaires are mostly completed in a face-to-face interview within the respondent's household. Since 2009, the survey has been extended to children aged 10-15 years old. Further information may be found on the ONS Crime Survey for England and Wales webpage and for the previous BCS Methodology webpage.

7. The Community Life Survey (CLS) is an annual household survey which was first commissioned by the Cabinet Office in 2012-13. Individuals aged 16 years and over and resident in England are interviewed face-to-face, with a sample size of around 5-6,000 individuals per year. The survey provide data on behaviours and attitudes within local communities, such as volunteering, charitable giving, neighbourhood, civic engagement, social action and personal well-being. The aim of the survey is to inform and direct policies to encourage social action and empower communities. Further information may be found on the Community Life Survey webpage.

8. © Crown copyright 2015

You may use or re-use this information (not including logos) free of charge in any format or medium, under the terms of the Open Government Licence, write to the Information Policy Team, The National Archives, Kew, London TW9 4DU, or email: psi@nationalarchives.gsi.gov.uk.

9. Details of the policy governing the release of new data are available by visiting www.statisticsauthority.gov.uk/assessment/code-of-practice/index.html or from the Media Relations Office email: media.relations@ons.gsi.gov.uk

Copyright

Office for
National Statistics

Measuring National Well-being: Our Relationships, 2015

Author Name(s): **Chris Randall, Office for National Statistics**

Abstract

This article focuses on people's relationships with both family and friends. However, these relationships do not operate in isolation, and relationships within the wider community and the workplace are also analysed. The ONS Measuring National Well-being programme aims to produce accepted and trusted measures of the well-being of the nation - how the UK as a whole is doing.

Introduction

Previous research has shown that the amount and quality of social connections with people around us are vitally important to an individual's well-being and should be considered when making any assessment of National Well-being.

'Social connections, including marriage, of course, but not limited to that, are among the most robust correlates of subjective well-being. People who have close friends and confidants, friendly neighbours and supportive co-workers are less likely to experience sadness, loneliness, low self-esteem and problems with eating and sleeping' (Helliwell and Putnam, 2004).

'The frequency of contact with others and the quality of personal relationships are crucial determinants of people's well-being' (Kahneman and Krueger, 2006).

This article will further explore relationships with family, friends, relationships within the wider community and relationships within the workplace. It will also focus on our satisfaction with our social life, and loneliness.

Key points

Relationships with family

- Just under a third (32%) of adults aged 16 and over in the UK who were married or in a civil partnership rated their satisfaction with life as very high (9 to 10 out of 10) in 2013–14.
- The average (mean) rating of family life given by adults aged 18 and over in the UK in 2011 was 8.2 out of 10.

- Money worries were reported as the main factor that puts a strain on a relationship by 62% of people aged 16 and over in the UK in 2014.
- In 2010/11, 87% of people in the UK reported that they had someone to rely on if they had a serious problem.

Relationships with friends

- Over half (53%) of adults aged 16 and over in the UK in 2011/12 reported that all their friends were of the same ethnic group. A third (33%) reported that all their friends were of a similar age while 39% reported their friends had a similar level of education.
- Around 9 in 10 adults aged 16 and over in the UK in 2011/12 had one or more friends that they could confide in (93%), supported them (92%) or they could escape with/have fun with (90%).

Relationships within the community

- Over half (55%) of adults aged 16 and over in the UK agreed or strongly agreed that friendships and associations with other people in their community meant a lot to them.
- In England in 2013–14, 85% of people aged 16 and over agreed that their local area is a place where people from different backgrounds get on well together.

Relationships at work

- Of adults aged 16 and over in the UK in full-time work, 62% were about as likely to have daily contact with their work colleagues than with their children.
- Just under two-thirds (64%) of employees in the UK reported the relationship between themselves and their managers as good or very good, while 13% reported relations as poor or very poor.

Social life and loneliness

- Adults aged 18 and over in the UK reported their average (mean) rating of satisfaction with their social life as 7.1 out of 10 in 2011.
- In the UK in 2011, 36% of adults aged 18 and over wished they could spend more time with their family and 36% more time with their friends.
- In April and June 2014, over half (53%) of people in Great Britain reported some feeling of loneliness (answers of 1 or more out of 10).

Relationships with family

'Of all the rocks upon which we build our lives, we are reminded today that family is the most important' (Barack Obama, 2008).

Strong family relationships can give the support needed to make it through difficult times and, in turn may improve the well-being of all family members.

According to 2011 Census data, under half (47%) of all adults aged 16 and over in the UK were married or in a registered same-sex civil partnership, while 3% were separated (but still legally married). Just over a third (35%) were single (never married), 9% were divorced and 7% were widowed or their civil partner had died.

Figure 1: Legal marital status of population aged 16 and over for the UK and constituent countries, 2011 (1,2)

United Kingdom

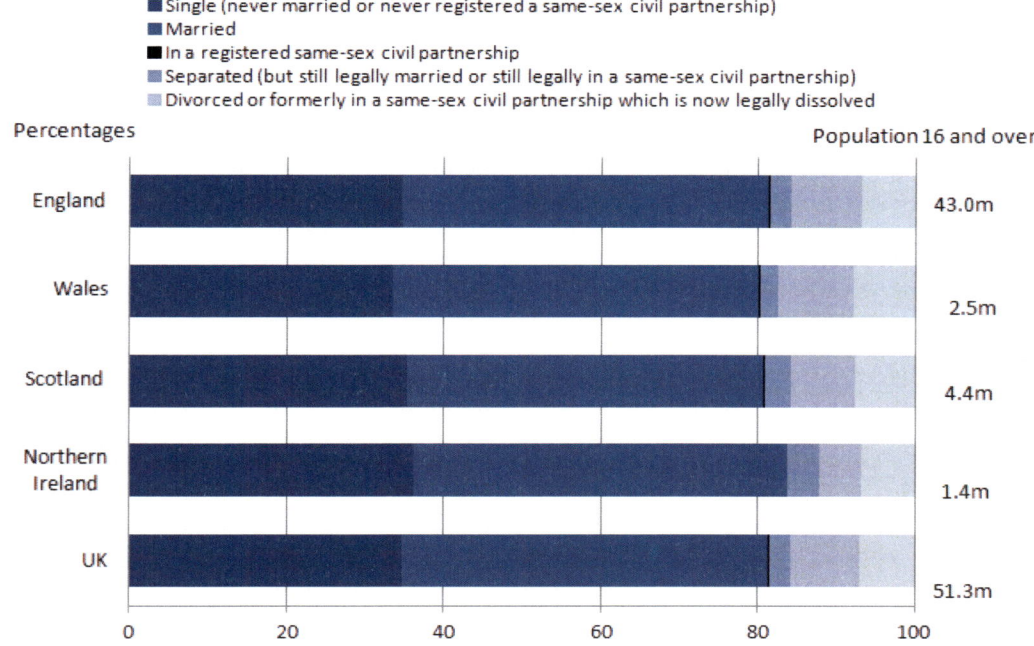

Source: Office for National Statistics, Northern Ireland Statistics and Research Agency and National Records for Scotland

Notes:
1. Percentages in the category 'In a registered same-sex civil partnership' were very small for all four UK countries ranging from: 0.09 per cent (Northern Ireland) to 0.23 per cent (England).
2. Census 2011 table DC1107EW, NISRA table DC1103NI and NRS table KS103SC were used to produce this chart.

Download chart

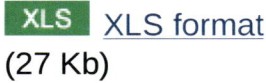 XLS format
(27 Kb)

Figure 1 summarises the marital status patterns, for adults aged 16 and over, of the four UK countries. The proportions of single and married people varied little between the countries and almost half (45% to 48%) of the populations of all four countries were married. The proportions of the populations in civil partnerships were highest in England (0.2%). Northern Ireland had the highest proportion separated (4%) and the lowest proportion divorced (5%); by contrast, Wales had the lowest proportion separated (2%) and highest proportion divorced (10%). The proportion widowed varied little across the UK (between 7% in Northern Ireland and 8% in Wales).

Table 1: Life Satisfaction(1): by marital status, 2013–2014 (2)

United Kingdom (% in each category on 11 point scale)

	Low (0–4)	Medium (5–6)	High (7–8)	Very High (9–10)
Married or Civil partnership	3.4	12.3	52.2	32.2
Cohabiting or same sex couple	3.9	14.1	55.9	26.1
Single	6.9	19.3	53.0	20.7
Widow or surviving civil partner	8.1	20.5	44.4	27.0
Divorced or separated or former/ separated civil partner	11.9	23.5	46.2	18.4

Source: April 2013 to March 2014, Annual Population Survey Personal Well-being Experimental dataset, Office for National Statistics

Table notes:
1. Respondents were asked 'Overall, how satisfied are you with your life nowadays? Where 0 is 'not at all satisfied' and 10 is 'completely satisfied'.
2. All estimates weighted.

Download table

XLS XLS format
(25.5 Kb)

The nature of our relationships may have an important influence on personal well-being. According to the Annual Population Survey, people who are married or in a civil partnership were more likely to rate their satisfaction with life as very high (9 to 10 out of 10)[1] in 2013–14 **(Table 1)**. Just under a third (32%) of adults aged 16 and over in the UK who were married or in a civil partnership rated their satisfaction with life as very high. This compared to 26% who were cohabiting or same sex couples and 21% who were single. Conversely those who were divorced or separated were more likely to have a low (0 to 4) rating of life satisfaction at (12%).

The average rating of satisfaction with family life is one of the three measures of National Well-being looked at as part of the 'Our relationships' domain. Adults aged 18 and over in the UK were asked on the European Quality of Life Survey to rate their satisfaction with family life. The average (mean) rating in 2011 (the latest data available) was 8.2[2]. This rating is the same as 2007 when the survey was last run, the rating was 8.0 in the 2003 survey.

Although this high satisfaction rating indicates that all may be well in our family relationships, there are many external factors that can put pressure on them.

Figure 2: Top 10 problems that place a strain on a relationship (1), 2014

United Kingdom

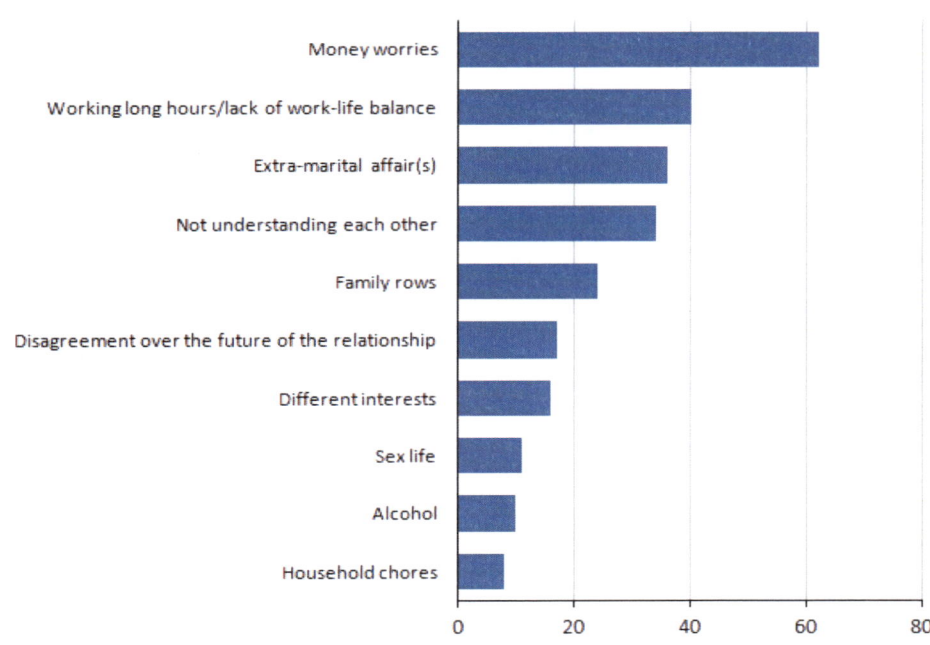

Source: The Way We Are Now, Relate

Notes:

1. Respondents aged 16 and over were asked 'Which three of the following 17 problems do you think places the most strain on a relationship?' (Please rank these options in order). This chart shows the first ten problems only and does not include those who stated 'Don't know'.

Download chart

 XLS format
(26 Kb)

People aged 16 and over in the UK were asked in a survey published by Relate in 2014 to identify the top three challenges (from a list of 17) to their family relationships. Around three-fifths (62%) of people reported money worries as the main factor that placed the most strain on their relationship **(Figure 2)**. This was followed by working long hours or maintaining a work-life balance (40%), infidelity (36%) and not understanding each other (34%). Just under a quarter (24%) reported that family rows put a strain on their relationship.

Most of us like to know that if we had a problem we could turn to someone. Another headline measure of National Well-being under the 'Our Relationships' domain is the proportion of people that had a spouse, family member or friend to rely on if they had a serious problem. According to the

2010/11 UK Household Longitudinal Survey, 87% of adults aged 16 and over did have someone to rely on.

In the UK in 2013, there were an estimated 12 million children aged 0 to 15, making up nearly a fifth of the population. Children require positive, loving relationships with the people closest to them. In the Good Childhood Report 2013, The Children's Society highlighted the importance of family relationships to children's subjective well-being. It found that a measure of family harmony was substantially more indicative of children's well-being than family structure.

The 2011/12 UK Household Longitudinal Survey asked people aged 16 and over how often they and their child(ren) spend time together on leisure activities or outings outside the home. Over a third (36%) of people reported that they spend time together with their children on leisure activities several times a week or almost every day. Just under a third (32%) took their children on outings about once a week, while 16% reported once a month or less or never or rarely.

Figure 3: Children's frequency of quarrelling and talking with parents, 2011/12 (1,2)

United Kingdom

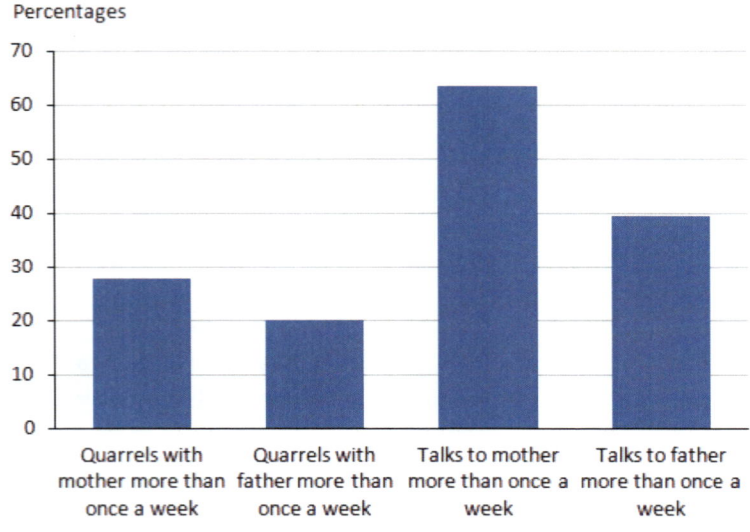

Source: Understanding Society, the UK Household Longitudinal Survey

Notes:
1. Children aged 10 to 15 years.
2. Respondents were asked: How often do you quarrel with your mother/father? How often do you talk to your mother/father about things that matter? Response options were: Most days, more than once a week, less than once a week, hardly ever, don't have mother/father.

Download chart

XLS XLS format
(26 Kb)

In 2011/12, around 28% of children aged 10 to 15 years reported quarrelling with their mother more than once a week, according to UK Household Longitudinal Survey data **(Figure 3)**. This compares with 20% of children reporting quarrelling with their father more than once a week; most children reported hardly ever quarrelling with their father (60%). It should be noted that more children live with their mothers than with their fathers, which may explain some of the variation. Nearly all children who reported hardly ever quarrelling with their mother reported the same with their father (91%). However, among those children reporting quarrelling frequently with their mother, around half (51%) reported the same with their father.

Children were more likely to report talking frequently to their mother than to their father about things that matter. In 2011/12, nearly two-thirds (63%) of children aged 10 to 15 years talked to their mother more than once a week about things that matter. This compares with nearly two-fifths (40%) who reported talking to their father. Among children aged 10 to 15 who reported talking with their mother more than once a week about things that matter, 58% also reported talking frequently with their father about things that matter. Around 3 in 20 (15%) children in this age group reported hardly ever talking to either parent about things that matter in 2011/12.

Notes

1. Where 0 is 'not at all satisfied' and 10 is 'completely satisfied'.

2. Using a scale from 1 to 10 where 1 indicates 'very dissatisfied' and 10 indicates 'very satisfied'.

Relationships with friends

'The number of real-life friends is positively correlated with subjective well-being even after controlling for income, demographic variables and personality differences' (Helliwell and Huang, 2013)

Friends provide support and companionship during bad times and can prevent loneliness. Friends can also increase a sense of belonging and purpose and may improve self-confidence and self-worth.

In 2011/12, 95% of adults aged 16 and over in the UK reported having at least one close friend according to the UK Household Longitudinal Survey. Over two-thirds (68%) reported having between 2 and 6 close friends[1].

Figure 4: Proportion of friends that have similar demographics (1), 2011/12

United Kingdom

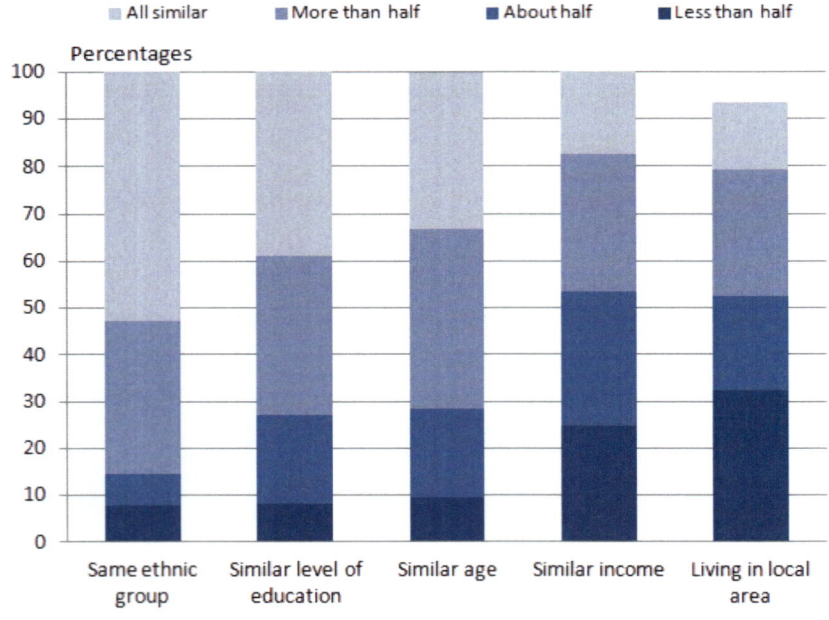

Source: Understanding Society, the UK Household Longitudinal Survey

Notes:

1. 'Similar age' does not include those that reported 'no friends (2.0%). 'Living in local area' does not include 'none' (6.4%).

Download chart

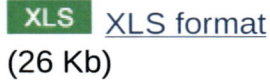 XLS format
(26 Kb)

Figure 4 shows the proportion of friends with different characteristics that people aged 16 and over reported they had. Over half (53%) reported that all their friends were of the same ethnic group. A third (33%) reported that all their friends were of a similar age while 39% reported they had a similar level of education. Under a fifth stated that their friends received a similar income or lived in their local area (17% and 14% respectively).

On a survey run by YouGov in 2012, adults aged 18 and over in Great Britain were asked to agree or disagree with the following statement 'I feel I need a core group of people (people who inspire, mentor me, who I can confide in and who support me) to help me achieve my goals in life (for example, job aspirations and education)'. Nearly half (48%) strongly agreed or tended to agree with the statement, while 43% tended to disagree or strongly disagree with the statement.

Table 2: Characteristics of friends (1): by number of friends, 2012

Great Britain (Percentages)

	0	1	2	3	4 or more
Someone you can confide in	7	17	24	18	34
Someone that supports you	8	21	21	15	35
Someone you can escape with/ have fun with	10	22	21	11	36
Someone that inspires you	24	24	22	12	18
Someone who will mentor you/ guide you	29	31	20	9	11

Source: YouGov

Table notes:

1. Respondents aged 18 and over were asked 'Thinking about your core friends (i.e. those who support and help you to achieve your goals)... Approximately, how many, if any, friends do you have who you feel possess each of the following characteristics? (If you're unsure, please give your best estimate). Fieldwork was 30th March to 2nd April 2012.

Download table

XLS XLS format
(17.5 Kb)

On the same survey, respondents were asked how many of their friends possessed certain characteristics. Around 9 in 10 had one or more friends that they could confide in (93%) or that supported them (92%) or they could escape with (90%) **(Table 2)**. Just over three-quarters (76%) of people had one or more friend that inspired them and 71% reported that they had one or more friend that would mentor or guide them.

Meeting face-to-face is still the preferred means of personal communication with friends and family, despite the rising use of digital communications according to Ofcom. In 2012, 48% of people in the UK aged 16 and over who made any sort of contact with friends and family did so face-to-face, while 12% did so by a voice call using a fixed landline and a further 12% used email. However, the number of social network users, and the amount of time spent on social networking sites, continues to rise; in 2013, 66% of all internet users were active on a social networking site.

On an online survey by YouGov in 2012, respondents aged 18 and over in Great Britain were asked to approximate how many friends they had on their social media sites, in total. Just under a quarter (24%) reported they had fewer than 50 friends, 12% reported 51 to 100 friends and 10% reported 101 to 150 friends. Just under a quarter (24%) reported having more than 150 friends, and 28% reported that they were not a member of a social media site. However, 27% of those who had social media accounts reported that at least half of these friends were just acquaintances (a person they only see occasionally or don't know very well). Just 8% stated that none of their friends on these sites were just acquaintances.

Notes

1. Personal relationships are a measure of 'Social Capital' more information can be found here: An Analysis of Social Capital in the UK

Relationships within the community

'For a community to be whole and healthy, it must be based on people's love and concern for each other' (Millard Fuller, Habitat for Humanity founder).

A community can be described as a place where friends, neighbours and strangers live, work, play and experience everyday life. People need to know that they are part of a community. They need to feel that they have others around them that they can connect with and share commonalities. This in turn may contribute to an individual's sense of well-being[1].

Figure 5: Proportion of people who agreed that they belonged to their neighbourhood (1): by age, 2011/12

United Kingdom

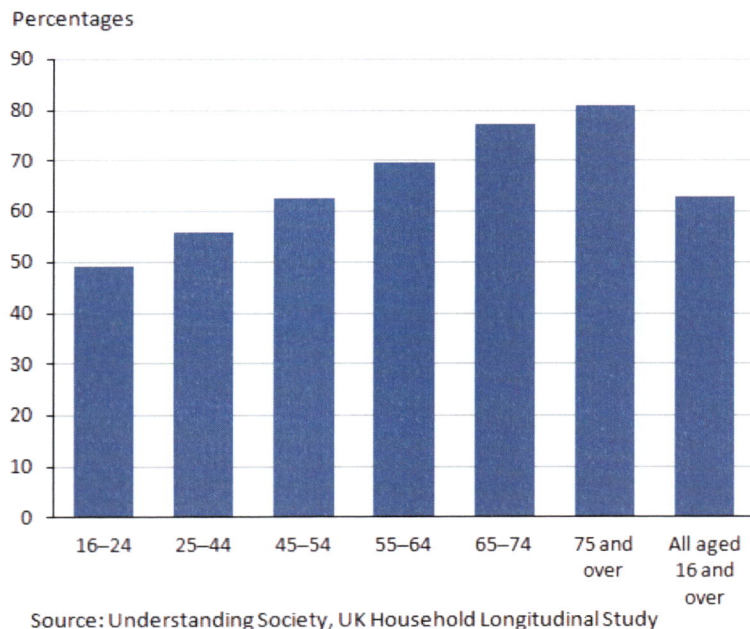

Source: Understanding Society, UK Household Longitudinal Study

Notes:

1. Respondents were asked to rate their sense of belonging to their neighbourhood from "strongly disagree" to "strongly agree". The chart shows those who agreed or strongly agreed.

Download chart

 XLS format
(26 Kb)

In 2011/12, over 6 in 10 (63%) people aged 16 and over agreed or strongly agreed that they belonged to their neighbourhood according to the UK Household Longitudinal Survey **(Figure 5)**. The proportion of people who felt strongly they belonged to a neighbourhood increased by age. Just under half (49%) of those aged 16 to 24 agreed or strongly agreed that they belonged to their neighbourhood compared to 81% of those aged 75 and over. People in Northern Ireland (73%) and Scotland (69%) were more likely to agree that they belonged to their neighbourhood, while those living in London (59%) were least likely to agree.

The 2011/12 UK Household Longitudinal Survey asked adults aged 16 and over whether the friendships and associations they have with other people in their neighbourhood meant a lot to them. Over half (55%) reported that they strongly agreed or agreed with the statement. When split by gender, friendships and associations in the neighbourhood meant a lot to 52% of men compared with 57% of women.

Figure 6: Proportion that agree that friendship and associations in the local neighbourhood mean a lot (1): by age-group, 2011/12

United Kingdom

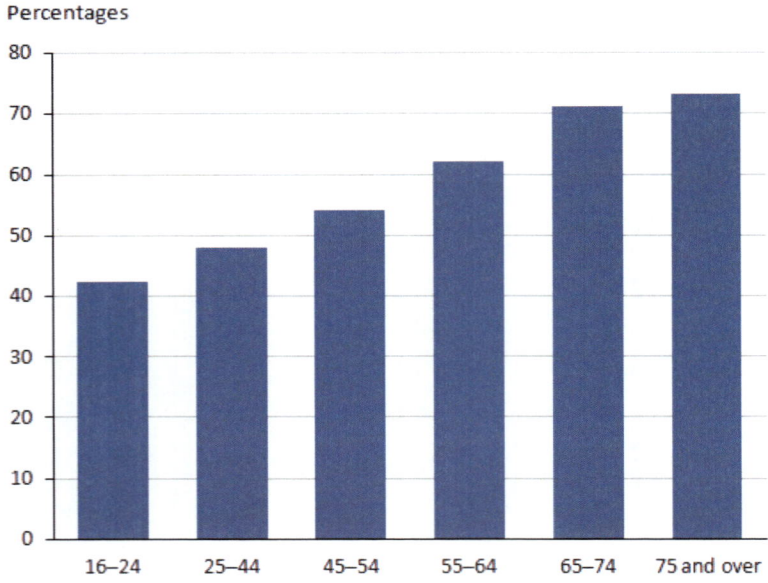

Source: Understanding Society, the UK Household Longitudinal Survey

Notes:

1. Adults aged 16 and over were asked 'The friendships and associations I have with other people in my neighbourhood mean a lot to me'. The chart shows those that strongly agreed or agreed with the statement.

Download chart

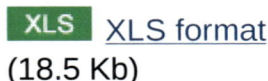 XLS format
(18.5 Kb)

The proportion of people in the UK who strongly agreed or agreed that the friendships and associations they have with other people in their neighbourhood meant a lot to them increased with age **(Figure 6)**. Under half (42%) of people aged 16 to 24 agreed with the statement increasing to nearly three-quarters (73%) of those aged 75 and over.

Taking the time to establish good terms with neighbours in the community may have numerous benefits, such as a friendlier community and a safer neighbourhood which in turn would make it a more comfortable place to live. Three-quarters (75%) of people aged 16 and over in England reported on the 2013–14 Community Life Survey that they chat to their neighbours (more than just to say hello) at least once a month. Just over a fifth (22%) reported that they chat to their neighbours on most days.

A cohesive community is a place where different types of people live and get on well together. It may be a place where there is respect and trust, differences might be celebrated and in turn those living in the community may have a greater sense of belonging. According to the Community Life

Survey, 85% of people aged 16 and over in England in 2013–14 thought that their community was cohesive, agreeing that their local area is a place where people from different backgrounds get on well together. There is no significant difference from levels in 2008–09 to 2012–13, but this is a significant increase compared to 2003 when the proportion was 80%.

Figure 7: Community cohesion (1), by age

England

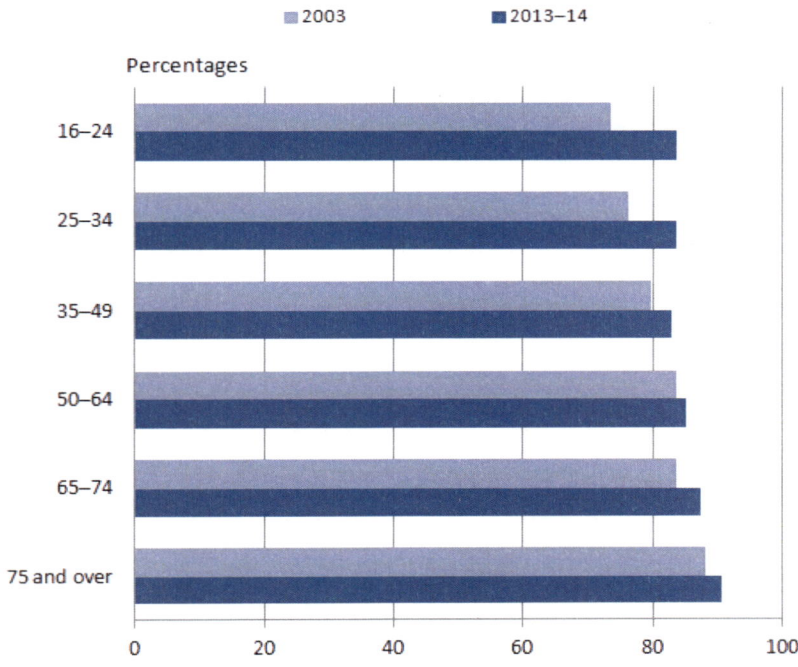

Source: Community Life Survey, Cabinet Office

Notes:
1. 2003 data collected through the Citizenship Survey. Respondents were asked 'To what extent do you agree or disagree that this local area is a place where people from different backgrounds get on well together?' The chart shows those that 'definitely' or 'tended to' agree with the statement.

Download chart

XLS XLS format
(26.5 Kb)

The proportion of people in England who reported that their local area is a place where people from different backgrounds get on well together varied slightly by age group from 84% for those aged 16 to 24 and 25 to 34 to 91% of those aged 75 and over **(Figure 7)**. Between 2003 and 2013–14 there was an increase in the proportion of people who thought that their local area was cohesive in all age groups. These increases were most notable among young people aged 16 to 24 (10 percentage points) and 25 to 34 (7 percentage points).

Notes

1. Neighbourhood social cohesion are measures of Social Capital, more information can be found here: An Analysis of Social Capital in the UK

Relationships at work

'Workplace relationships are unique interpersonal relationships with important implications for the individuals in those relationships and the organizations in which the relationships exist and develop. Various studies conducted in this respect have indicated that workplace relationships directly affect a worker's ability to work and produce' (Mamta Gaur, School of Business, Galgotias University, 2013).

For many people, a lot of their life is spent in the workplace and therefore in the company of their work colleagues. Good workplace relationships may add to a person's well-being and also may help productivity.

According to the report The Way We Are Now published by Relate in 2014, the amount of contact between those working full-time with work colleagues and bosses exceeds the amount of contact with many other family members or friends in the UK. The report highlighted that employees aged 16 and over were about as likely to have daily contact with work colleagues (62%) than they were their own children (64%). Over 4 in 10 (44%) were more likely to have daily contact with their bosses than with mothers (26%) or friends (16%)[1].

Over half (58%) of people at work had at least one close friend at work with over a fifth (22%) having three or more close friends. However, just over two-fifths (42%) of people in work did not count any colleagues as close friends[2].

Figure 8: Relations between managers and employees, 2011

United Kingdom

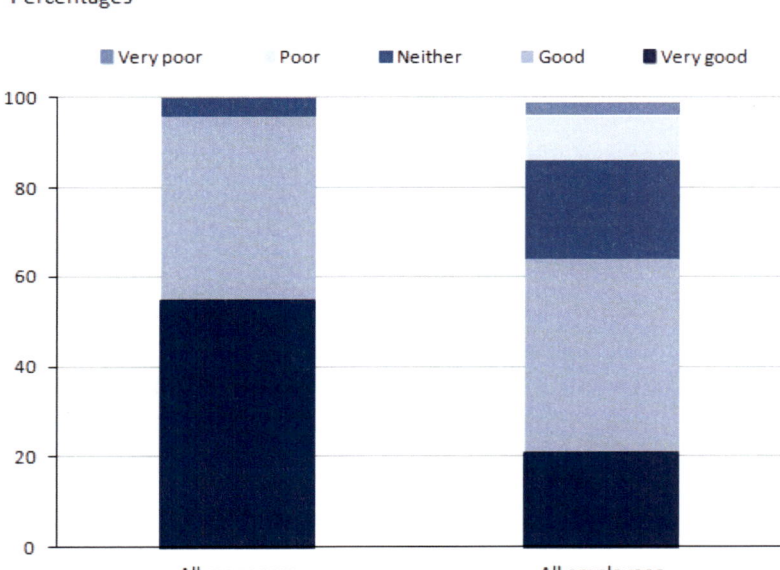

Source: The 2011 Workplace Employment Relations Study, Department for Business, Innovation and Skills (BIS), the Economic and Social Research Council (ESRC), the Advisory, Conciliation and Arbitration Service (Acas), the UK Commission for Employment and Skills (UKCES), and the National Institute of Economic and Social Research (NIESR)

Download chart

 XLS format
(25.5 Kb)

The quality of the relationship between a manager and employee can significantly impact the performance of the workforce. According to the 2011 Workplace Employment Relations Survey, managers were generally positive about their relationships with their employees with 96% rating their relationships as very good or good in the UK **(Figure 8)**. Just under two-thirds (64%) of employees reported the relationship between themselves and their managers as good or very good, while 13% reported relations as poor or very poor.

Notes

1. Participants were asked: 'On average, how often, if at all, do you have contact with each of the following people (including face-to-face, via phone, text, email, online etc.)? Of those who were full-time employed, 62%, said that they have contact with their colleagues daily. Of those who were full-time employed and had a relationship with their children, 64% said they had contact with their children daily. Of those who were full-time employed and had a relationship with their mothers, 26% of respondents said they had contact with their mothers daily. Of those who were

full-time employed and had a relationship with their boss, 44% reported they had contact with their boss daily.

2. These figures are based on the response to the question "How many, if any, of your colleagues do you count as close friends? Refers to people in work who did not say that the question was inapplicable (e.g. in cases where they had no colleagues).

Social life and loneliness

Research from the Universities of Exeter and Queensland shows that the quality of a person's social life could have an even greater impact than diet and exercise on their health and well-being[1].

Another of the measures of National Well-being in the 'Our relationships' domain is the average rating of satisfaction with social life. The 2011 European Quality of Life Survey asked adults aged 18 and over in the UK to rate their satisfaction with their social life[2]. The average (mean) rating in 2011 (the latest data available) was 7.1 out of 10, compared to 7.0 in 2007 and 6.8 in 2003. Satisfaction with a social life varied slightly by age. Those aged 18 to 24 and 65 and over reported the highest average (mean) rating with their social life at 8.0 and 7.6 out of 10 respectively. People aged 25 to 34 reported an average (mean) rating of 7.0 and those aged 35 to 64 a rating of 6.6 out of 10.

Figure 9: Meeting socially (1) at least once a week with friends, relatives or work colleagues (2), 2012

United Kingdom

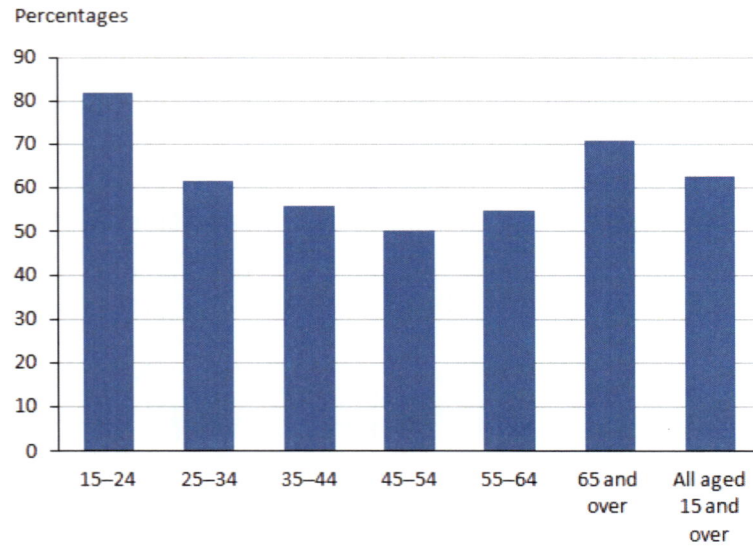

Source: ESS Round 6: European Social Survey Round 6 Data (2012). Data file edition 2.1. Norwegian Social Science Data Services, Norway

Notes:

1. 'Meeting socially' implies meet by choice rather than for reasons of either work or pure duty.

2. Respondents were asked 'Using this card, how often do you meet socially with friends, relatives or work colleagues'?

Download chart

 XLS format
(26.5 Kb)

The 2012 European Social Survey People asked those aged 15 and over in the UK how often they met socially with friends, relatives or work colleagues. Over 6 in 10 (63%) reported that they met socially once a week or more[3] **(Figure 9)**. Unsurprisingly, those aged 15 to 24 were more likely than other age groups to report that they met socially at least once a week, while those aged 35 to 64 were least likely to socialise with friends, relatives or work colleagues once a week or more. This was probably due to people in this age group having childcare or work commitments.

According to the 2011 European Quality of Life Survey, around 6 in 10 adults aged 18 and over in the UK reported that they were satisfied with the time they currently spent with family (61%) and friends (60%). Over 3 in 10 (36%) wished they could spend more time with family and 36% wished they could spend more time with friends. However, 3% reported that they wished they spent less time with family and 4% less time with friends.

Figure 10: Feeling of loneliness (1), 2014 (2)

Great Britain

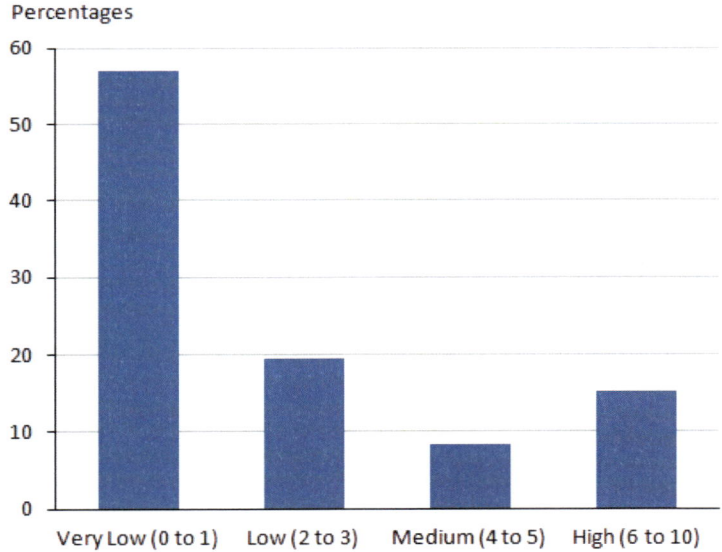

Source: Opinions and Lifestyle Survey - Office for National Statistics

Notes:

1. Respondents aged 16 and over were asked 'On a scale where 0 is not at all lonely and 10 is extremely lonely , how lonely do you feel in your daily life?'
2. April and July 2014.

Download chart

 XLS format
(25.5 Kb)

Inadequate levels of social relationships may lead to people experiencing loneliness in life. However the feeling of loneliness is subjective; a person may feel lonely even when in the company of family and friends. The ONS Opinions and Lifestyle Survey asked adults aged 16 and over in Great Britain on a scale of 0 to 10 how lonely they felt in daily life where 0 is not at all lonely and 10 is extremely lonely. Interestingly, over half (53%) of people reported some feeling of loneliness (answers of 1 or more out of 10) in April and July 2014, while 47% reported no feeling of loneliness. A high feeling of loneliness (6 to 10 out of 10) was reported by 15% of people **(Figure 10)**, while 57% reported a very low feeling of loneliness in their daily life (0 to 1 out of 10).

Notes

1. psychology.exeter.ac.uk/latestnews/archivenews/2009/title_41580_en.html

2. Using a scale from 1 to 10 where 1 indicates 'very dissatisfied' and 10 indicates 'very satisfied'.

3. Once a week, several times a week or every day.

Background notes

1. Details of the policy governing the release of new data are available by visiting www.statisticsauthority.gov.uk/assessment/code-of-practice/index.html or from the Media Relations Office email: media.relations@ons.gsi.gov.uk

Copyright

Sources related to 'Our Relationships, 2015'

Cabinet Office (Community Life Survey) - www.gov.uk/government/collections/community-life-survey

Department for Business, Innovation and Skills (The 2011 Workplace Employment Relations Study) - BIS: Workplace Employment Relations Survey

European Quality of Life Survey - eurofound.europa.eu/surveys/european-quality-of-life-surveys-eqls/european-quality-of-life-survey-2012

European Social Survey - www.europeansocialsurvey.org/

Good Childhood Report 2013 - www.childrenssociety.org.uk/good-childhood-report-2013-online/index.html

Office for National Statistics (2011 Census) - Census 2001

Office for National Statistics (Social Capital)- An Analysis of Social Capital in the UK

Relate (The Way We Are Now) - www.relate.org.uk/policy-campaigns/publications/way-we-are-now-state-uks-relationships-2014

Understanding Society, the UK Longitudinal Survey - Understanding Society

YouGov - Yougov archives

25 March 2015

Measuring National Well-being: Life in the UK, 2015

Author Name(s): **Joanne Evans, Ian Macrory and Chris Randall, Office for National Statistics**

Abstract

Provides a snapshot of life in the UK today across the 10 domains of national well-being. It is the third annual summary to be delivered by the Measuring National Well-being programme.

Key points

- Assessment of change in measures of national well-being are presented for the first time. Compared with a year earlier, 33% of indicators had improved, 42% showed no overall change, 21% were not assessed and 5% deteriorated
- The proportion of people in the UK giving the highest ratings for each aspect of personal well-being increased significantly in the financial year ending 2014
- Healthy life expectancy in the UK improved between 2006 to 2008 and 2009 to 2011, while the proportion of people satisfied with their health in the financial year ending 2013 (59.3%) showed no overall change
- Adult participation in 30 minutes of moderate intensity sport at least once a week in the UK improved over 3 years between 2010 to 2011 (35.2%) and 2013 to 2014 (35.8%) but deteriorated compared with 2012 to 2013 (36.2%)
- In the financial year ending 2013, 21% of people in the UK lived in households with less than 60% of median income
- In the financial year ending 2013, 10.1% of people found it difficult to get by financially in the UK, an improvement since the financial years ending 2012 (10.9%) and 2010 (12.3%)

Introduction

The Measuring National Well-being (MNW) programme began in November 2010 with the aim to "develop and publish an accepted and trusted set of National Statistics which help people understand and monitor well-being". We describe well-being as "how we are doing" as individuals, as communities and as a nation, and how sustainable this is for the future.

Life in the UK presents the full set of 41 headline measures of national well-being, organised by the 10 domains, or areas, such as Health, Where we live, What we do and Our relationships. The measures include both objective data (for example, number of crimes against the person per 1,000 adults) and subjective data (for example, percentage who felt safe walking alone after dark). The report also shows for the first time how measures of national well-being have changed over time and highlights which measures have "improved", "deteriorated" or show "no overall change".

By examining the headline measures, for example, ratings of life satisfaction, our sense of belonging to our neighbourhoods, and measures of inflation, the report considers "how we are doing" across each of the domains. There is reference to how sustainable our well-being is for the future through measures such as green house gas emissions, but the majority of measures focus on current well-being, how we are doing now. How sustainable national well-being is for the future is examined by looking at the work of the MNW programme around stocks of things like education, natural resources and community cohesion, known as "capitals". Valuing the stocks we have now provides important benchmark information to help ensure they can be sustained for the future.

Measures are updated in March and September. Where possible, data are presented for the UK. Where this is not the case, the best available geography is used. Data are the latest available at March 2015.

Feedback is welcome at nationalwell-being@ons.gov.uk

Also released today:

- National Well-being Measures spreadsheet (1.05 Mb Excel sheet) containing the latest data, time series data and detailed information on assessments of change as well as links to data sources
- Interactive wheel of measures which includes data for the latest and previous periods plus time series charts.
- Wheel of measures PDF (809 Kb Pdf) "print and keep" version showing the latest data and assessments of change
- Interactive charts showing the latest data for selected measures by region and country.

Assessing change in National Well-being

The Measuring National Well-being (MNW) programme set out to establish measures which would help people to understand national well-being, and also help them monitor it. This report includes for the first time assessments showing the direction of change for each of the measures, whether they have improved, shown no overall change, or deteriorated. Comparisons have been made with the previous year's data, or the previously published figure where year on year data are not available, as well as an assessment of change over a three year period. In future years, as more data become available, we will publish assessments of change over a longer time series.

Figure 1 summarises the assessments of change in measures of national well-being. Measures of healthy life expectancy and feeling safe walking alone after dark are presented for both men and women, and so there are 43 measures to assess.

Figure 1: Assessments of change - National Well-being measures

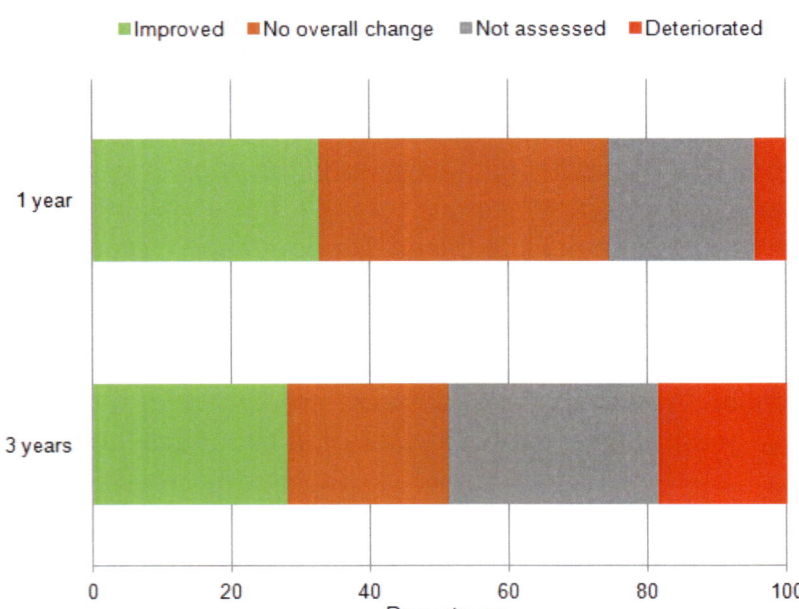

Download chart

XLS XLS format
(24 Kb)

Looking at the most recent change[1]:

- 33% (14 measures) had improved
- 42% (18 measures) showed no overall change
- 5% (2 measures) had deteriorated
- 21% (9 measures) were not assessed for this publication

Over the three year period[1]:

- 28% (12 measures) had improved
- 23% (10 measures) showed no overall change
- 19% (8 measures) had deteriorated
- 30% (13 measures) were not assessed

A number of measures have not been assessed, because data are not available for comparison, or where the direction of change is not a clear indication of either improvement or deterioration.

Individual measures of change can be viewed in the Wheel of measures PDF (809 Kb Pdf). Details of how each measure has been assessed are available in the National Well-being Measures spreadsheet (1.05 Mb Excel sheet).

It is recognised that the measures on which assessments of change have been made are headline measures and therefore only provide a snapshot of how national well-being is changing. There are many other measures that will affect national well-being that have not been considered here. However, it is hoped that assessing change in this way will help to signpost areas in need of closer evaluation and intervention.

Your opinions matter to us, and we would welcome your feedback on the way in which change has been assessed. Please email: nationalwell-being@ons.gov.uk

Notes

1.   Figures may not add to 100% due to rounding.

Summary of Life in the UK, 2015

Assessments of change show that overall 74% of measures had improved or shown no overall change in the short term, while 5% had deteriorated and the remaining 21% were not assessed. Over the 3 year period, just over half (51% of measures) had improved or shown no overall change, while 19% had deteriorated. The remaining 30% were not assessed. It is important to examine the detail beneath these assessments to better understand "how we are doing".

In the financial year ending 2014, more people in the UK were feeling positive about their lives than in the financial year ending 2012, according to questions on personal well-being. Young people were less likely than adults to feel a sense that the things they do in life are worthwhile, but more likely to report higher feelings of life satisfaction and happiness.

We are generally living longer and healthier lives. However, a significant proportion of the population have health concerns: 3 in 10 people (31.4%) were dissatisfied with their health in the financial year ending 2013 and around 2 in 10 people (18.8%) reported having a long-term illness or a disability that was either work-limiting or limited their day to day activities in July to September 2014.

Research also shows that people with higher levels of personal well-being make better health and lifestyle choices – they are more likely to eat healthily, be physically active, and are less likely to smoke[1]. Conversely, where the quality and quantity of relationships is poor, people can feel lonely, which is bad for both individual well-being and health. The influence of social relationships is similar to other, well-understood, mortality risk factors, such as smoking and alcohol consumption, and is even greater than the influence of physical activity and obesity[2].

Most of us have good relationships with friends, family and neighbours, with over 8 in 10 (86.7%) reporting that they had a spouse, family member or friend to rely on a lot if they had a serious problem in the financial year ending 2011.

How we use our time has obvious links to our well-being. Active pursuits, such as engaging with the arts, being physically active and volunteering, boosts well-being, while inactivity can have a negative impact. In spite of this, more than half (58.1%) did not participate in 30 minutes or more of moderate intensity sport on a regular basis between October 2013 and October 2014, and 8 in 10

(81.1%) reported that they never, or almost never, did unpaid voluntary work in the financial year ending 2013. However, most of us reported engagement or participation in an arts or cultural activity (83.4%) in the financial year ending 2014, and more than three-quarters of us (77.6%) were at least somewhat satisfied with our work in the financial year ending 2013.

Most of us are either fairly or very satisfied with where we live (in terms of accommodation and the local area). However, there are important differences. For example, in 2012 to 2013 94.9% of owner occupiers in England were very or fairly satisfied with their accommodation and 90.7% were very or fairly satisfied with their local area, compared with 80.6% and 81.9% of social renters.

Around 2 in 10 (21%) of people lived in relative poverty (in households with less than 60% of median income after housing costs) in the financial year ending 2013. One in 10 (10.1%) of us reported finding our financial situation difficult, and median household income in the financial year ending in 2013 was at its lowest level since the financial year ending 2003.

Increases in GDP suggest that the economy is getting stronger. However, since 2011, net national disposable income – that is, the income that is available to the government, businesses and households through production at home and abroad – has remained broadly flat, at £21,888 in 2013, compared with £22,146 in 2011. This suggests that while production in the UK is increasing, the income available to us from that net national disposable income is not increasing in the same way.

The value of human capital in 2013, while broadly stable compared with 2012, has deteriorated over the 3 year period and remains at its lowest since 2005. The proportion of people aged 16 to 64 with no qualifications has fallen significantly over the past decade, and the proportion of pupils gaining 5 or more GCSEs at grades A* to C, including English and Mathematics, has increased over this period. However, the gender gap for GCSE attainment widened over the last few years.

Data from autumn 2014 suggest that the majority of people in the UK are not politically engaged. Almost two-thirds (62%) of people in the UK tend not to trust the government, but this is not a particularly high proportion when compared to other EU countries and is considerably lower than, for example, France, Italy and Spain, where the proportion is closer to three-quarters. Voter turnout at the last general election, while higher than the last two general elections, was the third lowest since 1945. In comparison, however, more than 8 in 10 people voted in the Scottish Independence Referendum in 2014.

The UK is making progress towards key targets such as emissions of greenhouse gasses, renewable energy production and recycling. For example, the UK has a target to recycle compost or reuse at least 50% of the waste generated by households by 2020. In 2012, this figure was 43.9%, an increase of almost 4 percentage points compared with 2010. This figure varies across the constituent countries, and Wales has already exceeded the 2020 target, having recycled, composted or reused 52.5% of household waste in 2012.

How sustainable is our future

Stocks of things like education, natural resources and buildings are known as capitals and provide one means by which to assess how sustainable our future is. This report shows that the value of human capital has remained broadly flat over the last few years, but is below pre-recession levels.

Research shows that the greater a country's human capital, the greater potential for economic growth. Valuation of natural capital is still in development but appears to show long term decline. In 2011, the value of selected components of UK natural capital was £1,573 billion. This had declined by 4.1% since 2007. Measures of social capital, which were published for the first time in January 2015, look at personal relationships, social network support, civic engagement and trust, and cooperative norms, show that in 2011/12, 95% of people had at least one close friend, and in 2012, voluntary activity in the UK was valued at £23.9 billion, which is equivalent to 1.5% of GDP.

Development of natural, human and social capital is still relatively new. By measuring the stocks of things which are important, we develop benchmarks so that decision makers can better consider the impact of their decisions on the nation's future well-being and in turn, how sustainable it is.

Notes

1. Well-being and health policy, Department of Health

2. Holt-Lunstad J, Smith TB, Layton JB (2010) Social Relationships and Mortality Risk: A Meta-analytic Review. *PLoS Medicine* 7(7).

How do we evaluate our own lives?

Assessments of change - Personal well-being

	1 year	3 year
Very high rating of satisfaction with their lives overall	Improved	Not assessed
Very high rating of how worthwhile the things they do are	Improved	Not assessed
Rated their happiness yesterday as very high	Improved	Not assessed
Rated their anxiety yesterday as very low	Improved	Not assessed
Population mental well-being	Not assessed	No overall change

Download table

XLS XLS format
(17 Kb)

Personal well-being is a subjective assessment of how people feel about their own lives. How satisfied people are with their lives, their levels of happiness and anxiety, and whether or not they think the things they do are worthwhile are strongly associated with numerous aspects of national well-being, for example, people's health, education and employment.

Personal well-being

Most UK government departments and the devolved administrations are actively engaged in well-being research. Analysis is focused on how people's ratings of their personal well-being are associated with particular policy areas including housing, crime, adult learning, sport, culture, volunteering and health.

In the financial year ending 2014, over a quarter (26.8%) of people aged 16 and over in the UK rated their life satisfaction at the highest levels[1] compared to 5.6% at the lowest. Just under a third (32.6%) rated their sense that what they do in life is worthwhile at the highest levels, compared to 4.2% at the lowest levels. Similarly, just under a third (32.6%) rated their happiness at the highest levels, while 9.7% rated their happiness at the lowest levels and a higher proportion (39.4%) rated their anxiety at the lowest levels, and 20.0% rated it at the highest levels.

Figure 2: Distribution of personal well-being ratings, financial year ending 2012 to financial year ending 2014 (1,2,3,4)

United Kingdom

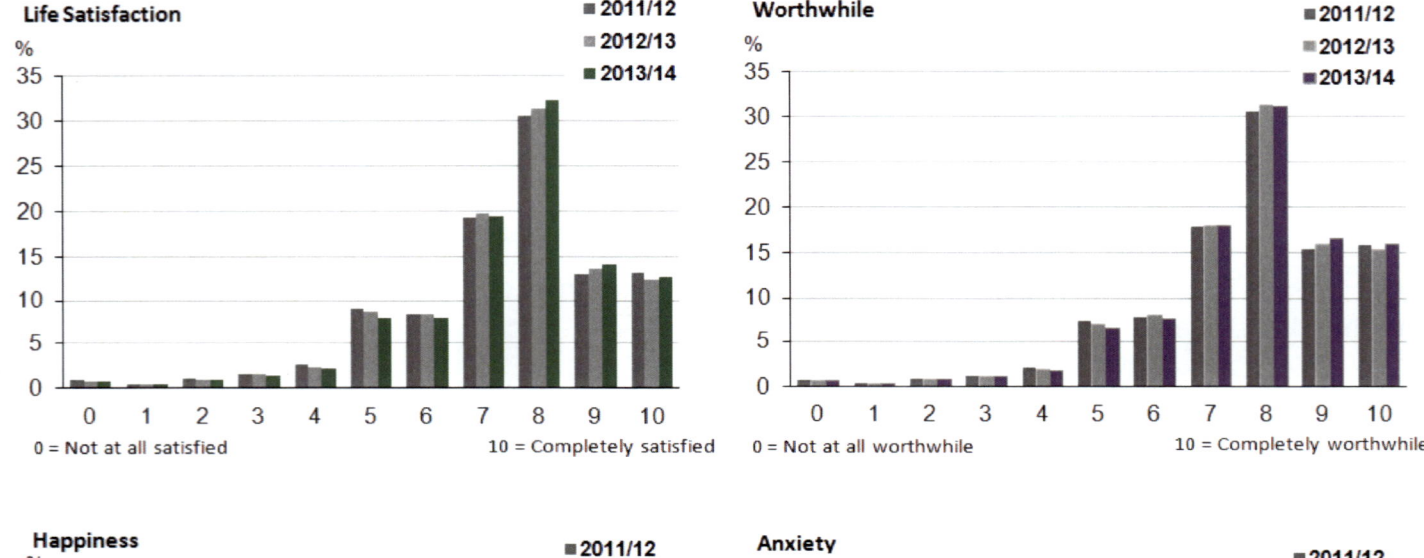

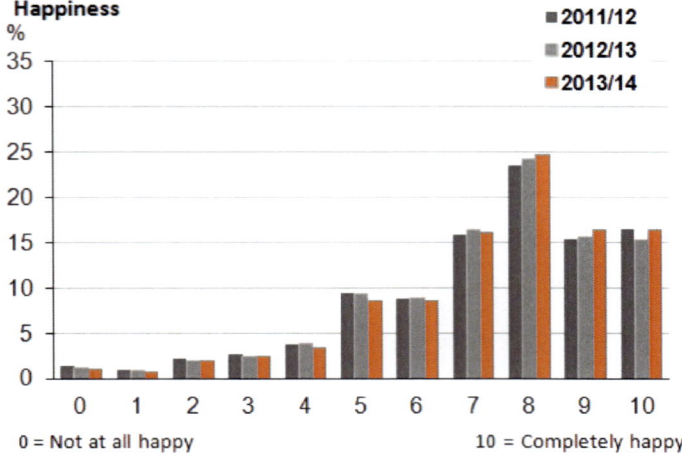

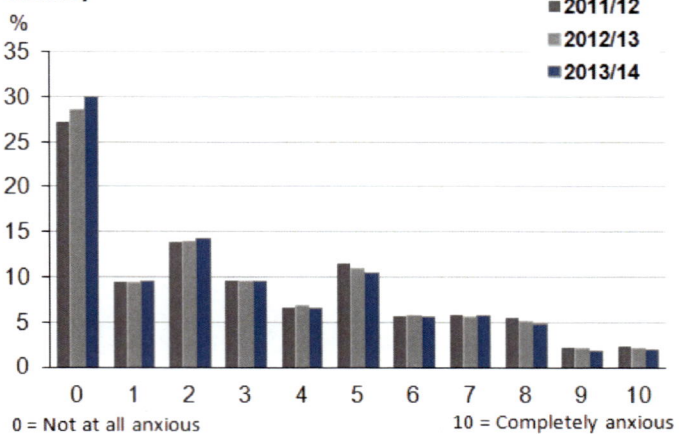

Source: Annual Population Survey (APS) - Office for National Statistics

Notes:

1.   Adults aged 16 and over were asked 'Overall, how satisfied are you with your life nowadays?', 'Overall, to what extent do you feel the things you do in your life are worthwhile?', 'Overall, how happy did you feel yesterday?' and 'Overall, how anxious did you feel yesterday?' where 0 is 'not at all' and 10 is 'completely'.
2.   Data are for financial year ending 2012, 2013 and 2014.
3.   All data weighted.
4.   Please click on the image to view a larger version.

Download chart

XLS XLS format
(28.5 Kb)

The proportion of people giving the highest ratings for each aspect of personal well-being increased significantly in the financial year ending 2014, compared to the previous year (Figure 2). This suggests that more people in the UK are feeling positive about their lives. For those reporting lowest personal well-being, the picture is more mixed. There were significant reductions in the proportions of people giving the lowest ratings of happiness (down 0.7 percentage points) and highest ratings of anxiety (down 0.9 percentage points). The proportions rating their life satisfaction and the sense that what they do in life is worthwhile at the lowest levels remained stable in the financial year ending 2014, compared to the previous year.

Looking at how ratings have changed over the period 2012 to 2014, there have been statistically significant gains in the proportions of people reporting very high personal well-being for each of the 4 measures. The largest gain was in the proportion of people rating their anxiety as very low (up 2.8 percentage points). The smallest gain was in the proportion of people giving the highest ratings of life satisfaction (up 0.6 percentage points). The proportions of people rating their personal well-being at the lowest levels decreased significantly for all 4 measures. The reductions in very low personal well-being ratings ranged from 0.7 percentage points in the case of low ratings for "worthwhile" to 1.8 percentage points in the case of very high ratings of "anxiety".

Children's and young people's well-being

Children and young people make up around 30% of the population of the UK. The Children's Society reported that "Improving levels of subjective well-being and preventing the resulting negative outcomes will reduce the personal impact to children and their families, and help ensure every child growing up in the UK has a good childhood, and positive life chances. It could also avoid the wider social and economic costs of low subjective well-being".

In 2013, just over three-quarters (77%) of children aged 10 to 15 in Great Britain rated their life satisfaction as moderate to high according to data from the Children's Society's Household Survey[2]. Similarly, three-quarters (75%) reported that they felt the things they did in their lives were worthwhile as moderate to high. Just under three-quarters (74%) reported a moderate to high level of happiness yesterday.

Figure 3: Personal well-being measures 1,2 (moderate to high ratings 3,4): by those aged 16 to 24 and all aged 16 and over, financial year ending 2014

United Kingdom

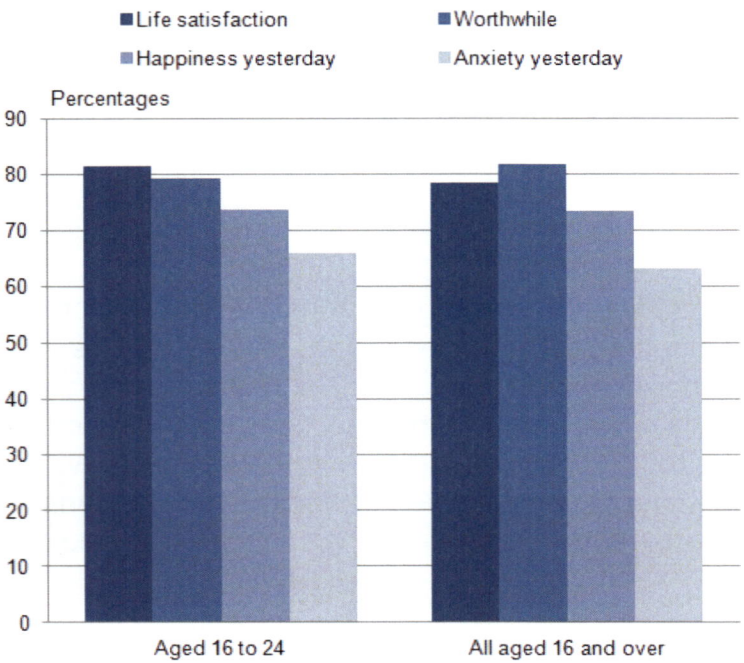

Source: Annual Population Survey (APS) - Office for National Statistics

Notes:
1. The data presented are derived from a customised weighted 12 month Annual Population Survey (APS) micro dataset. This dataset is not part of the regularly produced APS datasets and was produced specifically for the analysis of subjective well-being data.
2. Adults aged 16 and over were asked: "Overall, how satisfied are you with your life nowadays?", "Overall, to what extent do you feel the things you do in your life are worthwhile?", "Overall, how happy did you feel yesterday?" and "Overall, how anxious did you feel yesterday?" where 0 is "not at all" and 10 is "completely".
3. Life satisfaction, Worthwhile and Happiness percentages relate to those who responded 7 to 10 on a scale of 0 to 10 where 0 was not at all and 10 was completely.
4. Anxiety percentage relates to those who responded 0 to 3 on a scale of 0 to 10 where 0 was not at all and 10 was completely.

Download chart

XLS XLS format
(27.5 Kb)

A higher proportion of young people reported having low or very low levels (0 to 3 out of 10) of anxiety than all adults (Figure 3). Just under two-thirds (65.8%) of 16 to 24 year olds reported low or very low anxiety in the financial year ending 2014, compared to 63.1% of all adults aged 16 and over. Young people were also more likely to report higher levels of satisfaction with their life compared with all adults with 81.3% of 16 to 24 year olds reporting high or very high levels (7 to 10 out of 10), compared with 78.5% of all adults. This may relate to the increase in freedom, independence and self-focus associated with emerging adulthood. A similar proportion of young people reported high or very high levels of happiness yesterday, compared with all adults in this period (73.6% and 73.3% respectively).

Despite larger proportions of young people reporting higher levels of life satisfaction and happiness and lower levels of anxiety, young people are less likely than all adults to consider the things they do in their life are worthwhile. In the financial year ending 2014, 79.1% of 16 to 24 year olds considered the things they do in life to be worthwhile as high or very high, compared with 81.8% of all adults.

Notes

1. The highest levels of life satisfaction, worthwhile and happiness include ratings of 9 or 10 out of 10. For anxiety, ratings of 0 or 1 out of 10 indicate the lowest levels of anxiety and therefore the highest well-being. The lowest levels of life satisfaction, worthwhile and happiness include ratings of 0 to 4 out of 10. For anxiety, ratings of 6 or more out of 10 indicate the highest levels of anxiety and therefore the lowest well-being.

2. The survey asks children to rate their happiness yesterday, their satisfaction with life overall, and whether they consider the things they do are worthwhile. The rating is on a scale of 0 to 10, where "0" is not at all and "10" is completely. The ONS measure of "anxiety yesterday" is not included for children, due to ethical considerations. The proportion of children with a moderate to high level of well-being, which is defined as a score of 7 or more is used as the "headline" measure.

How good are our relationships?

Assessments of change - Our relationships

	1 year	3 year
Average rating of satisfaction with family life	Not assessed	No overall change
Average rating of satisfaction with social life	Not assessed	No overall change
Has a spouse, family member or friend to rely on if they have a serious problem	Not assessed	Not assessed

Download table

XLS XLS format
(25 Kb)

Good social relationships and connections with people around us are vitally important to individual well-being. This is important to national well-being because the strength of these relationships helps generate social values such as trust in others and social cooperation between people and institutions within our communities.

Satisfaction with family life and social life

In 2011, adults aged 18 and over in the UK scored their satisfaction with family life as 8.2 out of 10[1] (on average) and 7.1 out of 10 for satisfaction with social life. These ratings were broadly unchanged since the previous surveys in 2007 and 2003.

Figure 4: Distribution of satisfaction with family life and satisfaction with social life ratings, 2011

United Kingdom

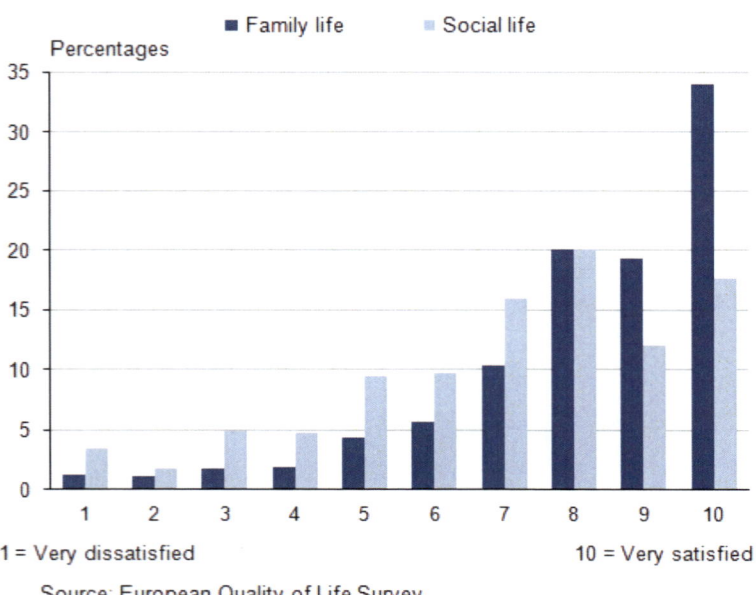

Source: European Quality of Life Survey

Download chart

XLS XLS format
(27.5 Kb)

A higher proportion of people aged 18 and over (53.3%) rated their satisfaction with family life as very high (rating of 9 or 10 out of 10), compared to their satisfaction with social life (29.7%) (Figure 4). Similarly a higher proportion of people (15.1%) rated their satisfaction with their social life as low (rating of 1 to 4 out of 10), compared to their satisfaction with family life (6.2%).

Those aged 18 to 24 and 65 and over reported the highest average (mean) rating with their social life at 8.0 and 7.6 out of 10 respectively. People aged 25 to 34 reported an average (mean) rating of 7.0 and those aged 35 to 64 a rating of 6.6 out of 10. Those aged 65 and over and 18 to 24 reported the highest average (mean) rating with their family life at 8.6 and 8.4 out of 10 respectively. People aged 25 to 34 reported an average (mean) rating of 8.2 and those aged 35 to 64 a rating of 8.0 out of 10.

Family and friends are important because of the support they can provide, either in times of need or on a more regular basis. Over 8 in 10 (86.7%) adults aged 16 and over had a spouse, family member or friend to rely on a lot if they had a serious problem in the financial year ending 2011 according to the UK Household Longitudinal Survey. People reported being able to rely a lot on their partner (83.3%) and on their family (62.4%), but less than half of people (44.8%) felt they could also rely a lot on their friends. A report published by us in 2014, 'Exploring the Well-being of Young People in the UK', showed that 82% of 16 to 24 year olds had someone to rely on a lot, less than the proportion of all other age groups. The difference may be accounted for by the higher levels of marriage and partnerships in older age groups.

Children's relationships with family

We also published 'Exploring the Well-being of Children in the UK' in 2014. This report cited that "children tend to have higher levels of well-being when they have good social relationships with family and friends..." The report also stated that children who reported relatively high satisfaction with life overall also reported better communication patterns with their parents.

In 2011 to 2012, nearly 70% of children aged 10 to 15 who reported being relatively satisfied with their life overall quarrelled less than once a week with both parents according to the UK Household Longitudinal Survey. This compares with just over 40% of children who reported being relatively unsatisfied quarrelling more than once a week with both parents. Children who were relatively unsatisfied with life overall were almost twice as likely to quarrel with both parents more than once a week as children who were relatively satisfied with life overall (24% compared with 13% respectively). Also, children who reported being relatively satisfied with life overall were around 2 and a half times more likely to talk to both of their parents about things that matter more than once a week than children who reported being relatively unsatisfied with life overall. The link between parents and children's well-being is strong, and persists after children leave home[2].

Friends and associations in the local neighbourhood

Having friends and associations in the local neighbourhood means that people can contribute to, and feel part of, a community. Over half (54.5%) of adults aged 16 and over reported that they strongly agreed or agreed that the friendships and associations they have with other people in their neighbourhood meant a lot to them. When split by gender, friendships and associations in the neighbourhood meant a lot to 52.0% of men compared with 56.9% of women.

Figure 5: Proportion that agree that friendship and associations in the local neighbourhood mean a lot (1): by age-group, financial year ending 2012

United Kingdom

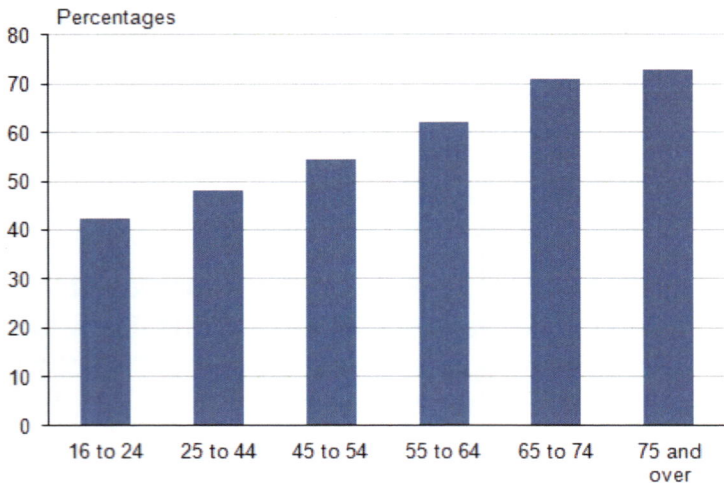

Source: Understanding Society, The UK Household Longitudinal Survey

Notes:

1. Adults aged 16 and over were asked 'The friendships and associations I have with other people in my neighbourhood mean a lot to me'. The chart shows those that strongly agreed or agreed with the statement.

Download chart

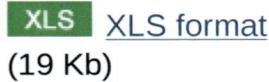 XLS format

(19 Kb)

The proportion of people in the UK who strongly agreed or agreed that the friendships and associations they have with other people in their neighbourhood meant a lot to them increased with age (Figure 5). Under half (42.5%) of people aged 16 to 24 agreed with the statement increasing to nearly three-quarters (73.1%) of those aged 75 and over. This could be because neighbourhood relations are more important to the generation of people who are currently aged 75 and over, or it could be that we value these types of relationships more as we age.

Notes

1. Using a scale from 1 to 10 where 1 indicates "very dissatisfied" and 10 indicates "very satisfied".

2. Predicting well-being, report commissioned by the Department of Health and available at Nat Cen Social Research

How good is our health?

Assessments of change - Health

	1 year	3 year
Healthy life expectancy at birth (male)	Improved	Improved
Healthy life expectancy at birth (female)	Improved	Improved
Reported a long term illness and a disability	Not assessed	Not assessed
Somewhat, mostly or completely satisfied with their health	No overall change	Deteriorated
Some evidence indicating depression or anxiety	No overall change	Deteriorated

Download table

 XLS format
(17.5 Kb)

During the Measuring National Well-being debate[1], health was the thing people routinely said was most important to their own, and to national well-being. The relationship between health and well-being is a cyclical one. Good physical and mental health enables people to deal with the challenges of everyday life, for example, having good health makes it easier to work, to care for yourself and others and to have an active social life, all of which contribute to higher levels of individual, and, in turn, national well-being. In return, positive well-being can lead to good health. Good well-being is associated with positive health behaviours in both adults and children, it improves recovery from illness and it can add years to your life. Improving the nation's well-being could ultimately reduce the cost of national healthcare.

Satisfaction with health

Over half (59.3%) of adults aged 16 and over were somewhat, mostly or completely satisfied with their health in the financial year ending 2013. This was broadly unchanged since the financial year ending 2012 and a decrease of 9.0 percentage points since the financial year ending 2010 according to data from the UK Household Longitudinal Survey. Health problems generally develop with age, so it is reasonable to expect young people to be more satisfied with their health than older people. Just under two-thirds (65.1%) of those aged 16 to 24 reported being somewhat, mostly or completely satisfied with their health in the financial year ending 2013 compared to 56.3% of those aged 75 and over. Further data from the same survey published by us in December 2014, gives an indication of good physical health for a large majority of children in the UK. In the financial year ending 2011, 93.0% of children aged 10 to 15 perceived their health as excellent, very good or good.

Figure 6: Average personal well-being, by self reported health, financial year ending 2014 (1,2,3,4,)

United Kingdom

Source: Annual Population Survey (APS) - Office for National Statistics

Notes:
1. Adults aged 16 and over were asked "Overall, how satisfied are you with your life nowadays?", "Overall, to what extent do you feel the things you do in your life are worthwhile?", "Overall, how happy did you feel yesterday?" and "Overall, how anxious did you feel yesterday?" where nought is "not at all" and 10 is "completely".
2. Data from April 2013 to March 2014.
3. All data weighted.
4. Non-respondents not included.

Download chart

 XLS format
(27 Kb)

Figure 6 shows that in general, the better people say their health is, the higher they rate their life satisfaction, worthwhile and happiness and the lower they rate their anxiety[2].

Between the financial years ending 2012 and 2014, the average well-being for people reporting "very good" and "good" health has significantly improved across all 4 well-being questions. There was no significant change in the average for any of the personal well-being measures among those rating their health as "bad" or "very bad". For those who rated their health as "fair" there was a significant improvement in average life satisfaction and anxiety ratings, but no significant change in average worthwhile and happiness ratings[3].

Healthy life expectancy

People are living longer than ever before; a boy or girl born today could expect to live 78.9 and 82.7 years respectively, if mortality rates remain the same as they were in 2011 to 2013 throughout their lives. It is important to measure how many of these years can be expected to be lived in good general health.

In the UK, a newborn baby in 2009 to 2011 is expected to live more years in "good" health than a baby born in 2000 to 2002 (an increase of 3.7 years for females and 3.5 years for males). The proportion of life spent in "good" health at birth has increased over the same period by 2.6 and 1.7 percentage points for females and males, respectively.

In the UK, females born in 2009 to 2011 are estimated to live 66.1 years in "good" health (80.2% of their life), for males it is 64.2 years (81.9% of their life). The gender gap in healthy life expectancy at birth is 1.9 years, with males living fewer years in "good" health compared with females.

Long-term health problem or disability

In July to September 2014, 18.8% of people aged 16 to 64 in the UK reported either having a long-term health problem or disability or a disability that limited their day-to-day activities. The proportion of people that reported a long term illness and a disability varied between men and women at 17.3% and 20.3% respectively. Many of the long-term health problems that people suffer with are linked to lifestyle and ageing, and, with both an ageing and growing population, it is likely that the number of people who will end up with a long-term condition will also increase. Strategies to cope with this include: targeting known risk factors, such as drinking, smoking and obesity; giving patients control; integrating care; and integrating mental and physical health care[4].

Mental health

Positive mental health is people thinking and feeling good about themselves and feeling able to cope with their problems. A current measure of national well-being is the percentage of those with some indication of anxiety and depression. This uses the General Health Questionnaire (GHQ) which asks respondents 12 questions about their recent feelings. A high score on the GHQ indicates that the respondent may have a mild to moderate mental illness - the types of mental illness which might be indicated on this scale don't include severe mental disorders characterised by derangement of personality, loss of contact with reality or deterioration of normal social functioning.

Figure 7: Evidence indicating depression or anxiety (1): by age, financial year ending 2013

United Kingdom

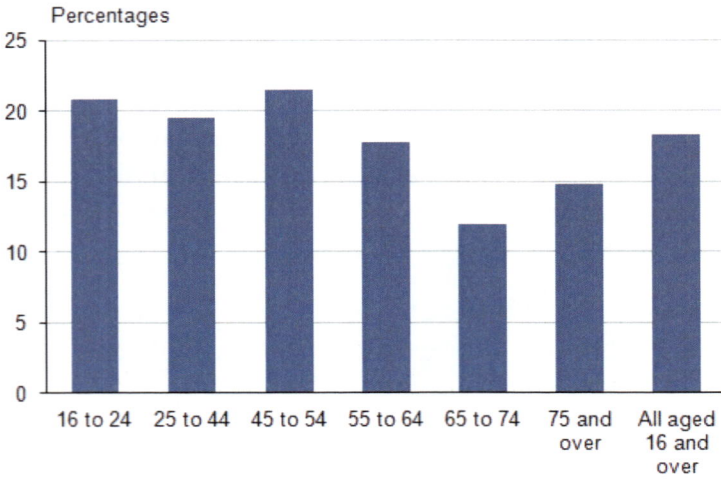

Source: Understanding Society, The UK Household Longitudinal Survey

Notes:

1. Responses are made on a scale of 0 to 12. Responses of 4 or more are regarded as indications of mental ill health. For more information see www.gl-assesment.co.uk/products/general-health-questionnaire/general-health-questionnaire-faqs

Download chart

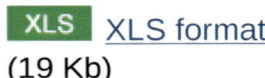 XLS format

(19 Kb)

In the financial year ending 2013, nearly 1 in 5 (18.3%) of people in the UK aged 16 and over had a GHQ score of 4 or more indicating some evidence of anxiety or depression, unchanged from the financial year ending 2012. The percentage was higher for women (21.5%) than for men (14.8%). There was also variation by age group, with those aged 16 to 54 more likely to have a GHQ score of 4 or more than those aged 65 and over (Figure 7).

Notes

1. Findings from the National Well-being Debate (407.1 Kb Pdf)

2. It is important to highlight that the measure of health used here is based on people's views of their health rather than on objective information about people's health. As such, it is likely to reflect people's emotional as well as physical state and the degree of optimism they have about their health. Similarly, people's ratings of their well-being reflect their emotional state and

optimism about life. For this reason, it is perhaps not surprising that people's perceptions of their health are strongly related to their perceptions of their life.

3. Significance in this instance has been calculated on the basis of non-overlapping 95% confidence intervals on unrounded data.

4. "We are living longer-fact-Dr Martin Mcshane", NHS England

How do we spend our time and are we satisfied with its use?

Assessments of change - What we do

	1 year	3 year
Unemployment rate	Improved	Improved
Somewhat, mostly or completely satisfied with their job	No overall change	No overall change
Somewhat, mostly or completely satisfied with their amount of leisure time	No overall change	Deteriorated
Volunteered more than once in the last 12 months	No overall change	Not assessed
Engaged with/participated in arts or cultural activity at least 3 times in last year	No overall change	Improved
Adult participation in 30 mins of moderate intensity sport, once per week	Deteriorated	Improved

Download table

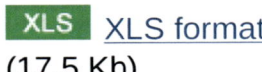 XLS format
(17.5 Kb)

How we spend our time and how we feel about it contributes to national well-being because it shapes our lifestyles, our relationships with others, our health and our collective individual well-being. Across the UK people live their lives based on individual choices, personal preferences and circumstances. Individuals divide their time between various tasks and activities, including paid or unpaid employment, volunteering and various leisure activities.

Employment

Work is an important part of most people's lives, it can provide structure and routine and a sense of self-worth which is essential for our well-being. There is also evidence that happy and satisfied workers are more productive at work. In terms of national well-being, changing demographics such as an ageing population mean that having more people in work is increasingly important for our communities and the economy[1]. Latest data from the Labour Force Survey shows that between the 3 months ending January 2014 and the 3 months ending January 2015 the proportion aged 16 to 64 in work grew from 72.1% to 73.3%.

Job satisfaction

Job satisfaction is considered a strong predictor of overall individual well-being (Diaz-Serrano and Cabral Vieira, 2005). Many factors can contribute to people's feelings of satisfaction about their job such as the nature of the work, their pay and their hours of work. In the financial year ending 2013 nearly 8 in 10 (77.6%) adults aged 16 and over in the UK reported that they were somewhat, mostly or completely satisfied with their job according to the UK Household Longitudinal Survey. This compares with 77.3% in the financial year ending 2012 and 78.5% in the financial year ending 2011. Just under 1 in 10 (9.4%) adults reported that they were neither satisfied nor dissatisfied in the financial year ending 2013, while 13.0% reported being somewhat, mostly or completely dissatisfied.

Unemployment

There is strong evidence showing that work is generally good for physical and mental health and well-being. Worklessness is associated with poorer physical and mental health and well-being[2]. For example, in 2014 research by the Department for Work and Pensions (DWP) and NatCen Social Research found that Jobseeker's Allowance claimants had lower personal well-being than other people of employment age. DWP are now researching support packages for the very long-term unemployed with the aim of reducing anxiety associated with work placements.

Figure 8: Unemployment rate (1) (aged 16 and over), seasonally adjusted

United Kingdom

Source: Labour Force Survey - Office for National Statistics

Notes:

1. The unemployment rate is calculated as the number of unemployed people aged 16 and over divided by the economically active population for that age group.

Download chart

 XLS format
(40.5 Kb)

In the UK, the unemployment rate fell between the three months ending January 2014 and the three months ending January 2015 from 7.2% to 5.7%; this decrease was equivalent to 479,000 people (Figure 8).

Volunteering

Apart from paid employment, individuals may spend time on things that might be considered as unpaid work or voluntary work. A report by the Cabinet Office, 'Wellbeing and Civil Society'[3] stated that "Volunteering is vital to charities and civil society, helps to strengthen local communities, and improves the wellbeing of individuals who participate"

According to the UK Household Longitudinal Survey, 17.3% of adults aged 16 and over had done some form of voluntary work more than once in the 12 months prior to interview in the financial year ending 2013. Over 8 in 10 (81.1%) had never, or almost never, done any voluntary work, while 1 in 10 (9.3%) worked voluntarily at least once a week. Women were more likely than men to have done some form of voluntary work more than once in the 12 months prior to interview, 18.6% and 16.1% respectively.

We published a report 'Valuing Voluntary Activity in the UK'[4] in December 2013 showing the volume of non market activity associated with volunteering in the financial year ending in 2013. UK residents formally volunteered 2.12 billion hours and the value of frequent volunteering[3] was £23.9 billion in the financial year ending 2013. This value is an estimate of what the same number of hours would cost if they were being provided by a paid person in the market. Research by the charity Join-in shows that accounting for the well-being benefits of volunteering significantly increases its value; their estimates of the value of sport volunteering in the UK are 30 times higher when you factor in well-being benefits compared with wage-replacement estimates.

Participation in both physical and non-physical leisure activities

Participation in both physical and non-physical leisure activities has been shown to increase general psychological well-being and life satisfaction as it helps to release the stress of work and everyday life[5].

Over half (58.2%) of adults aged 16 and over were somewhat, mostly or completely satisfied with their amount of leisure time in the financial year ending 2013 – no overall change from a year earlier according to the UK Household Longitudinal Survey. Over a quarter (27.6%) reported that they were somewhat, mostly or completely dissatisfied with their amount of leisure time.

According to the Taking Part Survey run by the Department for Culture, Media and Sport over 8 in 10 (83.4%) adults aged 16 and over in England engaged with, or participated in, arts or cultural activity at least three times in the year prior to interview in the financial year ending 2014. More women than men participated or engaged at 85.4% and 81.3% respectively. Between the financial years ending 2009 and 2014, the proportion of engagement and participation in an arts or cultural activity rose in most age groups, most notably by 6 percentage points for those aged 16 to 24 and 5 percentage points for those aged 65 to 74[6,7].

Between October 2013 and October 2014, over a third (35.8%) of adults aged 16 and over in England participated in at least 30 minutes of sport at moderate intensity at least once a week according to the Active People Survey, equivalent to 15.6 million people. However, more than half (58.1%) did not participate in at least 30 minutes of moderate intensity sport on a regular basis. Men were more likely than women to participate once a week (40.8% and 31.0% respectively).When analysed by age group over the same period, 3.8 million young people (54.7%) aged 16 to 25 participated once a week compared with 11.8 million adults (32.2%) aged 26 and over. The NHS recommends that adults aged 19 to 64 should try to be active daily and should do at least 150 minutes of moderate intensity aerobic activity every week, as well as muscle strengthening activities on 2 or more days a week[8].

Notes

1. "New study shows we work harder when we are happy" - Warwick University

2. Gordon Waddell, A Kim Burton - Is Work Good for your Health and Well-being?

3. Frequent voluntary activity is those who volunteer at least once a month.

4. Wellbeing and civil society: Estimating the value of volunteering using subjective wellbeing data

5. Household Satellite Accounts - Valuing Voluntary Activity in the UK

6. Haworth - Life, Work, Leisure and Enjoyment: the role of social institutions.

7. Similar data for arts and culture for the devolved administrations are available from the Scottish Household Survey, the Welsh Omnibus Survey and the Arts and Culture in Northern Ireland 2012 report.

8. Physical activity guidelines for adults, NHS Choices

How do we feel about where we live?

Assessments of change - Where we live

	1 year	3 year
Crimes against the person (per 1,000 adults)	Improved	Improved
Felt fairly/very safe walking alone after dark (men)	No overall change	No overall change
Felt fairly/very safe walking alone after dark (women)	No overall change	Deteriorated
Accessed natural environment at least once a week in the last 12 months	No overall change	Improved
Agreed/agreed strongly they felt they belonged to their neighbourhood	Deteriorated	Not assessed
Households with good transport access to key services or work (2010 = 100)	No overall change	No overall change
Fairly/very satisfied with their accommodation	No overall change	No overall change

Download table

XLS XLS format
(18 Kb)

Given the amount of time that we spend at home and in our local neighbourhood, how we feel about where we live is vital to our overall well-being. The 2014 Legatum report on well-being and policy argues that ensuring our built environment is sociable and green should be a priority: "Spaces that create opportunities for people to dwell and meet, be they parks, porches, or post offices, provide the soil for the seeds of friendship and connection to grow"[1]. Positive feelings about where we live can also create a strong, inclusive community where people feel that they belong, and where they feel safe. In turn communities that are strong are more likely to deliver higher rates of social and civic participation, lower rates of crime, and improved physical and mental health among its inhabitants.

Satisfaction with accommodation and local area

Housing represents the largest consumption item and investment in a person's lifetime and it is a place where people spend a lot of their time. It is therefore important to measure a person's satisfaction with their accommodation as it is a factor in assessing a person's quality of life.

Just over 9 in 10 (90.6%) of households in England in 2012 to 2013 reported that they were very or fairly satisfied with their accommodation, no overall change from a year earlier, but variations exist by tenure. In 2012 to 2013, 94.9% of owner occupiers said that they were either very or fairly satisfied with their accommodation while 2.6% stated they were either slightly or very dissatisfied. In comparison, 80.6% of social renters and 84.3% of private renters were either very or fairly satisfied.

Households were also asked to rate their levels of satisfaction with their local area using a five-point scale from "very satisfied" through to "very dissatisfied". Over half (55.5%) were very satisfied with their local area, while just under a third (32.1%) were fairly satisfied in 2012 to 2013. The majority of owner occupied households (90.7%) were satisfied with their local area. This was higher than the proportion of private renters (87.2%) and social renters (81.9%).

Belonging to a neighbourhood

Having a sense of belonging to a neighbourhood is an important factor not only to personal well-being but also to the local community because people are more inclined to live, work and invest in an area they have an affinity with.

In the financial year ending 2012, over 6 in 10 (62.8%) people aged 16 and over agreed or strongly agreed that they belonged to their neighbourhood, a fall of 3.2 percentage points since the financial year ending 2010 according to the UK Household Longitudinal Survey . The proportion of people who felt strongly that they belonged to a neighbourhood increased by age. Just under half (49.5%) of those aged 16 to 24 agreed or strongly agreed that they belonged to their neighbourhood compared to 81.0% of those aged 75 and over. People in Northern Ireland (72.3%) and Scotland (69.1%) were more likely to agree that they belonged to their neighbourhood, while those living in London (59.5%) were least likely to agree.

Access to key services

The proximity of housing to a range of employment, services and facilities, as well as the public transport infrastructure determines how far and how long people have to travel. This could have a bearing on the satisfaction level with the area in which they live. The Department for Transport measures access to 8 key services[2] in England by public transport and walking[3] that are used in accessibility planning by local authorities.

Between 2011 and 2013 travel times to the nearest local services showed little change. The average minimum travel time to the selection of key services in 2013 by public transport or walking was 12 minutes. Looking at these trips in more detail, the average minimum travel time to the nearest service by public transport or walking was lowest for primary schools and food stores (7 minutes) and highest for hospitals (25 minutes). However, there was considerable variation in these times between those living in rural areas and those living in urban areas. The average minimum travel times across the range of key services by public transport or walking were 10 minutes for urban areas and 19 minutes for rural areas.

Access to the natural environment

Various studies have demonstrated associations between access to local green space and people's health and well-being. Those living in areas with high quantities of green space have been found to have better health, as measured using both self-reported data from surveys and records of morbidity and mortality rates[4].

The adult population of England made approximately 2.93 billion visits to natural environments between March 2013 and February 2014 – the highest 12 month total recorded to date[5]. Around 6 in 10 (58%) adults aged 16 and over in England reported that they visited the outdoors, away from home, at least once a week, in the 12 months prior to interview. Just over 1 in 10 (11%) reported that they visited on a daily basis, while 8% stated that they had not visited in the previous 12 months. Walking was the most popular activity on visits to the natural environment and was a selected activity on just over three-quarters of all visits (76%). Walking with a dog was undertaken on a half (50%) of all visits and walking without a dog on 26%.

Crime

High or increasing crime levels have a negative effect on local communities. This can result in residents increasing desire to move house and a weaker attachment and satisfaction with their neighbourhood, which may culminate in lower house values.

There were an estimated 7.3 million incidents of crime against households and resident adults (aged 16 and over) for the year ending March 2014 according to the Crime Survey for England and Wales. This represents a 14% decrease from 8.5 million incidents compared with the previous year's survey and continues the long downward trend seen since the mid-1990s.

Figure 9: Crimes against the person (1)

England and Wales

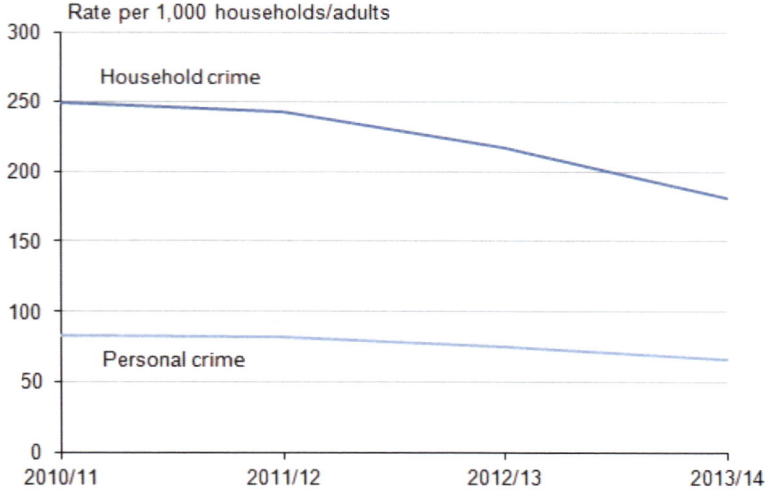

Source: Crime Survey for England and Wales - Office for National Statistics

Notes:

1. Years in chart are financial years.

Download chart

XLS XLS format
(26.5 Kb)

In the financial year ending 2014 there were an estimated 181 crimes per 1,000 households and 66 personal crimes per 1,000 adults aged 16 and over. This compares to 249 crimes per 1,000 households and 83 personal crimes per 1,000 adults in the financial year ending 2011 (Figure 9).

Feeling safe

Feeling safe in a local area can be an important factor for a person's sense of satisfaction in the area around them. A good indicator of this is to find out whether a person feels safe walking alone after dark. The perception of safety is not necessarily directly correlated to local crime rates but is linked to a person's trust in the safety of the area around them.

According to the Crime Survey for England and Wales 85.1% of men and 58.0% of females aged 16 and over in the financial year ending 2014 reported that they felt fairly or very safe walking alone after dark, broadly unchanged from a year earlier. Among the English regions, both men and women were more likely to report that they felt fairly or very safe walking alone after dark in the South West (91.2% and 66.1% respectively). Men were least likely to report that they felt fairly or very safe walking alone after dark in London (76.1%), while women reported feeling less safe in the West Midlands (52.6%). In Wales, 91.1% of men and 56.9% of women reported that they felt fairly or very safe walking alone after dark.

Notes

1. O"Donnell GC, Deaton A, Durand M, Halpern D, Layard R. Wellbeing and policy. London: Legatum Institute, 2014.

2. Employment centres; primary schools; secondary schools; further education institutions; GPs; hospitals; food stores; and town centres.

3. Data on other modes of transport, for example, cycle and car are also collected.

4. Maas et al., 2006, 2009; Mitchell and Popham, 2007, 2008.

5. Similar data for Scotland are available from Scotland's People and Nature Survey and for Wales from the Welsh Outdoor Recreation Survey.

How are we coping financially?

Assessments of change - Personal finance

	1 year	3 year
Individuals in households with less than 60% of median income after housing costs	No overall change	No overall change
Median wealth per household, including pension wealth	Not assessed	Not assessed
Real median household income	No overall change	Deteriorated
Somewhat, mostly or completely satisfied with the income of their household	No overall change	Deteriorated
Report finding it quite or very difficult to get by financially	Improved	Improved

Download table

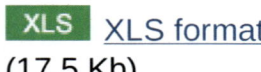 XLS format
(17.5 Kb)

As household income rises, life satisfaction and happiness also tend to rise, while anxiety levels tend to fall. However, what makes most difference to personal well-being is the level of individual's income relative to those around them; wealthier people tend to have better well-being than poorer people in the same society, but if wealth increases for everyone then average levels of personal well-being are likely to stay the same[1]. On average, those living in the poorest households report lower well-being. They are also are more likely to have poorer physical health and less healthy behaviours[2].

Median household income

Median household income[3] is the income of the middle household if all households are ranked from the lowest income to the highest, and therefore it gives us an indication of the income of the "typical" household.

Latest available data shows that between the financial years ending 2012 and 2013 median income fell 1.4% to £23,316. This is a continuation of the downward trend that has been seen in median income since the financial year ending 2010. Median income in the financial year ending 2013 was at its lowest level since the financial year ending 2003. However, the rate of decline has slowed over the last two years.

More recent data on household income are available from the National Accounts. Real Household Disposable Income (RHDI) per head is a measure of average household income adjusted for price changes to allow comparison over time. In the 3 months ending September 2014, RHDI per head decreased slightly (0.2%) on the quarter, but remains broadly in line with its pre-recession levels.

In 2008, Gross Domestic Product (GDP) began to fall but real household income per head remained fairly buoyant. In the 3 months ending June 2009, real household income per head was 3.8% above its pre-recession level. This was mainly due to historically low interest rates, falling employment and rising unemployment which meant that real household incomes were supported by rising social security benefits and reduced taxes. In early 2011 the impact of these factors had worn off and inflation had risen which eroded the growth of household incomes. Since 2011 real household income per head has remained broadly flat.

Although looking at average income (either median income or RHDI per head) is useful, it is also important to consider how income is distributed around the middle. In particular, it is important to look at those who have lower than average incomes as a way of understanding what percentage of the population are "in poverty". Poverty may have an effect on individuals ability to participate in social, economic, political and cultural life and their relationships with others close to them and in the wider community.

Proportion of individuals living in households with less than 60% of median income

One measure of poverty is to consider relative low income – those households with less than 60% of the median net household income, before and after housing costs. This type of relative indicator does not measure absolute poverty, but low income in comparison to other people, which in itself does not necessarily imply a low standard of living.

In the financial year ending 2013 the proportion of individuals living in households with less than 60% of median income after housing costs was 21%. This has been on a general downward trend since the financial year ending 1999, including through the economic downturn. This shows the gap between those at the bottom of the income distribution and the median has narrowed. However, this is as a result of a fall in the median income rather than increased income for those at the bottom of the income distribution.

Households with above average poverty rates include large families, workless households, lone parents and those without educational qualifications.

As well as considering levels of household income, it is important to consider individuals perceptions of their own income. It is individuals' perceptions of their own incomes, and their ability to make ends meet, that will influence their own assessment of their well-being.

Satisfaction with the level of income in the household

In the financial year ending 2013, over half (53.4%) of adults aged 16 and over in the UK were somewhat, mostly, or completely satisfied with the level of income in their household according to data from the UK Household Longitudinal Study[4].

Satisfaction with income saw a downward trend between the financial years ending 2007 and 2012, with a fall of 4.7 percentage points between the financial years ending 2011 and 2012. At the same time, household incomes were falling. More recently, the increase to 53.4% in the financial year ending 2013 shows some improvement in satisfaction with income. However, it remains below the levels seen prior to the economic downturn.

People who find their financial situation quite or very difficult

Respondents aged 16 and over in the UK were asked to rate how they were coping financially from "finding it very difficult" to "living comfortably" on the UK Household Longitudinal Study. In the financial year ending 2013 the proportion of people aged 16 and over in the UK who reported that they were finding their financial situation quite or very difficult was 10.1%, a continuation of the downwards trend seen since the peak in the financial year ending 2010.

The proportion finding their financial situation quite or very difficult varied between the age groups in the financial year ending 2013.

Figure 10: Percentage who report finding it quite or very difficult to get by financially: by age group, financial year ending 2013

United Kingdom

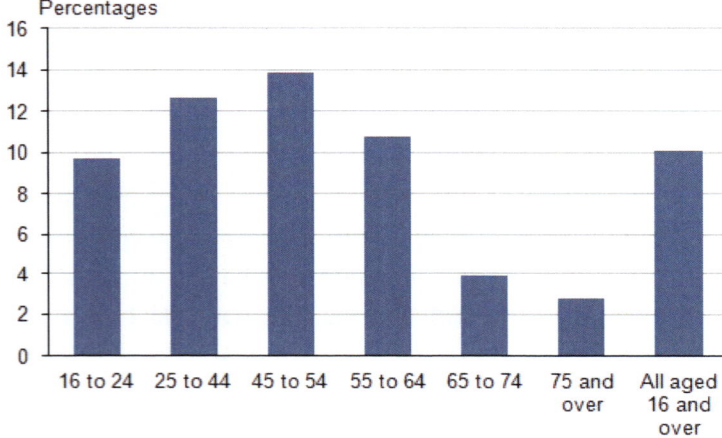

Source: Understanding Society, The UK Household Longitudinal Survey

Download chart

XLS XLS format
(17 Kb)

A higher percentage of those aged 25 to 64 reported finding their financial situation quite or very difficult than the average for all aged 16 and over (Figure 10). For those aged 65 and over a considerably smaller proportion of each age group reported that they were finding their financial situation quite or very difficult.

Wealth

Wealth is an important component of the economic well-being of households as it can be used to fund future consumption and can provide a "safety net" against loss of income. Therefore, when looking at how people are coping financially it is necessary to look further than household income. Home ownership, investment schemes, the ownership of shares and the accumulation of wealth, for instance through pensions, all contribute to the changing composition of wealth. Wealth inequality seems to be much greater than income inequality and therefore may have different implications for well-being.

The median household wealth for Great Britain, including pension wealth was £218,400 between July 2010 and July 2012 compared to £204,300 between July 2008 and July 2010 according to the Wealth and Assets Survey. The median value of household wealth masks considerable variation in wealth for households. For example, between July 2010 and July 2012 households a quarter of the way from the top of the distribution of all wealth (at the 75th percentile) had around 9 times more wealth than those households a quarter of the way up the distribution from the bottom (at the 25th percentile).

Figure 11: Distribution of household wealth including pension wealth (1): by region, July 2008 to July 2010

Great Britain

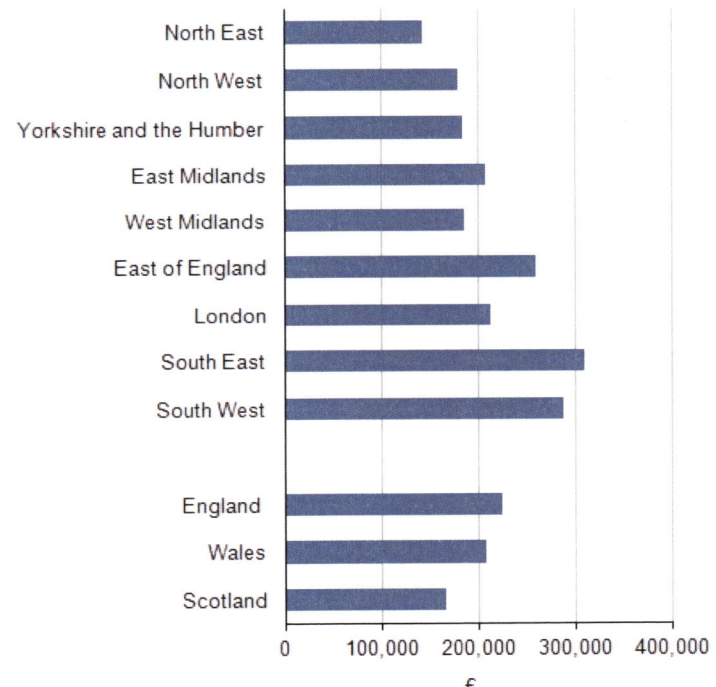

Source: Wealth and Assets Survey - Office for National Statistics

Notes:
1. Excludes assets held in Trusts (except Child Trust Funds) and any business assets held by households. Based on individual responses within households.

Download chart

XLS XLS format
(32 Kb)

Median total household wealth in the South East of England was more than double that in the North East of England between July 2010 and July 2012, the difference between the two medians being around £167,000 (Figure 11).

Across Great Britain, the North East of England and Scotland had the lowest median total household wealth, at £142,700 and £165,500 respectively. The greatest median total household wealth was in the South East of England, at £309,700, followed by the South West at £288,300 and the East of England at £259,900.

Notes

1. Dolan, P., Peasgood, T. and White, M. (2008). Do we really know what makes us happy? A review of the economic literature on the factors associated with subjective well-being.

2. "Low-Income Britons Struggle With Their Wellbeing", Gallup

3. Median equivalised household disposable income. Data are Organisation Economic Co-operations and Development (OECD) equivalised and at 2011/12 prices. The median household income is the income of what would be the middle household, if all households in the UK were sorted in a list from poorest to richest. As it represents the middle of the income distribution, the median household income provides a good indication of the standard of living of the "typical" household in terms of income.

4. Respondents were asked how they felt about the income of their household and responded on a seven point scale from "completely dissatisfied" to "completely satisfied".

How strong is our economy?

Assessments of change - Economy

	1 year	3 year
Real net national disposable income per head	No overall change	No overall change
UK public sector net debt as a percentage of Gross Domestic Product	Not assessed	Not assessed
Inflation rate (as measured by the Consumer Price Index)	Not assessed	Not assessed

Download table

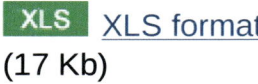 XLS format
(17 Kb)

The economy is an important contextual measure of national well-being. Typically, economic progress is assessed by looking at changes in Gross Domestic Product (GDP), and, for many years, this measure was used as a proxy for "how society is doing". However, it has long been recognised that GDP does not capture everything that determines society's well-being, nor was it designed to do so. The measures in this report supplement GDP to give a fuller picture of national well-being.

There are a range of measures that can be used when assessing economic performance other than GDP, including net national disposable income (NNDI).

Net national disposable income

Figure 12: Real net national disposable income and GDP per head

United Kingdom

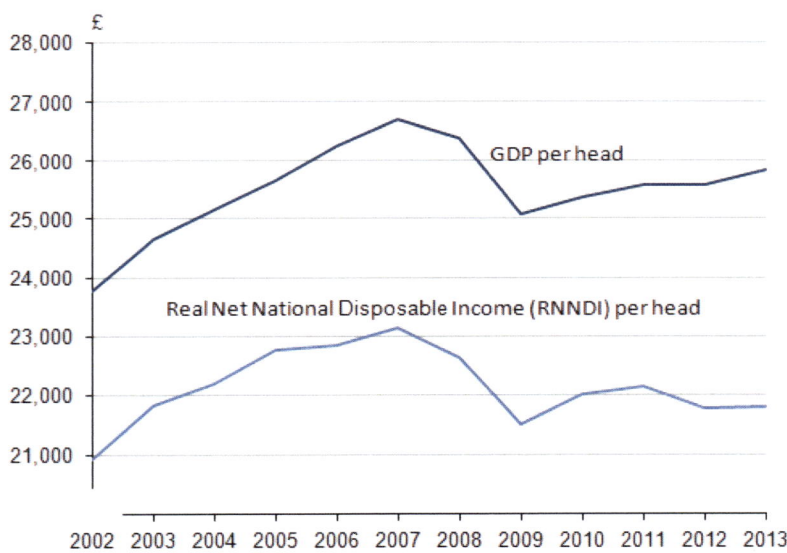

Source: Office for National Statistics

Download chart

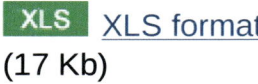 XLS format
(17.5 Kb)

NNDI adjusts GDP to reflect the income actually available to residents of the country from production (either at home or abroad). This measure includes income that is available to businesses and the government, as well as households.

In 2013 real (adjusted for inflation) NNDI per head was £21,888. Looking over the last decade, real NNDI per head peaked at £23,125 in 2007, and was at its lowest in 2009 at £21,508 (Figure 12).

Prior to 2011, the experience of NNDI per head and GDP per head was fairly similar. However since 2011, NNDI has remained broadly flat, despite growth in GDP. This suggests that while production in the UK is increasing, the economy as experienced by individuals is less rosy because the income available to residents of the UK has not grown in the same way. This is reflected in some degree in personal finance. When asked about satisfaction with income and how they were coping financially respondents showed a decline in satisfaction in 2008. Satisfaction levels for both measures remain below those reported before the financial crisis of 2008.

Table 1: Public sector net debt as a proportion of GDP (1,2)

UK

	Percentage of GDP
2000/01	30.1
2001/02	29.3
2002/03	30.3
2003/04	31.7
2004/05	34.3
2005/06	35.4
2006/07	36.0
2007/08	36.7
2008/09	49.0
2009/10	62.0
2010/11	68.7
2011/12	72.3
2012/13	76.7
2013/14	79.1

Table source: Office for National Statistics

Table notes:
1. Public Sector Net Debt excluding temporary effects of financial interventions as a proportion of GDP.
2. Annual figures reported here are financial years.

Download table

 XLS format
(27 Kb)

In the financial year ending 2008 public sector net debt (total gross financial liabilities less liquid financial assets) stood at 36.8% of GDP (Table 1). By the financial year ending 2014 this had more than doubled to 76.3% of GDP.

A high level of government borrowing will result in money having to be spent repaying that debt. This can lead to both a reduction in investment and a requirement on future generations to continue paying off these debts, which could in turn have a negative impact on national well-being and reduce their ability to make further investments. However, public sector debt increases are not necessarily bad for national well-being. For example, a government may borrow to invest in infrastructure projects or training that will benefit individuals and businesses in the long term. An investment in infrastructure may have environmental benefits such as reduced congestion which leads to improved transport access to key services or work, cleaner air and less harmful emissions. An investment in training, more schools or a reduced teacher to pupil ratio may lead to an increase in human capital stock, all of which are beneficial to well-being

Inflation rate

The consumer prices index (CPI) is the inflation measure used in the government's target for inflation. The Bank of England has responsibility for keeping CPI close to a target set by the government (2% as of 2011). The primary aim of this is price stability and to prevent inflation from being too high or low as zero inflation or deflation are also undesirable.

In January 2015, the rate of inflation was 0.3%, a record low. This was 1.6 percentage points lower than in January 2014, and much lower than during 2011 and 2012. The fall in the rate of inflation seen during late 2014 is a continuation of a downward trend that started in mid-2013. Much of this moderation in inflation has come about as a consequence of decreasing energy costs and food and drink prices.

The rate of inflation is important for well-being because of its effect on income and net wealth.

When prices increase faster than income, over time, incomes can buy less and households feel worse off. Equally, if incomes increase faster than prices, over time, incomes can buy more and households feel better off. The income section of this release considers the evolution of household income, adjusted for inflation.

In addition, inflation can impact on households through its effect on net wealth. If inflation is lower than the interest rates offered to households by banks, then the real value of savings increases. If inflation is higher the real value of savings decreases, since 2013 the lower inflation rate has benefitted savers. However, higher levels of inflation can also act to decrease debt, as the amount owed becomes worth less in real terms over time.

Spending patterns differ, meaning the inflation experienced by different households may not be the same. Some households may experience faster rates of price growth than others.

Our analysis in December 2014[1] indicates that the price experience of different types of UK household has varied widely between 2003 and 2014. Households that spend relatively little each month have experienced faster price growth than households who spend more. This may in part be due to food and fuel costs forming a larger proportion of their expenditure than wealthier household groups, food and fuel having experienced stronger than average inflation. This is reflected throughout each income decile as inflation decreases with every decile apart from the 2 wealthiest, 9 and 10, which have the same rate of inflation. Lowest-spending households experienced average annual inflation of 3.3% between 2003 and 2013, compared with 2.3% for among the highest spending households. These differences compound over this period, and consequently the prices of products purchased by the lowest-spending households have risen by 45.5%, compared with just 31.2% for the highest spending households.

Average CPI between 2003 and 2013 was 2.6%. However, looking at household composition, households with children typically experienced an inflation rate of 2.4% while retired households experienced a higher inflation rate of 2.8%. This is in part because retired households were more affected by the changes of energy and food prices than other household groups. Non-retired households as a whole experienced an inflation rate of 2.5%.

Notes

1.   Variation in the inflation experience of UK households index

How skilled are we?

Assessments of change - Educational and skills

	1 year	3 year
Human capital - the value of individuals' skills, knowledge and competences in labour market	No overall change	Deteriorated
Five or more GCSEs A* to C including English and Maths	No overall change	Improved
UK residents aged 16 to 64 with no qualifications	Improved	Improved

Download table

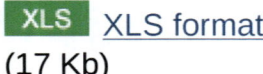 XLS format
(17 Kb)

Having a good education plays a crucial role in enabling people to maximise the opportunities available to them, achieve their potential and make a contribution to the country's economy. Educational qualifications are a key determinant of future employment and income. A wide variety of studies have investigated a positive relationship between education and well-being[1].

Educational attainment

Table 2: GCSE (1) and SCQF (2) attainments (3)

UK (Percentages)

GCSE	2008/09	2009/10	2010/11	2011/12	2012/13
All pupils	49.8	52.9	58.5	59.0	58.9
Boys	45.9	48.9	54.8	54.3	53.7
Girls	54.0	57.1	62.4	63.9	64.4
Gender gap	8.1	8.2	7.6	9.6	10.7
SCQF	**2008/09**	**2009/10**	**2010/11**	**2011/12**	**2012/13**
Level 3 or better	91.5	92.4	92.7	93.9	94.6
Level 4 or better	77.6	78.3	78.8	80.2	82.1
Level 5 or better	35.4	36.1	36.4	37.4	39.4

Source: Department for Education; Welsh Government; Scottish Government; Northern Ireland Department of Education

Table notes:
1. Pupils achieving 5 or more GCSE grades at A*-C including English and mathematics (England, Wales and Northern Ireland).
2. Pupils in last year of compulsory education achieving 5 or more qualifications at SCQF: by level (Scotland).
3. Years are academic years.

Download table

XLS XLS format
(133.5 Kb)

Table 2 shows that the percentage of pupils gaining 5 or more GCSE grades at A* to C including English and Mathematics in England, Wales and Northern Ireland has remained constant since the academic year ending 2012 and rose by around 9 percentage points since the academic year ending 2009[2]. In the academic year ending 2013, girls continued to outperform boys at GCSE with 64.4% of girls achieving 5 or more GCSE grades at A* to C including English and Mathematics compared to 53.7% for boys. The gender gap has widened over each of the last 3 academic years. In Scotland the proportion of pupils in their last year of compulsory education achieving 5 or more qualifications at SCQF level has increased year on year for each level between the academic years ending 2009 and 2013.

Research suggests that non-cognitive skills, such as empathy, non-verbal communication and emotional intelligence, are as important to academic achievement as cognitive skills, such as memory, attention and reasoning. The "How to Thrive" team at Hertfordshire County Council[3] is currently working with academics and local schools to implement a series of programmes aimed at improving pupil's well-being, resilience and motivation. Such programmes could be particularly beneficial for disadvantaged pupils, as these children tend to have poorer non-cognitive skills than more advantaged pupils[4].

While people with qualifications may have a higher chance of securing employment or continuing their education, those without any qualifications may face years of unemployment, underachievement and never realise their full potential in life.

The proportion of people in the UK with no educational qualifications has been falling since 2002 according to data from the Labour Force Survey. In 2002, 15.5% of UK residents had no qualifications; by 2007 this had fallen to 12.9%. In 2014 under 1 in 10 (8.6%) reported that they had no educational qualifications, 6.9 percentage points lower than in 2002. People in Northern Ireland and the West Midlands were more likely to report that they had no qualifications in 2014 (17.0% and 13.4% respectively). People in the South East and South West were least likely to report that they had no qualifications (5.8% and 5.9% respectively).

Human capital

Human capital is a measure of individuals' skills, knowledge, abilities, social attributes, personality and health attributes. These factors enable individuals to work, and therefore produce something of economic value. Individual's labour market outcomes are linked to their human capital. In general, individuals with low skills or levels of education are more likely to be unemployed and face social exclusion. Higher human capital (in particular educational attainment) is also associated with higher earnings. Earnings have been found to be related to life satisfaction and happiness. Human capital can also have social impacts; in particular, higher levels of human capital are associated with improved health outcomes, lower crime rates, and higher rates of trust and social participation. In addition, human capital also has important economic impacts. Research on economic growth suggests that countries with higher levels of human capital, other things being equal, have greater potential output and income in the future.

Figure 13: Employed and full human capital (1,2,3)

United Kingdom

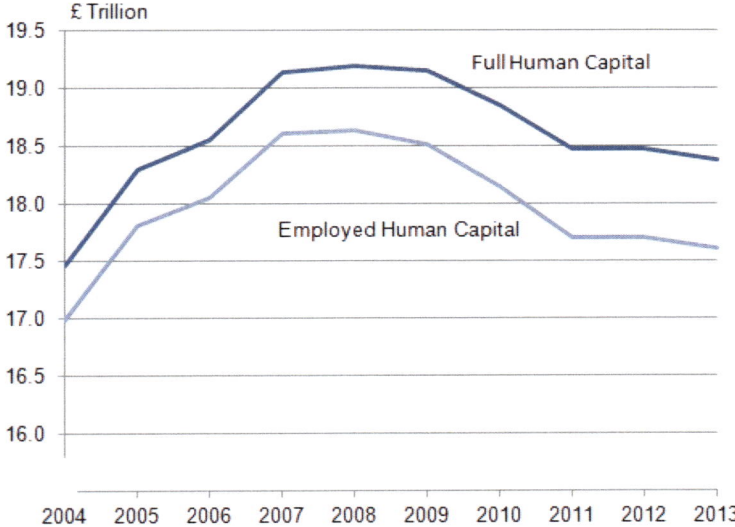

Source: Annual Population Survey (APS) - Office for National Statistics

Notes:
1. Figures in 2013 prices.
2. Labour productivity growth rate = 2%.
3. Discount rate = 3.5%.

Download chart

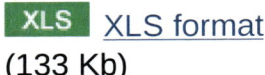 XLS format
(133 Kb)

Figure 13 shows the effect of the economic downturn on the UK's employed human capital stock. Between 2004 and 2007 the value of the UK's human capital stock increased steadily, at an average of 3.1% per year. This was driven by an increase in both the employed working-age population and the skills level of the population. Another important driver of the increase in the value of the UK's human capital stock was earnings growth, which generally grew in real terms between 2004 and 2007. Growth in employed human capital slowed into 2008 (0.2%) before falling slightly in 2009 (negative 0.7%), beginning to reflect the effect of the economic downturn on the UK's human capital stock. With falling employment rates and falls in real earnings, 2010 and 2011 saw further falls in the value of the UK's employed human capital stock (negative 2.0% and negative 2.4% respectively). Following these substantial falls in 2010 and 2011, the value of the UK's human capital stock began to stabilise from 2011.

Further information about human capital can be found in the 'How sustainable is our future well-being?' section of this report.

Notes

1. Dolan et al 2008.

2. In England, Northern Ireland, and Wales pupils take the GCSE (General Certificate of Secondary Education) at 16 and GCE A levels at 18. In Scotland pupils study for their first National Qualifications (NQ), typically at SCQF level 3 to 5, in the fourth year of secondary school. These include Access 3, National 3 to National 5 or Intermediates 1 and 2. NQ Higher grade (SCQF level 6), requires at least a further year of secondary schooling. Although Intermediates 1 and 2 can be taken in the fourth year of secondary school, they are designed primarily for candidates in the fifth and sixth years of secondary school.

3. Healthy Minds, How to Thrive

4. "Developing Healthy Minds in Teenagers", Education Endownment Foundation

How politically engaged are we?

Assessments of change - Governance

	1 year	3 year
Voter turnout (at UK General Elections)	Improved	Deteriorated
Those who have trust in national Government	Improved	Improved

Download table

 XLS format
(17 Kb)

Political engagement matters to our national well-being because it provides citizens with a voice and can help shape government activities which in turn helps build strong and resilient communities.

Voting is the most prominent form of political participation and, for many people, it is the only engagement with politics that they have. However, there are other ways that people can engage in the democratic process, such as contacting an elected representative, attending a public demonstration, attending a public meeting or involvement in decision-making about local services.

Trust in government

In the autumn of 2014, 31% of people aged 15 and over in the UK reported that they "tended to trust" their national government according to a Eurobarometer survey. Although this was a rise of 6 percentage points since spring 2014 and 7 percentage points since autumn 2013, it must be noted that just over 6 in 10 (62%) tended not to trust the government. This figure is comparable with a number of European countries, and lower than France, Italy and Spain, where the proportion that tend not to trust in government is closer to three-quarters. In the spring of 2007 the proportion of people that "tended to trust" the government, stood at over a third (34%) but fell to just under a fifth (19%) in the autumn of 2009. These proportional declines occurred around the time of the UK parliamentary expenses scandal and the start of the financial crisis. During the general election year of 2010, trust in government increased and by spring 2011 it stood at 32% before falling again to around 21% in the autumn of 2011.

Figure 14: Turnout in general elections, 1945 to 2010

United Kingdom

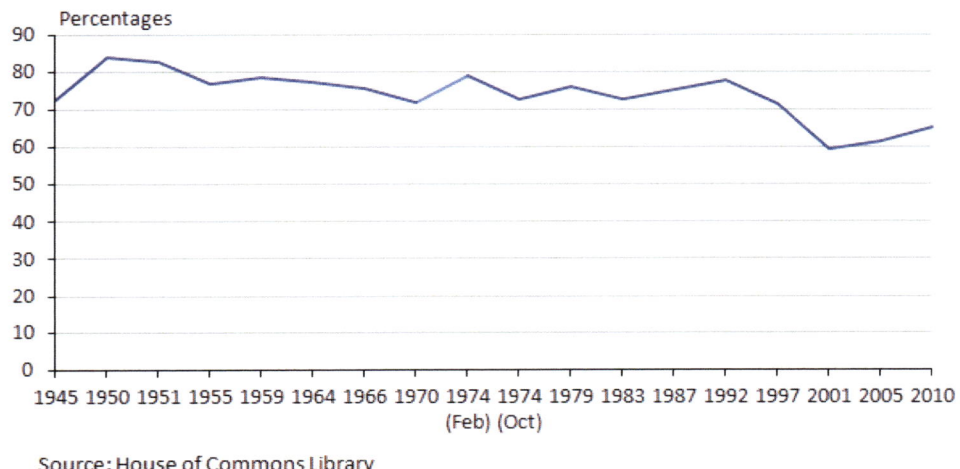

Source: House of Commons Library

Download chart

XLS XLS format
(25.5 Kb)

Voter turnout

Voter turnout can be used as a measure of people's trust in government, and in turn is another means with which to assess our attitudes to political engagement. Voter turnout in general elections in the UK has fallen from a high of 83.9% in 1950, to a low of 59.4% in 2001. The turnout for the last general election in 2010 was 65.1% - higher than the previous two elections, but still the third lowest since 1945 (Figure 14).

Figure 15 shows turnout at recent elections and referendums (not including local elections) between 2009 and 2014.

Figure 15: Voter turnout at elections and referendums held between 2009 and 2014

United Kingdom

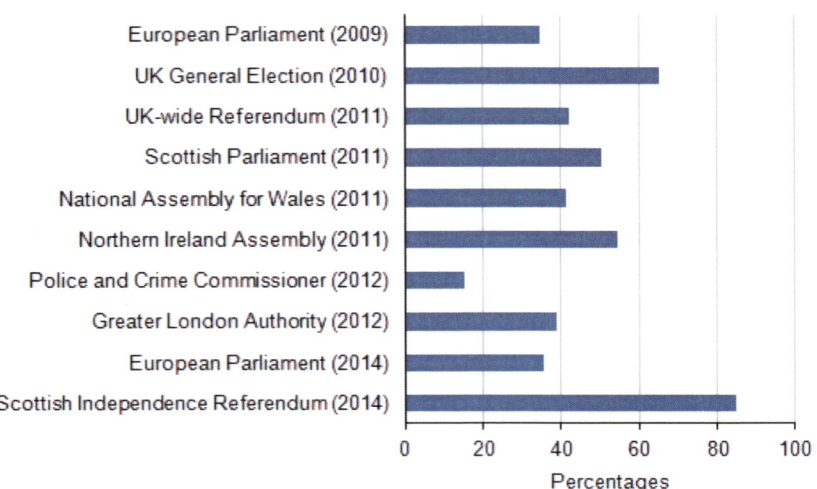

Source: House of Commons Library, The Electoral Commission, The Scottish Parliament

Download chart

 XLS format
(25.5 Kb)

The lowest turnout in the last 5 years was for the Police and Crime Commissioner Election in 2012, with a turnout of just 15.1% (Figure 15). This was the lowest recorded level of participation at a peacetime non-local government election in the UK.

The highest turnout in the last 5 years was for the Scottish Independence Referendum in 2014, where 84.6% of the electorate voted. This was the highest recorded turnout for an election or referendum in the UK since the introduction of universal suffrage[1]. The large proportion of people who voted suggests that people will turn out and vote for an issue where they believe they can make a difference.

Political engagement is also shown to vary by age with young people in the UK less likely to participate in elections than older people. Exact figures about the age of voters in general elections are not available in the UK because information about the identity of voters is kept secret. However, data from the British Election Study does provide age-based survey data.

Just 40.4% of eligible 18 to 24 year olds voted at the general election in 2001, falling further to 38.2% in 2005. Turnout within this group increased to 51.8% in 2010, yet this remains around 13 percentage points below the national average for all ages, and suggests that a large number of these young people who registered to vote opted not to do so. It is also a significantly lower turnout rate than recorded in earlier elections, for example, 66.6% in 1987 and 67.3% in 1992 and 76.4% in 1964.

The UK House of Commons, Political and Constitutional Reform Committee - Voter Engagement Inquiry, is looking into voter registration and turnout in the UK. A report was published in November 2014 that considered changes, such as compulsory voting, online voting, and extending the franchise to younger people. The inquiry asked the public to consider the proposals put forward in the report on what would make people more engaged or make it easier for them to turn out and vote. A follow up based on responses to the consultation was published on 5 February 2015 and is awaiting government response[2].

Civic engagement

Some other measures of civic engagement are captured on the Community Life Survey[3] commissioned by the Cabinet Office. The three measures of civic engagement on this survey are:

- civic participation
- civic consultation
- civic activism

In 2013 to 2014, 30% of people aged 16 and over in England engaged in some form of civic participation at least once in the 12 months prior to interview, while 16% took part in some form of civic consultation and 9% participated in some form of civic activism.

Notes

1. Universal suffrage means that every citizen above the age of 18 is allowed to vote.

2. Proposals on voter engagement, UK Parliament

3. Civic participation – engagement in democratic processes (both in person and online), such as contacting an elected representative or attending a public demonstration. Civic consultation – taking part in consultations about local services such as completing questionnaires, attending public meetings or being involved in discussion groups (both in person and online). Civic activism – involvement in decision-making about local services or in the provision of these services (both in person and online) such as being a school governor or magistrate.

How sustainable is our natural environment?

Assessments of change - Natural environment

	1 year	3 year
Total green house gas emissions (millions of tonnes)	Improved	Improved
Protected areas in the UK (Millions hectares)	Not assessed	Not assessed
Energy consumed within the UK from renewable sources	Improved	No overall change
Household waste that is recycled	No overall change	Not assessed

Download table

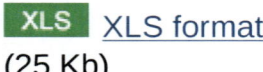 XLS format
(25 Kb)

The natural environment is vital to life on earth. Environmental sustainability is about protecting these natural resources from depletion, so they support existence now and for future generations.

Greenhouse gas emissions

Emissions of greenhouse gases (GHG) are widely believed to contribute to global warming and climate change. Carbon dioxide is responsible for the largest amount of GHG emissions, accounting for 82% of the total in 2013.

The UK has both international and domestic targets for reducing GHG emissions. For example, the Kyoto Protocol (an international agreement adopted in 1997, under the UN Framework Convention on Climate Change), and UK carbon budgets, which were established by the UK Climate Change Act 2008.

Figure 16: Emissions of greenhouse gases (1)

United Kingdom

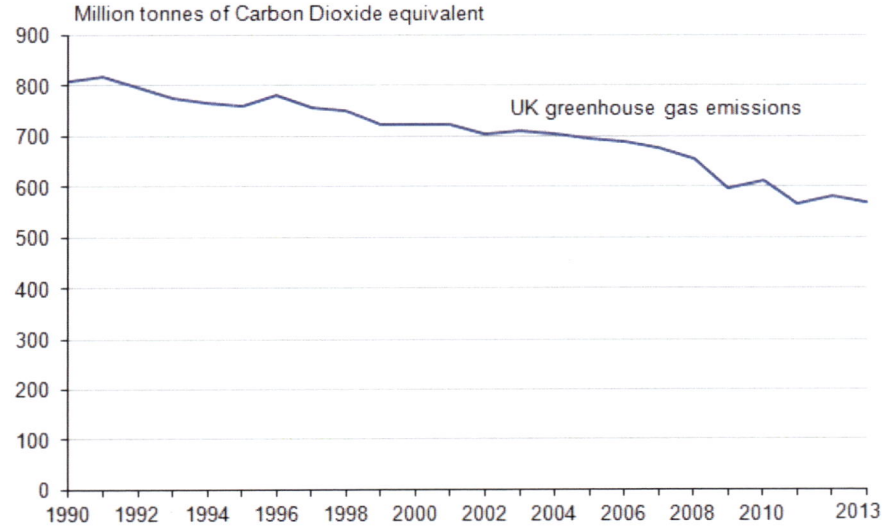

Source: Energy and Climate Change

Notes:

1. The chart shows UK greenhouse gas emissions only, and excludes emissions from UK Crown Dependencies or Overseas Territories. Geographical coverage of the UK's emissions reductions targets varies – for example the UK's Kyoto Protocol target includes the Crown Dependencies and some Overseas Territories, while UK carbon budgets cover the UK only.

Download chart

 XLS format
(33 Kb)

Since 1990, UK greenhouse gas emissions have decreased by 30% (Figure 16). This is due to a number of factors including changes in the mix of fuels used for electricity generation, and greater energy efficiency resulting from improvements in technology. In 2014, the UK confirmed that it had met the first carbon budget (for the period 2008-2012), with emissions of 36 million tonnes carbon dioxide equivalent (MtCO2e) below the cap of 3,018 MtCO2e over the first carbon budget period.

Energy from Renewable Sources

Renewable energy is energy that is naturally replenished and is therefore sustainable. It is sourced from natural resources such as sunlight, wind, rain, tides and geothermal heat. Renewable energy technologies have a much lower environmental impact than conventional energy technologies. In June 2009, the UK signed up to the European Union (EU) Renewable Energy Directive (RED). This includes a target that the UK has to provide 15% of energy from renewable sources by 2020 for electricity, heat and transport.

Provisional figures indicate that during 2013, 5.2% of final energy consumption was from renewable sources. This is an increase from the 2012 figure of 4.2%, and 3.8% in 2011. The RED introduced interim targets for member states to achieve on their route to attaining the 2020 proportion. The UK was broadly in line with its first interim target of 4.04% across 2011 to 2012, achieving 4.01%.

Protected areas

Protected areas are locations that are conserved because of landscape, ecological and/or cultural reasons, with the main purpose of protecting biodiversity. In the UK, there are some protected areas which have international designations, such as World Heritage Sites, and some areas, including National Parks, which have national designations. Protected areas also include Marine Protected Areas, which are zones of the seas and coasts where wildlife is protected from damage and disturbance.

The overall total extent of land and sea protected in the UK through national and international protected areas, and through wider landscape designations, has increased by 12.7 million hectares, from 8.7 million hectares in December 2009 to 21.4 million hectares at the start of August 2014 (an increase of 245%). This increase is largely due to designation of inshore and offshore marine sites under the Habitats Directive, designation of marine conservation zones in English and Welsh waters, and designation of nature conservation marine protected areas in Scottish Waters. The area of protected areas at sea increased by 12.5 million hectares between 2009 and 2014.

Recycling

Recycling supports sustainability by conserving raw materials and protecting natural habitats for the future. Using recycled materials in the manufacturing process also uses considerably less energy than that required for producing new products from raw materials. Under the Waste Framework Directive, the UK have a target to recycle, compost or reuse at least 50% of waste generated by households by 2020[1].

Figure 17: Household recycling rates (1,2,3) 2012

United Kingdom

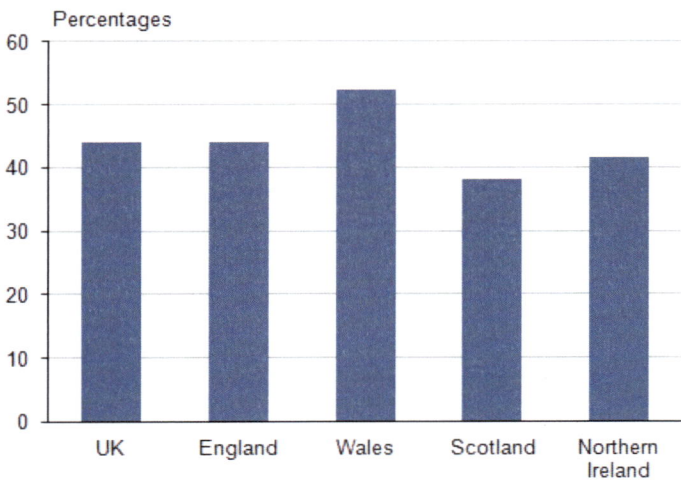

Source: Environment, Food and Rural Affairs

Notes:

1. UK estimates for "Waste from households" have been calculated in accordance with the Waste Framework Directive.
2. "Waste from households" includes waste from: Regular household collection, civic amenity sites, "bulky waste" and "other household waste". "Waste from households" excludes waste from: street cleaning/sweeping, gully emptying, separately collected healthcare waste and asbestos waste.
3. While the general approach is consistent across UK countries, aggregation method and the wording of some questions completed by Local Authorities varies.

Download chart

 XLS format
(32 Kb)

In 2012, around 26.4 million tonnes of household waste was produced in the UK, of which 11.6 million tonnes (43.9%) was recycled, composted or reused (Figure 17). The remainder went to landfill or was incinerated. Between 2010 and 2012 the recycling rate increased by 4 percentage points from 40.3%. Recycling rates in 2012 varied across the countries of the UK. In Wales, more than half (52.5%) of household waste was recycled, composted or reused, compared to 44.1% in England, 38.3% in Scotland and 41.7% in Northern Ireland.

Notes

1. Set out in the Waste Framework Directive (2008/98/EC).

How sustainable is our future well-being?

The decisions we make today will affect the resources and opportunities for future generations, which is why the definition of national well-being includes not just "how we are doing" as individuals, as communities and as a nation, but also how sustainable this is for the future. The OECD's 'How's Life? Measuring Well-being' report says that the most useful approach to assessing sustainability over time is to consider the stocks we have of things like education and skills, our natural resources, community cohesion – things that "can generate a stream of benefits to society over time". These are known as capitals and they help us to understand sustainability because they link the present with the future.

Natural capital

As part of the Measuring National Well-being programme, we have determined estimates of natural capital. Natural capital involves valuing our natural assets so that we can determine current stocks and monitor future impacts. In 2011, selected components of UK natural capital were valued at £1,573 billion. This included mineral reserves valued at £14.0 billion, agricultural land valued at £45.1 billion, and timber valued at £6.9 billion. It also included the value of the annual benefits of recreational ecosystem services (the benefits people get from the natural environment), which was £77.4 billion, and the monetary asset value of recreational ecosystem services, which was £1,353 billion. This estimate is 4.1% lower than in 2007, mainly due to a fall in the value of sub-soil assets. These estimates are experimental and do not currently value all of the material benefits of nature that make up the UK's natural capital. There are also other, non-material benefits of nature, such as positive physical and mental health impacts, improving community cohesion, and enhancing our living environment (Faculty of Public Health, 2010), which are not included in natural capital accounts. Further information on natural capital can be found in UK Natural Capital[1].

Human capital

The Measuring National Well-being programme also measures human capital, which refers to the economic value of people – the value of our skills, knowledge, abilities, social attributes, personality and health attributes. These are the things that enable us to work and produce something of economic value. In practical terms, the focus of measuring human capital is limited to people's skills, knowledge and competencies, with particular consideration paid to the role of formal education and training. In 2013 the value of the UK's employed human capital stock was £17.61 trillion, and the value of full human capital stock (which includes the unemployed) was £18.38 trillion.

Analysis of the distribution of human capital shows that those with higher qualifications hold a greater proportion of human capital stock. In 2013, more than a third (35.4%) of the UK's human capital stock was among the 26.2% of the working age population whose highest educational attainment was a degree, or equivalent. In comparison, the proportion of the working age population who have no formal qualifications (9.6%) held just 5.4% of the UK's human capital stock.

The stock of employed human capital per head of working-age population rose steadily between 2004 and 2007, where it peaked at £472,657 (Figure 18). Even though the total stock of human capital began to stabilise from 2011, the per head figure began to decline in 2008 and was valued at £437,561 in 2013, more than £35,000 lower than in 2007. This is because the size of the working age population had grown, while the stock of human capital had not. As the population increases, total human capital needs to increase for human capital per head to stay the same.

These changes show how the value of our population's skills, knowledge and competencies has changed between 2004 and 2013. Measuring human capital is important to national well-being because it helps us understand the level of skills we have as a nation. However, we can also see how it affects individuals because lower skill levels among the labour force may ultimately translate into lower wages.

Figure 18: Employed human capital per head

United Kingdom

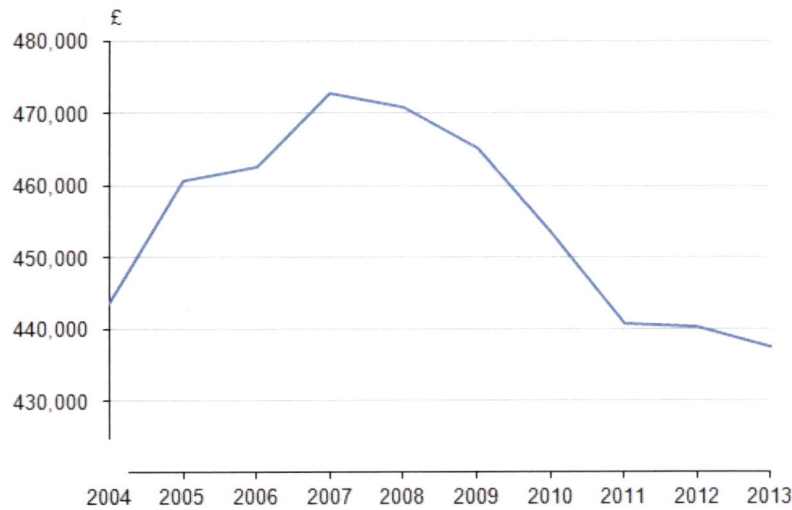

Source: Office for National Statistics

Download chart

XLS XLS format
(16.5 Kb)

Because women tend to spend less time in paid employment, and have lower average earnings, the total value of women's human capital stock in 2013 was equivalent to around 59% of men's human capital stock (£6.53 trillion and £11.08 trillion respectively). Further information on human capital can be found in Human Capital Estimates, 2013[2].

Social capital

Social capital refers to social connections and the benefits they generate. Social capital is associated with civic participation, civic-minded attitudes and values which help people cooperate, such as tolerance or trust. Unlike natural or human capital, we don't put a financial value on social capital. In January 2015[3], we published a set of 25 measures that cover 4 key aspects: personal relationships, social network support, civic engagement and trust, and cooperative norms. In terms of personal relationships, the report showed that most of us (95%) had at least one close friend in the financial year ending 2012. However, the report also showed that in the financial year ending 2012, 11% of people felt lonely at least half of the time over the previous two weeks. People who regularly feel lonely are more likely to feel left out of society, and that the things they do are not recognised. They are also less likely to feel that what they do is worthwhile.

Social network support is about perceived and actual support that people give and receive. The social capital report found that most people felt that they can rely "a lot" on their partner (83%) and their family (62%) in case of a serious problem, but less than half (45%) felt that they could also rely "a lot" on their friends.

Volunteering and political participation are forms of civic engagement. The role of volunteering is important to national well-being because it impacts on society and the economy. At the individual level, volunteering is known to have positive impacts not only on the people being supported but on the volunteer as well. At the national level, the report showed that voluntary activity in the UK in 2012 was valued at £23.9 billion which, at around 1.5% of GDP, means volunteering is also important to the UK economy.

Trust and cooperative norms are key for the effective functioning of society and, therefore, are important for national well-being. For example, people who trust others in their local area are more likely to feel safe walking alone after dark. People who trust others are also more likely to have trust in public institutions. Conversely, people who have low ratings of trust in government are more likely to report being dissatisfied with their own lives. Therefore, actions taken at national level to improve, for example, trust in institutions may also impact individual well-being.

A nation that has high levels of social capital stocks is a nation where people are connected to one another, trust and help each other, are tolerant, and are empowered to shape the society they live in. More information on social capital can be found in the publication "An Analysis of Social Capital in the UK" (ONS, January 2015).

Economic Capital

We also publish the value of economic capital, although not as part of the Measuring National Well-being programme. Economic capital is the combined value of physical and financial capital, otherwise known as non-financial assets and financial net worth. At the end of 2013, economic capital was valued at £7.6 trillion, which is equivalent to £119,000 per person, or £289,000 per household.

Physical capital, which includes the machinery, equipment and buildings, was valued at £7.9 trillion at the end of 2013. Dwellings are by far the most valuable non-financial asset at 61% of the UK"s net worth, or £4.7 trillion.

Financial capital is the value of financial assets minus financial liabilities. Although the value of financial capital (which includes currency and deposits, shares, bonds and derivatives) was £28.7 trillion at the end of 2013, the value of financial liabilities was larger at £29.0 trillion. This means that financial capital was valued at minus £0.3 trillion[4].

Sustainable development

We reported measures of human and social capital stocks, along with a wide range of indicators in July 2014 in the publication 'Sustainable Development Indicators'[5], which provides an overview of progress towards a sustainable economy, society and environment. This publication assessed the short and long term changes in the report's economic, social and environmental measures. These changes are reflected in Figure 19. In terms of the economy, looking only at measures where data could be assessed, more measures had deteriorated than improved over the short term (the latest 5-year period). In comparison, an assessment of the social and environmental measures shows that more measures have improved than deteriorated over the short term.

Figure 19: Assessment of change - Sustainable Development Indicators, 2014

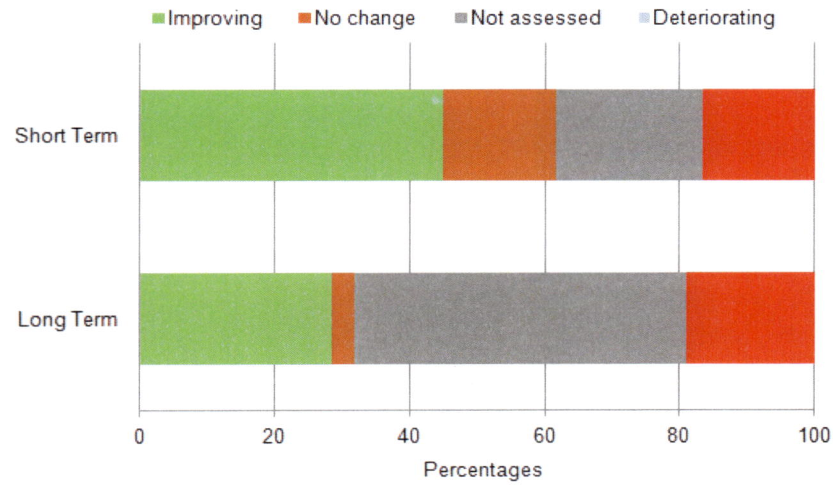

Source: Sustainable Development Indicators, July 2014, Office for National Statistics

Download chart

XLS XLS format
(16.5 Kb)

In 2015, the Millennium Development Goals (MDGs) for developing countries will expire and a new set of development goals are currently being negotiated internationally. The United Nations Statistical Division has been asked following Rio+20 Summit, to lead work on Sustainable Development Goals (SDGs) (for both developed and developing countries). We are coordinating the Government Statistical Service input into this development process to ensure consistent and considered advice is given to UK policy officials and international statistical groups on measurement capabilities, issues and data gaps. The final set of Sustainable Development Goals will be agreed at a UN Summit in September 2015 and we are positioned to monitor and report UK progress against these goals and targets from 2016.

Although our work on natural, human and social capital is still in development, it has already drawn attention to areas that are important for understanding future well-being. For example, work on human capital has highlighted inequalities in the distribution of human capital stocks, and that widening inequalities are detrimental to national well-being. The natural environment, as well as being an economic resource we need to sustain, can have significant impacts on our physical and mental health, leading to higher individual, and therefore national well-being. Higher social capital stocks mean people are more likely to act for the good of their community.

The Commission for Economic Performance and Social Progress likened the people leading our economies and societies to pilots trying to "steer a course without a reliable compass", and said that in order for them to make good decisions, they need good measurements that are well understood (Stiglitz, Sen, Fitoussi, 2009). Measures such as the capital stocks will enable such people to be better informed when making decisions.

Notes

1. Natural Capital

2. Human Capital Estimates - 2013

3. An Analysis of Social Capital in the UK

4. More information about non-financial assets and financial net worth is available here The National Balance Sheet index

5. Sustainable Development indicators - July 2014

Background notes

1. Details of the policy governing the release of new data are available by visiting www.statisticsauthority.gov.uk/assessment/code-of-practice/index.html or from the Media Relations Office email: media.relations@ons.gsi.gov.uk

Copyright

Sources, reports and surveys related to 'Life in the UK, 2015'

Summary

Well-being and health policy, Department of Health - www.gov.uk/government/publications/wellbeing-and-health-policy

How do we evaluate our own lives?

Children's Well-being, 2014

Childrens Society - www.childrenssociety.org.uk

Personal Well-being in the UK, 2013/14

Young People's Well-being, 2014

How good are our relationships?

European Quality of Life Survey - //eurofound.europa.eu/surveys/eqls

Exploring the Well-being of Children in the UK, 2014

Exploring the Well-being of Young People in the UK, 2014

Predicting well-being, report commissioned by the Department of Health and available at www.natcen.ac.uk/

Understanding Society, the UK Household Longitudinal Survey - Understanding Society

How good is our health?

Children's Well-being, 2014

Personal Well-being in the UK, 2013/14

"We are living longer-fact-Dr Martin Mcshane", NHS England -www.england.nhs.uk/2014/02/25/martin-mcshane-6/

How do we spend our time and are we satisfied with its use?

Department for Culture, Media and Sport - DCMS - Taking Part Survey

"New study shows we work harder when we are happy" - www.warwick.ac.uk/newsandevents/pressreleases/new_study_shows/

Physical activity guidelines for adults, NHS Choices - www.nhs.uk/Livewell/fitness/Pages/physical-activity-guidelines-for-adults.aspx

Sport England - //sportengland.org/

Understanding Society, the UK Household Longitudinal Survey - Understanding Society

Valuing Voluntary Activity in the UK

Wellbeing and civil society: Estimating the value of volunteering using subjective wellbeing data -www.gov.uk/government/publications/wellbeing-and-civil-society-estimating-the-value-of-volunteering-using-subjective-wellbeing-data-wp112

How do we feel about where we live?

Department for Communities and Local Government - www.gov.uk/government/collections/english-housing-survey

Understanding Society, the UK Household Longitudinal Survey - Understanding Society

Department of Transport accessibility statistics - www.gov.uk/government/collections/transport-connectivity-and-accessibility-of-key-services-statistics

Natural England - Natural England

Crime Survey for England and Wales - Crime in England and Wales

How are we coping financially?

Department for Work and Pensions - DWP: Households Below Average Income

"Low-Income Britons Struggle With Their Wellbeing", Gallup - www.gallup.com/poll/148151/Low-Income-Britons-Struggle-Wellbeing.aspx

Wealth and Assets Survey - Wealth and Assets Survey

Understanding Society, the UK Household Longitudinal Survey - Understanding Society

How strong is our economy?

Measuring National Well-being, Economic Well-being

National accounts - National Accounts - all releases

How skilled are we?

"Developing Healthy Minds in Teenagers", Education Endownment Foundation -www.educationendowmentfoundation.org.uk/projects/developing-healthy-minds/

Healthy Minds, How to Thrive - www.howtothrive.org/healthy-minds/

Human capital - Human Capital Estimates index

Department for Education - Department for Education

How politically engaged are we?

Eurobarometer - Eurobarometer

House of Commons Library (elections turnout) www.parliament.uk/business/publications/research/briefing-papers/SN01467/elections-turnout

Proposals on voter engagement, UK Parliament - www.parliament.uk/business/committees/committees-a-z/commons-select/political-and-constitutional-reform-committee/inquiries/parliament-2010/proposals-on-voter-engagement/

How sustainable is our natural environment?

Department for Energy and Climate Change - Digest of UK Energy Statistics (DUKES)

Department for Environment, Food and Rural Affairs - DEFRA website

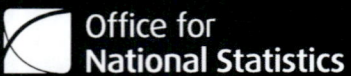

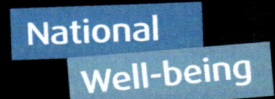

Assessment of Change
March 2015 release

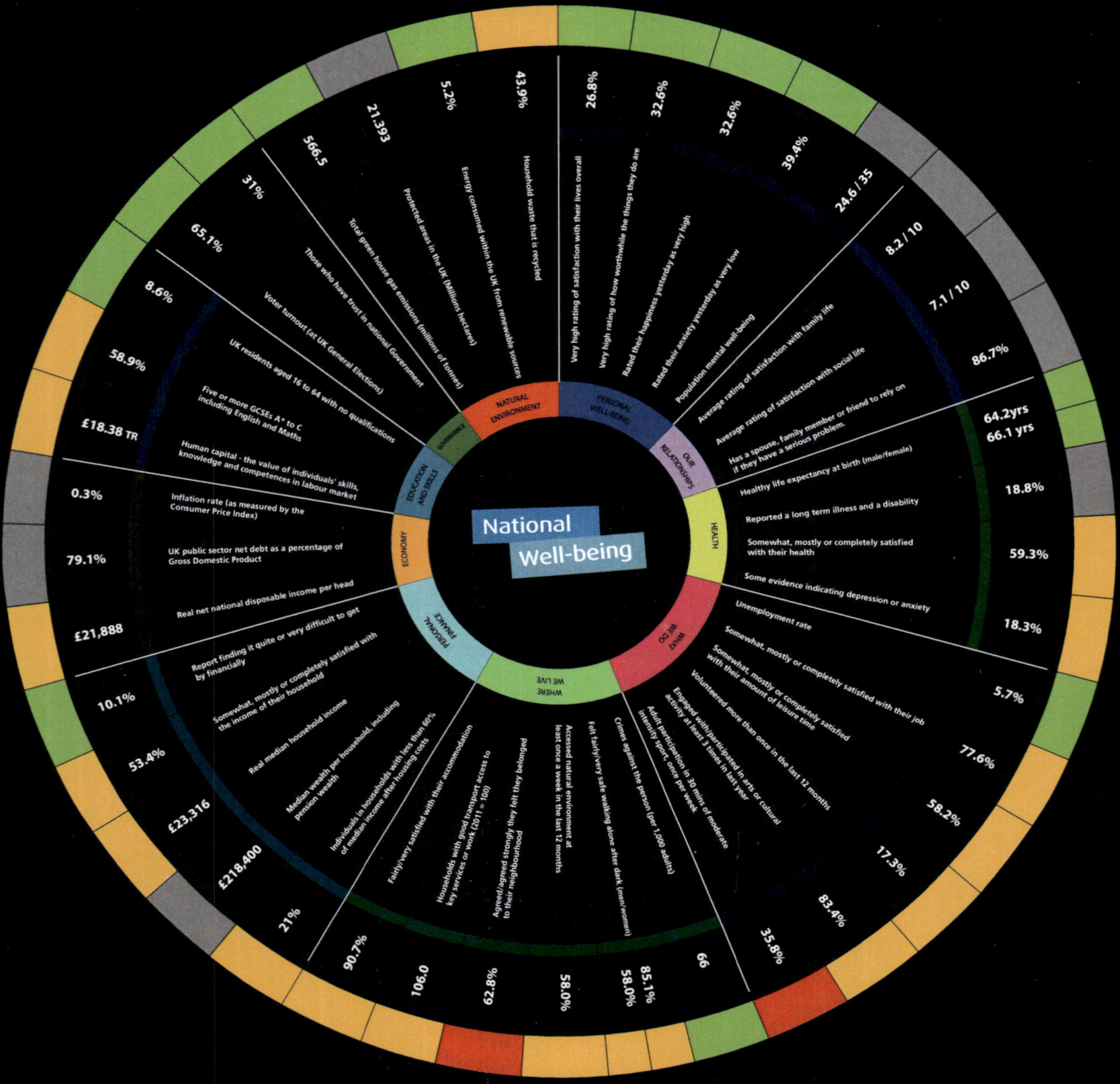

National Well-being

NATIONAL ENVIRONMENT
- 43.9% — Household waste that is recycled
- 5.2% — Energy consumed within the UK from renewable sources
- 21,393 — Protected areas in the UK (millions of hectares)
- 566.5 — Total greenhouse gas emissions (millions of tonnes)

GOVERNANCE
- 31% — Those who have trust in national government
- 65.1% — Voter turnout (at UK General Elections)

EDUCATION AND SKILLS
- 8.6% — UK residents aged 16 to 64 with no qualifications
- 58.9% — Five or more GCSEs A* to C including English and Maths
- £18.38 TR — Human capital - the value of individuals' skills, knowledge and competences in labour market

ECONOMY
- 0.3% — Inflation rate (as measured by the Consumer Price Index)
- 79.1% — UK public sector net debt as a percentage of Gross Domestic Product
- £21,888 — Real net national disposable income per head

PERSONAL FINANCE
- 10.1% — Report finding it quite or very difficult to get by financially
- 53.4% — Somewhat, mostly or completely satisfied with the income of their household
- £23,316 — Real median household income
- £218,400 — Median wealth per household, including pension wealth
- 21% — Individuals in households with less than 60% of median income after housing costs

WHERE WE LIVE
- 90.7% — Fairly/very satisfied with their accommodation
- 106.0 — Households with good transport access to key services or work (2011 = 100)
- 62.8% — Accessed natural environment at least once a week in the last 12 months
- 58.0% — Agreed/agreed strongly they felt they belonged to their neighbourhood

WHAT WE DO
- 58.0% — Felt fairly/very safe walking alone after dark (men/women)
- 85.1% — Crime against the person (per 1,000 adults)
- 66 — Adult participation in 30 mins of moderate intensity sport, once per week
- 35.8% — Engaged with/participated in arts or cultural activity at least 3 times in last year
- 83.4% — Volunteered more than once in the last 12 months
- 17.3% — Somewhat, mostly or completely satisfied with their amount of leisure time
- 58.2% — Somewhat, mostly or completely satisfied with their job
- 77.6% — Unemployment rate
- 5.7% — Some evidence indicating depression or anxiety

PERSONAL WELL-BEING
- 26.8% — Very high rating of satisfaction with their lives overall
- 32.6% — Very high rating of how worthwhile the things they do are
- 32.6% — Rated their happiness yesterday as very high
- 39.4% — Rated their anxiety yesterday as very low
- 24.6 / 35 — Population mental well-being

OUR RELATIONSHIPS
- 8.2 / 10 — Average rating of satisfaction with family life
- 7.1 / 10 — Average rating of satisfaction with social life
- 86.7% — Has a spouse, family member or friend to rely on if they have a serious problem

HEALTH
- 64.2yrs / 66.1 yrs — Healthy life expectancy at birth (male/female)
- 18.8% — Reported a long term illness and a disability
- 59.3% — Somewhat, mostly or completely satisfied with their health
- 18.3% — Unemployment rate

	1 year	Previous year change	3 year	
14		Improving		12
18		Little or no overall change		10
9		Not assessed		13
2		Deteriorating		8

More data and interactive version available at: **www.ons.gov.uk/well-being**

Data latest available: at March 2015

Office for
National Statistics

Personal Well-being Three Year Dataset Maps (Interactive and Static)

Coverage: **UK**
Date: **27 March 2015**
Geographical Area: **Local Authority**
Theme: **People and Places**

Introduction

In October 2014 we released the first ever combined 3 year Personal Well-being Annual Population Dataset. The enhanced sample size of the 3 year dataset compared with the annual has allowed for more detailed analysis at lower levels of geography. For the first time, we have released maps with Personal Well-being data at local authority district level.

This release displays the estimates from this dataset in both interactive and static maps.

Interactive maps

To explore the data and find out what personal well-being is like in your area please see our interactive maps.

Life satisfaction (Static)

Overall, people in the UK said that their average life satisfaction was 7.5 out of 10. Looking at responses across local authorities in the UK, these estimates ranged from 6.9 to 8.2 out of 10. When looking at the percentage of people responding along the 0 to 10 scale, more people answered on the positive end of the scale (7 to 10) than the negative (0 to 6), at 77.1% and 22.9% respectively.

Life Satisfaction

United Kingdom

How satisfied are you with your life nowadays?
2011/12 to 2013/14 by local authority district, United Kingdom

Average score (out of 10)

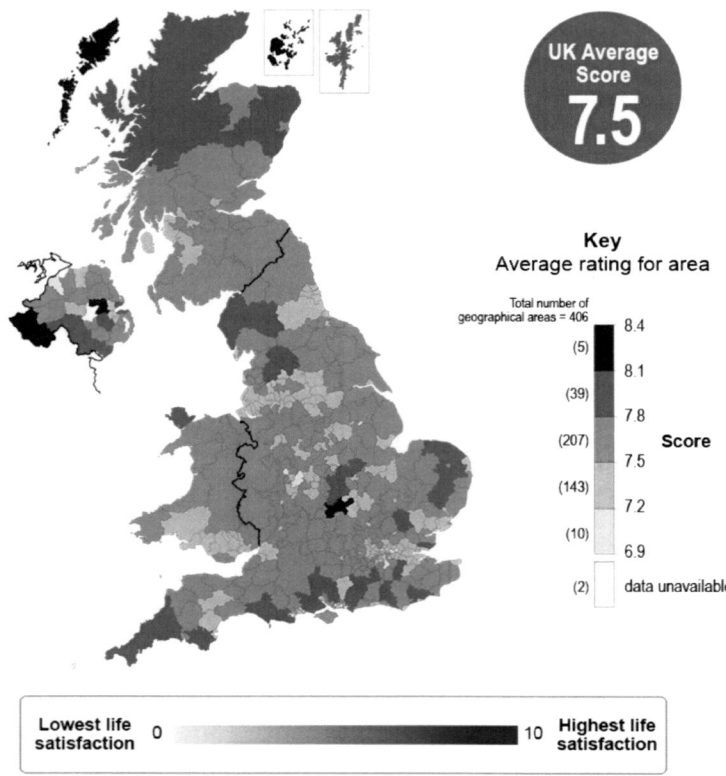

UK Average Score 7.5

Key
Average rating for area

Total number of geographical areas = 406

	Score
(5)	8.4
(39)	8.1
(207)	7.8
(143)	7.5
(10)	7.2
(2)	6.9
	data unavailable

Lowest life satisfaction 0 — 10 Highest life satisfaction

Percentage answering High and Very High score (7 to 10)

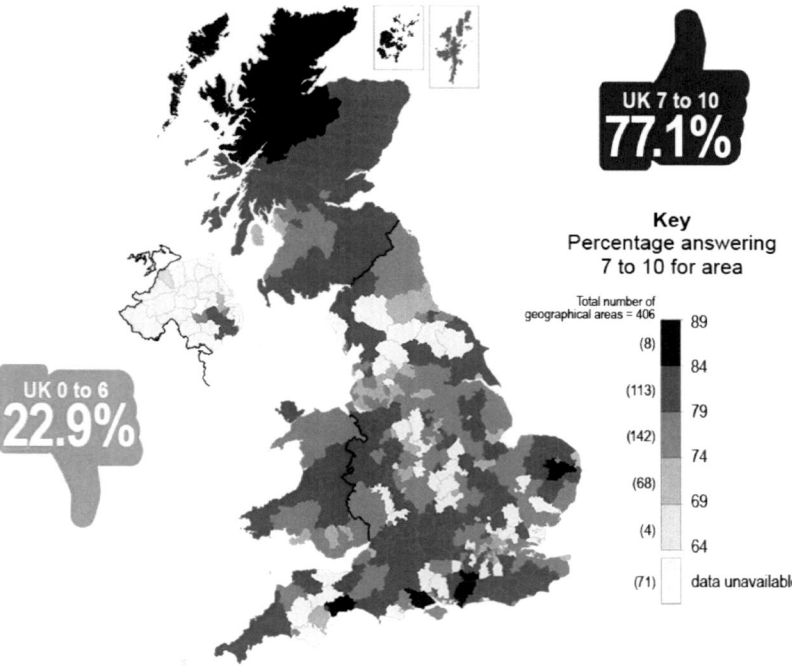

UK 7 to 10 77.1%

UK 0 to 6 22.9%

Key
Percentage answering 7 to 10 for area

Total number of geographical areas = 406

(8)	89
(113)	84
(142)	79
(68)	74
(4)	69
(71)	64
	data unavailable

What else you need to know:

1. Adults aged 16 and over were asked 'Overall, how satisfied are you with your life nowadays?' where 0 is 'not at all satisfied' and 10 is 'completely satisfied'.
2. All data are weighted.
3. Thresholds have been combined to provide more robust estimates.
4. Any sample size less than 50 has been suppressed for quality reasons.
Source: Office for National Statistics licensed under the Open Government Licence v.3.0.
Contains Ordnance Survey data © Crown copyright and database right 2015

Source: Annual Population Survey (APS) - Office for National Statistics

Notes:

1. Adults aged 16 and over were asked 'Overall, how satisfied are you with your life nowadays?' where 0 is 'not at all satisfied' and 10 is 'completely satisfied'.
2. All data are weighted.
3. Thresholds have been combined to provide more robust estimates.
4. Any sample size less than 50 has been suppressed for quality reasons.

Download map

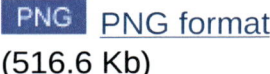 PNG format
(516.6 Kb)

Worthwhile (Static)

When looking at all questions, more people answered at the positive end of the scale (7 to 10) for worthwhile than for any other question, at 80.8%. Worthwhile also generated the highest average of all the 4 questions, at 7.7 out of 10.

Worthwhile

United Kingdom

To what extent do you feel the things you do in your life are worthwhile?

2011/12 to 2013/14 by local authority district, United Kingdom

Average score (out of 10)

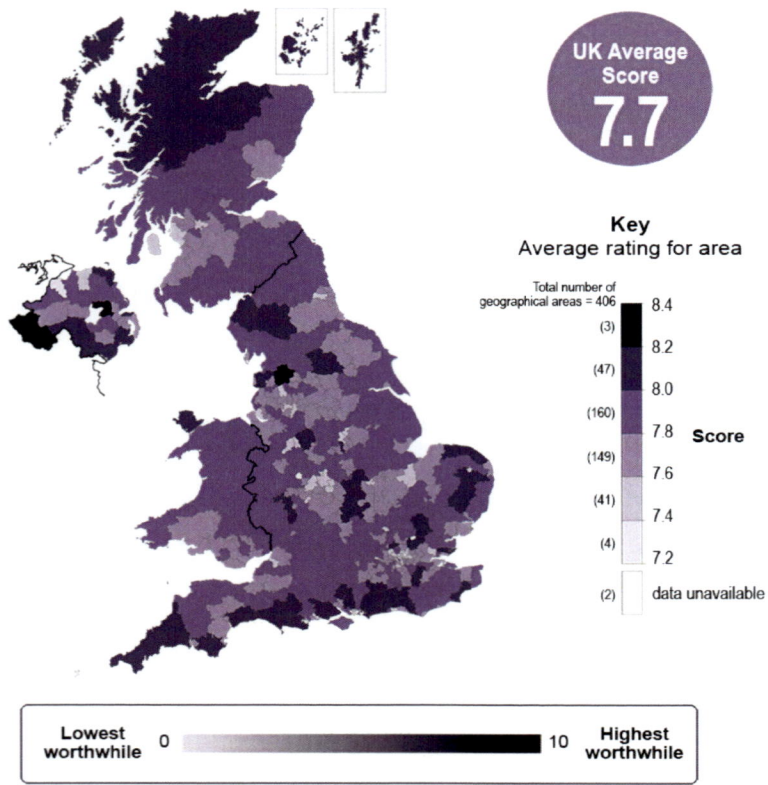

UK Average Score
7.7

Key
Average rating for area

Total number of geographical areas = 406

(3)	8.4
(47)	8.2
(160)	8.0
(149)	7.8 **Score**
(41)	7.6
(4)	7.4
(2)	7.2
	data unavailable

Lowest worthwhile   0 — 10   Highest worthwhile

Percentage answering High and Very High score (7 to 10)

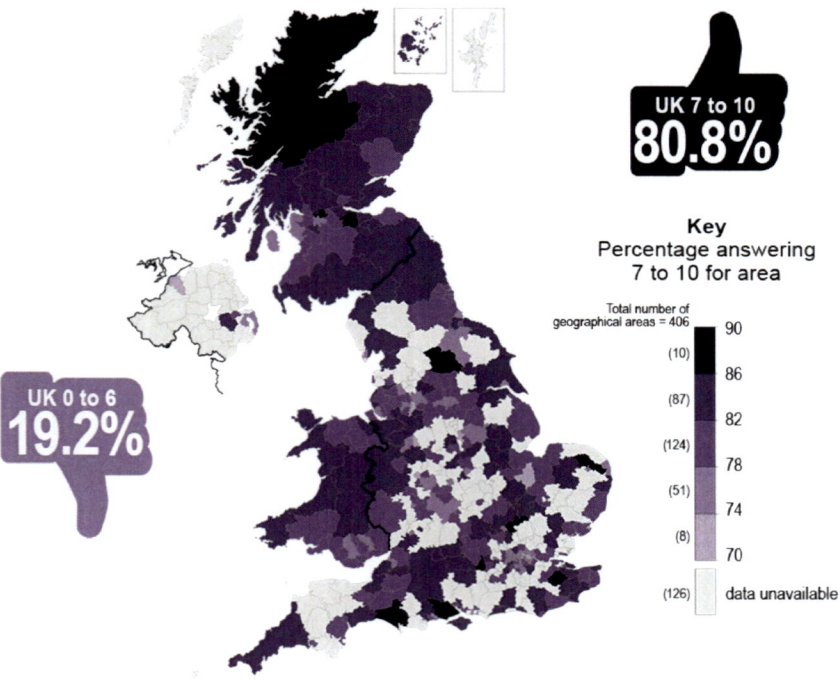

UK 7 to 10
80.8%

UK 0 to 6
19.2%

Key
Percentage answering
7 to 10 for area

Total number of geographical areas = 406

(10)	90
(87)	86
(124)	82
(51)	78
(8)	74
(126)	70
	data unavailable

What else you need to know:

1. Adults aged 16 and over were asked 'Overall, to what extent do you feel the things you do in your life are worthwhile?' where 0 is 'not at all worthwhile' and 10 is 'completely worthwhile'.
2. All data are weighted.
3. Thresholds have been combined to provide more robust estimates.
4. Any sample size less than 50 has been suppressed for quality reasons.

Source: Office for National Statistics licensed under the Open Government Licence v.3.0.
Contains Ordnance Survey data © Crown copyright and database right 2015

Source: Annual Population Survey (APS) - Office for National Statistics

Notes:

1. Adults aged 16 and over were asked 'Overall, to what extent do you feel the things you do in your life are worthwhile?' where 0 is 'not at all worthwhile' and 10 is 'completely worthwhile'.
2. All data are weighted.
3. Thresholds have been combined to provide more robust estimates.
4. Any sample size less than 50 has been suppressed for quality reasons.

Download map

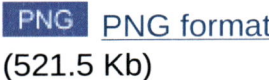 PNG format
(521.5 Kb)

Happiness (Static)

Happiness had the lowest average of the questions, at 7.3 out of 10. Happiness also had the highest percentage of people answering on the lower end of the scale (0 to 7), at 27.9%

Happiness

United Kingdom
How happy did you feel yesterday?
2011/12 to 2013/14 by local authority district, United Kingdom

Average score (out of 10)

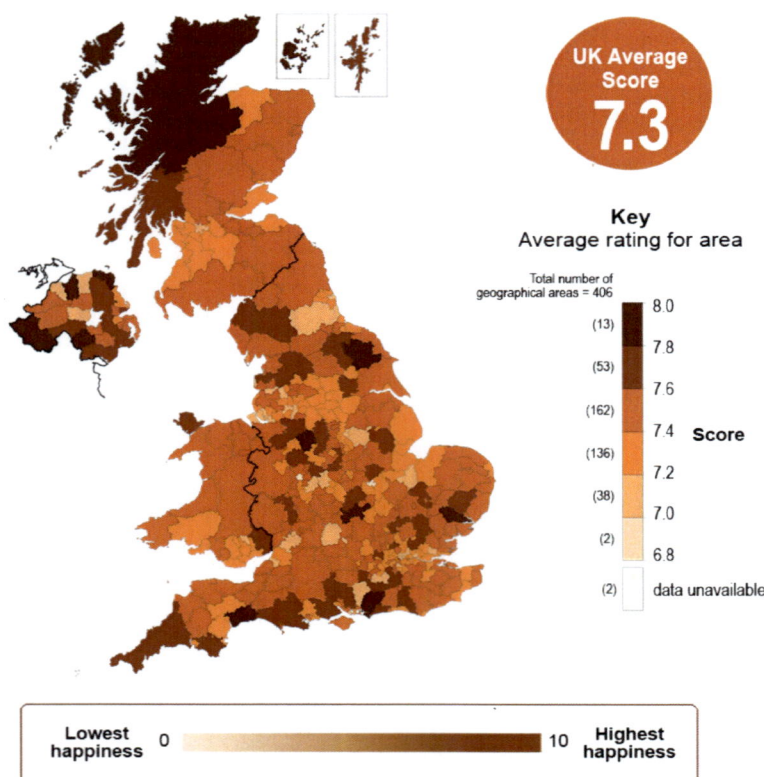

UK Average Score

7.3

Key
Average rating for area

Total number of geographical areas = 406

(13)	8.0
(53)	7.8
(162)	7.6
(136)	7.4 **Score**
(38)	7.2
(2)	7.0
(2)	6.8
	data unavailable

Lowest happiness 0 ———————— 10 Highest happiness

Percentage answering High and Very High score (7 to 10)

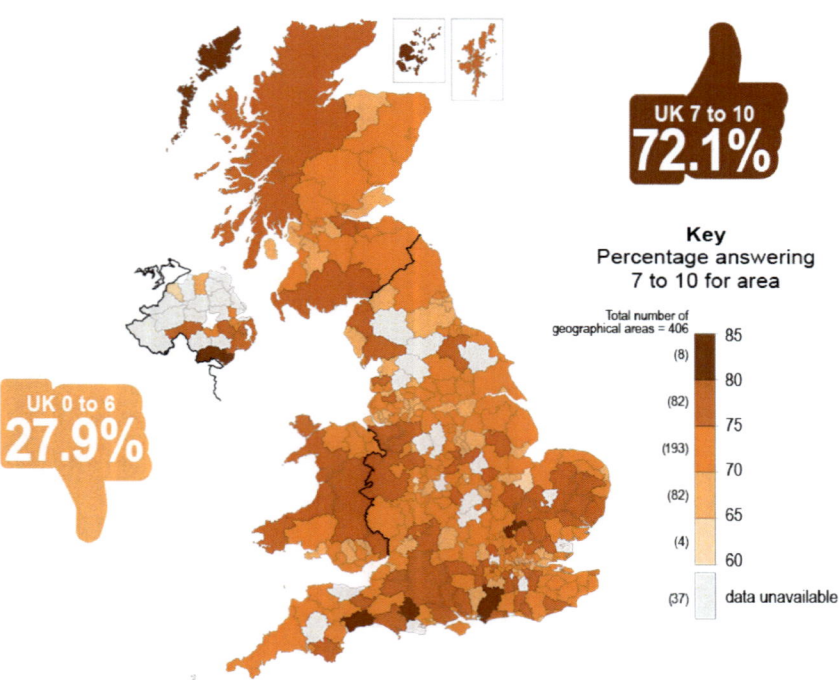

UK 7 to 10
72.1%

UK 0 to 6
27.9%

Key
Percentage answering 7 to 10 for area

Total number of geographical areas = 406

(8)	85
(82)	80
(193)	75
(82)	70
(4)	65
	60
(37)	data unavailable

What else you need to know:

1. Adults aged 16 and over were asked 'Overall, how happy did you feel yesterday?' where 0 is 'not at all happy' and 10 is 'completely happy'.
2. All data are weighted.
3. Thresholds have been combined to provide more robust estimates.
4. Any sample size less than 50 has been suppressed for quality reasons.
Source: Office for National Statistics licensed under the Open Government Licence v.3.0.
Contains Ordnance Survey data © Crown copyright and database right 2015

Source: Annual Population Survey (APS) - Office for National Statistics

Notes:

1. Adults aged 16 and over were asked 'Overall, how happy did you feel yesterday?' where 0 is 'not at all happy' and 10 is 'completely happy'.
2. All data are weighted.
3. Thresholds have been combined to provide more robust estimates.
4. Any sample size less than 50 has been suppressed for quality reasons.

Download map

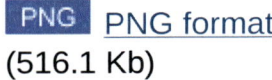 PNG format
(516.1 Kb)

Anxiety (Static)

For anxiety, the results on the lower end of the scale (0 to 6) represent lower anxiety and the results at the higher end of the scale (7 to 10) represent higher anxiety. Out of 10, on average people in the UK rated their level of anxiety yesterday as 3.0. More people answered on the lower end of the scale (0 to 6, representing high well-being), than the higher end of the scale (representing lower well-being) at 61.8% and 38.3% respectively.

Anxiety

United Kingdom

How anxious did you feel yesterday?

2011/12 to 2013/14 by local authority district, United Kingdom

Average score (out of 10)

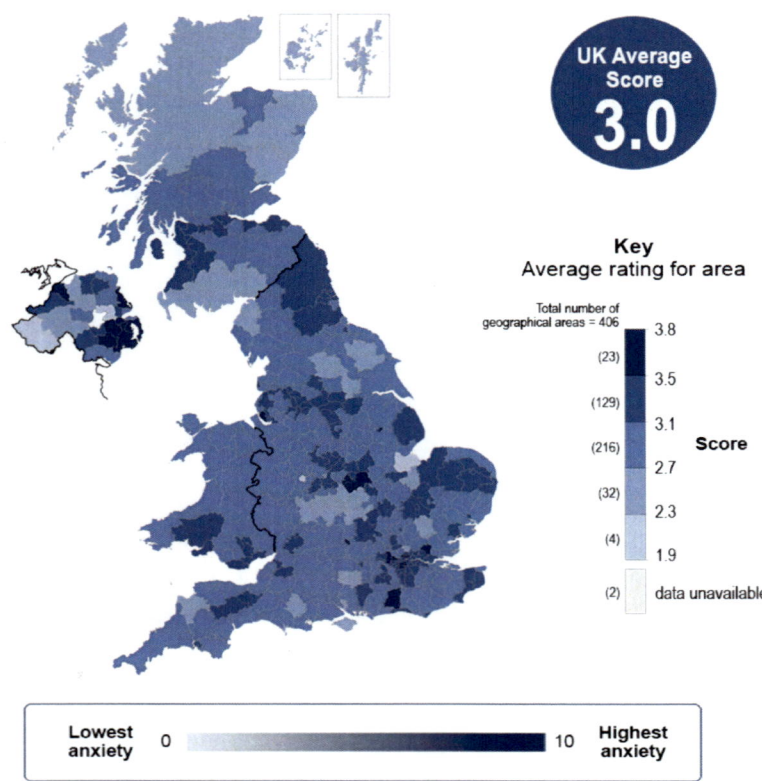

UK Average Score
3.0

Key
Average rating for area

Total number of geographical areas = 406

	Score
(23)	3.8
(129)	3.5
(216)	3.1
(32)	2.7
(4)	2.3
(2)	1.9
	data unavailable

Lowest anxiety 0 —————— 10 Highest anxiety

Percentage answering Very Low and Low score (0 to 6)

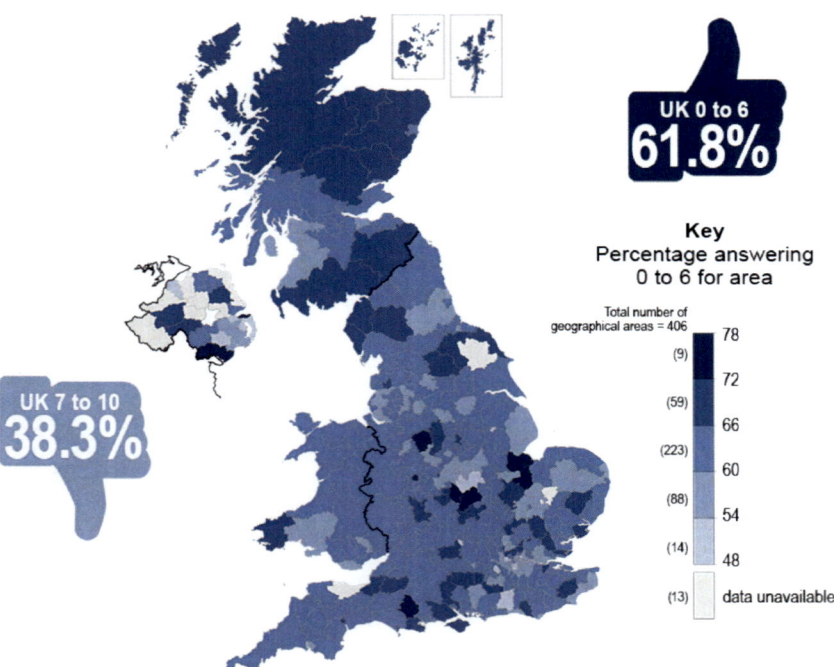

UK 0 to 6
61.8%

UK 7 to 10
38.3%

Key
Percentage answering 0 to 6 for area

Total number of geographical areas = 406

(9)	78
(59)	72
(223)	66
(88)	60
(14)	54
(13)	48
	data unavailable

What else you need to know:

1. Adults aged 16 and over were asked 'Overall, how anxious did you feel yesterday?' where 0 is 'not at all anxious' and 10 is 'completely anxious'.
2. All data are weighted.
3. Thresholds have been combined to provide more robust estimates.
4. Any sample size less than 50 has been suppressed for quality reasons.
5. Thresholds do not add up to 100 because of rounding.

Source: Office for National Statistics licensed under the Open Government Licence v.3.0.
Contains Ordnance Survey data © Crown copyright and database right 2015

Source: Annual Population Survey (APS) - Office for National Statistics

Notes:

1. Adults aged 16 and over were asked 'Overall, how anxious did you feel yesterday?' where 0 is 'not at all anxious' and 10 is 'completely anxious'.
2. All data are weighted.
3. Thresholds have been combined to provide more robust estimates.
4. Any sample size less than 50 has been suppressed for quality reasons.

Download map

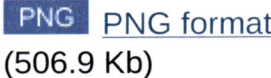 PNG format
(506.9 Kb)

Background notes

1. Approved researchers can access the datasets at the UK Data Archive.

2. If you have comments on the ONS approach to measuring personal well-being and/ or the presentation of the personal well-being data, please email us at personal.wellbeing@ons.gsi.gov.uk.

3. The data analysed in this report was collected from the Annual Population Survey (APS) which is the largest constituent survey of the Integrated Household Survey. The sample size of the 3 year APS dataset is approximately 305,000 adults aged 16 and over and living in residential accommodation in the UK (England, Scotland, Wales and Northern Ireland). Data used are weighted to be representative of the population and to take account of the fact that responses made on behalf of other household members are not accepted.

4. The UK Statistics Authority has designated these statistics as National Statistics, in accordance with the Statistics and Registration Service Act 2007 and signifying compliance with the Code of Practice for Official Statistics.

   Designation can be broadly interpreted to mean that the statistics:

   - meet identified user needs;
   - are well explained and readily accessible;
   - are produced according to sound methods; and
   - are managed impartially and objectively in the public interest.

   Once statistics have been designated as National Statistics it is a statutory requirement that the Code of Practice shall continue to be observed.

5. Details of the policy governing the release of new data are available by visiting www.statisticsauthority.gov.uk/assessment/code-of-practice/index.html or from the Media Relations Office email: media.relations@ons.gsi.gov.uk

These National Statistics are produced to high professional standards and released according to the arrangements approved by the UK Statistics Authority.

Copyright

Office for
National Statistics

How Does Personal Well-being Vary by Sex, Disability, Ethnicity and Religion?

Coverage: **UK**
Date: **27 March 2015**
Geographical Area: **UK**
Theme: **People and Places**

How does personal well-being vary by sex, disability, ethnicity and religion?

We started collecting data on personal well-being in April 2011 and have now made available a combined 3 year dataset, which provides a much larger sample size and allows for more detailed analysis for subgroups such as religion and lower levels of geography, for example, Local Enterprise Partnership (LEP) areas. We also published data tables and maps. We have explored this dataset to find out how personal well-being ratings compare for different equality groups: sex, disability, ethnicity and religion.

The findings show different equality groups have different personal well-being ratings. Women are more likely than men to find the things that they do in their lives are worthwhile, but are also more likely to report higher anxiety. People who report being disabled have lower personal well-being scores than people without a disability. Some ethnic minority and religious minority groups reported lower personal well-being scores than others. This is likely to be due to a number of factors, including differences in social and economic characteristics.

As well as providing information on the different personal well-being ratings, the data provides important information on the scale of differences among the different groups examined and benchmark information on which the success of future interventions could potentially be assessed.

Why evaluate personal well-being by equality groups?

Generally, people in the UK are reasonably content. Current average ratings for the four Office for National Statistics (ONS) measures of personal well-being are:

- 7.5 points out of 10 for life satisfaction
- 7.7 out of 10 for feeling that what one does in life is worthwhile
- 7.3 out of 10 for happiness yesterday
- 3.0 out of 10 for anxiety yesterday

Exploring differences for different population groups is important as it informs debate about why inequalities exist and can help policy makers target policy at groups in most need.

How does personal well-being compare for the different equality groups?

Sex

There are differences in how men and women rate their personal well-being. Average ratings show that women have slightly higher life satisfaction (7.5 compared with 7.4 out of 10 for men), consider their activities to be more worthwhile (7.8 compared with 7.6) and rate their happiness slightly higher than men (7.4 compared with 7.3). However, women also rate their anxiety levels significantly higher than men (3.1 compared with 2.9).

It is useful to look at the proportions of people who rated their well-being at the highest and lowest levels. Figure 1 shows that women are far more likely to report feeling the highest ratings of things in their life being worthwhile than men (35.8% compared to 28.4%). Further, when reporting how happy they were yesterday, women are over-represented in the highest and lowest proportions. This indicates that women are more prone to feeling and/or reporting more extremes in happiness than men.

Figure 1: Percentages rating personal well-being at highest and lowest levels: by sex, 2011 to 2014 (1,2,3)

United Kingdom

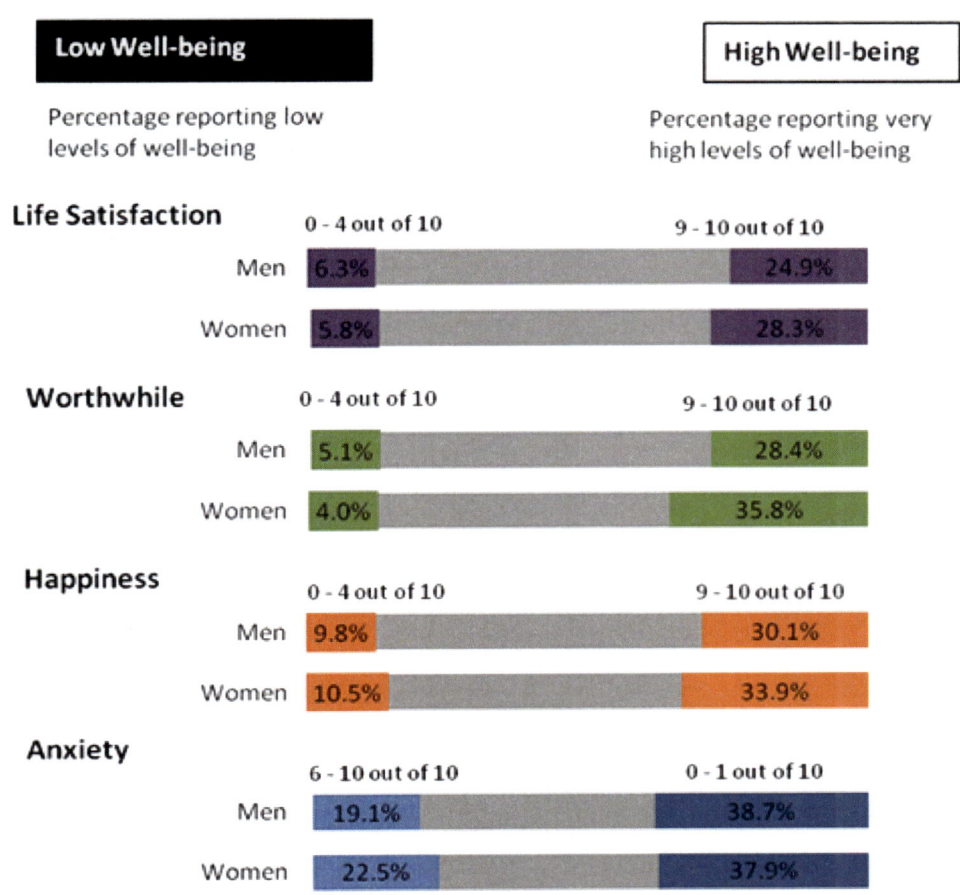

Source: Annual Population Survey (APS) - Office for National Statistics

Notes:

1. Adults aged 16 and over were asked 'Overall, how satisfied are you with your life nowadays?', 'Overall, to what extent do you feel the things you do in your life are worthwhile?', 'Overall, how happy did you feel yesterday?' and 'Overall, how anxious did you feel yesterday?' where 0 is 'not at all' and 10 is 'completely'.
2. Data from April 2011 to March 2014.
3. All data weighted.

Download chart

XLS XLS format
(28 Kb)

Disability and Health

There are also differences in how disabled people rate their personal well-being compared to those without a disability. People who report a disability rate their life satisfaction (6.8 out of 10 compared to 7.7), worthwhile (7.2 out of 10 compared to 7.9) and happiness yesterday (6.8 out of 10 compared to 7.5) lower than those who do not report a disability. They are also more likely to report feeling anxious yesterday (3.7 compared to 2.8) (Figure 2). The large distinctions are considerable with personal well-being data, indicating a sizeable difference in how personal well-being is experienced between the two groups.

Figure 2: Average personal well-being ratings: by disability, 2011 to 2014 (1,2,3)

United Kingdom

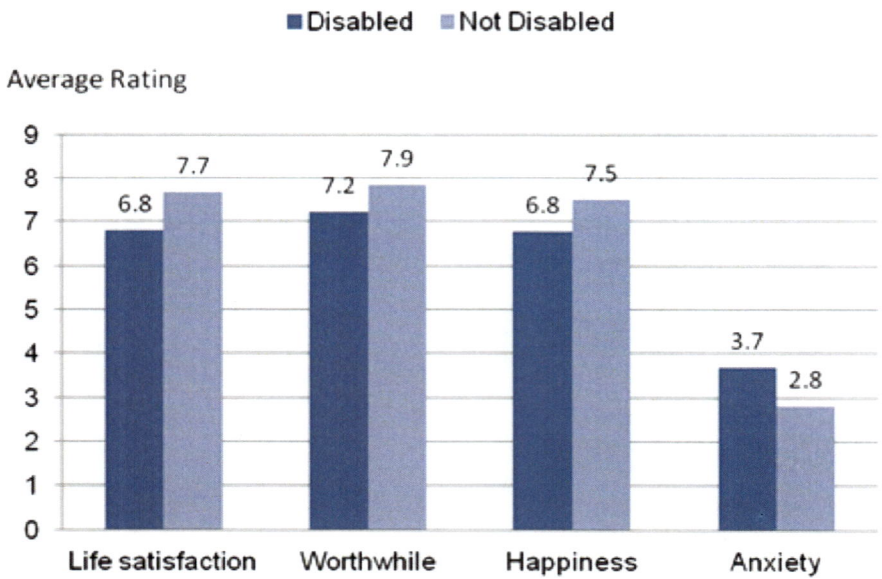

Source: Annual Population Survey (APS) - Office for National Statistics

Notes:
1. Adults aged 16 and over were asked 'Overall, how satisfied are you with your life nowadays?', 'Overall, to what extent do you feel the things you do in your life are worthwhile?', 'Overall, how happy did you feel yesterday?' and 'Overall, how anxious did you feel yesterday?' where 0 is 'not at all' and 10 is 'completely'.
2. Data from April 2011 to March 2014.
3. All data weighted.

Download chart

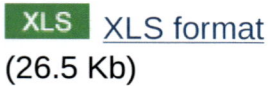 XLS format
(26.5 Kb)

This pattern is repeated with self-reported health across the population; people who reported bad health had lower ratings of life satisfaction, feelings that things were worthwhile, levels of happiness, and higher ratings of anxiety, on average, than those who said their health was good (ONS, 2013c).

We (2013c) found that when other characteristics were held equal, self-reported health has the strongest association with all the measures of personal well-being. This is not surprising; self-reported health is based on people's views of their health rather than objective information. As such, it is likely to reflect people's emotional as well as physical state and the degree of optimism they have about their health. Similarly, people's well-being ratings reflect their emotional state and their optimism about life (ONS, 2013b).

Ethnicity

Consistent with our previous reports (ONS, 2013a), people from the Black ethnic group are, on average, least satisfied with their lives out of all the ethnic groups in the UK (6.8 out of 10) (Figure 3). Mixed/multiple ethnic groups (7.1 out of 10) and the Arab ethnic group (7.2 out of 10) also gave lower ratings, on average. The Other Asian, Indian, White and Chinese ethnic groups were most likely to report being satisfied with their lives (all 7.5 out of 10).

The White ethnic group are most likely to feel that the things they do in life are worthwhile (7.7 out of 10). The Arab ethnic group (7.4 out of 10), the Other ethnic group (7.5 out of 10) and the Chinese ethnic group (7.5 out of 10) gave the lowest average ratings.

Day-to-day emotions including happiness and anxiety, also differ by ethnic group. The Arab ethnic group (3.6 out of 10) and the Mixed or multiple ethnic group (3.4 out of 10) are the most anxious, compared to the Chinese and the White ethnic groups (3.0 out of 10) who are least likely to have felt anxious the previous day. The Arab ethnic group (7.0 out of 10) and the Black ethnic group (7.1 out of 10) are the least likely to report feeling happy yesterday. The Indian and the Other Asian ethnic groups are most likely to report feeling happy (7.4 out of 10).

Figure 3: Average personal well-being ratings compared to UK averages: by ethnic group, 2011 to 2014 (1,2,3,4)

United Kingdom

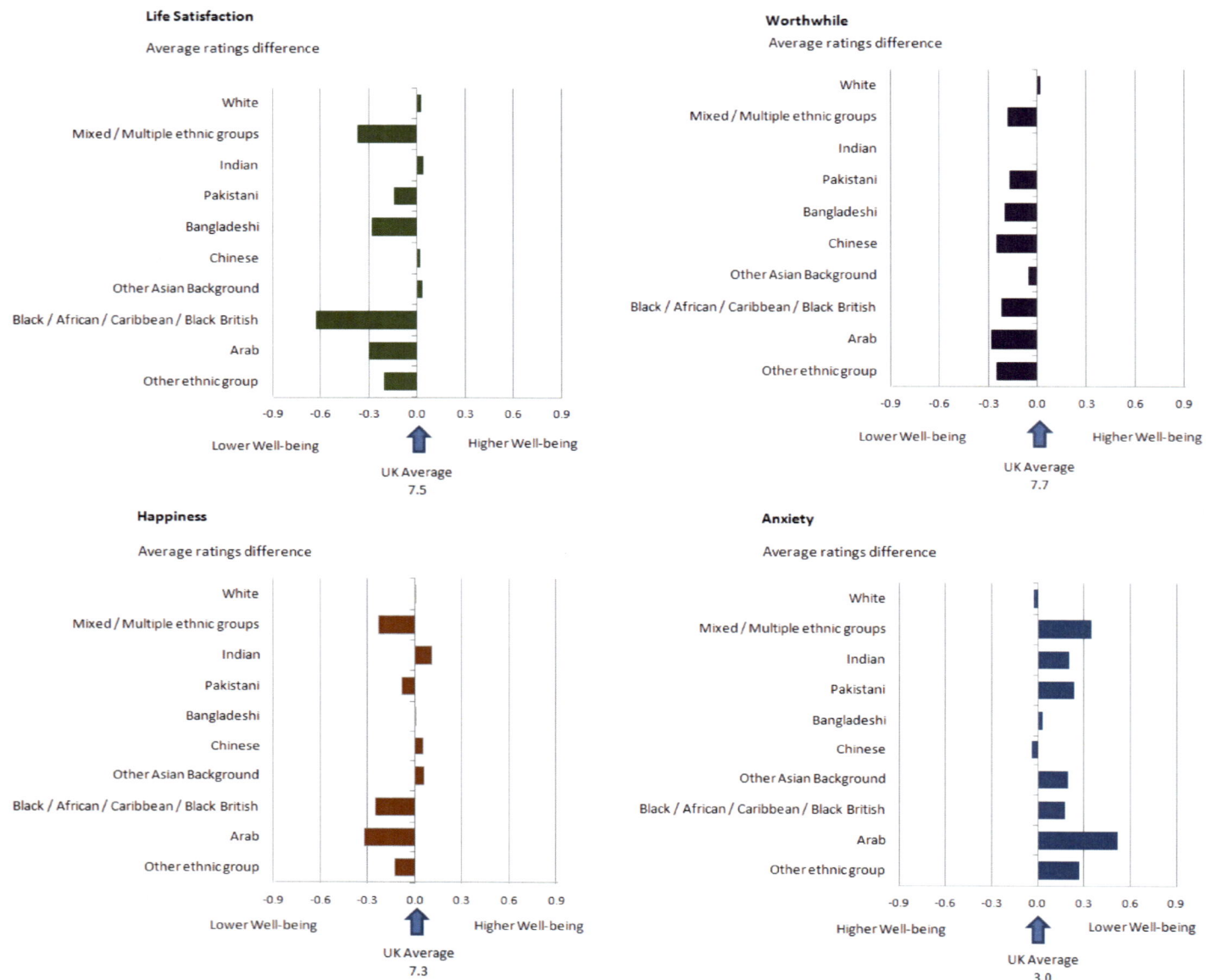

Source: Annual Population Survey (APS) - Office for National Statistics

Notes:

1. Adults aged 16 and over were asked 'Overall, how satisfied are you with your life nowadays?', 'Overall, to what extent do you feel the things you do in your life are worthwhile?', 'Overall, how happy did you feel yesterday?' and 'Overall, how anxious did you feel yesterday?' where 0 is 'not at all' and 10 is 'completely'.
2. Data from April 2011 to March 2014.
3. All data weighted.
4. The Gypsy/Traveller/Irish Traveller group have not been included in analysis due to small sample sizes.
5. Please click on the image to view a larger version.

Download chart

Religion

Religion is an important defining characteristic of people's identity. Christians have the highest average life satisfaction ratings (7.5 out of 10). People who identify as Muslim and Buddhist and those who identify with no religion are least satisfied with their lives (7.3 out of 10) (Figure 4).

Christians and Jewish people are most likely to report that they feel that the things they do in life are worthwhile (both 7.8 out of 10). Whereas, Muslims and those who identify with no religion, are the least likely to feel that the things they do in life are worthwhile (both 7.5 out of 10).

Day-to-day emotions also vary for religious groups. Hindus and Christians are more likely to report being happy (7.5 and 7.4 out of 10 respectively), whereas those who identify with no religion and Muslims are less likely to report being happy (both 7.2 out of 10). Conversely, those who identify with no religion, along with Christians, are also less likely to report feeling anxious (3.0 out of 10), compared to people who identify as Jewish, Muslim, Any other religion and Hindu, who report the highest averages for anxiety (3.3 out of 10).

Figure 4: Average personal well-being ratings compared to UK averages: by religion, 2011 to 2014 (1,2,3)

United Kingdom

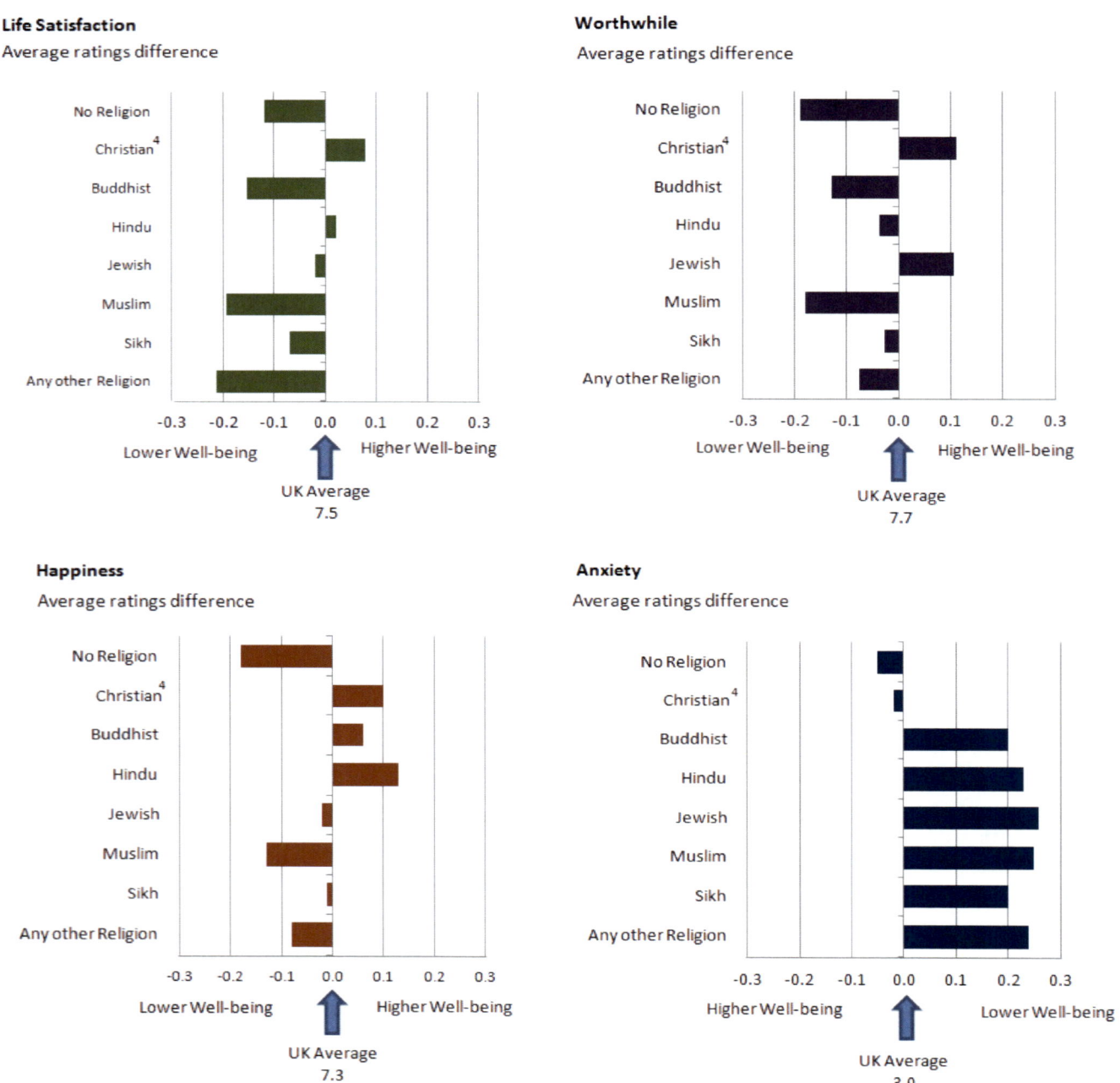

Source: Annual Population Survey (APS) - Office for National Statistics

Notes:

1. Adults aged 16 and over were asked 'Overall, how satisfied are you with your life nowadays?', 'Overall, to what extent do you feel the things you do in your life are worthwhile?', 'Overall, how happy did you feel yesterday?' and 'Overall, how anxious did you feel yesterday?' where 0 is 'not at all' and 10 is 'completely'.

2. Data from April 2011 to March 2014.

3.   All data weighted.
4.   All denominations.
5.   Please click on the image to view a larger version.

Download chart

`XLS` XLS format
(33 Kb)

Why might personal well-being ratings be higher for some equality groups than others?

There are distinct differences in the average ratings between equality groups. The varied responses could, in part, reflect the way different people respond to questions, the different circumstances that people find themselves in, or other characteristics that are common within the equality group, such as age.

In order to determine the individual impact a personal characteristic or circumstance can have on personal well-being more complicated analysis is required. In 2013 we carried out a regression analysis and found that when all else was kept equal self-reported health had the strongest association with all the measures of personal well-being, the second strongest association was employment status and the third was relationship status. As such, if people from different equality groups were more likely to have low self-reported health, be unemployed, or single, this may explain some of the variation in personal well-being ratings (ONS, 2013c).

However, the analysis also found that, after taking into account personal characteristics and circumstances, there was evidence that factors such as an individual's sex, ethnic group and religious affiliation had an impact on personal well-being ratings in different ways, albeit on a smaller scale (ONS, 2013c).

Where can I find out more?

If you'd like to find out more about the latest personal well-being statistics, please explore our new reference tables and maps or see our publications. We also have a range of census publications on religion and ethnicity.

References

1.   OECD (2013) OECD Guidelines on Measuring Subjective Well-being, OECD Publishing

2.   ONS (2013a) Differences in well-being by ethnicity

3.   ONS (2013b) Personal Well-being in the UK 2012/13

4.   ONS (2013c) Measuring National Well-being – What matters most to Personal Well-being?

5.   ONS (2014) Personal Well-being in the UK 2013/14

Background notes

1. Since April 2011, APS has included 4 questions which are used to monitor personal well-being in the UK:

   - Overall, how satisfied are you with your life nowadays?
   - Overall, to what extent do you feel the things you do in your life are worthwhile?
   - Overall, how happy did you feel yesterday?
   - Overall, how anxious did you feel yesterday?

2. The data analysed in this report are derived from a customised, weighted 3 year combined dataset from April 2011 to March 2014. All data can be found in the reference tables.

3. Findings reported here are based on survey estimates and are subject to a degree of uncertainty. They should therefore be interpreted as providing a good estimate, rather than an exact measure of personal well-being in the UK. There is more information about how the statistics are produced and implications for the accuracy of the estimates, in section 8 of Personal Well-being in the UK 2013/14.

4. For ease of reference the majority of this publication refers to averages given by the sample respondents. This does not account for variability between groups. We cannot assume that just because the sample has a certain rating of personal well-being, everyone with that characteristic will give the same rating. Further the direction of causation is not implied. There is more information about how the statistics are produced and implications for the accuracy of the estimates in section 8 of Personal Well-being in the UK 2013/14.

5. The highest levels of personal well-being for life satisfaction, worthwhile and happiness are defined as 9 or 10 out of 10. For reported anxiety, ratings of 0 or 1 out of 10 are used because lower levels of anxiety suggest better personal well-being. Lowest levels of personal well-being are defined as ratings of 0 to 4 for life satisfaction, worthwhile and happiness. For reported anxiety, ratings of 6 to 10 are used because higher levels of anxiety suggest lower personal well-being.

6. It is important to note that people who report a disability are a diverse group of people which includes those with a disability that substantially limits their day-to-day activities, as well as those with a disability that limits the type or amount of work they do, but does not limit their day-to-day activities.

7. The Black ethnic group is made up of Black, African, Caribbean and Black British people.

8. Caution is advised when considering the Arab ethnic group as sample sizes are small, as such confidence intervals are large.

9. The APS asks "what is your religion?" and gathers information on religious affiliation, that is how we connect or identify with a religion, irrespective of actual practise or belief. Religion is a many sided concept and there are other aspects of religion such as religious belief, religious

practice or belonging that are not covered in this analysis. Further information can be found on our Guidance and Methodology pages.

10. Regression analysis – a statistical technique which analyses variation in well-being outcomes by specific characteristics and circumstances, while holding all other characteristics equal.

11. The Gypsy / Traveller / Irish Traveller group have not been included in analysis due to small sample size.

12. All analysis is done on more than 1 decimal place.

13. Differences in personal well-being estimates are described only where they are statistically significant, based on non-overlapping 95 per cent confidence intervals. That is, where the change is not likely to be only due to variations in sampling.

14. Approved researchers can access the datasets at the UK Data Archive.

15. If you have comments on the ONS approach to measuring personal well-being and/ or the presentation of the personal well-being data, please email us at personal.wellbeing@ons.gsi.gov.uk.

16. The data analysed in this report was collected from the Annual Population Survey (APS) which is the largest constituent survey of the Integrated Household Survey. The sample size of the 3 year APS dataset is approximately 305,000 adults aged 16 and over and living in residential accommodation in the UK (England, Scotland, Wales and Northern Ireland). Data used are weighted to be representative of the population and to take account of the fact that responses made on behalf of other household members are not accepted.

17. The UK Statistics Authority has designated these statistics as National Statistics, in accordance with the Statistics and Registration Service Act 2007 and signifying compliance with the Code of Practice for Official Statistics.

Designation can be broadly interpreted to mean that the statistics:

- meet identified user needs;
- are well explained and readily accessible;
- are produced according to sound methods; and
- are managed impartially and objectively in the public interest.

Once statistics have been designated as National Statistics it is a statutory requirement that the Code of Practice shall continue to be observed.

18. Details of the policy governing the release of new data are available by visiting www.statisticsauthority.gov.uk/assessment/code-of-practice/index.html or from the Media Relations Office email: media.relations@ons.gsi.gov.uk

These National Statistics are produced to high professional standards and released according to the arrangements approved by the UK Statistics Authority.

Copyright

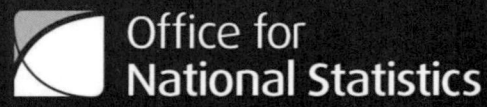
Office for
National Statistics

Opinions and Lifestyle Survey: Methodological Investigation into Response Scales in Personal Well-being

Vicky Palmer and Eleanor Evans

Office for National Statistics

A National Statistics publication

National Statistics are produced to high professional standards set out in the Code of Practice for Official Statistics. They are produced free from political influence.

About us

The Office for National Statistics

The Office for National Statistics (ONS) is the executive office of the UK Statistics Authority, a non-ministerial department which reports directly to Parliament. ONS is the UK government's single largest statistical producer. It compiles information about the UK's society and economy, and provides the evidence-base for policy and decision-making, the allocation of resources, and public accountability. The Director-General of ONS reports directly to the National Statistician who is the Authority's Chief Executive and the Head of the Government Statistical Service.

The Government Statistical Service

The Government Statistical Service (GSS) is a network of professional statisticians and their staff operating both within the Office for National Statistics and across more than 30 other government departments and agencies.

Contacts

This publication

For information about the content of this publication, contact Vicky Palmer
Tel: 01633 656528
Email: personal.well-being@ons.gsi.gov.uk

Other customer enquiries

ONS Customer Contact Centre
Tel: 0845 601 3034
International: +44 (0)845 601 3034
Minicom: 01633 815044
Email: info@statistics.gsi.gov.uk
Fax: 01633 652747
Post: Room 1.101, Government Buildings,
Cardiff Road, Newport, South Wales NP10 8XG
www.ons.gov.uk

Media enquiries

Tel: 0845 604 1858
Email: press.office@ons.gsi.gov.uk

Copyright and reproduction

Introduction

Personal Well-being questions have been asked on Office for National Statistics (ONS) surveys since April 2011. ONS has 4 headline questions to measure personal well-being that were decided upon after consultation, research and testing. These are:

"Overall, how satisfied are you with your life nowadays?"

"Overall, to what extent do you feel the things you do in your life are worthwhile?"

"Overall, how happy did you feel yesterday?"

"Overall, how anxious did you feel yesterday?"

These questions are measured on an 11-point scale, where 0 is 'not at all' and 10 is 'completely'. In other non-ONS household surveys, for example, the UK Household Longitudinal Survey (hereon referred to as "Understanding Society") and the "Which? Consumer Insight" Survey different response scales are used for questions about life satisfaction.

This report examines the findings from the Opinions and Lifestyle survey where questions about life satisfaction were asked using 3 response scales. Measuring the same questions using different scales can give us an indication of the extent to which we can compare ONS' Personal Well-being questions to similar questions on different scales.

Background and Approach

The scale used for the ONS personal well-being questions was chosen because 11-point scales of this nature are more commonly used across other surveys of interest (ONS 2011a). This scale was applied to all 4 questions to ensure that the scales between the questions are consistent, in order to help respondents answer the questions more easily and to aid analysis across separate questions.

Life Satisfaction questions on the Understanding Society survey use a 7-point scale, whereas a 5-point scale is used on the "Which? Consumer Insight" Survey. Different lengths and labelling of scale points require careful consideration, as a different scale may affect how people respond to the question. In addition, the use of different scales in different surveys means that it can be difficult to compare responses across different sources of data.

The 3 questions and response scales investigated in this report are:

- 11-point scale

Overall how satisfied are you with your life nowadays where 0 is 'not at all satisfied' and 10 is 'completely satisfied'.

This question is asked by ONS on the 'Annual Population Survey'.

- 7-point scale

Please choose the number which you feel best describes how dissatisfied or satisfied you are with the following aspects of your current situation...your life overall.

1. Completely dissatisfied
2. Mostly dissatisfied
3. Somewhat dissatisfied
4. Neither satisfied or dissatisfied
5. Somewhat satisfied
6. Mostly satisfied
7. Completely satisfied

This question is used on the 'Understanding Society' Survey.

- 5-point scale

Taking everything into consideration how satisfied or dissatisfied are you with your life overall at the moment?

1. Very satisfied
2. Fairly satisfied
3. Neither satisfied or dissatisfied
4. Fairly dissatisfied
5. Very dissatisfied

This question is used on the 'Which? Consumer Insight' Survey.

For the purpose of this release the questions above will be referred to as "11-point scale", "7-point scale" and "5-point scale".

The data analysed in this paper are from the Opinions and Lifestyle Survey (OPN). For more information on the OPN survey, please see methods notes 1 and 2. The question scales here were tested as a split trial, so each individual in the monthly sample was asked either the 11-point scale, the 7-point scale or the 5-point scale question.

Results

Descriptive Statistics

Each question assesses an individual's perception of their own life satisfaction on a different scale. Table 1 shows the mean, median and mode for the different scales. For all 3 scales, the median score is equal to the mode and the mean value is just below that of the median and mode. It is not easy to make comparisons across the 3 scales using these measures due to the scales being of different lengths, but this analysis is still beneficial to give us insight into the responses of each question and gives an understanding of the shape of the data along each scale. It also helps in providing context for the further analysis seen in this report.

Table 1: Average responses for each question

Great Britain, adults aged 16 and over

	11-point scale	7-point scale	5-point scale
Mean	7.6	5.4	1.9
Median	8	6	2
Mode	8	6	2

Source: Opinions and Lifestyle Survey, Office for National Statistics

Distribution of responses

The average estimates above summarise the overall responses for each question, but do not show how the data is distributed along each scale. It is beneficial for us to look at how the data is distributed along the scale, as it could indicate whether the responses are similarly distributed, and it helps to show whether the length of the scale has an impact on the interpretation of the question. Figure 1 shows histograms of the proportion of responses in each of the response categories for each of the 3 scales.

<u>Figure 1: Histograms displaying the distribution of responses across the 11-point, 7-point and 5-point scale</u>[1,2]

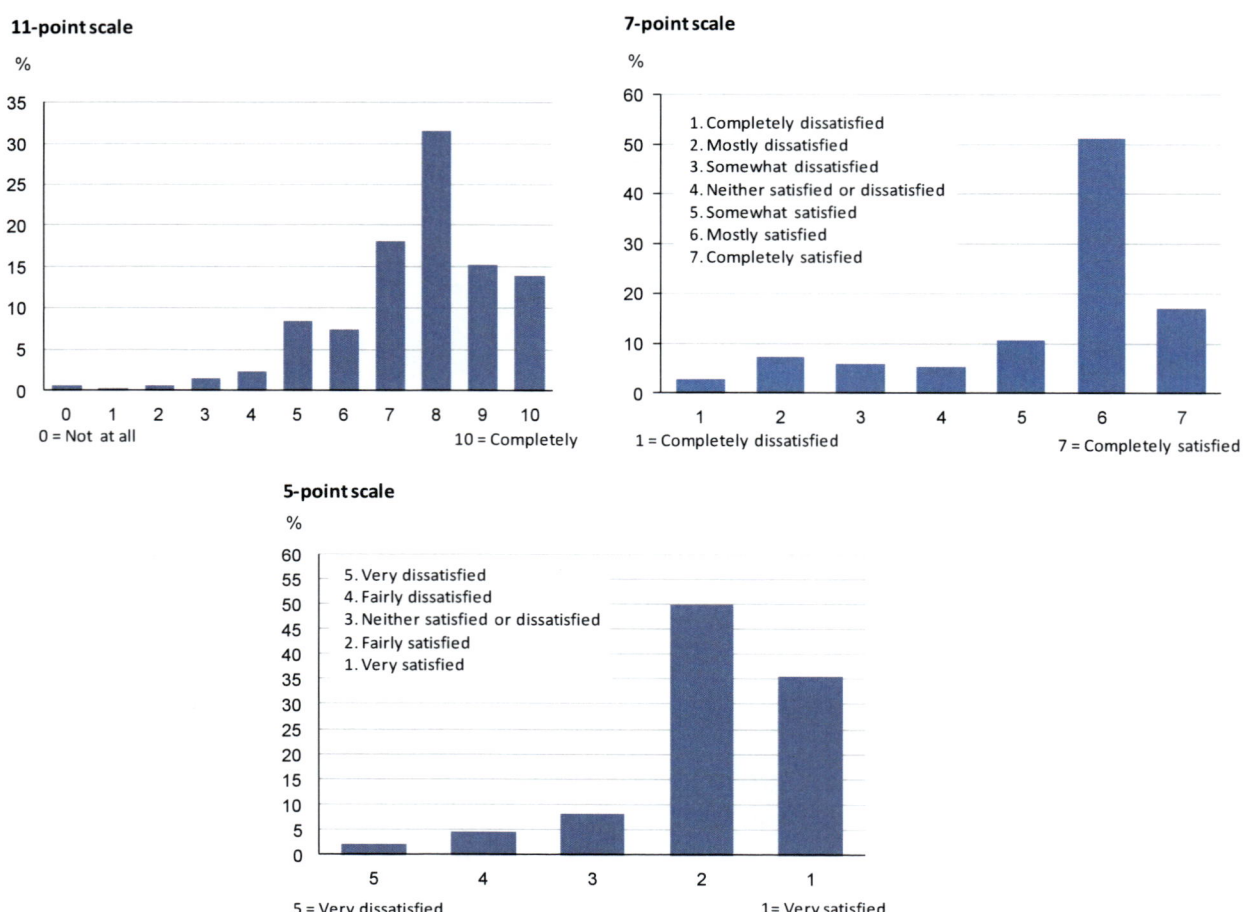

Source: Opinions and Lifestyle Survey, Office for National Statistics

Notes:
1. The 5-point scale has been reversed to ease comparisons.
2. Due to the nature of the survey, some samples are small and therefore may be less reliable.

Figure 1 shows a larger proportion of people answered the questions on the positive side (i.e. to the right of the median) of the well-being scale.

The distributions of the data are quite varied across the 3 scales. For example, the proportion of people answering 0,1 or 2 (the negative end of the well-being scale) on the 11-point scale is extremely small and the scale shows a gentle curve building up to the modal response value of 8. The 7 point scale shows a clear and distinct spike at the modal value of 6 (the positive end of the well-being scale) and the 5-point scale shows a peak at both scale points 1 and 2 (the positive end of the well-being scale).

Figure 2: Cumulative frequency of responses across the 11-point, 7-point and 5-point scale[1,2]

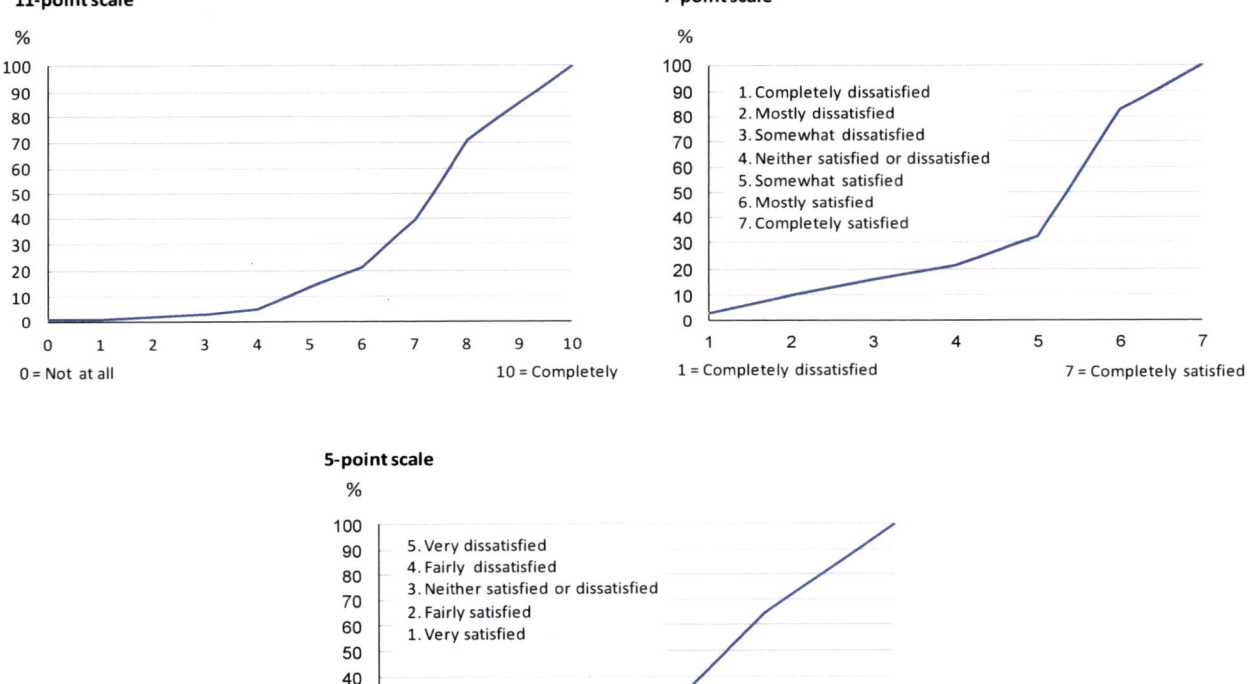

Source: Opinions and Lifestyle Survey, Office for National Statistics

Notes:
1. The 5-point scale has been reversed to ease comparisons.
2. Due to the nature of the survey, some samples are small and therefore may be less reliable.

The cumulative frequency charts above are an alternative way to display the distribution of the data. The distributions are different but hard to compare to one another as they are on different scales. Again, we can clearly see from Figure 2 that the proportion of people who answered 0, 1, 2 and 3 (low levels of life satisfaction) on the 11 point scale is very small. The 5-point scale shows a sharp increase in the number of people answering 2 and 1 (high levels of life satisfaction) compared to the number of people answering 3 or below. The cumulative frequency of the 7-point scale looks slightly different to the other 2, with a steady upwards trend in the proportion of people answering 1 – 5 and then a very sharp increase between the number of people answering 5 and the number of people answering 6. This echoes the findings discussed when looking at the histograms earlier in this report.

Proportions above, below and on the midpoint

An alternative way to investigate distributions of responses is by assessing the proportion of responses above or below defined thresholds. Thresholds are useful to present the proportion of people who fall above and below a certain point on the scale (ONS 2011a). This allows comparison of proportions of people who reported high well-being against people who reported lower well-being across the 3 different scales. The scales have therefore been split to show the proportion of people who answered the midpoint of the scale, gave a response which was above the midpoint, or gave a response which was below the midpoint.

Figure 3: Proportions answering above, below and on the midpoint for each of the 3 scale questions

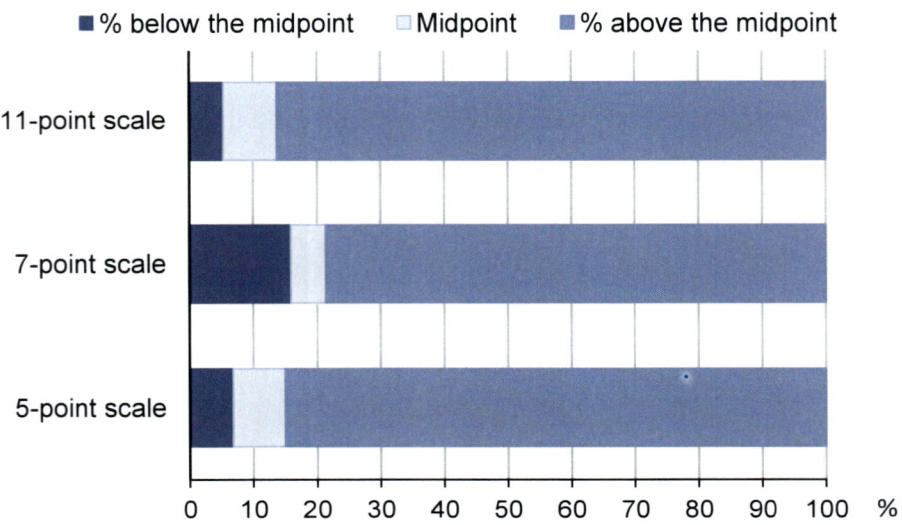

Source: Opinions and Lifestyle Survey, Office for National Statistics

- For the 11-point scale the midpoint of the scale is response category 5, the proportion above the midpoint are the people who answered response categories 0-4 and the proportion below the midpoint are the people who answered 6-10.
- For the 7-point scale the midpoint of the scale is 4, the proportion of people above the midpoint are the people who answered 1-3 and the proportion below the midpoint are the people who answered 5-7.
- For the 5-point scale the midpoint of the scale is 3, the proportion who answered below the midpoint is 4-5 and the proportion of people who answered below the midpoint is those people who answered 1-2. Please note that the 5-point scale is different because the scale has been flipped for ease of analysis.

The 5-point scale and the 11-point scale show fairly similar results, and again, these are quite dissimilar to the results that are displayed by the 7-point scale. A larger proportion of people who answered the 7-point life satisfaction scale gave a score which was below the midpoint than the proportion for those people who answered the 5-point and the 11-point scale. These results appear to indicate that the results given on the 5-point scale are more comparable with the 11-point scale than the 7-point scale. This pattern can also be seen from the distribution charts displayed earlier. However, there are some differences between the distribution of responses given on the 5-point and the 11-point scale; these are not identical by any means. A larger proportion of people who answered the 5-point scale answered below the midpoint than the proportion of those answering the 11-point scale. This information informs us of the similarities but also the differences between the scales, which give an indication that perhaps the scales are measuring life satisfaction in different ways. This could be indicating that people understand the 5-point scale and the 11-point scale in a similar way. Possible reasons for this are discussed in the conclusion.

Normality

Data can be normally distributed, positively skewed or negatively skewed. If the majority of the data is clustered around the right hand side of the scale (usually the higher scores), then the data is negatively skewed. Likewise, data that is mostly clustered around the left hand side of the scale (usually the lower scores) is positively skewed. Skewness is the extent to which data is not symmetrical around the mean.

Table 2: Test of Normality using the Shapiro-Wilk test

Great Britain, Adults aged 16 and over

	Shapiro-Wilk Statistic	Skewness	Kurtosis
11-point scale	0.895*	-1.156	2.000
7-point scale	0.800*	-1.199	0.420
5-point scale	0.781*	1.298	1.811

Source: Opinions and Lifestyle Survey, Office for National Statistics

Notes:
* Significant at the 99% level.

A Shapiro-Wilk test was conducted on the data, which measures the extent to which data are normal, or alternatively, the extent to which the data deviates from the normal distribution. The significant Shapiro-Wilk test statistics show that all 3 questions failed the normality assumption. Both the 11-point and the 7-point scale were negatively skewed, and the 5-point scale was positively skewed. This was expected as the numerical scoring scale for this question runs in the opposite direction to the other 2 questions, where a higher number indicates a more negative response. Skewness increased slightly with more scale points, with the 5-point scale showing the smallest skew of the 3 and the 11-point scale showing the largest skew of the 3. This is as expected because longer scales are naturally more likely to result in a greater spread of the data, which would result in a larger variance.

This pattern did not hold for Kurtosis however. Kurtosis refers to the shape of the data around the mean and the tails of the distribution. A normal distribution has a kurtosis of zero, whereas data that exhibit positive kurtosis are more peaked about the mean and have shorter tails (Dawes, 2008). It was found in this analysis that the 11-point scale had the highest kurtosis of the 3 scales, but the 7-point scale had the lowest kurtosis. This suggests that people were most likely to use all 7 of the points on the 7-point scale than they were to use all 11 of the points for the 11-point scale. For example, very few people answered "0", "1" or "2" on the 11-point scale. We would expect to see a pattern here, with the 5-point scale showing the smallest kurtosis and the 11-point scale showing the largest kurtosis of the 3, but this pattern does not hold. Again, this seems to be implying that people answered the 7-point scale in a different way to the way in which they answered the 11-point scale and the 5-point scale. It also highlights the fact that it is not easy to make comparisons across the 3 scales by examining them as they are. Therefore in the next section of this paper, an alternative way to examine these scales using a rescaling method has been investigated.

Rescaling

In order to examine the differences between the scales in more detail it is useful to rescale the data so that the 3 scale formats are comparable to one another. For these calculations, ratings from the 7-point scale and the 5-point scale were rescaled[*] to make them comparable with the 11-point scale. The following formula was used, which is based on a formula by Preston and Colman (2000):

$$(\text{Rating} - 1)/(\text{Number of response categories} - 1) \times 10.$$

For more detail about this rescaling procedure, please see methods note 6. For the purpose of the analysis in this release we are assuming linearity across each scale. Rescaling is the best way in which we can compare the scales against one another, however, it should be noted that it still may not lead to completely comparable results because the assumption of linearity may not hold. For more detail on this, please see methods note 7.

Figure 4: Average[1] scores of rescaled variables on the 0-10 scale

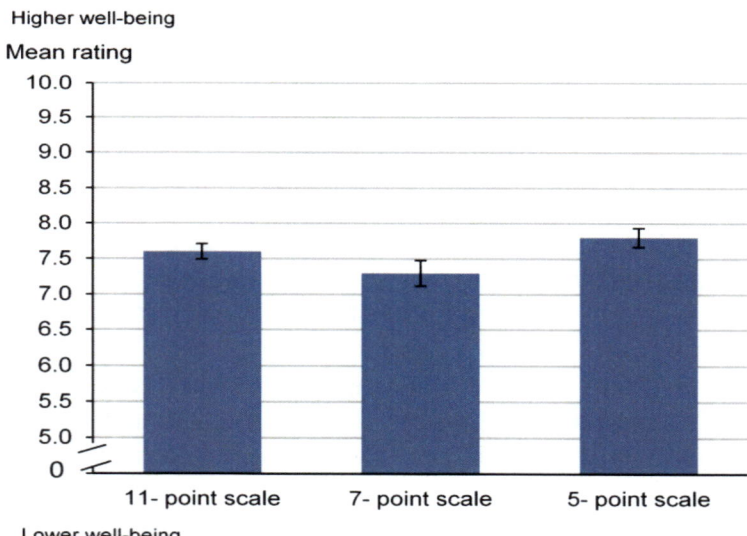

Source: Opinions and Lifestyle Survey, Office for National Statistics

Notes:
  1. Average score is based on the mean.

---

[*] The purpose of this rescaling is to facilitate comparison between the scale formats, not to find a specific functional transformation that will minimize any rescaled differences.

Figure 4 shows the average scores for each of the rescaled variables. The differences between all 3 scales are statistically different from one another at the 5% level. The highest mean was seen for the 11-point scale, and the lowest mean was seen for the 7-point scale. Once again here, we can see a big difference between the results on the 7-point scale compared to the other 2 scales, although all 3 are statistically different from one another based on an f-test. For more detail about significance testing see methods note 5.

Past research on well-being has shown that scores often tend to be negatively skewed (ONS 2013, ONS 2014). This means that there are more responses at the positive end of the well-being scale than there are at the negative end of the well-being scale. This is consistent with the results that have been found in this paper, and can clearly be seen from the histograms displayed above. More scale points mean that there are more positive responses to choose from, so the fact that respondents tend to give responses that are positive may mean that a finer scale with more response options could result in a slightly lower mean score. This is consistent with the results found for the 11-point and 5-point scale, but again the 7-point scale is showing a different pattern.

Conclusions

Great care should be taken when comparing results across scales. The results from this analysis show that responses are not equal when asked across different scales, suggesting that individuals are likely to answer differently depending on the scale that they are presented with (Dawes, 2008).

One reason for this may be translation ease. According to Krosnick and Presser (2010), the scale length can impact on the ease at which people are able to map their attitudes onto the response alternatives. For example, if an individual has an extremely positive or negative attitude, a dichotomous scale such as "like" or "dislike" easily allows the individual to report their attitude, however, if an individual has a more neutral attitude, this scale would not easily permit them to express how they feel. Therefore, the value of adding more points to a rating scale may depend on the extent to which people's mental representations of the construct are refined.

It is also worth noting that the 3 response scales investigated in this release may not be comparable to one another due to the fact that the questions were worded differently. Even small changes in question wording can sometimes lead to a change in the way that people respond or express particular attitudes (Iarossi, 2006). Further research would be needed to investigate the extent to which this would affect the results, testing differing response scales using the same question wording for each.

Other studies suggest that reliability between response scales is higher when all points are labelled with words than when only some are (Krosnick and Bernet,1993). In this analysis, the 11-point scale did not have all points labelled with words, whereas the 7-point and 5-point scale did. This could be a factor that led to the significant differences which were found. Krosnick and Fabrigar (1997) found that labels on every data point were more cognitively demanding than end-labelled scales because they require the respondent to remember a lot of information. Questions without labels are therefore much less of a burden to answer. This may explain why our 7-point scale showed such different results to the other 2 scales, as it was the most burdensome for individuals to answer, especially due to the interviewer led mode of question asking that is used on the OPN survey.

References

Dawes, J. (2008) Do data characteristics change according to the number of scale points used? An experiment using 5-point, 7-point and 10 point scales. International Journal of Market Research, Vol. 50, Issue 1.

Iarossi, G. (2006) The Power of Survey design. The World Bank, Washington D.C. Krosnick, J.A., & Berent, M.K. (1993) Comparisons of party identification and policy preferences: The impact of survey question format. American Journal of Political Science, 37, 941-964.

Krosnick, J.A., & Fabrigar, L.R. (1997). Designing Rating Scales for Effective Measurement in Surveys (Chapter 6) in Lyberg L, Biemer P, Collins M, De Leeuw E, Dippo C, Schwarz N and Trewin D (Eds.) Survey Measurement and Process Quality (1997) Wiley. New York: pp141-164.

Krosnick J A and Presser S (2010) Question and Questionnaire Design (chapter 9) in Marsden P V and Wrights J D (Eds.) (2010) Handbook of Survey Research. 2nd Edition. Emerald. pp.263-313.

ONS (2011a) Measuring Subjective Well-being. Office for National Statistics.

ONS (2011b) Initial investigation into Subjective Well-being from the Opinions Survey. Office for National Statistics.

ONS (2012) Summary of results from testing of experimental subjective well-being questions.

ONS (2013) Personal well-being in the UK 2012/13.

ONS (2014) Personal well-being in the UK 2013/14.

ONS (2015) Opinions and Lifestyle Survey: Methodological Investigation into the Societal Module.

Opinions and Life Style Survey Technical Report. Office for National Statistics.

Osgood, C. E., Suci, G. J., & Tannenbaum, P. H. (1957) The measurement of meaning. Urbana, IL: University of Illinois Press.

Preston, C.C. & Colman, A. (2000) Optimal number of response categories in rating scales: reliability, validity, discriminating power, and respondent preferences. Acta Psycholohica, 104, 1-15.

Schuman, H. and Presser. (1981) Questions and Answers in Attitude Surveys . New York: Academic Press.

Thurstone, L. L. (1928) Attitudes can be measured. American Journal of Sociology, 33, 529–554.

Methods Notes

1. The data presented in this report are taken from the March, May, August and November 2014 OPN Survey and relate to Great Britain. The sample used for this analysis is an aggregation of these 4 months of data, giving an overall sample size of around 4,200. The 3 questions analysed in this report were asked in the same way for each of these months.

2. The OPN has been used as a testing vehicle for well-being analysis since April 2011 (ONS, 2012). Question testing using the OPN has continued since the development of the 4 headline personal well-being in order to explore and investigate additional personal/subjective well-being questions. The OPN is ONS' omnibus survey which covers Great Britain, running monthly to allow quick and reliable information on topics of immediate policy interest. It is for this reason it was chosen for testing questions on personal/subjective well-being. This forms part of the broader suite of Personal/Subjective Well-being question testing on the OPN (ONS, 2011b; ONS, 2012; ONS, 2015) .

   The OPN is sampled from the Royal Mail's small user postcode address file. The survey is purely voluntary and asks questions to those over the age of 16 and selects an adult from a household on the basis of a Kish grid. Each month's achieved interviews are roughly 1,000 - 1,100 adults. The estimates in this release are weighted to take account of the uneven probability of selection from a household in the OPN and to calibrate responses so that they are representative of the whole population (Opinions and Lifestyle Survey).

3. Response rates

   Table 3: Response rates for each of the 3 scale questions

	Response rate (%)
11-point scale	99.0
7-point scale	99.8
5-point scale	99.6
Total	99.5

   Source: Opinions and Lifestyle Survey, Office for National Statistics

4. All estimates have been calculated with the weight (indwgt) applied. The weight was adjusted to take account of there being 4 datasets combined to run this analysis (Opinions and Lifestyle Survey). Standard Errors (used to calculate confidence intervals, CI) have been calculated taking into account the complex survey design and post-stratification weighting.

5. Significant differences when noted in the text have been calculated on the basis of F-tests. Note: F-tests are treating the well-being scores as continuous. Please see methods note 7.

6. Reverse scoring and Rescaling

For the 11-point scale and the 7-point scale, a higher response score indicated higher life satisfaction. However, due to the wording of the scale, this was not the case for the 5-point scale. For the 5-point scale a higher response score indicated lower life satisfaction. Therefore in places throughout this analysis the 5 point scale has been reverse scored for ease of analysis.

The 7-point scale and the 5-point scale were rescaled for part of the analysis in order to make them comparable with the 11-point scale. The 11-point scale was unaltered for this analysis. The rescaling was based on a formula by Preston and Coleman (2000) who used the formula (rating-1)/(number of response categories-1) x100 to rescale to a common score out of 100. For the purpose of this analysis, a similar formula was used which rescaled the original 7-point and 5-point scales to a scale from 0-10, in order to make them comparable with the 11-point scale.

Firstly, the 5-point scale was reverse scored. Each scale point on the 7-point scale and the 5-point scale was then inserted into the formula below, to create new scale points.
Formula: (rating − 1)/(number of response categories − 1) × 10.
Table 5 displays the old values, and new values following the rescaling.

Table 5: Rescaling and Reverse Scoring Detail

11-point scale (original)	11-point scale used in analysis (unchanged)	7-point scale (original)	7-point scale used in analysis (rescaled)	5-point scale (original)	5-point scale (reverse scored)	5-point scale used in analysis (rescaled)
0	0	1	0	5	1	0
1	1	2	1.6666667	4	2	2.5
2	2	3	3.333333	3	3	5
3	3	4	5.0	2	4	7.5
4	4	5	6.6666667	1	5	10
5	5	6	8.333333			
6	6	7	10			
7	7					
8	8					
9	9					
10	10					

Source: Opinions and Lifestyle Survey, Office for National Statistics

7. The methods used in this paper assume that the scales are linear, and therefore treat the well-being data as continuous. The linearity assumption assumes that each scale point is

an equal distance away from the scale point preceding it. This means for example that we assume that the difference between a score of 1 and 2 is exactly equal to the difference between a score of 2 and 3, and so on. This in practice is unlikely to be the case but there is no way of adjusting the methodology to account for this.

8. For more information on Personal Well-being, please contact:
Personal Well-being Team, ONS
Telephone: 01633 455713
Email: personal.well-being@ons.gsi.gov.uk

9. Details of the policy governing the release of new data are available by visiting the UK Statistics Authority or from the Media Relations Office

10. © Crown copyright 2015. You may use or re-use this information (not including logos) free of charge in any format or medium, under the terms of the Open Government Licence, write to the Information Policy Team, The National Archives, Kew, London TW9 4DU, or email: psi@nationalarchives.gsi.gov.uk.

11. Details of the policy governing the release of new data are available by visiting www.statisticsauthority.gov.uk/assessment/code-of-practice/index.html or from the Media Relations Office email: media.relations@ons.gsi.gov.uk

12. These statistics are experimental. Should users have comments on the ONS approach to the measurement of personal well-being and or the presentation of the personal well-being questions they can email ONS at national.well-being@ons.gov.uk.

Annex 1

Data for Figure 1: Histograms displaying the distribution of responses across the 11-point, 7-point and 5-point scale[1,2]

11-point scale		7-point scale		5-point scale	
Scale point	%	Scale point	%	Scale point	%
0	0.7	1	2.9	5	2.1
1	0.3	2	7.3	4	4.7
2	0.6	3	5.8	3	8.1
3	1.4	4	5.4	2	49.8
4	2.3	5	10.0	1	35.4
5	8.3	6	51.1		
6	7.4	7	17.0		
7	18.2				
8	31.6				
9	15.2				
10	14.0				

Source: Opinions and Lifestyle Survey, Office for National Statistics

Notes
1. The 5-point scale has been reversed to ease comparisons.
2. Estimates may not add up to 100 due to rounding.

Data for Figure 2: Cumulative frequency of responses across the 11-point, 7-point and 5-point scale[1]

11-point scale		7-point scale		5-point scale	
Scale point	%	Scale point	%	Scale point	%
0	0.7	1	2.9	5	2.1
1	1.0	2	10.1	4	6.8
2	1.6	3	15.9	3	14.9
3	3.0	4	21.3	2	64.6
4	5.3	5	31.9	1	100.0
5	13.6	6	83.0		
6	21.1	7	100.0		
7	39.2				
8	70.8				
9	86.0				
10	100.0				

Source: Opinions and Lifestyle Survey, Office for National Statistics

Notes
1. The 5-point scale has been reversed to ease comparisons.

Data for Figure 3: Proportions of the population answering above, below and on the midpoint for each of the 3 scale questions

	% below the midpoint	Midpoint	% above the midpoint
11 point scale	5.3	8.3	86.4
7 point scale	15.9	5.4	78.7
5 point scale	6.8	8.1	85.1

Source: Opinions and Lifestyle Survey, Office for National Statistics

Data for Figure 4: Average[1] scores of rescaled variables on the 0-10 scale

	Mean	95% Confidence Interval
11 Point scale	7.6	0.1
7 Point scale	7.3	0.2
5 Point scale	7.8	0.1

Source: Opinions and Lifestyle Survey, Office for National Statistics

Notes:
1. Average score is based on the mean.

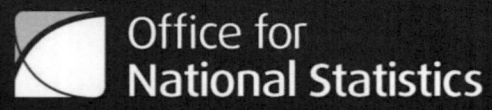

Opinions and Lifestyle Survey: Methodological Investigation into the Societal Module

Eleanor Evans and Vicky Palmer

Office for National Statistics

A National Statistics publication

National Statistics are produced to high professional standards set out in the Code of Practice for Official Statistics. They are produced free from political influence.

About us

The Office for National Statistics

The Office for National Statistics (ONS) is the executive office of the UK Statistics Authority, a non-ministerial department which reports directly to Parliament. ONS is the UK government's single largest statistical producer. It compiles information about the UK's society and economy, and provides the evidence-base for policy and decision-making, the allocation of resources, and public accountability. The Director-General of ONS reports directly to the National Statistician who is the Authority's Chief Executive and the Head of the Government Statistical Service.

The Government Statistical Service

The Government Statistical Service (GSS) is a network of professional statisticians and their staff operating both within the Office for National Statistics and across more than 30 other government departments and agencies.

Contacts

This publication

For information about the content of this publication, contact Eleanor Evans
Tel: 01633 651631
Email: personal.well-being@ons.gsi.gov.uk

Other customer enquiries

ONS Customer Contact Centre
Tel: 0845 601 3034
International: +44 (0)845 601 3034
Minicom: 01633 815044
Email: info@statistics.gsi.gov.uk
Fax: 01633 652747
Post: Room 1.101, Government Buildings,
Cardiff Road, Newport, South Wales NP10 8XG
www.ons.gov.uk

Media enquiries

Tel: 0845 604 1858
Email: press.office@ons.gsi.gov.uk

Copyright and reproduction

Introduction

The National Statistics Measuring National Well-being Programme launched in November 2010. The programme looked to provide a fuller understanding of 'how society is doing' across society, the economy, and the environment.

The National Statistics Measuring National Well-being Programme started the national debate on "What matters to you?" to ask what should be included in measures of the nation's well-being. Amongst the things emerging from the debate community was suggested as an area that people felt was particularly important.

This article focuses on questions about community which can be found in the societal module of the Opinions and Lifestyle Survey (OPN). For more information on the OPN see methods note 1. Many of these questions can be used to assess Social Capital. For the latest work on Social Capital see ONS (2015a) Measuring National Well-being – An Analysis of Social Capital in the UK.

This analysis will focus on the 7 community related questions tested as part of the broader suite of Personal/ Subjective Well-being question testing on the OPN (ONS, 2011b; ONS, 2012; ONS, 2015b) .

This module was selected for analysis due to inclusion in 8 months of testing allowing us for the first time to assess community related question responses by demographic characteristics. Other modules have been run assessing Evaluative, Eudemonic and Experience aspects of well-being. These are more detailed modules following on from the Office for National Statistics' (ONS) 4 headline Personal Well-being questions, which are:

"Overall, how satisfied are you with your life nowadays?"

"Overall, to what extent do you feel the things you do in your life are worthwhile?"

"Overall, how happy did you feel yesterday?"

"Overall, how anxious did you feel yesterday?"

The 7 community related questions tested on the OPN and investigated in this release are:

1. To what extent do you feel most people can be trusted?

2. To what extent do you feel you have any relatives, friends or neighbours that you can ask for help?

3. Overall, how satisfied are you with the local area where you live? (When answering, please consider the area to be within 15-20 minutes walking distance from your home)

4. To what extent do you feel that you are involved in the local area where you live?

5. To what extent do you feel you belong in the local area where you live?

6. Overall, how satisfied are you with the public gardens, parks, commons or other green spaces in the local area where you live? (When answering, please consider the area to be within 15-20 minutes walking distance from your home)

7. How safe would you feel walking alone in this local area after dark?

In this article these questions will be referred to in short form (see background note 1). The responses to these questions ranged from 0 to 10 with 0 being 'not at all' and 10 being 'completely'[1].

This analysis investigates the way people respond to these questions, for example, the distribution of responses along the 0 to 10 scale, question response rates, the way different sub-groups respond to the questions, as well as the extent to which the questions are correlated with each other (e.g. picking up similar concepts).

The primary purpose of testing the questions in this way is to ascertain whether these questions are collecting information about the same or different topics relating to community.

It is worth remembering that the responses to these questions are subjective, therefore they measure people's self - reported feelings and thoughts on the topics asked.

Results

Average estimates for all indicators

Each question assesses a different aspect of community. To get an overall review of the responses for each question we can assess the mean average for each.
Looking at the average response to each question the highest average was for "*To what extent do you feel you have any relatives, friends or neighbours that you can ask for help?*" at 8.3 out of 10. The second highest average was for "*Overall, how satisfied are you with the local area where you live?*" at 7.6.

The lowest average was for "*To what extent do you feel that you are involved in the local area where you live?*" at 4.1 out of 10. This is considerably lower than all other estimates, with the next lowest estimate being 6.0 out of 10 ("*To what extent do you feel most people can be trusted?*"). This shows that on average, people feel that their involvement in their area is less than how satisfied they are with their local area.

The question "*To what extent do you feel you belong in the local area where you live?*" had an average of 6.6 out of 10, showing that people are more likely to say that they belong in the area that they live, than they are to say that they are involved in the area that they live.

---

[1] These questions were always asked after the 4 ONS headline personal well-being questions on the OPN. The introduction of the well-being section of the survey begins as follows "Next I would like to ask you four questions about your feelings on aspects of your life. There are no right or wrong answers. For each of these questions I'd like you to give an answer on a scale of nought to 10, where nought is 'not at all' and 10 is 'completely'."

The averages indicate that these questions, although asking about similar topics, are answered differently by respondents indicating that the questions are collecting information about different and distinct community related concepts.

Figure 1: Average Estimates of the Community Questions

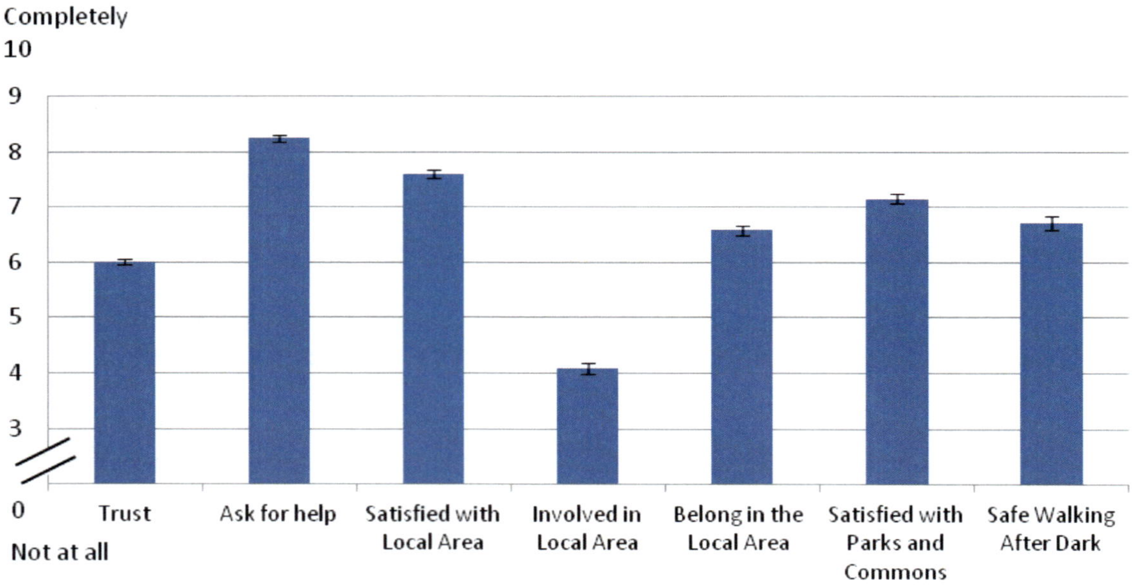

Notes:
1. There are 11 response categories available for these questions ranging from 0 to 10. "On a scale where nought is '[not at all]' and 10 is '[completely]',"
2. Average has been calculated on the basis of the mean.

Source: Opinions and Lifestyle Survey, Office for National Statistics.

Response Rates

Figure 2: Response Rates to the Community Questions

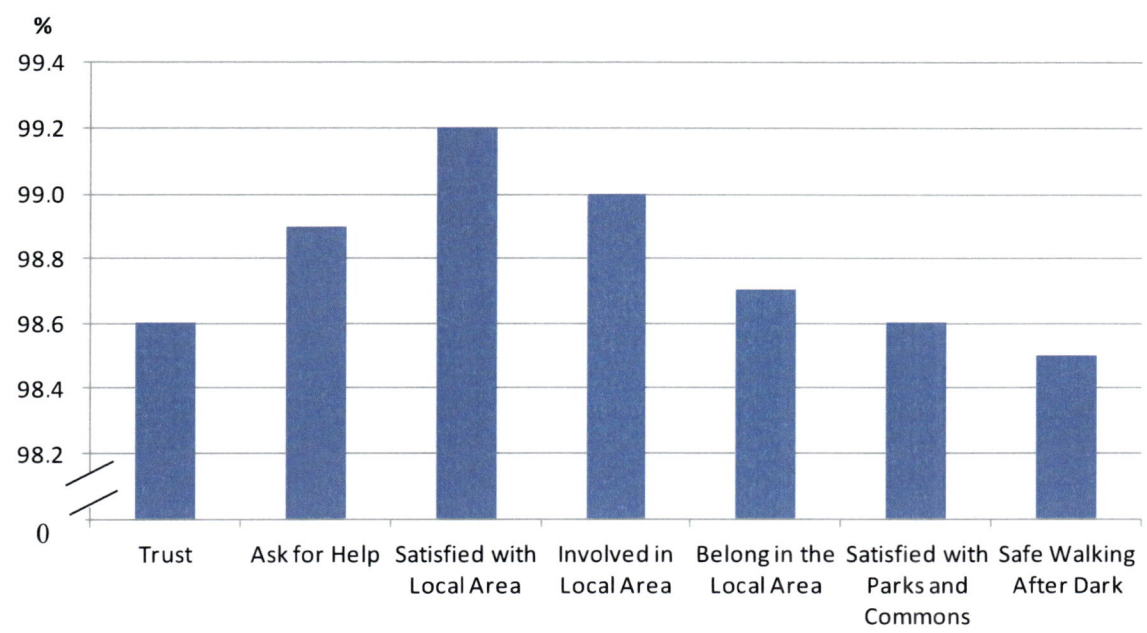

Source: Opinions and Lifestyle Survey, Office for National Statistics.

Of the 7 questions tested the highest response rate was seen for *'Satisfied with local area'* at 99.2%, this is the third question in the module of questions asked. The smallest response rate was seen for *'Safe walking after dark'* which is the last question in the series at 98.5%. There is not a great deal of difference between the questions with the difference between the most and least answered question being 0.7% of the sample. Potential explanations for the differing response rates for the questions include:

- how people interpret the questions against the scale (are they better able to place their level of satisfaction against the 0 to 10 scale than they are their ability to ask a friend or neighbour for help for example) (Krosnick and Presser, 2010);

- not having a 'Don't know' category and therefore forcing people to answer or not respond (Krosnick and Presser, 2010); and

- concern for social desirability (would people be happy to note that their area is less desirable for example) (Krosnick and Presser, 2010).

Distribution of responses

The average scores presented above provide a good summary of the overall responses for each question; however they do not show how the data are distributed along the 0 to 10 scale, specifically whether the responses are evenly distributed or how people answer at the top and bottom ends of the scale. Figure 3 shows histograms of the proportion of responses in each of the 11 response categories for the 7 community related questions analysed here.

Figure 3 shows there are differing distributions of responses for each question. There is a varied pattern for the 'Involved in local area' question responses, where more people reported 'not at all' than any other option. 'Involved in local area' was also the only question that followed a negative gradient with its responses with an exception for those answering 5 out of 10, for example the responses were highest for '0' and gradually declined to 9/10. 'Satisfied with local area' and 'Satisfied with parks and commons' had very similar distributions, both following a positive gradient peaking at 8 out of 10, and with 10 out of 10 having a higher proportion than 9 out of 10. This could indicate a strong correlation between the two variables, something we will look at further on in this article. The highest response category for all the questions was seen in 'Ask for help'. This question saw 39.3% of people giving a rating of 10 out of 10 when asked if they feel they can ask someone for help.

When comparing the proportion answering in the top half of the distribution (5 to10), compared to the bottom half of the distribution (0 to 4) we see that it is common place for people to answer in the top half of the distribution (5 to10). The biggest skew[2] was seen for 'Ask for help' where 93.1% answered 5 to 10 and 6.9% answered 0 to 4. A similar pattern is seen for 'Satisfied with local area'.

The only question that does not follow this pattern is 'Involved in local area' where 53.7% of the sample answered 0 to 4 and 46.3% answered 5 to 10.
When assessing the mode for each question, which is the most common response out of 10, 8 out of 10 is the most common, with 4 of the 7 questions having 8 as the mode. Interestingly, the question 'Trust' has a similar proportion of people saying that they felt that most people can be trusted completely (10) at 2.0% as not at all (0) at 1.8%. The question 'Ask for help' has more people answering 'completely' (10 out of 10) than any other response for any questions.

Again, this indicates that respondents are interpreting these questions as distinct from each other and altering their responses for each question accordingly, with the possible exceptions being 'Satisfied with local area' and 'Satisfied with parks and commons'.

---

[2] Skewness refers to the extent to which data deviates from the normal distribution.

Figure 3: Distribution of responses to the Community Questions

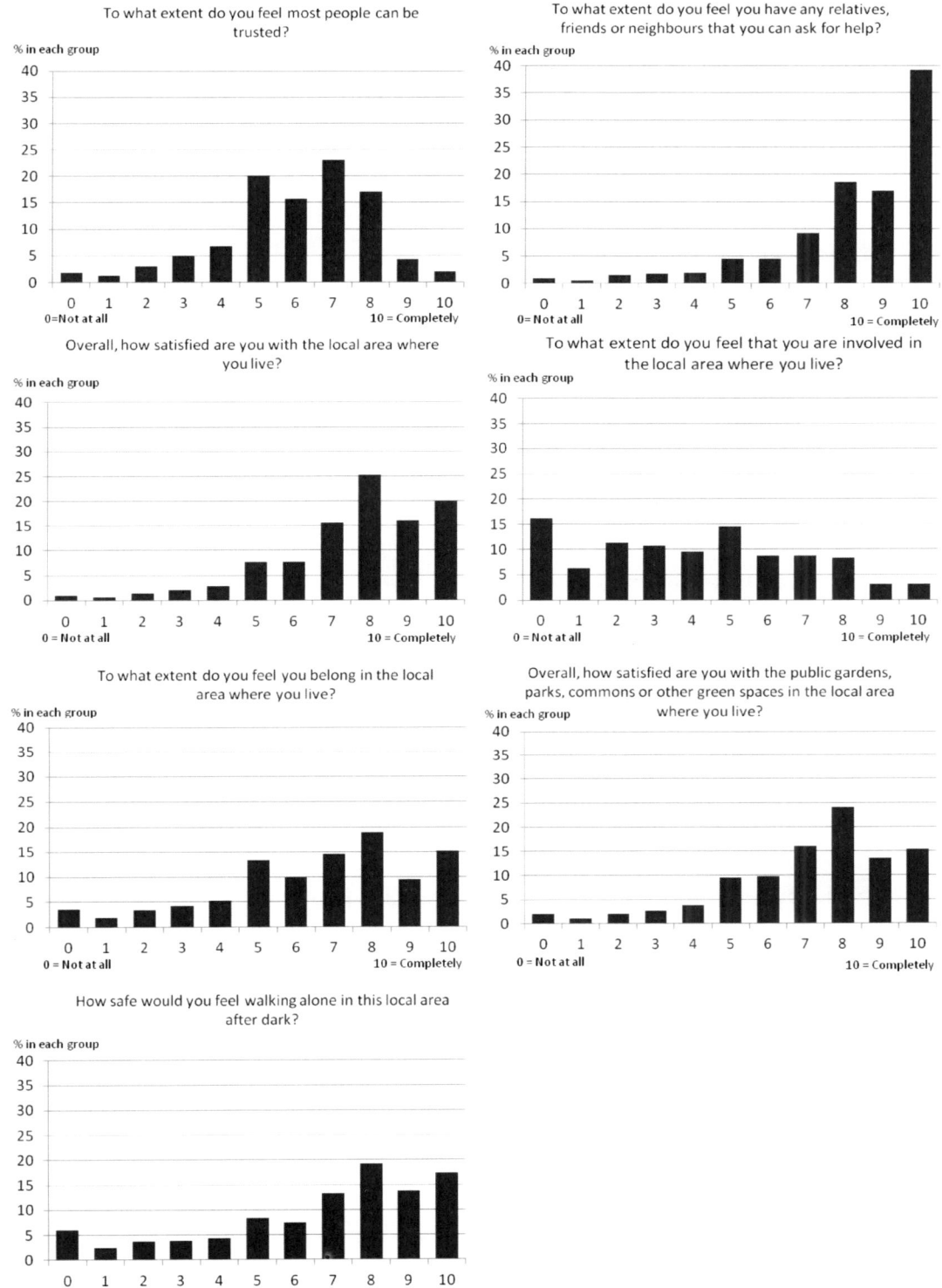

Notes:

1. There are 11 response categories available for these questions ranging from 0 to 10. "On a scale where nought is '[not at all]' and 10 is '[completely]',"

Source: Opinions and Lifestyle Survey, Office for National Statistics.

Thresholds

Figure 4: Proportion of the population in each threshold category

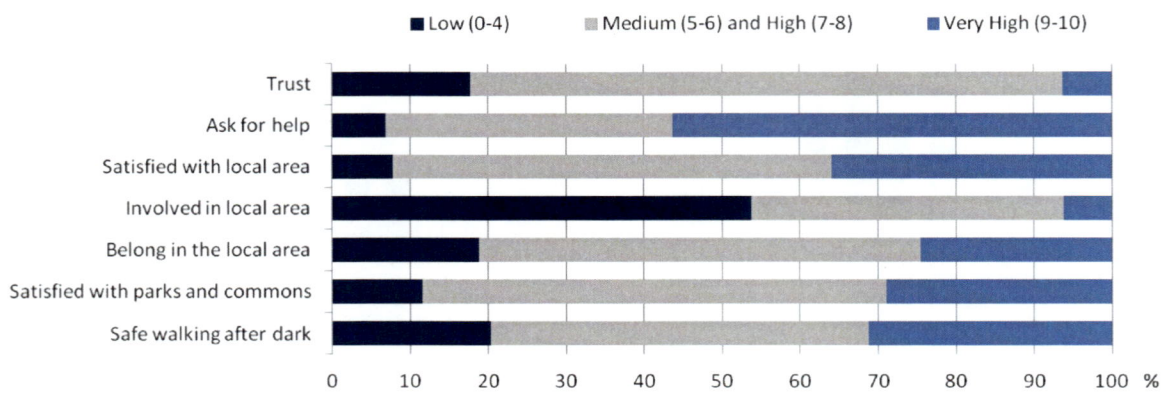

Notes:
1. There are 11 response categories available for these questions ranging from 0 to 10. "On a scale where nought is '[not at all]' and 10 is '[completely]',"

Source: Opinions and Lifestyle Survey, Office for National Statistics.

An alternative way to investigate distributions of responses is through assessing the proportion of people answering certain responses through thresholds. These thresholds are 0 to 4 out of 10, 5 to 6 out of 10, 7 to 8 out of 10 and 9 to10 out of 10. The above graph demonstrates some of the patterns we saw in the histograms. The majority of people (53.7%) responded with low scores (0 to 4 out of 10) for 'Involved in local area'. The inverse is seen for 'Ask for Help' where a majority (56.3%) gave a very high rating (9 to 10 out of 10).

The questions 'Trust' and 'Involved in local area' have a similar proportion of people giving a very high rating (9 or 10 out of 10) at 6.3% and 6.2% respectively, however when assessing those two questions for those who reported low ratings (0 to 4 out of 10) only 17.7% of people gave a low rating to 'Trust' compared to 53.7% for 'Involved in the local area'.

Estimates by gender

Figure 5: Average Estimates of the Community Questions by gender

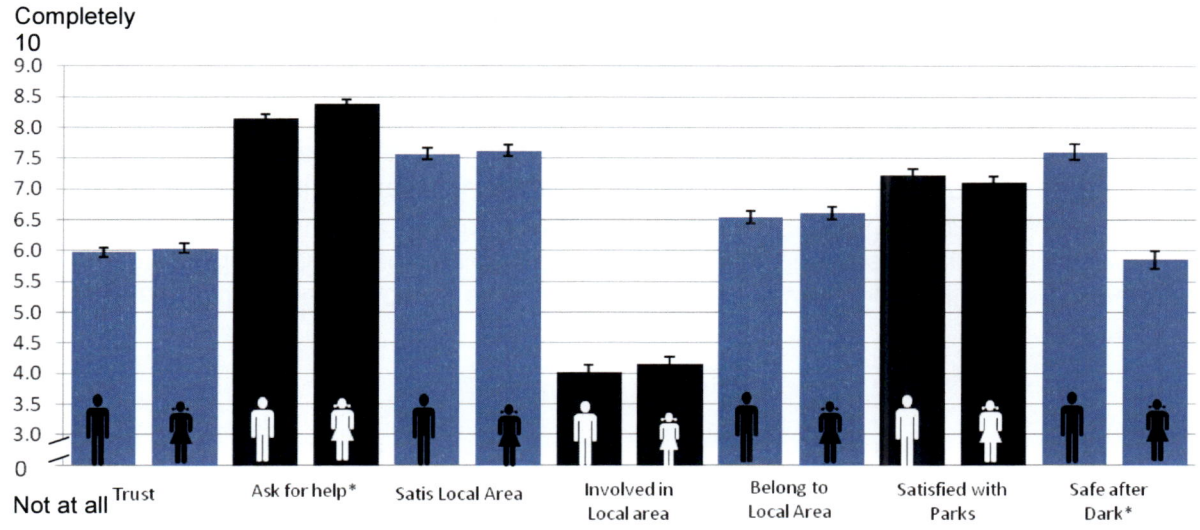

Notes:
1. * Denotes statistical significance where statistical significance is calculated on the basis of a t-test at the 95% level.

2. Average has been calculated on the basis of mean.

Source: Opinions and Lifestyle Survey, Office for National Statistics.

The difference between the responses of men and women to personal/subjective well-being questions has previously been reported (ONS, 2013, ONS, 2014b). Studies investigating this difference at older ages have suggested potential explanations for this could be, that women are more likely to disclose negative feelings than men and older women are more likely to be widowed than older men (Pinquart and Sorensen, 2001). When the community questions are assessed by gender (Figure 5) statistically significant differences are observed for 'Ask for help' and 'Safe walking after dark'. For 'Ask for help' the estimate was significantly higher for women (8.4) than for men (8.1).
There is a large difference between men and women's estimates for "Safe walking after dark?". The estimate for men is significantly higher (1.7 percentage points) than that for women at 7.6 and 5.9 respectively, this is not unexpected and similar results have been shown on the ONS Well-being Wheel from the Crime Survey for England and Wales.

Overall, when assessing the estimates to the community questions by gender we see little difference with the exception of 'Ask for help' and 'Safe after dark'.

<u>Estimates by age</u>

The ONS 4 headline measures of Personal Well-being (Life Satisfaction, Worthwhile, Happiness and Anxiety) have been shown to vary by age (ONS, 2011b; ONS, 2013; ONS 2014b).

Differences in responses to these questions by age groups could be due to a number of factors which includes life course effects and those over 65 being more likely to be retired and therefore have more time to be involved in their areas. Generational and cohort factors are also worth noting, research suggests that there is evidence of cohort effects in personal well-being analysis, citing that those living through the Great Depression experienced lower well-being than those cohorts living in a prosperous time (Sutin et al., 2013).

Figure 6: Average Estimates of the Community Questions by age.

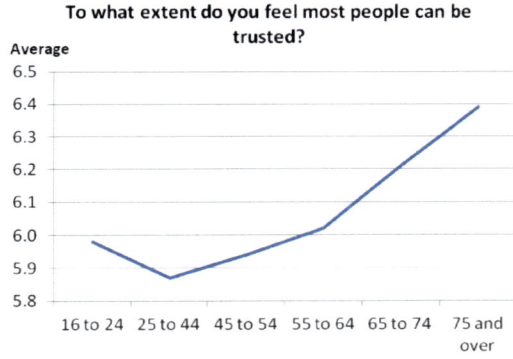

To what extent do you feel most people can be trusted?

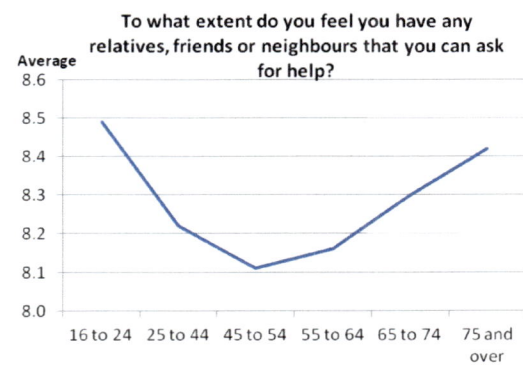

To what extent do you feel you have any relatives, friends or neighbours that you can ask for help?

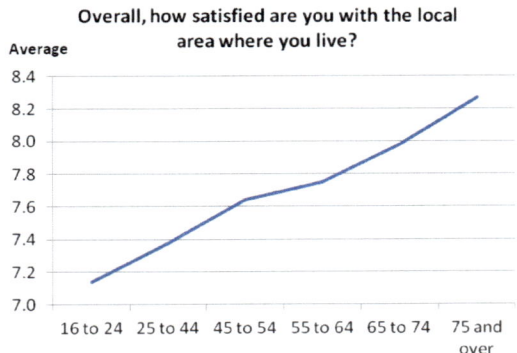

Overall, how satisfied are you with the local area where you live?

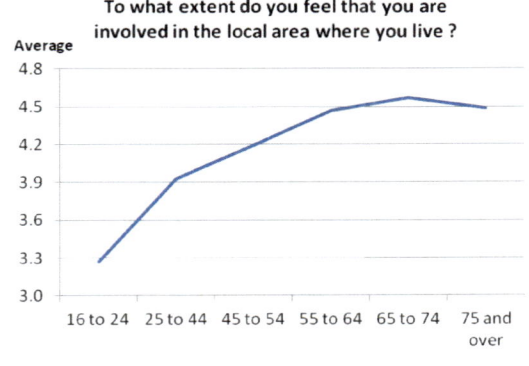

To what extent do you feel that you are involved in the local area where you live ?

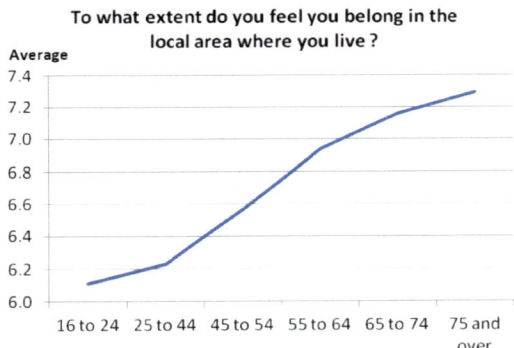

To what extent do you feel you belong in the local area where you live ?

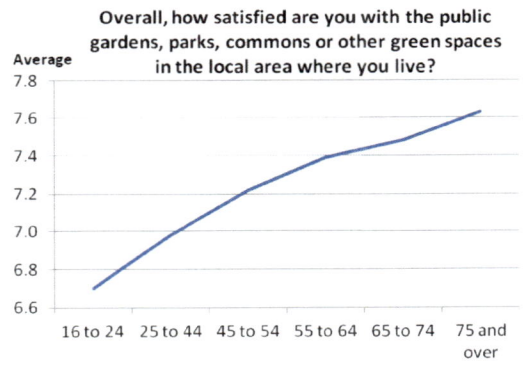

Overall, how satisfied are you with the public gardens, parks, commons or other green spaces in the local area where you live?

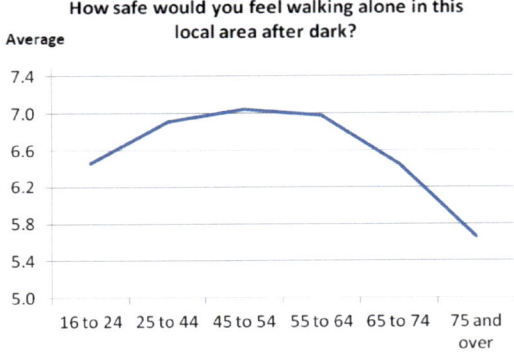

How safe would you feel walking alone in this local area after dark?

Notes:
1. Average has been assessed on the basis of mean.

Source: Opinions and Lifestyle Survey, Office for National Statistics.

Responses to each of the questions tested differ by age group. In general, 5 of the 7 questions show a gradual improvement in well-being as we move from the younger age groups to the middle age groups, with the highest well-being experienced by the oldest age groups; Only *'Safe walking after dark'* and *'Ask for help'* do not follow this trend. There is a positive gradient in 4 of the 7 questions, where the average estimate increases as age increases. This is seen for *'Belong to the local area'*, *'Satisfied with parks and commons'*, *'Satisfied with local area'* and *'Trust'*.

The lowest rating of *'Trust'* is observed for those aged 25 to 44. A positive gradient is observed from the age 25 – 44 to older ages, with the steepest gradient in this curve at the older ages, where the feeling that most people can be trusted improves at a faster rate. The drop seen in average response for those aged 25 to 44 can be seen somewhat in ONS' Life Satisfaction headline question where the biggest drop between ages (when age is assessed on a 5 year age group breakdown) is between 16 to 19 and 20 to 24 (ONS, 2013; ONS, 2014b). These results showing lower levels of *'Trust'* in the younger ages and higher in the older has also been noted elsewhere (HM Government, 2014).

'Ask for help', *'Involved in local area'* and *'Safe walking after dark'* are unique. The question *"To what extent do you feel you have any relatives, friends or neighbours that you can ask for help?"* generates responses on a U-shaped curve where those aged 16 to 24 and 75 and over feel that they can ask for help more than those aged 45 to 54. This is a relatively shallow curve however, with the difference between scores for those aged 45 to 54 and those 75 and over being 0.3.

This U-shaped curve has been documented in other well-being analysis (Clark et al,. 1996; Blanchflower and Oswald, 2008; Dolan et al., 2008) and was also seen for ONS' headline well-being questions (ONS, 2011b). When assessed against 5 year age bands, the shape of the curves for the 4 headline questions generally show a "U-shape" with those in the youngest and oldest age groups having the highest levels of life satisfaction and lowest anxiety (ONS, 2013; ONS, 2014b).

The question *"How safe would you feel walking alone in this local area after dark?"* is the inverse of this where those in the middle age bands (those aged between 25 and 64) feel the safest walking alone and with the youngest and the oldest reporting lower results. Those over 75 have the lowest estimates, with an average 1.4 lower than those aged 45 to 54.

Involvement in the local area also follows a curve but a positive curve. Where the extent you feel you are involved in your local area increases until age 64 to 74 and then drops slightly for those 75 and over, which could be due to poorer health. There is a large difference between those aged 16 to 24 and those aged 65 to 74 at 1.3.

When assessing responses to all 7 questions by age, *'Involved in local area'* had the lowest estimates over all ages. *'Ask for help'* had the highest estimates for every age. *'Ask for help'* also displays a U-shaped curve similar to the 'ONS 4' for the three positively worded questions.

The 4 ONS personal well-being questions traditionally see the youngest age band (16 – 24 year olds) reporting higher well-being compared to age bands in the middle years. This pattern is not necessarily reflected here with only *'Ask for help'* having the highest estimate for those aged 16 to 24. *'Belong to local area'*, *'Satisfied with parks and commons'*, *'Satisfied with local area'* and *'Involved in local area'* all have their lowest estimates for the 16 to 24 age group.

When assessing trends over these age bands we should also be noting that these age groups have been artificially formed. Should these ages be categorised differently a different story may emerge.

All of the community questions assessed here are impacted by age, where distinctions can be made between those in the younger, middle and older age groupings. These patterns could indicate towards a cohort or generational effect which has been evidenced in personal well-being analysis but further research using longitudinal data is required.

<u>Relationships between the variables.</u>

<u>Table 1: Relationship between Community questions</u>

	Satisfied with Local Area	Trust	Ask for Help	Involved in Local Area	Belong in the Local Area	Satisfied with Parks and	Safe Walking After Dark
Satisfied with Local Area							
Trust	0.058						
Ask for Help	0.053	0.283					
Involved in Local Area	0.042	0.094	-0.004				
Belong in the Local Area	0.254	0.020	0.155	0.340			
Satisfied with Parks and Commons	0.369	0.074	0.001	0.094	0.047		
Safe Walking After Dark	0.171	0.096	0.019	0.058	0.071	0.109	

Notes:
1. The correlations above are Pearson partial correlations. The relationship between each pair of variables has been assessed taking into account their relationships with the other five variables.

2. All correlations are significant at the 95% level.

Source: Opinions and Lifestyle Survey, Office for National Statistics.

Correlation is a method for assessing how similar the responses of two questions are. The results range from -1 through to +1, where -1 is a perfect negative correlation and +1 is a perfect positive correlation. Within this range 0 means no association and 1(or -1) is perfect association.

There are no exceptionally large correlations (those over 0.5) between the 7 community questions investigated in this article. The strongest correlation was seen between *'Satisfied with local area'* and *'Satisfied with parks and commons'* at .369. The second strongest was between *'Involved in local area'* and *'Belong in the local area'* at .340. This was followed by *'Trust'* and *'Ask for help'* at .283. The smallest correlation was seen between *'Ask for help'* and *'Satisfied with parks and commons'* at .001. All correlations were positive apart from *'Ask for help'* and *'Involved in local area'* but this was very small at -.004.

The questions that have the highest correlations (*'Satisfied with local area'* and *'Satisfied with parks and commons'*; and *'Involved in local area'* and *'Belong in the local area'*) tell us that they are related and there is the potential of one being a predictor of the other. Further research would be needed into this, as in future it could indicate that when assessing community we may not need to include both of the questions.

Conclusions

This analysis has investigated the responses from 7 community related questions tested on the Opinions and Lifestyle survey.

This analysis has shown that within the questions tested here, there is a range of different aspects to sense of and contentment with community and that the responses capture differing opinions and aspects of one's life.

Interestingly these questions do not always follow the traditional "U-shape" in responses across age groups that are seen in personal well-being data.

When assessing responses by gender, only 2 of the 7 questions show significantly different responses, showing little difference in the responses between men and women. It should still be noted however that *"Safe after dark"* did have a large difference between men and women.

Background notes

1. Within the report the 7 questions are referred to in their short form. This is for ease of interpretation. The long and short hand terms are listed below.

    1. To what extent do you feel most people can be trusted? – Trust

    2. To what extent do you feel you have any relatives, friends or neighbours that you can ask for help? - Ask for help

    3. Overall, how satisfied are you with the local area where you live? - Satisfied with local area

    4. To what extent do you feel that you are involved in the local area where you live? - Involved in local area

    5. To what extent do you feel you belong in the local area where you live? - Belong in the local area

    6. Overall, how satisfied are you with the public gardens, parks, commons or other green spaces in the local area where you live? - Satisfied with parks and commons

    7. How safe would you feel walking alone in this local area after dark? - Safe walking after dark

2. These statistics are experimental. Should users have comments on the ONS approach to the measurement of personal well-being and or the presentation of the personal well-being questions they can email ONS at national.well-being@ons.gov.uk.

3. All data (unless otherwise stated) is from the Opinions and Lifestyle Survey. All data is weighted and non-respondents are not included.

4. Details of the policy governing the release of new data are available by visiting the UK Statistics Authority or from the Media Relations Office

5. © Crown copyright 2015. You may use or re-use this information (not including logos) free of charge in any format or medium, under the terms of the Open Government Licence, write to the Information Policy Team, The National Archives, Kew, London TW9 4DU, or email: psi@nationalarchives.gsi.gov.uk.

6. Details of the policy governing the release of new data are available by visiting www.statisticsauthority.gov.uk/assessment/code-of-practice/index.html or from the Media Relations Office email: media.relations@ons.gsi.gov.uk

Methods notes

1. Opinions and Lifestyle Survey (OPN)

The OPN has been used as a testing vehicle for personal/subjective well-being question analysis since April 2011. Question testing using the OPN has continued since the development of the 4 headline personal well-being in order to explore and investigate additional personal/subjective well-being questions. The OPN is ONS' omnibus survey which covers Great Britain, running monthly to allow quick and reliable information on topics of immediate policy interest, it is for this reason it was chosen for testing questions on personal/subjective well-being.

The OPN is sampled from the Royal Mail's small user postcode address file. The survey is purely voluntary and asks questions to those over the age of 16 and selects an adult from a household on the basis of a Kish grid. Each month's achieved interviews are roughly 1,000 - 1,100 adults. The estimates in this release are weighted to take account of the uneven probability of selection from a household in the OPN and to calibrate responses so that they are representative of the whole population (Opinions and Lifestyle Survey).

2. Questions asked with responses available 0-10

Questions asked on the Opinions and Lifestyle survey had the option to answer on a scale from 0 to 10 with the introduction being "On a scale where nought is '[not at all]' and 10 is '[completely]',"

3. Sample construction

The sample used for this analysis is an aggregation of 8 months of data from the OPN. The sample was drawn from across 2011 – 2014, covers an even distribution of months over the year and was chosen for their inclusion of the Societal module. The monthly datasets used are September 2011, January 2012, May 2012, October 2013, November 2013, April 2014, July 2014 and October 2014. The total sample size for the analysis was around 8,500.

4. Testing Impacts on Sample

The data used in this analysis is from the OPN survey for the months September 2011, January 2012, May 2012, October 2013, November 2013, April 2014, July 2014 and October 2014. As well as the differing events happening over this three year period there are also testing impacts we need to be aware of in the sample.

The first of which is the use of generic show cards. The Societal module in October 2013, November 2013, April 2014, July 2014 and October 2014 had generic show cards used to aid respondents when answering the questions and September 2011, January 2012 and May 2012 did not have generic show cards.

Secondly for the same split of months listed above, there was a different question ordering and placement of the questions in the survey as noted by the table below.

Table 2: Question Ordering and Placement in OPN Survey

	Sample 1 Question Number in Survey	Question Order in Sample 1	Sample 2 Question Number in Survey	Question Order in Sample 2
To what extent do you feel most people can be trusted?	5	1	14	1
To what extent do you feel you have any relatives, friends or neighbours that you can ask for help?	7	2	15	2
Overall, how satisfied are you with the local area where you live?	8	3	17	3
To what extent do you feel that you are involved in the local area where you live?	9	4	19	5
To what extent do you feel you belong in the local area where you live?	10	5	20	6
Overall, how satisfied are you with the public gardens, parks, commons or other green spaces in the local area where you live?	14	6	18	4
How safe would you feel walking alone in this local area after dark?	15	7	21	7

Notes:
1. Sample 1 refers to September 2011, January 2012 and May 2012.

2. Sample 2 refers to October 2013, November 2013, April 2014, July 2014 and October 2014.

The impact of these changes cannot be disentangled due to them being tested over the same periods; however, we can assess the differences between the time points and investigate testing that has been done previously.

Show cards have been shown to help the understanding of the respondent (Ralph et al., 2011). The impact of their use has been assessed previously for ONS' 4 headline questions. These results showed that the means were significantly higher for life satisfaction (at the 5% level) and happy (at the 10% level) when show cards were used. However there was no significant difference for worthwhile or anxious yesterday (ONS, 2012).

It is widely acknowledged in survey design that question ordering impacts responses (Krosnick and Presser, 2010). For all of the monthly samples the first four questions asked were the ONS headline well-being questions (Life Satisfaction, Worthwhile, Happy yesterday and Anxious yesterday). It is worth noting that split trial and order testing for the headline questions happened in September 2011, January 2012, May 2012, October 2013 and November 2013. For the last 5 monthly datasets combined, being later in the survey, the answers for the Societal module need to be assessed in context of the further questions asked before them. For these 5 datasets respondents were also asked questions:

Table 3: Further questions in OPN survey

Question Number	
5	Overall, how satisfied are you with your relationships with family, including spouse/partner?
6	Overall, how satisfied are you with your relationships with friends?
7	Overall, how satisfied are you with your physical health?
8	Overall, how satisfied are you with your mental well-being?
9	Overall, how satisfied are you with the well-being of your child/children?
10	Overall, how satisfied are you with your financial situation?
11	Overall, how satisfied are you with your work situation?
12	Overall, how satisfied are you with your commute to work?
13	How satisfied are you with the balance between the time you spend on your paid work and the time you spend on other aspects of your life?
16	On a scale where 0 is not at all lonely and 10 is extremely lonely, how lonely do you feel in your daily life?

Due to the differences being across the same time spans we are unable to disentangle the potential interaction affects between the effect of show cards, question order and question placement. Therefore we must simply assess the extent of the difference between the 2 samples.

Table 4: Impact of differences between time points

		Overall, how satisfied are you with the local area where you live?	To what extent do you feel most people can be trusted?	To what extent do you feel you have any relatives, friends or neighbours that you can ask for help?	To what extent do you feel that you are involved in the local area where you live?	To what extent do you feel you belong in the local area where you live?	Overall, how satisfied are you with the public gardens, parks, commons or other green spaces in the local area where you live?	How safe would you feel walking alone in this local area after dark?
September 2011, January 2012 and May 2012	**Mean**	**7.49**	**5.80**	**8.32**	**4.09**	**6.61**	**6.93**	**6.47**
	Lower 95% CI	7.37	5.72	8.22	3.95	6.50	6.79	6.29
	Upper 95% CI	7.61	5.89	8.42	4.23	6.73	7.07	6.66
October 2013, November 2013, April 2014, July 2014 and October 2014	**Mean**	**7.66**	**6.13**	**8.22**	**4.08**	**6.56**	**7.30**	**6.86**
	Lower 95% CI	7.57	6.05	8.14	3.96	6.46	7.19	6.72
	Upper 95% CI	7.75	6.20	8.29	4.21	6.66	7.40	6.99
	P Value	0.031*	0.000*	0.107	0.933	0.501	0.000*	0.001*

Note: * = significant difference at the 95% level, where significant differences have been calculated on the basis of t-tests.

When assessing the differences between the 2 time points, there are significant differences at the 95% level for 4 of the 7 questions. Although there is a significant difference for "Overall, how satisfied are you with the local area where you live" the estimates do have overlapping confidence intervals.

Although there are significant differences between the two periods (due to show cards, ordering and placement) it is still advantageous to include all 8 months of data as it increases our sample sizes and the robustness of our results. These issues do need to be kept in mind, however, when analysing the results of the investigation.

5. All estimates have been calculated with the weight (indwgt) applied. The weight was adjusted to take account of there being 8 datasets combined to run this analysis (ONS). Standard Errors (used to calculate confidence intervals, CI) have been calculated taking into account the complex survey design and post-stratification weighting.

6. Significant differences when noted in the text have been calculated on the basis of t-tests. This gives a more robust estimate of statistical significance.

7. Partial correlations have been used to assess the relationship (correlation) between the variables to take into account the implicit link between the questions due to them being asked one after another, and to them all assessing a different aspect of community, therefore having an underlying connection.

For more information on Personal Well-being, please contact:

Personal Well-being Team, Office for National Statistics
Telephone: 01633 455713
Email: personal.well-being@ons.gsi.gov.uk

References

Blanchflower D G and Oswald A J (2008) Is well-being U-shaped over the life cycle? Social Science and Medicine. 66(8) 1733-49.

Clark A, Oswald A and Warr P (1996) Is job satisfaction U-shaped in age? Journal of Occupational and Organizational Psychology. 69(1) pp57-81

Dolan P, Peasgood T and White M (2008) 'Do we really need to know what makes us happy? A review of the economic literature on the factors associated with subjective well-being', Journal of Economic Psychology 29, pp94-122

Dolan P, Layard R, Metcalfe R and Office for National Statistics (2011) Measuring Subjective Well-being for Public Policy.

HM Government Cabinet Office (2014) Social Attitudes of Young People. A Horizon Scanning Research Paper by the Social Attitudes of Young People Community of Interest.

Krosnick J A and Presser S (2010) Question and Questionnaire Design (chapter 9) in Marsden P V and Wrights J D (Eds.) (2010) Handbook of Survey Research. 2nd Edition. Emerald. pp.263-313.

ONS (no date) National Statistics Opinions and Lifestyle Survey – Technical Report. Office for National Statistics

ONS (2011a) National Statistician's Reflections on the National Debate on Measuring National Well-being. Measuring what matters? Office for National Statistics.

ONS (2011b) Initial Investigation into Subjective Well-being from the Opinions Survey. Office for National Statistics.

ONS (2011c) Measuring Subjective Wellbeing. Office for National Statistics.

ONS (2012) Summary of results from testing of experimental subjective well-being questions.

ONS (2013) Measuring National Well-being – Personal Well-being in the UK, 2012/13.

ONS (2014a) Measuring Social Capital. Office for National Statistics.

ONS (2014b) Measuring National Well-being – Personal Well-being in the UK, 2013/14.

ONS (2015a) Measuring National Well-being – An Analysis of Social Capital in the UK. Office for National Statistics.

ONS (2015b) Measuring National Well-being: Methodological Investigation into Response Scales in Personal Well-being using the OPN.

Pinquart M and Sorensen S (2001) Gender Differences in Self-Concept and Psychological Well-being in Old Age. A Meta Analysis. The Journal of Gerontology Psychological Sciences and Social Sciences Series b. 56 (4) 195-213.

Ralph K, Palmer K and Olney J (2011) Subjective Well-being: a qualitative investigation of subjective well-being questions. Office for National Statistics.

Sutin A R, Terracciano A, Milaneschi Y, Yang A, Ferrucci L and Zonderman A B (2013) Cohort Effect on Well-being: The Legacy of Economic Hard Times. Psychological Science. 24: 379 – 385.

Annex 1

Data for Figure 1: Average Estimates of the Community Questions

	Average[2]	Lower 95% Confidence Interval	Upper 95% Confidence Interval
To what extent do you feel most people can be trusted?	6.0	6.0	6.1
To what extent do you feel you have any relatives, friends or neighbours that you can ask for help?	8.3	8.2	8.3
Overall, how satisfied are you with the local area where you live?	7.6	7.5	7.7
To what extent do you feel that you are involved in the local area where you live?	4.1	4.0	4.2
To what extent do you feel you belong in the local area where you live?	6.6	6.5	6.7
Overall, how satisfied are you with the public gardens, parks, commons or other green spaces in the local area where you live?	7.2	7.1	7.3
How safe would you feel walking alone in this local area after dark?	6.7	6.6	6.8

1. There are 11 response categories available for these questions ranging from 0 to 10. "On a scale where nought is '[not at all]' and 10 is '[completely]',"
2. Average is measured on the basis of mean.
Source: Opinions and Lifestyle Survey, Office for National Statistics

Data for Figure 2: Response Rates to the Community Questions

	Response Rates (%)
Trust	98.6
Ask for Help	98.9
Satisfied with Local Area	99.2
Involved in Local Area	99.0
Belong in the Local Area	98.7
Satisfied with Parks and Commons	98.6
Safe Walking After Dark	98.5

Source: Opinions and Lifestyle Survey, Office for National Statistics

Data for Figure 3: Distribution of responses to the Community Questions

	Proportion of the population in each response category %										
	0	1	2	3	4	5	6	7	8	9	10
To what extent do you feel most people can be trusted?	1.8	1.2	3.0	4.9	6.8	20.1	15.8	23.0	17.1	4.4	2.0
To what extent do you weel you have any relatives, friends or neighbours that you can ask for help?	1.0	0.6	1.5	1.8	2.0	4.6	4.5	9.2	18.6	17.0	39.3
Overall, how satisfied are you with the local area where you live?	1.0	0.6	1.4	2.0	2.9	7.6	7.7	15.6	25.2	16.1	19.9
To what extent do you feel that you are involved in the local area where you live?	16.1	6.2	11.3	10.7	9.4	14.5	8.6	8.7	8.2	3.1	3.1
To what extent do you feel you belong in the local area where you live?	3.7	2.0	3.5	4.2	5.4	13.4	9.8	14.5	18.9	9.4	15.2
Overall, how satisfied are you with the public gardens, parks, commons or other green spaces in the local area where you live?	2.0	1.0	2.1	2.7	3.8	9.5	9.7	16.1	24.0	13.6	15.5
How safe would you feel walking alone in this local area after dark?	6.0	2.4	3.7	3.9	4.4	8.4	7.5	13.4	19.2	13.8	17.4

1. There are 11 response categories available for these questions ranging from 0 to 10. "On a scale where nought is '[not at all]' and 10 is '[completely]'".
Source: Opinions and Lifestyle Survey, Office for National Statisitics

Data for Figure 4: Proportion of the population in each threshold category (%)

	Low (0-4)	Medium (5-6) and High (7-8)	Very High (9-10)
To what extent do you feel most people can be trusted?	17.7	76.0	6.3
To what extent do you feel you have any relatives, friends or neighbours that you can ask for help?	6.9	36.8	56.3
Overall, how satisfied are you with the local area where you live?	7.9	56.1	36.0
To what extent do you feel that you are involved in the local area where you live?	53.7	40.0	6.2
To what extent do you feel you belong in the local area where you live?	18.8	56.6	24.6
Overall, how satisfied are you with the public gardens, parks, commons or other green spaces in the local area where you live?	11.6	59.3	29.1
How safe would you feel walking alone in this local area after dark?	20.3	48.5	31.2

1. There are 11 response categories available for these questions ranging from 0 to 10. "On a scale where nought is '[not at all]' and 10 is '[completely]'".

2. Percentages may not sum due to rounding.

Source: Opinions and Lifestyle Survey, Office for National Statistics

Data for Figure 5: Average[2] Estimates of the Community Questions by gender

Question	Gender	Average[2]	Lower Confidence Limit	Upper Confidence Limit
To what extent do you feel most people can be trusted?	Male	6.0	5.9	6.1
	Female	6.0	6.0	6.1
To what extent do you feel you have any relatives, friends or neighbours that you can ask for help?	Male	8.1	8.1	8.2
	Female	8.4	8.3	8.5
Overall, how satisfied are you with the local area where you live?	Male	7.6	7.5	7.7
	Female	7.6	7.5	7.7
To what extent do you feel that you are involved in the local area where you live?	Male	4.0	3.9	4.1
	Female	4.2	4.0	4.3
To what extent do you feel you belong in the local area where you live?	Male	6.5	6.4	6.6
	Female	6.6	6.5	6.7
Overall, how satisfied are you with the public gardens, parks, commons or other green spaces in the local area where you live?	Male	7.2	7.1	7.3
	Female	7.1	7.0	7.2
How safe would you feel walking alone in this local area after dark?	Male	7.6	7.5	7.7
	Female	5.9	5.7	6.0

1. There are 11 response categories available for these questions ranging from 0 to 10. "On a scale where nought is '[not at all]' and 10 is '[completely]' .

2. Average has been calculated on the basis of the mean.

Source: Opinions and Lifestyle Survey, Office for National Statistics

Data for Figure 6: Average[2] Estimates of the Community Questions by age

	Age Group					
	16 to 24	**25 to 44**	**45 to 54**	**55 to 64**	**65 to 74**	**75 and over**
To what extent do you feel most people can be trusted?	6.0	5.9	5.9	6.0	6.2	6.4
To what extent do you feel you have any relatives, friends or neighbours that you can ask for help?	8.5	8.2	8.1	8.2	8.3	8.4
Overall, how satisfied are you with the local area where you live?	7.1	7.4	7.6	7.8	8.0	8.3
To what extent do you feel that you are involved in the local area where you live?	3.3	3.9	4.2	4.5	4.6	4.5
To what extent do you feel you belong in the local area where you live ?	6.1	6.2	6.6	6.9	7.2	7.3
Overall, how satisfied are you with the public gardens, parks, commons or other green spaces in the local area where you live?	6.7	7.0	7.2	7.4	7.5	7.6
How safe would you feel walking alone in this local area after dark?	6.5	6.9	7.1	7.0	6.5	5.7

1. There are 11 response categories available for these questions ranging from 0 to 10. "On a scale where nought is '[not at all]' and 10 is '[completely]' ".

2. Average has been calculated on the basis of the mean.

Source: Opinions and Lifestyle Survey, Office for National Statistics

Measuring National Well-being: International Comparisons, 2015

Author Name(s): **Rachel Beardsmore and Chris Randall, Office for National Statistics**

Abstract

This article explores how the UK is faring in key areas of well-being compared to the member countries of the Organisation for Economic Co-operation and Development (OECD) where available. It is published as part of the Office for National Statistics (ONS) Measuring National Well-being programme.

Introduction

This article explores how areas of well-being in the UK compare with the 34 member countries of the Organisation for Economic Co-operation and Development (OECD)[1] using national well-being measures if available or similar well-being measures where comparable if not. If international comparable data are not available then a comparison with countries in the European Union (EU)[1] is included if available. The article uses data from sources including the Charity Commission, Eurobarometer, European Quality of Life Survey, Eurostat, Gallup World Poll, International Social Survey Programme, OECD, Programme for International Students Assessment and the World Health Organisation.

Notes

1. For information on what countries belong to the OECD and EU - see 'OECD countries and member states of the EU' section.

Main points

- Life satisfaction scores have not recovered to pre-economic downturn levels for more than half of the Organisation for Economic Co-operation and Development (OECD) countries, although all countries except Greece have shown an increase in GDP per capita.
- The UK showed an increase of nearly 5% in GDP per capita but no change in life satisfaction between 2007 and 2014.
- Nearly three-quarters (74%) of people in the UK reported being in good or better health in 2013, higher than the OECD average of 68%.

- Over 9 in 10 (91%) of people in Great Britain reported being satisfied with their family life in 2012. People in Iceland were most satisfied (95%) while people in Korea were the least satisfied (65%).
- Over three-quarters (76%) of people in the UK felt safe walking alone at night in the area where they lived in 2012. People in Norway felt the safest (89%) while people in Greece were least likely to feel safe (47%).
- Nearly half (47%) of people aged 15 and over in the UK reported having confidence in the national government in 2012. This was higher than the OECD average of 40%.

Life satisfaction and the economic downturn

Introduction

GDP has long been recognised as just one way of measuring a country's progress (Thomas, J. And Evans, J., 2010)[1] and this is especially true as countries emerge from the most recent economic downturn. Many people, including organisations such as the Legatum Institute and the OECD, now recognise that economic indicators do not provide the whole picture of how societies were impacted by the economic downturn[2].

The idea that GDP (or on a more individual level, income) does not relate to life satisfaction was first put forward by R. A. Easterlin, and has become known as the Easterlin paradox[3]. Although people with higher income generally have higher life satisfaction, over time an increase in income (beyond a certain point) does not improve life satisfaction scores. This argument holds true at the national level as well as individually. Easterlin found that in the USA and across Europe, there was little or no trend of improved life satisfaction over many years of increasing GDP per capita.

Life satisfaction is one of the 41 measures of national well-being. As a measure of subjective well-being it can provide an additional picture of how a country has responded to the economic downturn, and potentially reveal problems that aren't apparent when only considering economic factors[4]. This section looks at how GDP per capita and life satisfaction scores have changed since 2007 for the 34 countries within the Organisation for Economic Co-operation and Development (OECD).

GDP per capita and life satisfaction

Figure 1: Average life satisfaction score for the top and bottom 5 OECD countries

Score out of 10   ■2007 ■2014

Source: Organisation for Economic Cooperation and Development

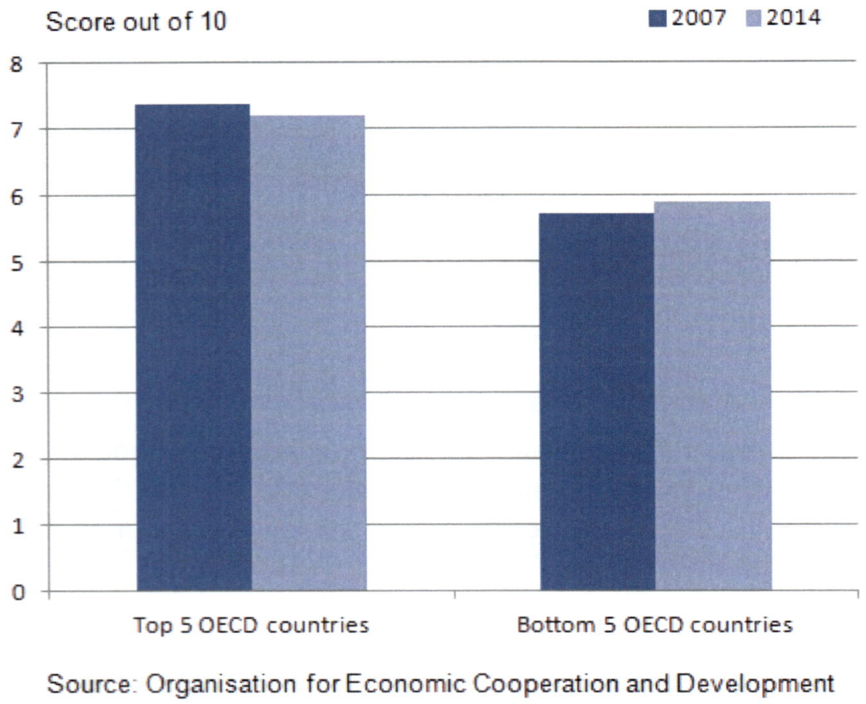

Notes:
1. Top 5 OECD countries by GDP per capita are Luxembourg, Norway, Switzerland, USA, Ireland
2. Bottom 5 OECD countries by GDP per capita are Hungary, Poland, Chile, Mexico, Turkey

Download chart

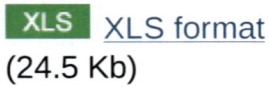 XLS format
(24.5 Kb)

Figure 1 clearly shows that those countries with a lower GDP per capita report lower life satisfaction scores than countries with a higher GDP per capita. The average life satisfaction for the 5 countries reporting the lowest GDP per capita (Hungary, Poland, Chile, Mexico and Turkey) was just 5.7 out of 10 in 2007, whereas the average score for the 5 countries reporting the highest GDP per capita (Luxembourg, Norway, Switzerland, USA and Ireland) was 7.4 out of 10[5].

In 2014, the countries reporting the highest and lowest GDP per capita were the same as in 2007. Between 2007 and 2014 GDP per capita for the bottom 5 countries rose by 33%, and life satisfaction scores rose by 0.2 out of 10. The rise in GDP per capita was lower for the top 5 countries (an increase of 14%), but the average life satisfaction score fell by 0.2 out of 10.

Changes in GDP per capita and life satisfaction by country, 2007 to 2014

The period 2007 to 2014 encompasses the economic downturn which started in 2008. Each country in the OECD was affected differently by the downturn and so responded to the challenges differently. The OECD report, Society at a Glance 2014, considers data for a variety of social indicators, from unemployment and health to life satisfaction and tolerance, to provide a fuller picture of the social situation in OECD countries after the downturn. The OECD found that "life satisfaction deteriorated during the first years of the crisis between 2007 and 2012" - in aggregate accross all its member countries.

Using updated life satisfaction data, Figure 2 shows that for over half of the OECD countries, life satisfaction has still not recovered to pre-downturn levels. However, all of these countries except Greece have shown an increase in GDP per capita.

"In the OECD as a whole, the poor employment situation had a major impact on life satisfaction. This trend is not visible in the United Kingdom where, from 2007 to 2013, the percentage of British people declaring being very satisfied with their lives increased" (OECD, 2013).

According to OECD data, the UK has shown an increase in GDP per capita of nearly 5% and no change in life satisfaction score (6.8 out of 10) between 2007 and 2014 (ONS data shows that life satisfaction in the UK increased between 2011 and 2014).This compares with the OECD average, which shows an increase in GDP per capita of 14% but a decrease in life satisfaction of around 1% over the same period. The differences in these two measures over time illustrate why it is necessary to look at a whole range of measures when considering national well-being.

Figure 2: Percentage change in GDP per capita and life satisfaction between 2007 and 2014 in OECD member countries (1)

OECD countries

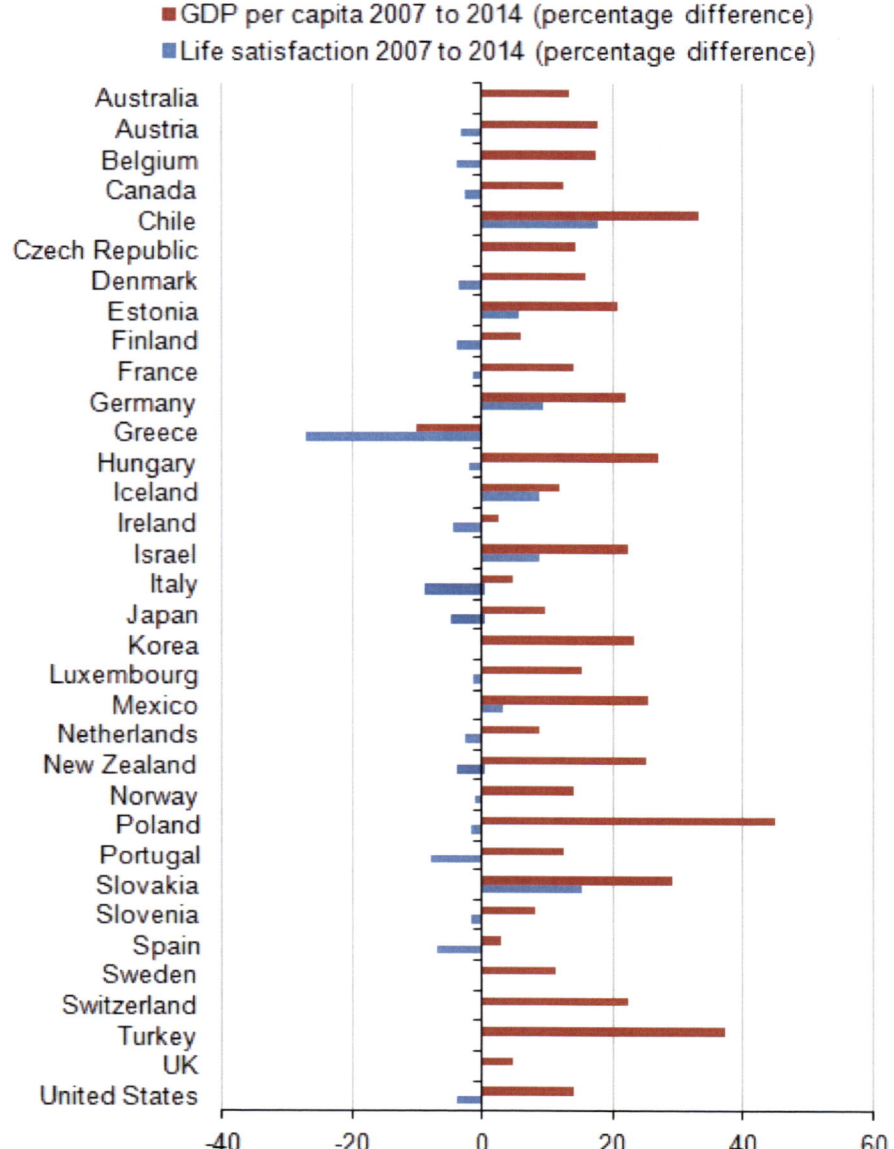

Source: Organisation for Economic Co-operation and Development

Notes:

1. All OECD countries except Greece showed an increase in GDP per capita between 2007 and 2014. Seven countries showed an increase in life satisfaction, seven showed no change, and 20 showed a decrease between 2007 and 2014.

Download chart

XLS XLS format
(20 Kb)

Why has life satisfaction improved in some countries but declined in others?

Of all the OECD countries, Poland shows the biggest increase in GDP per capita between 2007 and 2014 (an increase of 45.1%). During the global economic downturn, Poland experienced continuous growth, and increased its GDP per capita from 54% of the EU average in 2007 to 65% in 2011 (Orlowski, W.M). However, life satisfaction scores remained broadly flat, at 5.9 out of 10 in 2007 and 5.8 out of 10 in 2014.

Poland's economic growth has recently slowed and unemployment has increased as Poland's largest trading partners within Europe recovered from the downturn and decreased demand for Polish goods (Reichardt, 2011). Rural Poland is recognised as having higher levels of poverty than urban areas. It may be that some young Poles feel there are few prospects for them within Poland (Szczerbiak, 2015). This apparent lack of opportunity, together with growing inequality, may be impacting upon the life satisfaction of the Polish people, despite the growth of the economy as a whole.

Greece is the only OECD country to have experienced negative growth in GDP per capita between 2007 and 2014. Life satisfaction scores have also fallen over this period, from 6.6 to 4.8 out of 10 – the lowest life satisfaction score among OECD countries. The proportion of Greek people reporting that they trust the government in Greece fell from 38% to 13% between 2007 and 2012 (OECD), while the proportion of people who were optimistic about the future was just 20% in 2011 (Eurofound).

Chile saw the greatest improvement in life satisfaction scores (5.7 to 6.7 out of 10) along with the third highest percentage increase in GDP per capita (an increase of 33.2% from $16,709 (USD) to $22,254). This increase may be a reflection of a number of different factors: statistics from the OECD show that public social expenditure increased from 8.3% of GDP in 2007 to 10% in 2013, while the unemployment rate decreased from 7.1% of the total labour force to 6.4% in 2014. In addition, there was a presidential election in 2013.

Slovakia similarly saw a large improvement in life satisfaction scores (5.3 to 6.1 out of 10), and the fourth highest percentage increase in GDP. Slovakia reported one of the largest increases in real household disposable income in the OECD between 2007 and 2011 (the latest data available) and the overall employment rate fell by 1% between 2007 and 2012. At the same time, trust in government rose by 12 percentage points between 2006 and 2013, (OECD, 2014). However, there is considerable inequality in Slovakia: the average net adjusted disposable income of the top 20% of the population is around $30,700 compared with around $7,900 for the bottom 20%.

Iceland, Switzerland and Denmark had the highest life satisfaction scores in 2014 at 7.5 out of 10. While Switzerland's life satisfaction score remains unchanged from 2007, and Denmark's fell over the period, Iceland's life satisfaction score increased from 6.9 in 2007 to 7.5 in 2014. At the centre of the economic downturn in Iceland was a collapse of the banks (whose assets were worth nearly 1000% of GDP), and drops of 70% in the value of the currency and 80% in the stock market. Despite this, by 2014 Iceland's GDP per capita had increased by nearly 12%, and its life satisfaction score had increased from 6.9 out of 10 in 2007 to 7.5 out of 10.

Since 2009, despite cuts in government expenditure in Iceland, benefit payments have not been cut, and income inequality has fallen. Furthermore, OECD figures show that since 2008 Iceland has reported a 2 percentage point increase in its trust in government score.

Conclusion

The experiences of these selected countries illustrate that there are many factors contributing to their average life satisfaction scores, from the structure of the labour market and financial inequality to social freedoms and trust in political systems. Furthermore, they clearly show that GDP is only one of a number of measures which should be considered when assessing a country's progress.

ONS's work during the National Well-being debate (407.1 Kb Pdf) identified 10 areas, or domains, that people felt are key when considering well-being. These include areas such as health, education and skills, personal finance, and the environment. The rest of this report looks at the measures presented in each of these domains and identifies comparable data sources, where available, for OECD countries.

Notes

1. Stiglitz, J. E., et al., Report by the Commission on the Measurement of Economic Performance and Social Progress, 2009, also has details.

2. The Legatum Institute, Prosperity since the Financial Crisis, pg 13; and OECD, Society at a Glance, 2014, pg 16.

3. The Easterlin paradox has been disputed, most notably by Stevenson, B., and Wolfers, J. (2008).

4. The OECD suggests that "Waning life satisfaction could... be seen as a leading indicator that points to serious health or societal problems developing at a later date" (2014, pg 30).

5. Top 5 OECD countries by GDP per capita, 2007 and 2014; Luxembourg, Norway, Switzerland, USA, Ireland. Bottom 5 OECD countries by GDP per capita, 2007 and 2014; Hungary, Poland, Chile, Mexico, Turkey.

Personal well-being

"Subjective (or personal) well-being reflects the notion that how people experience a set of circumstances is as important as the circumstances themselves, and that people are the best judges of how their own lives are going" (OECD, 2011).

There are 5 measures in the National Well-being "Personal well-being" domain. International data are available for 2 of the measures using alternative measures from a different source, while EU data are included for 1 measure. There is more information in Comparison of National Well-being measures and international measures (621.5 Kb Excel sheet).

Table 1: International comparisons summary - Personal well-being

	UK (unless otherwise stated)	Highest ranked country	Lowest ranked country	Coverage
Average (mean) rating of life satisfaction Source: OECD, (2014)	6.8 out of 10	Denmark, Iceland and Switzerland (7.5 out of 10)	Greece (4.8 out of 10)	OECD countries
Completely, very or fairly happy on the whole Source: International Social Survey Programme, (2012)	Great Britain (87.2%)	Iceland (92.4%)	Korea (62.6%)	Some OECD countries[1]
I generally feel that what I do in life is worthwhile (strongly agree or agree) Source: Third European Quality of Life Survey, (2011–12)	81.9%	Denmark, Netherlands (91.4%)	Greece (47.8%)	EU–28

Table notes:

1. Data are not available for Belgium, Estonia, Greece, Hungary, Italy, Luxembourg, Netherlands, New Zealand and Portugal.

Download table

XLS XLS format (617.5 Kb)

Life satisfaction

According to data from the Organisation for Economic Co-operation and Development (OECD) conducted by Gallup World Poll, the average (mean) rating of life satisfaction of adults aged 16 and over in the UK was 6.8 out of 10 in 2014[1] (Figure 3). This was slightly higher than the OECD average of 6.6 out of 10 and was similar to Austria, Belgium and Luxembourg (6.9 out of 10) and Chile and Mexico (6.7 out of 10). The highest-ranked countries were Denmark, Iceland and Switzerland (7.5 out of 10), while Greece was the lowest ranked country (4.8 out of 10).

Figure 3: Average rating of life satisfaction (1), 2014 (2)

OECD countries (3)

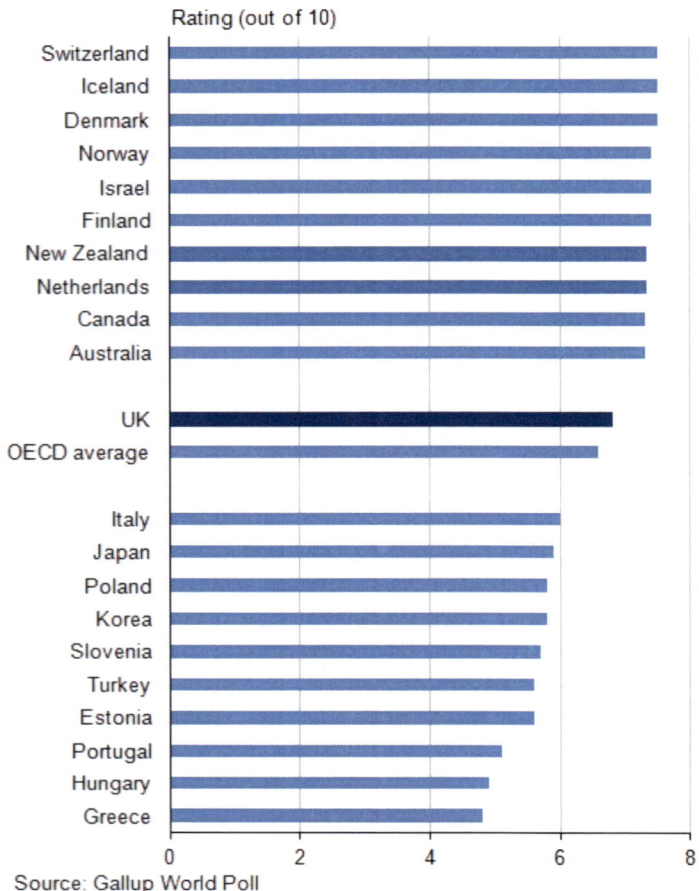

Source: Gallup World Poll

Notes:

1. Average rating of life satisfaction on an 11-step ladder from 0 to 10.
2. 2013 for Iceland and Hungary.
3. Chart shows the 10 top and bottom OECD countries along with the UK and OECD average.

Download chart

XLS XLS format
(618.5 Kb)

Happiness

Adults aged 18 and over were asked on the 2012 International Social Survey Programme (ISSP), "If you were to consider your life in general, how happy or unhappy would you say you are, on the whole?" In Great Britain, 87.2% of respondents reported that they were completely, very or fairly happy, a similar proportion to Australia (87.9%). The countries that had the largest proportion of people reporting that they were completely, very or fairly happy were Iceland (92.4%), Switzerland

(90.9%) and the United States (89.6%). Korea had the lowest proportion of people reporting that they were completely, very or fairly happy (62.6%).

Feeling worthwhile

According to the 2011–12 European Quality of Life Survey, over 8 in 10 (81.9%) adults aged 16 and over in the UK strongly agreed or agreed they generally felt that what they did in life was worthwhile. This was higher than the EU–28 average of 78.5%, and was similar to both Spain (81.5%) and Belgium (81.1%). The highest-ranking countries were Denmark and the Netherlands, where over 9 in 10 (91.4%) strongly agreed or agreed that they generally felt that what they did in life was worthwhile, while the lowest-ranking country was Greece (47.8%).

Notes

1. The Gallup World Poll asked respondents to: "Imagine an eleven-rung ladder where the bottom (0) represents the worst possible life for you and the top (10) represents the best possible life for you. On which step of the ladder do you feel you personally stand at the present time?"

Our relationships

"Beyond the intrinsic pleasure that people derive from spending time with others, social connections have positive spill-over effects for individual and societal well-being. People with extensive and supportive networks have better health, tend to live longer, and are more likely to be employed" (OECD, 2011).

There are 3 measures in the National Well-being "Our relationships" domain. Comparable international data are available for 1 of these measures using an alternative measure from a different source. For the remaining 2 measures an EU comparison is shown. There is more information in Comparison of National Well-being measures and international measures (621.5 Kb Excel sheet).

Table 2: International comparisons summary - Our relationships

	UK (unless otherwise stated)	Highest ranked country	Lowest ranked country	Coverage
Completely, very or fairly satisfied with family life	Great Britain (90.9%)	Iceland (95.1%)	Korea (65.3%)	Some OECD countries[1]
Source: International Social Survey Programme, (2012)				
Average (mean) rating of satisfaction with social life	7.0 out of 10	Denmark (8.3 out of 10)	Bulgaria (5.9 out of 10)	EU–28
Source: Third European Quality of Life Survey, (2011–12)				
Support if needed advice about a serious personal or family matter	88.7%	Slovakia (98.8%)	France (86.1%)	EU–28
Source: Third European Quality of Life Survey, (2011–12)				

Table notes:

1. Data are not available for Belgium, Estonia, Greece, Hungary, Italy, Luxembourg, Netherlands, New Zealand and Portugal.

Download table

XLS XLS format
(610 Kb)

Satisfaction with family life

People aged 18 and over were asked to rate their satisfaction with their family life on the International Social Survey in 2012. In Great Britain, over 9 in 10 (90.9%) reported that that they were completely, very or fairly satisfied with their family life (Figure 4). This was similar to Poland (90.4%) and Slovenia (90.3%). Iceland had the highest proportion of people completely, very or fairly satisfied with family life (95.1%), while the country with the lowest proportion was Korea (65.3%).

Figure 4: Satisfaction with family life (1), 2012

Selected OECD countries (2)

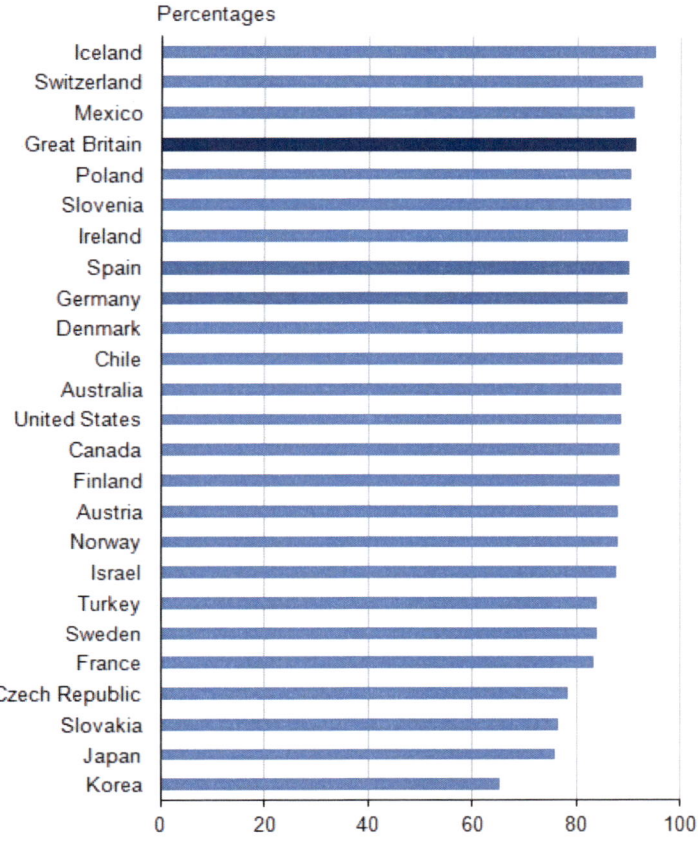

Percentages

Source: International Social Survey Programme: Family and Changing Gender Roles IV - ISSP 2012

Notes:
1.   Respondents were asked "All things considered, how satisfied are you with your family life?" Respondents were asked "All things considered, how satisfied are you with your family life?" The chart includes those who stated "completely satisfied" or "very satisfied" or "fairly satisfied".
2.   The selected countries are OECD countries that were included in this survey. Data are not available for Belgium, Estonia, Greece, Hungary, Italy, Luxembourg, Netherlands, New Zealand and Portugal.

Download chart

XLS XLS format
(618.5 Kb)

Satisfaction with social life

On the 2011–12 European Quality of Life Survey, people aged 16 and over were asked to rate their satisfaction with their social life out of 10. In the UK the average rating of satisfaction was 7.0 out of

10. This was lower than the EU–28 average of 7.3 out of 10 and similar to Ireland and Greece (both 7.1 out of 10) and Estonia and Croatia (both 6.9 out of 10). The country with the highest average rating was Denmark (8.3 out of 10), while the country with the lowest average was Bulgaria (5.9 out of 10).

Support if needed advice about a serious personal or family matter

On the same survey, people aged 16 and over were asked who would give them support if they needed advice about a serious personal or family matter. In the UK, 88.7% people said that they had support from family, friends, neighbours or someone else in 2011. This was lower than the EU–28 average of 93.0%. The highest-ranking country was Slovakia (98.8%), while the lowest-ranking countries were France (86.1%) and Denmark (88.1%).

Health

"Being healthy is one of the most valued aspects of people's lives, and one that affects the probability of having a job, earning an adequate income, and actively participating in a range of valued social activities" (OECD, 2011).

There are 4 measures in the National Well-being "Health" domain. Comparable international data are available for 3 of the measures using alternative measures from different sources. There is more information in Comparison of National Well-being measures and international measures (621.5 Kb Excel sheet).

Table 3: International comparisons summary - Health

	UK (unless otherwise stated)	Highest ranked country	Lowest ranked country	Coverage
Self reported health (good or better health) Source: OECD and Eurostat, (2013)	74%	New Zealand (90%)	Japan (30%)[1]	OECD countries
Reported a long-standing illness, chronic condition or disability Source: International Social Survey Programme, (2011)	Great Britain (33.3%)	Switzerland (21.3%)	Finland (43.7%)	Some OECD countries[2]
Healthy life expectancy at birth Source: World Health Organisation, (2013)	Male (69) Female (72)	Male - Japan (72) Female - Japan (78)	Male - Hungary (61) Female - Turkey (67)	OECD countries

Table notes:
1. 2010 for Japan.
2. Data are not available for Austria, Canada, Estonia, Greece, Hungary, Iceland, Ireland, Italy, Luxembourg, Mexico, New Zealand and Spain.

Download table

XLS XLS format
(618 Kb)

Self-reported health

According to data published by the Organisation for Economic Co-operation and Development (OECD) and Eurostat, just under three-quarters (74%) of adults aged 15 and over in the UK reported "good" or "better health" in 2013 (Figure 5). This was the same proportion as Belgium and Greece and higher than the OECD average of 68%. The highest-ranking country was New Zealand (90%), while the lowest-ranking country was Japan (30% in 2010).

Figure 5: Self-reported health (1), 2013 (2)

OECD countries (3)

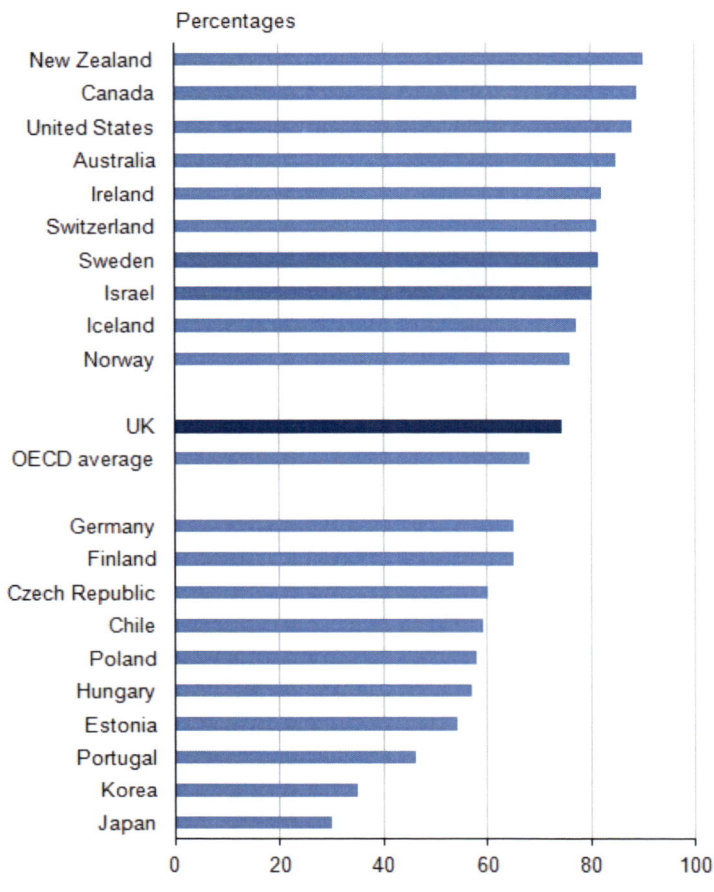

Source: OECD Health Database and
European Union Statistics on Income and Living Conditions (EU-SILC)

Notes:

1. The chart shows the percentage of the population aged 15 years old and over who report "good" or "better" health.
2. The reference year is 2013 with the exception of: 2012 for the United States; 2011 for Australia; 2010 for Japan; 2009 for Chile and New Zealand.
3. Chart shows the 10 top and bottom OECD countries, the UK and the OECD average.

Download chart

XLS XLS format
(622 Kb)

Reported a long-standing illness, chronic condition or disability

In 2011, a third (33.3%) of adults aged 18 and over in Great Britain reported a long-standing illness, chronic condition or disability according to data from the International Social Survey Programme.

This was similar for Denmark (33.6%) and Slovakia (33.8%). The highest proportion of people reporting a long-standing illness or health problem was in Finland (43.7%), while the lowest proportion was in Switzerland (21.3%).

Healthy life expectancy at birth

According to data from the World Health Organisation, males in the UK had an estimated 69 healthy life years[1] at birth in 2013. This was the same as Belgium, Denmark, France, Germany, Greece, Ireland and Norway. Females in the UK had an estimated 72 healthy life years at birth in 2013. This was the same as Belgium, Chile, the Netherlands, Norway and Slovenia. Japan was the highest-ranking country for both male and females (72 and 78 healthy life years respectively). Hungary was the lowest-ranking country for males (61 healthy life years), while Turkey was the lowest-ranking country for females (67 healthy life years).

Notes

1. Average number of years that a person can expect to live in "full health" by taking into account years lived in less than full health due to disease and/or injury.

What we do

"The amount and quality of leisure time is important for people's overall well-being, and can bring additional physical and mental health benefits" (OECD, 2011).

There are 6 measures in the National Well-being "What we do" domain. Comparable international data is available for 3 of these measures using alternative measures from a different source and 2 measures have an EU comparison. There is more information in Comparison of National Well-being measures and international measures (621.5 Kb Excel sheet).

Table 4: International comparisons summary - What we do

	UK (unless otherwise stated)	Highest ranked country	Lowest ranked country	Coverage
Harmonised unemployment rate Source: OECD, (2014)	6.2%	Norway and Korea (3.5%)	Greece (26.5%)	OECD countries
Percentage completely, very or fairly satisfied with their main job Source: International Social Survey Programme, (2012)	Great Britain (76.0%)	Mexico (89.7%)	Japan (59.8%)	Some OECD countries[1]
Participation in volunteering, 1 month prior to interview Source: Charity Commission, (2013)	29%	Canada, New Zealand and United States (44%)	Turkey (5%)	Some OECD countries[2]
Index of cultural participation (very high, high or medium) Source: Eurobarometer, (2013)	79%	Sweden (92%)	Greece (37%)	EU–27

	UK (unless otherwise stated)	Highest ranked country	Lowest ranked country	Coverage
Taking part in sports or physical exercise (every day or almost every day or at least once a week)	46.8%	Finland (72.5%)	Bulgaria (12.0%)	EU–28
Source: Third European Quality of Life Survey, (2011–12)				

Table notes:

1. Data are not available for Belgium, Estonia, Greece, Hungary, Italy, Luxembourg, Netherlands, New Zealand and Portugal.
2. Data are not available for Norway and Switzerland.

Download table

XLS XLS format
(618.5 Kb)

Harmonised unemployment rate

In 2014, the harmonised unemployment rate[1] for the UK was 6.2% according to data from the Organisation for Economic Co-operation and Development (OECD) (Figure 6). This was the same rate as the United States and a similar rate to the Czech Republic and Australia (6.1%). The countries with the largest harmonised unemployment rate were Greece (26.5%) and Spain (24.4%), while the countries with the lowest rate were Korea and Norway (both 3.5%).

Figure 6: Harmonised unemployment rate (1), 2014

OECD countries (2)

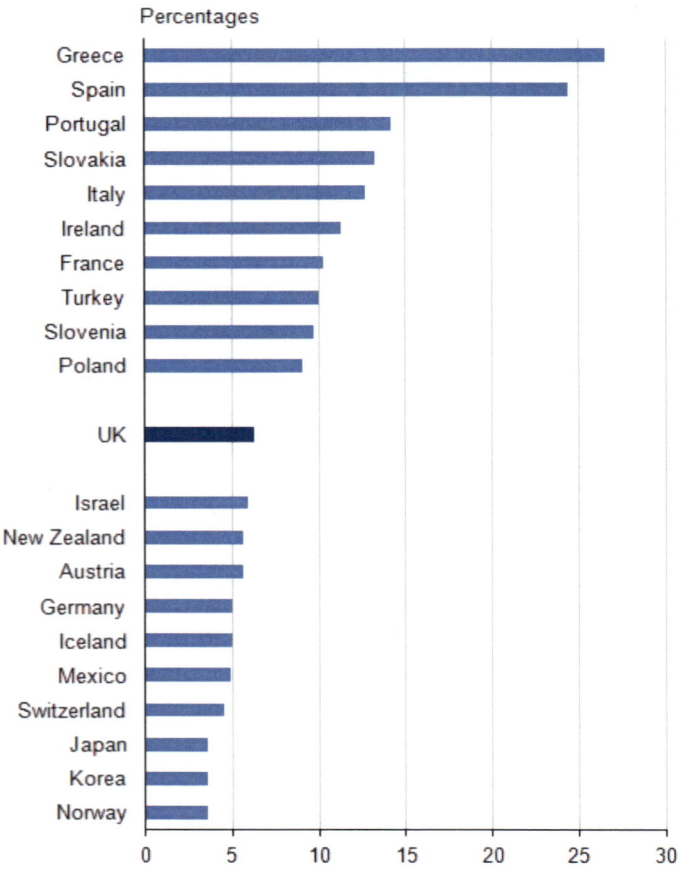

Source: Organisation for Economic Co-operation and Development

Notes:

1. Harmonised unemployment rates define the unemployed as people of working age who are without work, are available for work, and have taken specific steps to find work. The uniform application of this definition results in estimates of unemployment rates that are more internationally comparable than estimates based on national definitions of unemployment. This indicator is measured in numbers of unemployed people as a percentage of the labour force and it is seasonally adjusted. The labour force is defined as the total number of unemployed people plus those in civilian employment.

2. The chart shows the 10 top and bottom OECD countries and the UK.

Download chart

XLS XLS format
(611.5 Kb)

Satisfaction with main job

In 2012, just over three-quarters (76.0%) of adults aged 18 and over in Great Britain reported that they were completely, very or fairly satisfied with their main job according to data from the International Social Survey Programme. This was similar to Turkey (77.4%), Spain (77.7%) and

France (77.8%). Mexico had the highest proportion of people who were satisfied with their main job (89.7%), while the lowest proportion was in Japan (59.8%)[2].

Volunteering

According to data from the Charities Aid Foundation, just under 3 in 10 (29%) adults aged 15 and over in the UK participated in some kind of volunteering 1 month prior to interview in 2013. This was the same as proportion as Austria and Iceland. The highest ranked countries were Canada, New Zealand and the United States where 44% of adults participated in volunteering 1 month prior to interview, while the lowest ranked countries were Turkey (5%) and Italy and Poland (both 9%).

Cultural participation

A special Eurobarometer survey run from April to May 2013 looked at cultural access and participation. Just under 8 in 10 (79%) adults aged 15 and over in the UK had a combined score of very high, high and medium cultural engagement[3]. This was higher than the EU–27 average of 66% and similar to France and Luxembourg (both 81%). The country with the highest combined score of very high, high and medium cultural engagement was Sweden (92%) while the lowest was Greece (37%).

Taking part in sports or physical exercise

According to the European Quality of Life Survey, 46.8% of people aged 16 and over in the UK took part in sports or physical exercise at least once a week between September 2011 and February 2012. This was higher than the EU–28 average of 39.7% and similar to Germany (47.6%). The highest proportion of people who took part in sports or physical exercise at least once a week were in Finland and Sweden (72.5% and 70.4% respectively), while the lowest proportion was in Bulgaria (12.0%).

Notes

1. Harmonised unemployment rates define the unemployed as people of working age who are without work, are available for work, and have taken specific steps to find work. The uniform application of this definition results in estimates of unemployment rates that are more internationally comparable than estimates based on national definitions of unemployment. This indicator is measured in numbers of unemployed people as a percentage of the labour force and it is seasonally adjusted. The labour force is defined as the total number of unemployed people plus those in civilian employment.

2. The question was asked of those aged 16 and over in Japan.

3. A simple index of cultural practice was formed to help identify levels of engagement in cultural activities among citizens from the 27 EU Member States. This is based on the frequency of participation and access to the different cultural activities included in the survey. Each

respondent had been given a score based on their frequency of participation, and these scores were used to identify the different cultural index types of 'very high', 'high', 'medium' and 'low'. For more information see special Eurobarometer 399 available at Eurobarometer.

Where we live

"Where people live matters for their well-being and improving people's lives requires making where they live a better place" (OECD, 2014).

There are 6 measures in the National Well-being "Where we live" domain. Comparable international data are available for 1 of these measures using an alternative measure from a different source and 3 measures have an EU comparison. There is more information in Comparison of National Well-being measures and international measures (621.5 Kb Excel sheet).

Table 5: International comparisons summary - Where we live

	UK	Highest ranked country	Lowest ranked country	Coverage
Feeling safe walking alone at night in the city or area where lived Source: Gallup World Poll, (2012)	76.1%	Norway (88.9%)	Greece (46.7%)	OECD Countries
Very easy or easy access to recreational or green areas Source: Third European Quality of Life Survey, (2011–12)	90.6%	Denmark (97.0%)	Greece (74.7%)	EU–28
Strongly agree or agree feel close to people in the area where I live Source: Third European Quality of Life Survey, (2011–12)	58.4%	Cyprus (80.8%)	Germany (58.3%)	EU–28
Satisfaction with accommodation (7 or more out of 10) Source: Third European Quality of Life Survey, (2011–12)	80.2%	Finland (90.9%)	Latvia (55.2%)	EU–28

Download table

XLS XLS format
(618.5 Kb)

Feeling safe walking alone at night in the city or area where living

According to the 2012 World Gallup Poll, over three-quarters (76.1%) of people aged 15 and over in the UK felt safe walking alone at night in the city or area where they lived (Figure 7). This was higher than the OECD average of 72.2% and similar to Luxembourg (75.9%). People in Norway felt the safest (88.9%), while people in Greece felt the least safe (46.7%).

Figure 7: Feeling safe walking alone at night in the city or area where living, 2012 (1)

OECD countries (2)

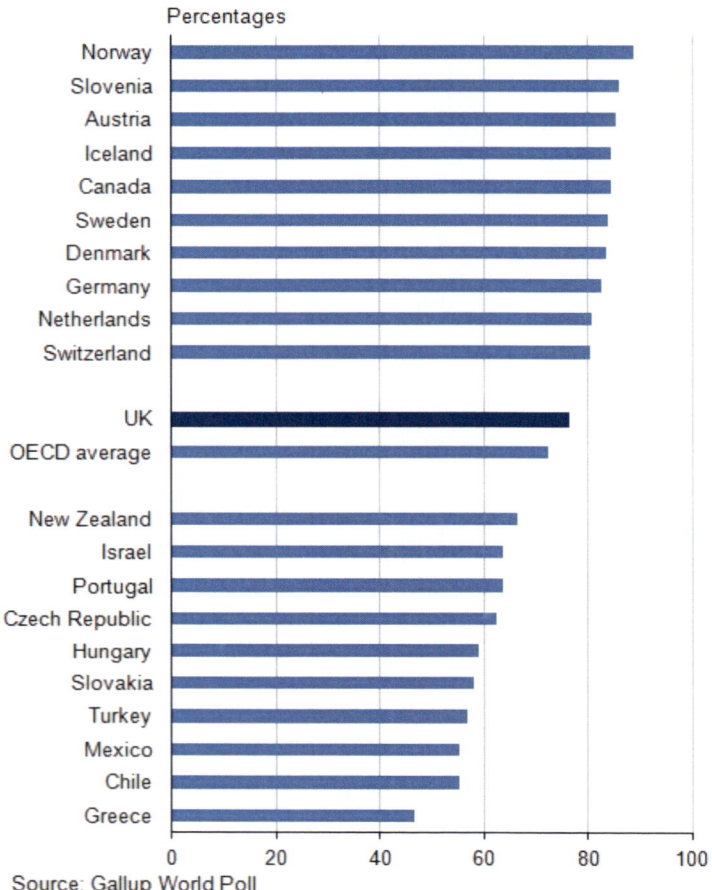

Source: Gallup World Poll

Notes:

1. The reference year is 2012 with the exception of: 2011 for Chile; 2006 for Austria, Norway, Portugal, Slovakia, Slovenia and Switzerland and 2008 for Iceland.
2. The chart shows the 10 top and bottom OECD countries, the UK and OECD average.

Download chart

XLS XLS format
(610 Kb)

Access to recreational or green areas

Research has shown that living in an urban area with green spaces has a long-lasting positive impact on people's mental well-being and generally beneficial to public health[1]. Therefore having ease of access to them is important. Just over 9 in 10 (90.6%) adults aged 16 and over in the UK reported that they had very easy or easy access to recreational or green areas on the 2011–12 European Quality of Life Survey. This was higher than the EU–28 average of 86.6% and was similar to France (90.9%) and Croatia (90.4%). The highest-ranking country was Denmark (97.0%), while the lowest-ranking country was Greece (74.7%).

Feeling close to people in the local area

Looking at whether people feel close to other people in the area where they live can give a sense of whether they feel a sense of belonging to their neighbourhood. According to the European Quality of Life Survey in 2011–12, 58.4% of people aged 16 and over in the UK reported that they felt close to other people in the area where they lived. This was lower than the EU–28 average of 66.6% and was similar to Germany (58.3%) which was the lowest-ranking country. The highest-ranked country was Cyprus (80.8%).

Satisfaction with accommodation

On the European Quality of Life Survey in 2011–12, 80.2% of people aged 16 and over in the UK rated their satisfaction with their accommodation as 7 or more out of 10. This was higher than the EU–28 average of 76.9%, and similar to Belgium (80.7%). Finland had the highest proportion of people who rated their satisfaction with their accommodation as 7 or more out of 10 (90.9%), followed by Denmark and Malta (both 89.7%). Latvia had the lowest proportion of people rating their satisfaction with their accommodation as 7 or more out of 10 (55.2%).

Notes

1. Research by the University of Exeter - Beyond green space: an ecological study of population general health and indicators of natural environment type and quality.

Personal finance

"While money may not buy happiness, it is an important means to achieving higher living standards and thus greater well-being. Higher economic wealth may also improve access to quality education, health care and housing" (OECD, 2011).

There are 5 measures in the National Well-being "Personal finance" domain. Comparable international data are available for 1 of these measures using an alternative measure from a different source and 3 measures have an EU comparison. There is more information in Comparison of National Well-being measures and international measures (621.5 Kb Excel sheet).

Table 6: International comparisons summary - Personal finance

	UK (unless otherwise stated)	Highest ranked country	Lowest ranked country	Coverage
Median net wealth per household[1] Source: OECD, (2010 or latest available year)	Great Britain ($187,380)	Luxembourg ($360,251)	Netherlands ($34,194)	Some OECD countries[2]
Median equivalised net income (Purchasing Power Standard) Source: Eurostat, (2013)	€16,826	Luxembourg (€28,030)	Romania (€3,936)	EU–28
Households making ends meet with difficulty or great difficulty Source: Eurostat, (2013)	21.1%	Sweden (6.6%)	Greece (78.3%)	EU–28
At-risk-of-poverty rate after deducting housing costs Source: Eurostat, 2013	32.4%	Malta (23.7%)	Greece (46.4%)	EU–28

Table notes:

1. Wealth values are expressed in 2005 USD.
2. Data are not available for Chile, Czech Republic, Denmark, Estonia, Hungary, Iceland, Ireland, Israel, Japan, Mexico, New Zealand, Poland, Slovenia, Sweden, Switzerland and Turkey.

Download table

XLS XLS format
(619 Kb)

Median net wealth per household

Financial wealth makes up an important part of a household's economic resources, and can protect from economic hardship and vulnerability. According to data from the Organisation for Economic Co-operation and Development (OECD), median net wealth per household[1] in Great Britain in 2012 was $187,380. This was higher than the OECD average (18 countries) of $132,615 and similar to Belgium ($188,149 in 2010). The country with the highest median net wealth per household was Luxembourg ($360,251 in 2010), while the Netherlands had the lowest median net wealth per household ($34,194 in 2010).

Median equivalised disposable income

Disposable income is the amount of money that households have available for spending and saving after direct taxes (such as income tax and council tax) have been accounted for, but before housing costs. It includes earnings from employment, private pensions and investments as well as cash benefits provided by the state. Equivalisation adjusts the income to take into account the size and composition of the household. Data from Eurostat shows that in 2013 the median equivalised household disposable income (expressed in PPS[2]) for the UK was €16,826, similar to Cyprus (€17,165) and Ireland (€15,968). Luxembourg had the highest median equivalised income (€28,030) while the lowest median equivalised income was in Romania (€3,936).

Households making ends meet with difficulty or great difficulty

In 2013, over a fifth (21.1%) of all households in the UK reported great difficulty or difficulty in making ends meet (Figure 8). This was lower than the estimated EU–28 average of 28.9%, and was similar to Belgium (21.0%) and France (20.5%). The countries with the highest proportion of households reporting great difficulty or difficulty in making ends meet were Greece (78.3%) and Bulgaria (65.2%), while the lowest proportion of households were in Sweden (6.6%) and Finland (6.9%).

Figure 8: Households making ends meet with difficulty or great difficulty

EU–28

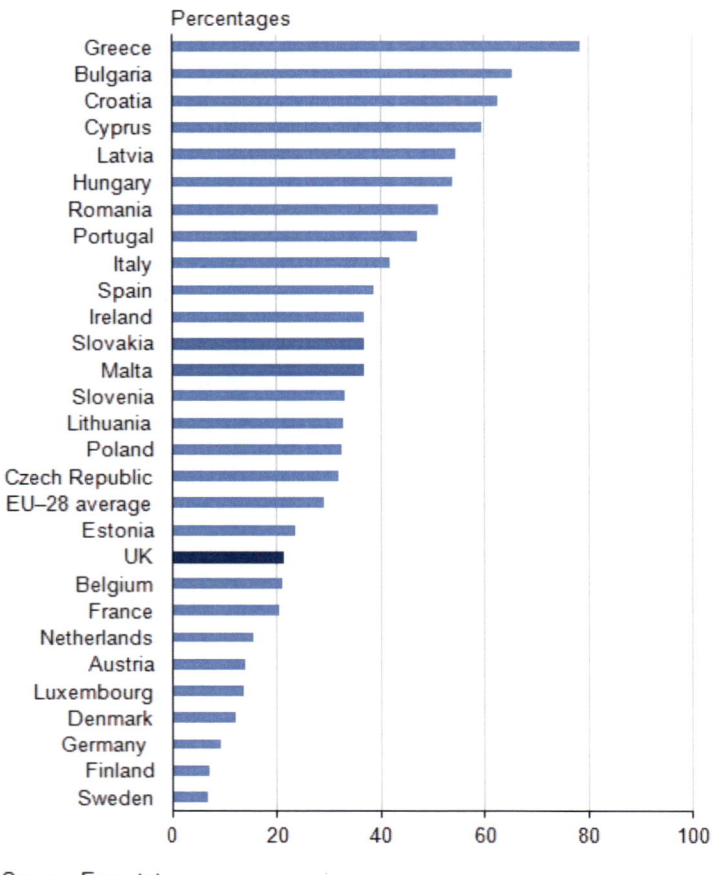

Source: Eurostat

Download chart

XLS XLS format
(617.5 Kb)

At-risk-of-poverty rate after deducting housing costs

In 2013, nearly a third (32.4%) of the population of the UK were at-risk-of-poverty[3] (after deduction of housing costs) according to data from Eurostat. This was slightly higher than the than the EU–28 average of 32.2%. The highest proportion of people at risk of poverty (after deduction of housing costs) was in Greece (46.4%), while the lowest proportion of people was in Malta (23.7%) and Cyprus (24.7%).

Notes

1. Wealth values are expressed in 2005 USD by, first, expressing values in prices of the same year (2005) through consumer price indexes and, second, by converting national values into a common currency through the use of purchasing power parities for household consumption.

2. The purchasing power standard, abbreviated as PPS, is an artificial currency unit. Theoretically, one PPS can buy the same amount of goods and services in each country. However, price differences across borders mean that different amounts of national currency units are needed for the same goods and services depending on the country.

3. An individual is considered to be in poverty if they live in a household with an equivalised disposable income below 60% of the national median. The after housing costs measure refers to the percentage of persons in the total population who are at-risk-of-poverty after housing costs have been deducted, i.e. with an equivalised disposable income without total housing cost below the at-risk-of-poverty threshold calculated in the standard way.

Economy

"Well-being has several dimensions of which money income is only one. It is nevertheless an important one, since richer economies are better placed to create and maintain other well-being-enhancing conditions..." (OECD, 2006).

There are 3 measures in the National Well-being "Economy" domain. Comparable international data are available for all these measures using alternative measures from a different source. There is more information in Comparison of National Well-being measures and international measures (621.5 Kb Excel sheet).

Table 7: International comparisons summary - Economy

	UK	Highest ranked country	Lowest ranked country	Coverage
Net national income per capita (Index numbers, OECD = 100) Source: OECD, (2012)	99.9%	Norway (184.3%)	Mexico (50.5%[1])	OECD countries[2]
General government total gross debt as a percentage of GDP Source: OECD, (Q4, 2014)	95.1%	Estonia (10.6%)	Japan (244.6%)	Some OECD countries[3]
Inflation rate Source: OECD, (2014)	1.5%	n/a	n/a	OECD Countries

Table notes:

1. Estimated data.
2. Data are not available for Turkey.
3. Data are not available for Chile, Greece, Iceland, Israel, New Zealand, Slovenia and Turkey.

Download table

XLS XLS format
(618 Kb)

Net national income per capita

In 2012, ranking countries by net national income (NNI)[1] per capita, 14 OECD member countries were above the OECD average (100%), and 19 were below. The UK was just below the OECD average at 99.9%. The 5 highest ranked countries were Norway (184.3%), Luxembourg (156.9%), Switzerland (144.8%), the United States (140.7%), and Sweden (121.1%). The lowest ranked countries were Mexico (an estimated 50.5%) and Hungary (55.8%).

Government consolidated gross debt

According to data from the OECD, the UK general government total gross[2] debt was 95.1% of gross domestic product (GDP) at current prices in October to December 2014. The highest rate of general government total gross debt as a percentage of GDP was in Japan (244.6%), while the lowest rate was in Estonia (10.6%).

Inflation rate

According to data from the OECD, the UK had a rate of inflation (Consumer Price Indices)[3] in 2014 of 1.5% which was similar to Austria and the United States (both 1.6%) (Figure 9). Turkey (8.9%) and Chile (4.7%) had the highest inflation rates, while some OECD countries experienced falling prices, for example, Greece (negative 1.3%) and Portugal (negative 0.3%).

Figure 9: Inflation rates, 2014 (1)

OECD countries (2)

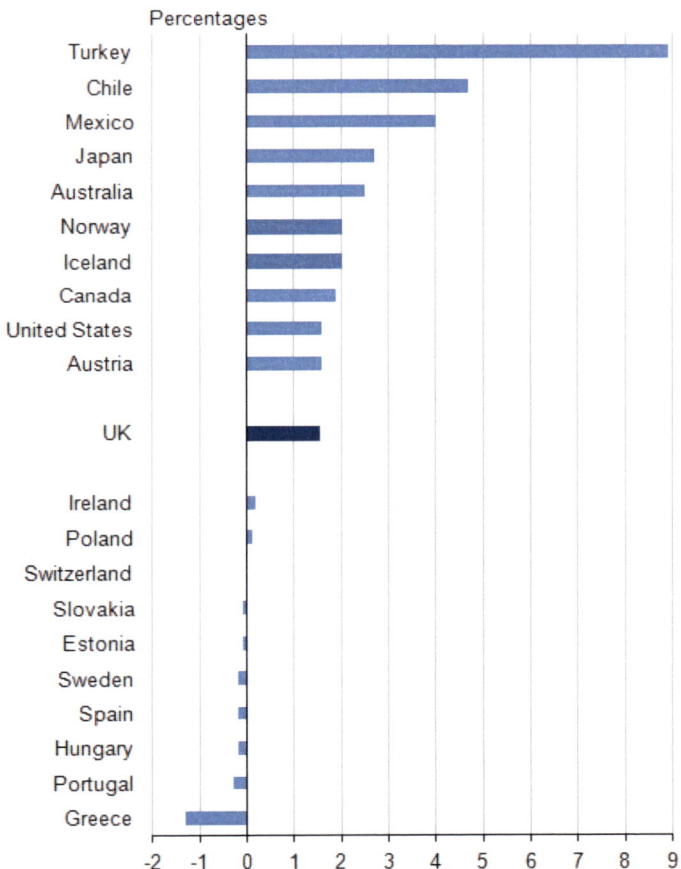

Source: Organisation for Economic Co-operation and Development

Notes:
1. Percentage change on the same period of the previous year. Consumer Price Indices (CPIs) measure the average changes in the prices of consumer goods and services purchased by households. In most instances, CPIs are compiled in accordance with international statistical guidelines and recommendations. However, national practices may depart from these guidelines, and these departures may impact on international comparability between countries.

2.   Chart shows OECD countries with highest and lowest rates of inflation and the UK.

Download chart

XLS XLS format
(618 Kb)

Notes

1.   Net national income (NNI) is equal to gross national income (GNI) net of depreciation. Gross National Income is defined as GDP plus net receipts from abroad of wages and salaries and of property income plus net taxes and subsidies receivable from abroad.

2.   The definition and more information about general government debt is available here stats.oecd.org/glossary/detail.asp?ID=1161

3.   Consumer Price Indices (CPIs) measure the average changes in the prices of consumer goods and services purchased by households (percentage change on the same period of the previous year). In most instances, CPIs are compiled in accordance with international statistical guidelines and recommendations. However, national practices may depart from these guidelines, and these departures may impact on international comparability between countries.

Education and skills

 "Education and skills have a strong influence on people's well-being. Education opens opportunities for people and brings a wide range of benefits to society, including higher economic growth, stronger social cohesion and less crime" (OECD, 2011).

There are 3 measures in the National Well-being "Education and skills" domain. Comparable international data are available for 1 of these measures using an alternative measure from a different source and a comparison of educational performance sourced from the Programme for International Students Assessment (PISA)[1] is also included. There is more information in Comparison of National Well-being measures and international measures (621.5 Kb Excel sheet).

Table 8: International comparisons summary - Education and skills

	UK	Highest ranked country	Lowest ranked country	Coverage
Mathematics, average (mean) score	494	Korea (554)	Mexico (413)	OECD countries
Source: Programme for International Students Assessment (PISA), 2012				
Reading, average (mean) score	499	Japan (538)	Mexico (424)	OECD countries
Source: Programme for International Students Assessment (PISA), 2012				
Science, average (mean) score	514	Japan (547)	Mexico (415)	OECD countries
Source: Programme for International Students Assessment (PISA), 2012				
Proportion of those aged 25 to 64 that attained below upper secondary education	20.8%	Czech Republic (7.2%)	Turkey (65.2%)	OECD countries
Source: OECD, (2013)				

Download table

XLS XLS format
(618.5 Kb)

Performance in mathematics, reading and science

The UK score for mathematics in 2012 was 494 points on average, the same as the Organisation for Economic Co-operation and Development (OECD) average. The UK's mean score was similar to Iceland (493) and France (495). Korea and Japan had the highest mean score among the OECD countries (554 and 536 respectively), while the lowest mean scores were in Mexico (413) and Chile (423).

The UK score for reading in 2012 was 499 points on average, slightly higher than the OECD average of 496. The UK's mean score was similar to the United States (498) and Denmark (496). Japan and Korea had the highest mean scores (538 and 536 respectively), while the lowest mean scores were in Mexico (424) and Chile (441).

The UK score for science in 2012 was 514 points on average, higher than the OECD average of 501. The UK's mean score was the same as Slovenia. Japan and Finland had the highest mean scores (547 and 545 respectively), while the lowest mean scores were in Mexico (415) and Chile (445).

Educational attainments below upper secondary education

According to data from the OECD, just over a fifth (20.8%) of people aged 25 to 64 in the UK had educational attainments below upper secondary education[2] in 2013 (Figure 10). This was lower than the OECD average of 23.5% and similar to Denmark (21.7%). Turkey and Mexico had the highest proportion of people who had educational attainments below upper secondary education (65.2% and 61.6% respectively). Conversely, 7.2% of people aged 25 to 64 in the Czech Republic and 8.2% in Slovakia had educational attainments below upper secondary education.

Figure 10: Proportion aged 25 to 64 who attained below upper secondary education, 2013

OECD countries (1)

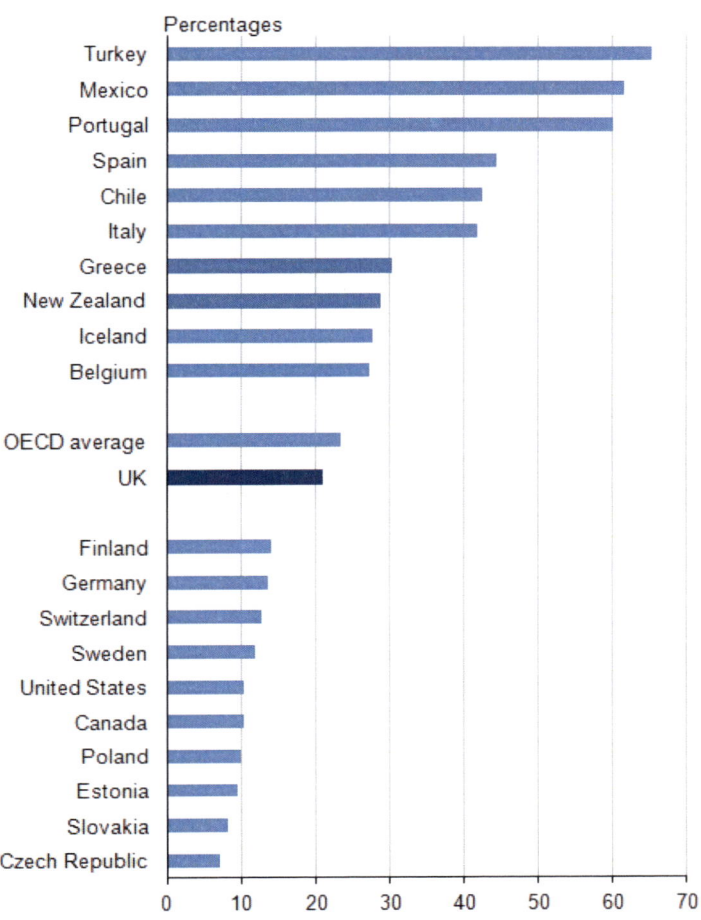

Source: Organisation for Economic Co-operation and Development

Notes:

1. The chart shows the 10 top and bottom OECD countries, the UK and the OECD average. 2011 for Chile. No data for Japan.

Download chart

XLS XLS format
(610 Kb)

Notes

1. The Programme for International Student Assessment (PISA) is an ongoing triennial survey. It assesses the extent to which 15-year-old students near the end of compulsory education have acquired key knowledge and skills that are essential for full participation in modern societies. The assessment does not just find out whether students can reproduce knowledge; it also

examines how well students can take what they have learned and apply it to unfamiliar settings, both in and outside of school.

2. Those who had, pre-primary and primary education, lower secondary education or ISCED 3C (short programme). More information is available at www.oecd.org/education/eag.htm

Governance

"Civic engagement allows people to express their voice and to contribute to the political functioning of their society. In turn, in well-functioning democracies, civic engagement shapes the institutions that govern people's lives" (OECD, 2011).

There are 2 measures in the National Well-being "Governance" domain. Comparable international data are available for these measures using alternative measures from different sources. There is more information in Comparison of National Well-being measures and international measures (621.5 Kb Excel sheet).

Table 9: International comparisons summary - Governance

	UK	Highest ranked country	Lowest ranked country	Coverage
Confidence in National Government	47%	Switzerland (77%)	Greece (13%)	OECD countries
Source: Gallup World Poll, (2012)				
Voter turnout in UK General Elections	66.1% (in 2015)	Australia (93.2 in 2013)	Poland (48.9% in 2011)	OECD countries
Source: The International Institute for Democracy and Electoral Assistance				

Download table

XLS XLS format
(609 Kb)

Confidence in national government

Nearly half (47%) of people aged 15 and over in the UK reported having confidence in the national government in 2012 according to data from the Gallup World Poll (Figure 11). This was higher than the Organisation for Economic Co-operation and Development (OECD) average of 40% and similar to France and Belgium (both 44%). Switzerland had the highest proportion of people reporting confidence in their national government (77%), while Greece had the lowest proportion of people reporting confidence in their national government at 13%.

Figure 11: Confidence in national government, 2012 (1)

OECD countries (2)

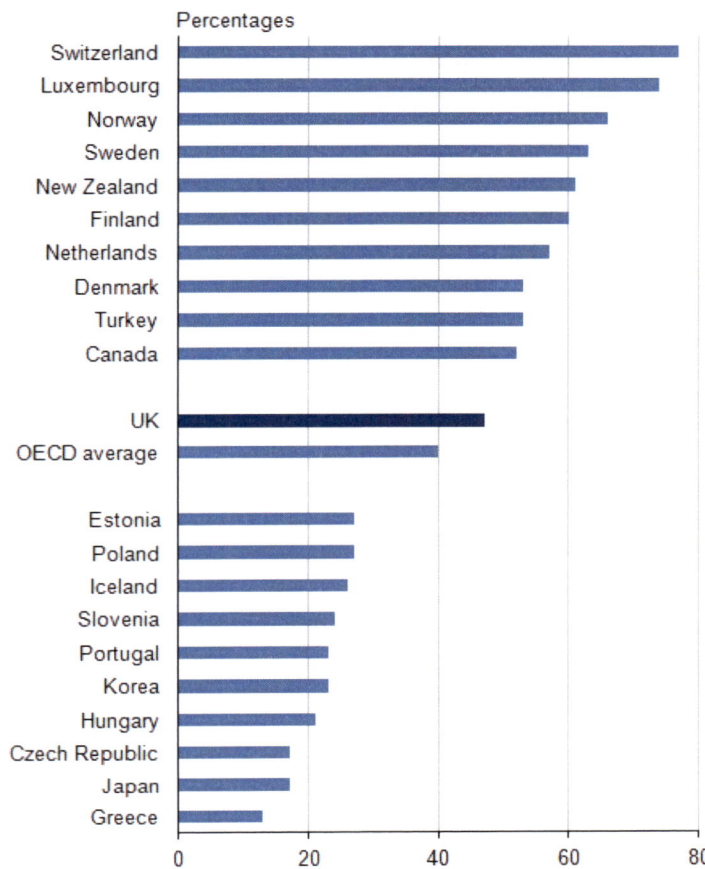

Percentages

Notes:

1. Data refer to the percentage who answered "yes" to the question: "Do you have confidence in national government?"
2. Chart shows the 10 top and bottom OECD countries, the UK and the OECD average. Data for the UK are for 2011.

Download chart

XLS XLS format
(610 Kb)

Voter turnout

According to data from the International Institute for Democracy and Electoral Assistance, two-thirds (66.1%) of registered voters in the UK voted in the parliamentary election in 2015. This was a similar proportion to Finland in 2015 (66.9%) and the United States in 2012 (68.0%). Among the OECD countries, Australia in 2013 (where there is compulsory voting) and Luxembourg in 2013 had the highest proportion of registered voters who actually voted at 93.2% and 91.2% respectively. Poland in 2011 and Switzerland in 2011 had the lowest proportion of registered voters who actually voted, at 48.9% and 49.1% respectively.

Natural environment

"The quality of our local living environment has a direct impact on our health and well-being. An unspoiled environment is a source of satisfaction, improves mental well-being, allows people to recover from the stress of everyday life and to perform physical activity" (OECD, 2013).

There are 4 measures in the National Well-being "Natural environment" domain. Comparable international data are available for 2 of these measures using measures from different sources and 1 measure has an EU comparison. There is more information in Comparison of National Well-being measures and international measures (621.5 Kb Excel sheet).

Table 10: International comparisons summary - Natural environment

	UK	Highest ranked country	Lowest ranked country	Coverage
Total green house gas emissions (million tonnes of Carbon Dioxide equivalent) Source: OECD, (2012)	584.3	Iceland (4.5)	United States (6,487.8)	OECD countries
Contribution of renewables to energy supply Source: OECD, (2012)	4.5%	Iceland (84.7%)	Korea (0.7%)	OECD countries
Recycling rate of municipal waste Eurostat, (2013)	43.5%	Germany (64.5%)[1]	Romania (2.6%)[1]	EU–28

Table notes:
1.   Estimated data.

Download table

XLS XLS format
(618.5 Kb)

Greenhouse gas emissions

Environmental statistics from the Organisation for Economic Co-operation and Development (OECD) show that the UK's greenhouse gas emissions[1] stood at 584.3 million tonnes of Carbon Dioxide equivalent (Mt of CO2e) in 2012. This figure was the fifth highest among OECD countries and was similar to Australia (543.6 Mt of CO2e). The United States (6,487.8 Mt of CO2e) and Japan (1,343.1 Mt of CO2e) had the highest total emissions, while Iceland (4.5 Mt of Mt of CO2e) and Luxembourg (11.8 Mt of Mt of CO2e) had the lowest.

Energy from renewable sources

In 2012, renewables accounted for 4.5% of the UK's total primary energy supply[2] according to data from OECD. This was lower than the OECD total of 8.5% and similar to Australia (4.6%) and the Netherlands (4.3%) (Figure 12). The highest shares of renewable energy as a percentage of primary energy supply in 2012 were found in Iceland (84.7%) and Norway (46.9%). The lowest percentage shares were in Korea (0.7%) and Luxembourg (3.2%).

Figure 12: Contribution of renewables (1) to primary energy supply, 2012

OECD countries (2)

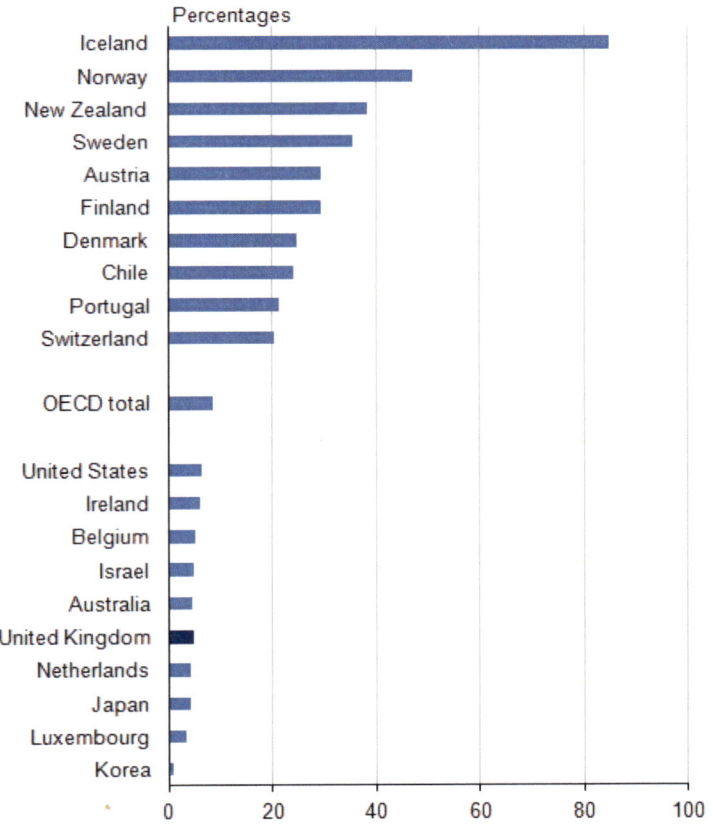

Source: Organisation for Economic Co-operation and Development

Notes:

1. Renewable energy is defined as the contribution of renewables to total primary energy supply (TPES). Renewables include the primary energy equivalent of hydro (excluding pumped storage), geothermal, solar, wind, tide and

wave sources. Energy derived from solid biofuels, biogasoline, biodiesels, other liquid biofuels, biogases and the renewable fraction of municipal waste are also included.

2. The chart shows the 10 top and bottom OECD countries and OECD total. Data for Chile, Germany and the UK are for 2011 rather than 2012.

Download chart

XLS XLS format
(618 Kb)

Recycling rate of municipal waste

According to data from Eurostat, an estimated 43.5% of the UK's municipal waste was recycled or composted[3] in 2013. This was above the EU–28 average of 41.8%. The country with the highest proportion of recycled or composted municipal waste was Germany (estimated at 64.5%). The countries with the lowest proportions were Romania (estimated at 2.6%), Malta (10.4%) and Slovakia (10.8%).

Notes

1. Data refer to total emissions of CO_2 (emissions from energy use and industrial processes, e.g. cement production), CH_4 (methane emissions from solid waste, livestock, mining of hard coal and lignite, rice paddies, agriculture and leaks from natural gas pipelines), nitrous oxide (N_2O), hydrofluorocarbons (HFCs), perfluorocarbons (PFCs) and sulphur hexafluoride (SF_6).

2. Renewable energy is defined as the contribution of renewables to total primary energy supply (TPES). Renewables include the primary energy equivalent of hydro (excluding pumped storage), geothermal, solar, wind, tide and wave sources. Energy derived from solid biofuels, biogasoline, biodiesels, other liquid biofuels, biogases and the renewable fraction of municipal waste are also included. Municipal waste comprises wastes produced by the residential, commercial and public service sectors that are collected by local authorities for disposal in a central location for the production of heat and/or power.

3. The recycling rate is the tonnage recycled from municipal waste divided by the total municipal waste arising. Recycling includes material recycling, composting and anaerobic digestion. Municipal waste consists to a large extent of waste generated by households, but may also include similar wastes generated by small businesses and public institutions and collected by the municipality; this latter part of municipal waste may vary from municipality to municipality and from country to country, depending on the local waste management system. This variation in scope across the Member States means that cross-country comparison is problematic. For areas not covered by a municipal waste collection scheme the amount of waste generated is estimated.

Background notes

1. Data from the International Social Survey Programme: These figures have been calculated using unweighted data. For information about data for each country, please see the study descriptions available on the GESIS website: //dbk.gesis.org/dbksearch/sdesc2.asp?no=5900

2. Details of the policy governing the release of new data are available by visiting www.statisticsauthority.gov.uk/assessment/code-of-practice/index.html or from the Media Relations Office email: media.relations@ons.gsi.gov.uk

Copyright

Sources used in 'International comparisons, 2015'

Charity Commision - www.cafonline.org/publications/2014-publications.aspx

Eurobarometer - Eurobarometer

European Quality of Life Survey - www.eurofound.europa.eu/surveys/eqls

Eurostat - Eurostat

Gallup World Poll - Gallup World Poll - Gallup Worldview

International Institute for Democracy and Electorial Assistance - www.idea.int/vt/

International Social Survey Programme - www.issp.org/

Organisation for Economic Co-operation and Development - OECD: Statistics

Programme for International Students Assessment - www.oecd.org/pisa/keyfindings/pisa-2012-results.htm

World Health Organisation - www.who.int/research/en/

OECD countries and member states of the EU

The Organisation for Economic Co-operation and Development (OECD)

The OECD is an international economic organisation of 34 countries, founded in 1961 to stimulate economic progress and world trade. It is a forum of countries describing themselves as committed to democracy and the market economy, providing a platform to compare policy experiences, seeking answers to common problems, identify good practices and coordinate domestic and international policies of its members.

OECD member countries are:

Australia, Austria, Belgium, Canada, Chile, Czech Republic, Denmark, Estonia, Finland, France, Germany, Greece, Hungary, Iceland, Ireland, Israel, Italy, Japan, Korea (South Korea), Luxemburg, Mexico, Netherlands, New Zealand, Norway, Poland, Portugal, Slovakia, Slovenia, Spain, Sweden, Switzerland, Turkey, the United Kingdom and the United States.

The European Union

The EU was created on 1 November 1993, when the Maastricht Treaty came into force. It encompasses the old European Community (EC) together with two intergovernmental 'pillars' for dealing with foreign affairs and with immigration and justice. The European Union consists of 28 member states (EU–28), where the EU–27 is referred to in this article, Croatia is not included.

The 28 member states are as follows:

Austria, Belgium, Bulgaria, Croatia, Cyprus, Czech Republic, Denmark, Estonia, Finland, France, Germany, Greece, Hungary, Ireland, Italy, Latvia, Lithuania, Luxembourg, Malta, Netherlands, Poland, Portugal, Romania, Slovakia, Slovenia, Spain, Sweden, and the United Kingdom.

Office for
National Statistics

Inequalities in Social Capital by Age and Sex, July 2015

Author Name(s): **Veronique Siegler, Rittah Njeru and Jennifer Thomas**

Abstract

This article provides an analysis of inequalities in social capital by age and sex in the UK, using the latest available data. The data are based on 25 headline measures, which cover 4 key aspects of social capital: personal relationships, social network support, civic engagement and trust and cooperative norms.

Main points

- Young people were the least likely to regularly stop and talk to their neighbours: less than half (45%) of those aged 18 to 24 regularly stopped and talked to their neighbours, compared to around 8 in 10 (83%) people aged 65 to 74 (2011 to 2012).
- Young people were the least interested in politics: around 4 in 10 (39%) of those aged 18 to 24 reported being quite or very interested in politics, compared to just under two-thirds (64%) of those aged 65 to74 (2012 to 2013).
- People aged 75 and over were the least likely to have at least one close friend; 11% of them reported having no close friend at all, compared to 2% of those aged 18 to 24 (2011 to 2012).
- Around 1 in 4 women (24%) and in 1 in 5 men (19%) aged 75 and over reported caring for someone sick, disabled or elderly within their household (2012 to 2013).
- Middle aged people (aged 45 to 54) were the most likely to feel lonely of all age groups (15% in 2011 to 2012) and the least likely to socialise, with nearly half (49%) reporting meeting socially with family, friends or colleagues less than once a week (2012 to 2013).
- Fewer women than men reported feeling safe walking alone in their local area (58% compared to 85% in 2013 to 2014).

Introduction

Social capital represents social connections and all the benefits they generate. High social capital means a society where people are connected, tolerant, help each other and spend time for the "common good". They have trust in others and in institutions, and are empowered to shape the society they live in. This has positive impacts on a range of areas, such as personal well-being, health, employment and crime.

Recent government evidence, submitted by the Cabinet Office to the UK Parliament's Environmental Audit Committee as part of their inquiry on well-being, highlighted the need for better evidence and further in-depth research to better understand social capital. Our current work, as part of the Measuring National Well-being Programme, is helping to better understand social capital, using data from existing sources.

This article explores inequalities in social capital by looking at differences in age and sex in the UK using the latest available data. It follows a baseline analysis of social capital in the UK published earlier in the year. It allows policy makers to identify the areas where action may be best targeted to address differences in social capital by age and sex.

Background

Around 64% of the 64.6 million of people living in the UK in mid-2014 were aged 16 to 64 , 9.6% were 65 to 74 years old and 8% were 75 and over, according to the latest population estimates. The UK has an ageing population: the proportion of the population aged 65 and over has increased over the past 30 years and this is projected to continue.

People of different age and sex might have different levels of social capital; for example, they might have a different range of social connections and resources; their civic attitudes, civic participation and the way they contribute to society might differ; their attitudes towards each other, their neighbours and institutions can also vary. Social capital can also make a difference at every stage of life, during the years in education, in the labour market and in older age, for both men and women. People of different age and sex can all shape the society and local area they live in.

A weakened social capital for people of different age and sex can in turn lead to inequalities in personal well-being (Eurofound report, 2014) and in accessing new opportunities or valuable resources for dealing with life challenges. A weakened social capital where people are less connected, integrated or civically engaged can also have an impact on community well-being and on social cohesion.

Personal relationships

This section looks at differences in the extent and nature of people's relationships with friends, family and neighbours, by age and sex.

Young people are less likely to interact with their neighbours

In 2011 to 2012, the proportion of people regularly stopping and talking with people in the neighbourhood increased steadily with age, with a slight decrease observed for those aged 75 and over (Figure 1). Only 45% of those aged 18 to 24 regularly stopped to talk with neighbours compared to 83% of those aged 65 to 74 and 79% of those aged 75 and over. Men were less likely to regularly stop and talk with people in the neighbourhood than women across all ages, with 63% of men doing so compared to 70% of women.

Positive attitudes in neighbourhoods, including taking the time to talk to neighbours, are important factors contributing to the building of communities in both urban and rural areas. More research is needed to understand what prevents a higher proportion of younger people, in particular younger men, from building relationships with neighbours. We also need better understanding of the benefits that talking to neighbours can generate (for example, wider social network) and for the communities (for example, safer communities) across different ages.

Further discussion of neighbourhood measures for young people can be found in the Trust and Cooperative Norms section.

Figure 1: Proportion of people who regularly stop and talk with people in neighbourhood by age and sex, 2011 to 2012

United Kingdom

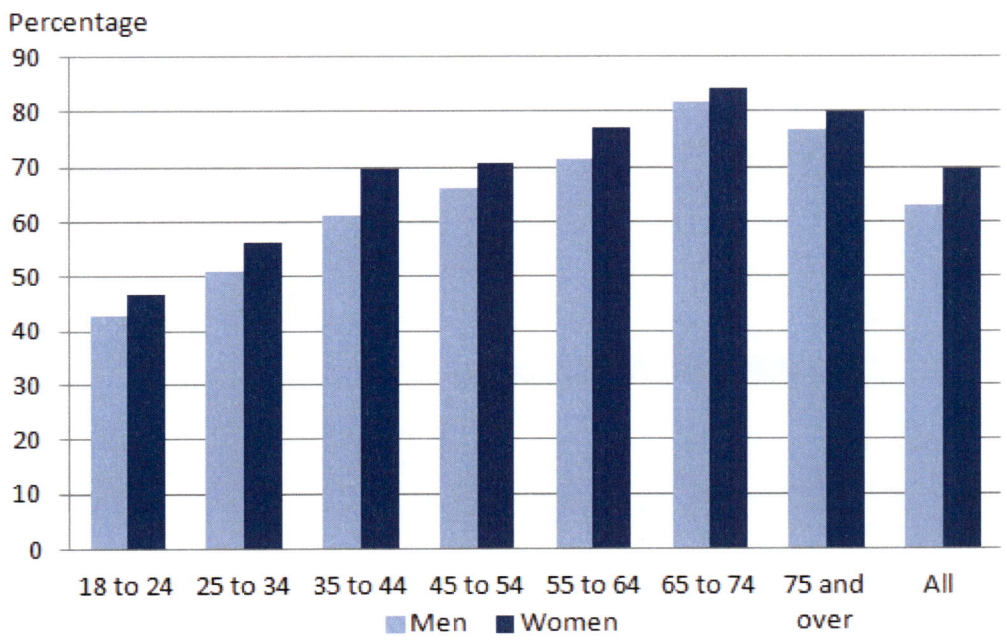

Source: Understanding Society

Download chart

XLS XLS format
(26 Kb)

People aged 45 to 54 are less satisfied about their social and family life, less likely to socialise often and more likely to feel lonely

Middle aged people rated their satisfaction with family and social life lower on average than other groups (Figure 2). A U-shape was observed for satisfaction with family life, with those aged 35 to 44 and 45 to 54 being the least satisfied with their family life on average (7.9 out of 10) (European Quality of Life Survey, EQLS, 2011 to 2012). Those aged 75 and over had the highest average rating

(8.8 out of 10) of all age groups for satisfaction with family life. This U-shape was more marked for satisfaction with social life, with those aged 45 to 54 rating their satisfaction with social life at 6.3 out of 10 on average (EQLS, 2011 to 12). Those aged 18 to 24 had the highest average rating (8.0 out of 10).

Satisfaction with both family life and satisfaction with social life have been shown to have a positive correlation with life satisfaction and happiness (Eurofound, 2012a). A similar U-shape in personal well-being with age has been widely reported in the literature over the last 40 years (ONS, 2013; Blanchflower and Oswald, 2008), with the drivers of this variation with age remaining largely unclear (ONS, 2013a).

Mid-life is an important transition and often a stressful time, burdened with simultaneous demands from work, childcare and ageing parents, but also a time where people re-evaluate and recalibrate their life, and might be more likely to suffer from mental health issues. Research across 27 European countries has shown a strong inverted U-shape in the use of antidepressants, peaking in people's late 40s (Blanchflower and Oswald, 2011). Also, the highest UK suicide rate in 2013 by broad age group was among people aged 45 to 59 (ONSc, 2015).

Figure 2: Deviations from the average ratings of satisfaction with family life and social life by age and sex, 2011 to 2012

United Kingdom

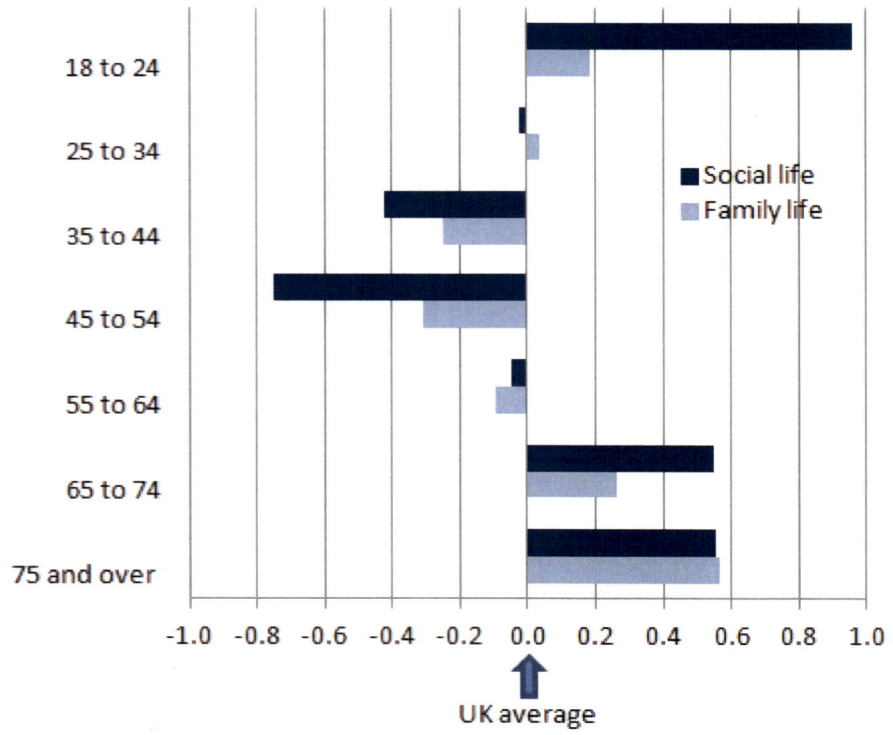

Source: Eurofound, Quality of Life Survey

Download chart

Loneliness is not necessarily about being alone, but about the perception of being alone and isolated. In 2011 to 2012 around 1 in 7 (15%) people aged 45 to 54 reported feeling lonely, the highest of all age groups (Figure 3). This compares to 6% of younger people aged 25 to 34. More research is required to understand the dynamics of loneliness with age, in particular in middle-age groups.

The proportion of those reporting socialising at least once a weekly basis was also the lowest in the middle-age groups, with only half (51%) of those aged 45 to 54 reporting meeting socially with friends, relatives or work colleagues at least once a week (Figure 3). This compares to 81% of those aged 18 to 24 and 75% of those aged 75 and over who reported socialising frequently. This U-shape in socialising with age is likely to be accounted for by external factors, such as the lack of time and opportunities, financial constraints and caring responsibilities, which are likely to impact middle-aged people in particular.

Figure 3: Proportion of people who report feeling lonely more than half, most or all the time by age, 2011 to 2012 and proportion of people who report meeting socially with friends, relatives or colleagues at least once a week by age, 2012 to 2013

United Kingdom

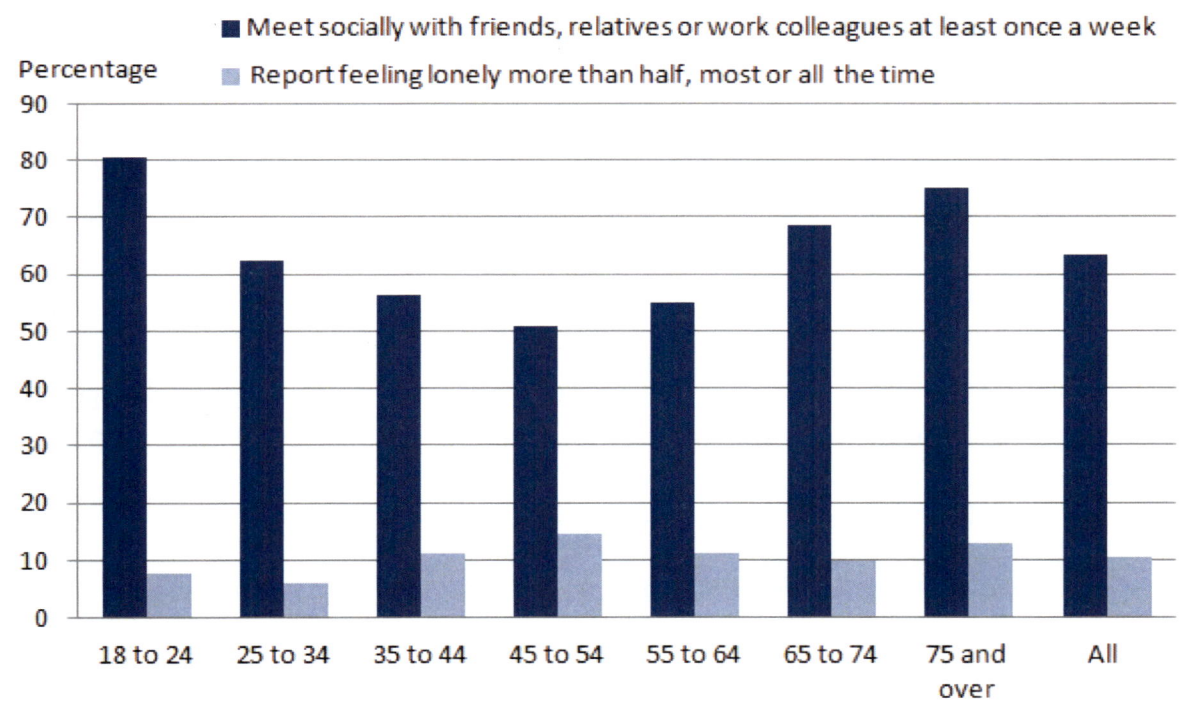

Sources: European Social Survey and Eurofound, European Quality of Life Survey

Download chart

1 in 8 people aged 75 and over feeling lonely and 1 in 4 socialising less than once a week

There were 1 in 8 (13%) people aged 75 and over who reported feeling lonely more than half, most or all the time in 2011 to 2012, the second highest proportion of all age groups (Figure 3). Personal circumstances, such as poor health, living alone, caring for someone else, going through a relationship break-up or loss, moving to a new area away from existing social networks can all be factors contributing to feelings of loneliness.

There were 1 in 4 (25%) people aged 75 and over who reported meeting with friends, relatives or work colleagues less than once week, in 2012 to 2013 (Figure 3) . It is known that older people, especially those aged 75 and over, are vulnerable to social isolation which can impact on their physical and mental health. People can become socially isolated for various reasons, including long-term health conditions and illnesses (Lloyd J, 2014), or the deaths of spouses and friends.

Similarly, there was a strong association between having at least one close friend and age. Around 11% of people aged 75 and over reported having no close friend at all in 2011 to 2012 (Source: Understanding Society), the highest proportion of all age groups. This compared to 2% of those aged 18 to 34. Another 10% of people aged 75 and over reported having 1 close friend only. More men than women reported having no close friend across all ages, with the difference between sexes being more marked at older age: around 14 % of men aged 75 and over reported having no close friend compared to 9% of women aged 75 and over.

The 2011 Census shows that 59% of those aged 85 and over and 38% of those aged 75 to 84 were living alone in England and Wales compared to 10% of those aged 25 to 34 (ONS, 2014). Around half of the 65 and over population in England were limited by a longstanding health condition or disability, with most people in this limited group living at home (93.5%) (Lloyd J and Ross A, 2014).

A small proportion of people aged 65 and over using social network websites

A social network website is defined as a platform to build social networks or social relations among people who share interest, activities, backgrounds or real-life connections. Social network websites can be a good way for people to keep in touch with family (such as grand-children for older people) and friends, to reconnect with old friends and to make new online friends. The use of the tablet computer can be particularly useful for people with limiting conditions.

In 2011 in 2012, 3% of those aged 75 and over and 11% of those aged 65 to 74 belonged to a social network website, compared to 90% of those aged 18 to 24 (Figure 4). The proportion of people belonging to a social network website decreased with age, which is likely to indicate a cohort effect: the older people are, the less they will have been exposed to the use of computer and new computer-mediated forms of social interactions.

The latest ONS internet use estimates show that the proportion of people aged 75 years and over who had never used the internet decreased from 76% in April to June 2011, to 61% of people in

January to March 2015. Around 41% of men aged 75 years and over were recent internet users compared with 27% of women aged 75 years and over.

Figure 4: Proportion of people who report belonging to a social website by age, 2011 to 2012

United Kingdom

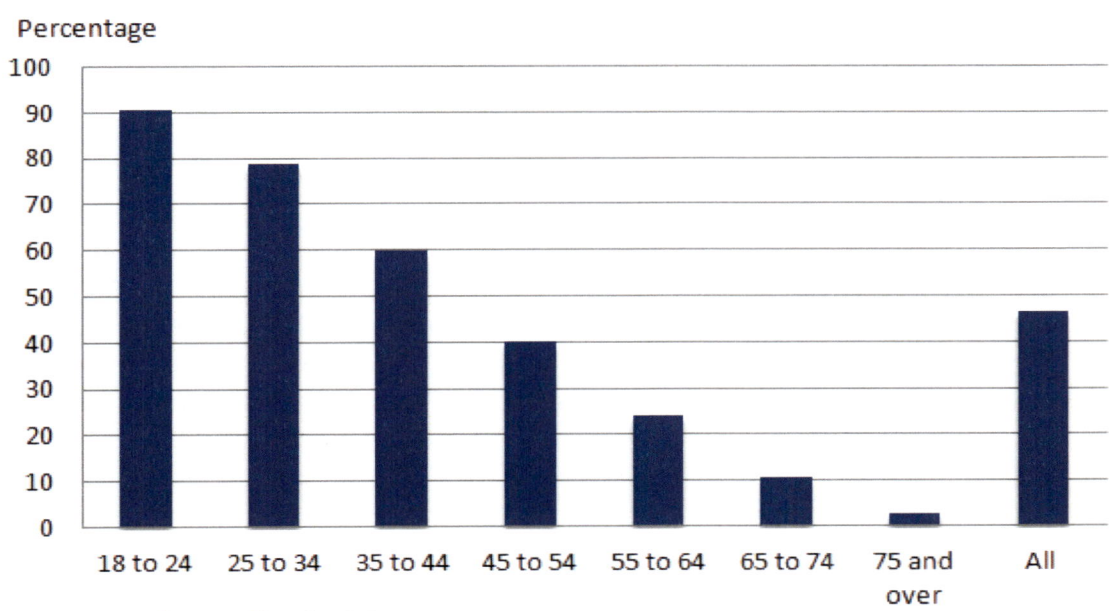

Source: Understanding Society

Download chart

XLS XLS format
(17.5 Kb)

Social network support

This section looks at differences in the extent to which people exchange resources or support within their own social network of family, friends and neighbours, by age and sex.

Fewer people aged 45 to 54, especially men, feel they can rely a lot on their family in case of a problem

The proportion of people who felt they can rely on their family in case of a serious problem formed a U-shape with age, which was more marked for men than women, in 2010 to 2011 (Figure 5).

Men were less likely than women to feel they could rely a lot on their family across all ages; the largest difference occurred at 55 to 64, where 55% of men and 68% of women felt they could rely a lot of their family. The lowest proportion of people who felt they could rely on their family a lot was found amongst those aged 45 to 54 for both men (47%) and women (57%). In comparison, the highest proportion of people who felt they could rely on their family a lot was found amongst those aged 75 and over for both men (73%) and women (82%).

Fewer men feel they can rely on their friends, but fewer women aged 35 and over feel they can rely on their partner in case of a serious problem

Men were also less likely than women to rely on their friends and this was the case across all ages. (Figure 5). In 2011 to 12 around a third (36%) of men of all ages felt they could rely a lot on their friends compared to half (52%) of women of all ages. The proportion of women who felt they could rely on their friends remained similar across all ages, whereas that of men was higher at ages 18 to 24 and 65 to 74.

Amongst those who had a husband, wife or partner with whom they live, the lowest proportion who felt they can rely a lot on their partner in case of a serious problem was found amongst those aged 18 to 24 (71%) for men and amongst those aged 35 to 44 (79%) for women (Figure 5). In comparison, the highest proportion of people who felt they could rely a lot on their partner was found among those aged 65 to 74, for both men (91%) and women (85%). A lower proportion of women than men felt that they can rely a lot on their partner from age 35 to 44 onwards; the largest difference occurred at age 75 and over where 88% of men and 80% of women felt they could rely a lot on their partner.

Figure 5: Proportion of people who feel they can rely a lot on their partner, family and friends in case of a serious problem by age and sex, 2010 to 2011

United Kingdom

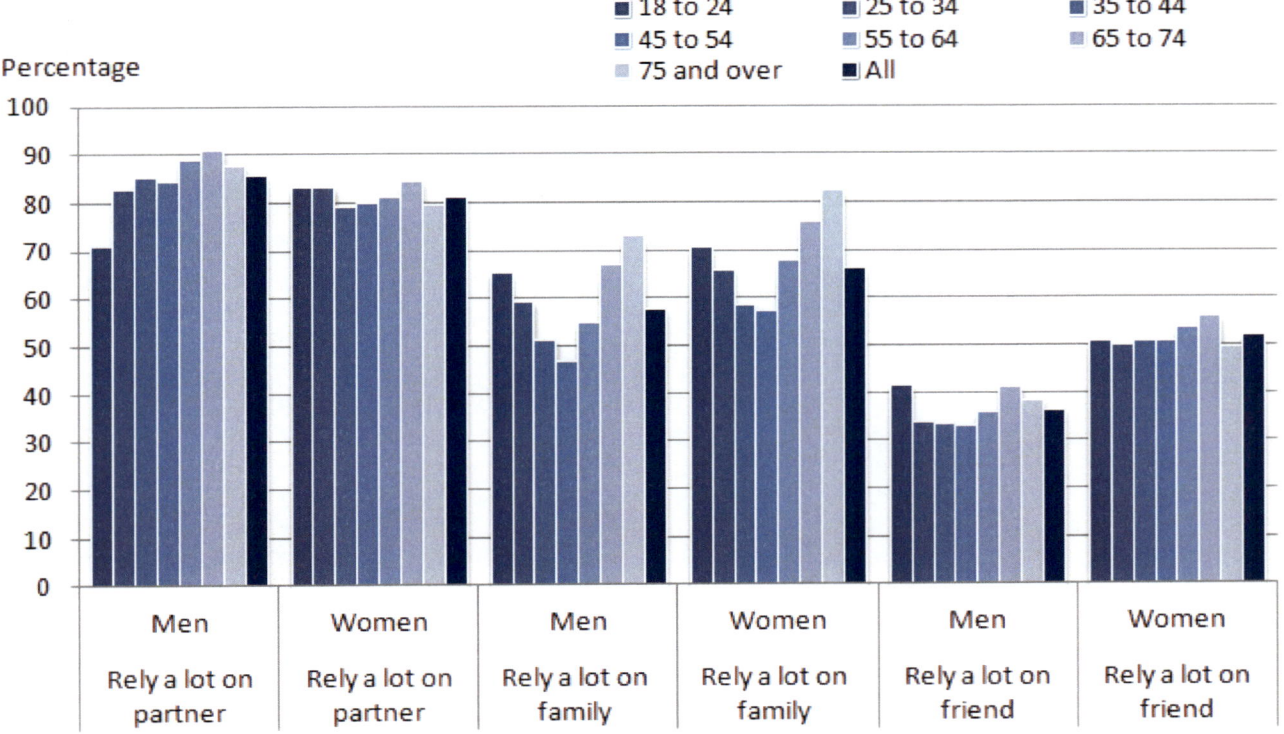

Source: Understanding Society

Download chart

XLS XLS format
(43 Kb)

Women, especially those aged 45 and over, are more likely than men to give special help to a sick, disabled or elderly person

Nearly 1 in 5 people (19%) reported looking after, or giving special help, to someone sick, disabled or elderly inside their household (7%), outside their own household (10%) or both (1%) in 2012 to 2013. Around 21% of women of all ages reported caring for someone sick, disabled or elderly inside or outside their household, compared to 16% of men of all ages (Figure 6).

The proportion of men and women who reported caring for someone sick, disabled or elderly within the household increased with age, and was significantly higher for those aged 75 and over than for any other age groups (Figure 6). A higher proportion of older women than older men cared for someone inside their household. Around 1 in 4 women (24%) and 1 in 5 men (19%) aged 75 and over cared for someone within their household, compared to around 1 in 10 women (10%) and 1 in 10 men (9%) aged 55 to 64.

The proportion of men and women caring for someone sick, disabled or elderly outside their household formed an inverse U-shape with age (Figure 6). The highest proportion of people caring for someone outside their household occurred at age 55 to 64 for both men (15%) and women (23%). The proportion of women caring for someone sick, disabled or elderly outside the household was significantly higher than that of men for those within the age groups 25 to 64. The largest difference occurred at age 45 to 54, where 21% of women care for someone outside their household compared 12% of men.

Figure 6: Proportion of people who give special help to at least one sick, disabled, elderly person living or not living with them, by age and sex, 2012 to 2013

United Kingdom

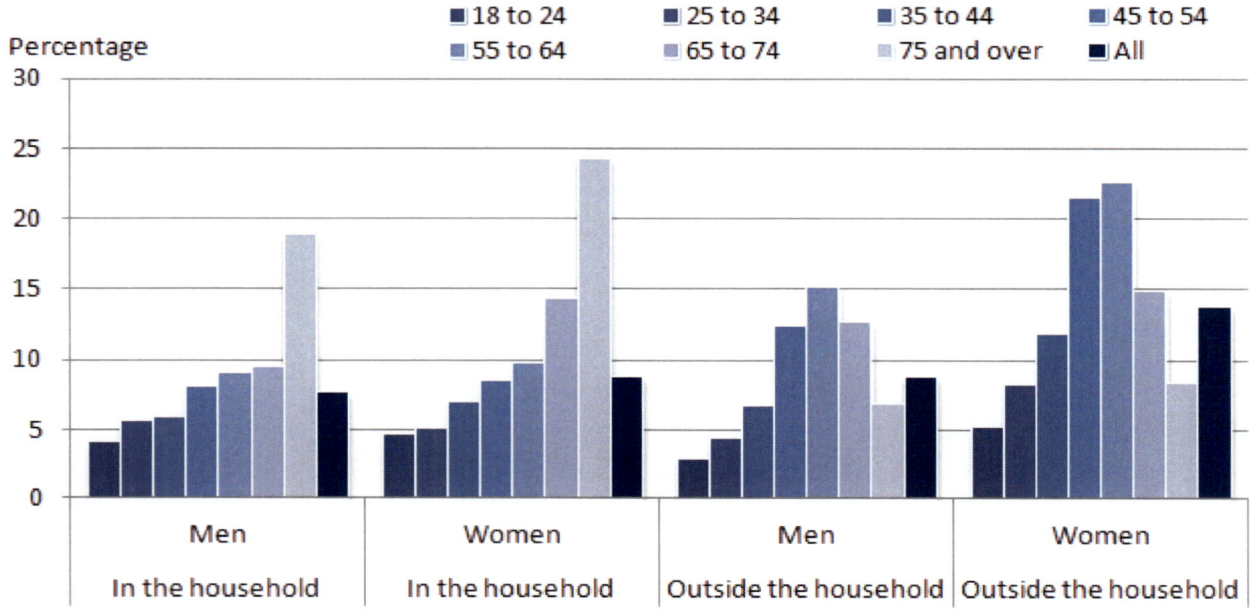

Source: Understanding Society

Download chart

XLS XLS format
(19.5 Kb)

Fewer men than women are receiving or giving help to their children who have grown up and left home

The proportion of parents who reported regularly receiving help from their children aged 16 or over not living with them increases with age (Understanding Society, 2011 to 2012). Around a third of people aged 55 to 64 (37%) and 45 to 54 (31%) report regularly receiving help, compared to 45% of people aged 65 to 74 and 60% of people aged 75 and over. A higher proportion of people gave than received help in the age groups before 75, but the reverse occurred for people over 75.

A lower proportion of men than women reported regularly receiving help across all ages. For example, 66% of women aged 75 and over and 50% of women aged 65 to 74 reported receiving help compared to 53% of men aged 75 and over and 50% of men aged 65 to 74.

Nearly 7 out of 10 parents aged 55 to 64 (70%) and 45 to 54 (69%) reported regularly giving help to a child aged 16 and over not living with them. Around 65% of men aged 45 to 54 and 67% of men aged 55 to 64 reported regularly giving help, compared to 72% of women aged 45 to 54 and 55 to 65.

Younger people are less likely to borrow things and exchange favour with their neighbours

The proportion of people regularly borrowing things and exchanging favour with their neighbours was lower for both men (32%) and women (31%) aged 18 to 24 than for people of any other groups (Understanding Society, 2011 to 2012). In comparison, around 45% of men and 49% of women aged 35 to 44 regularly borrowed things and exchanged favours with neighbours. This is in line with the finding that younger people were also less likely to stop and talk to neighbours, as described in the Personal Relationships section. Analysis of the feelings of young people about their local area can be found in the Trust and Cooperative Norms section.

Civic engagement

This section looks at differences in activities such as volunteering, political participation and other forms of community actions, by age and sex.

People aged 25 to 44 and 75 and over are less likely to volunteer

In 2012 to 2013, people aged 25 to 44 and 75 and over were less likely to be involved in volunteering than younger people (18 to 24) and people aged 45 to 74 (Figure 7). Around 15% of people aged 25 to 34 reported volunteering in the previous 12 months, compared to a quarter (25%) of those aged 65 to 74. Previous research has shown that the top 3 barriers to volunteering are work commitments, looking after children or the home and having other things to do with their own time (Cabinet Office, 2013). Health limitations are likely to restrict the ability to volunteer for people over 75.

There was a higher proportion of women volunteering than men, although these differences were not statistically significant; the only exception was for the age group 35 to 44, where a higher proportion of women (19%) than men (14%) had volunteered in the previous 12 months (Figure 7). At age 35 to 44, around a fifth (22%) of women also report being members of a parents/school association, compared to only 5% of men of that age. The higher volunteering rate of women aged 35 to 44 could potentially be associated with a higher involvement of mothers than fathers in activities of school-aged children, although this would need to be investigated further.

Figure 7: Proportion of people who volunteered in the last 12 months, by age and sex, 2012 to 2013

United Kingdom

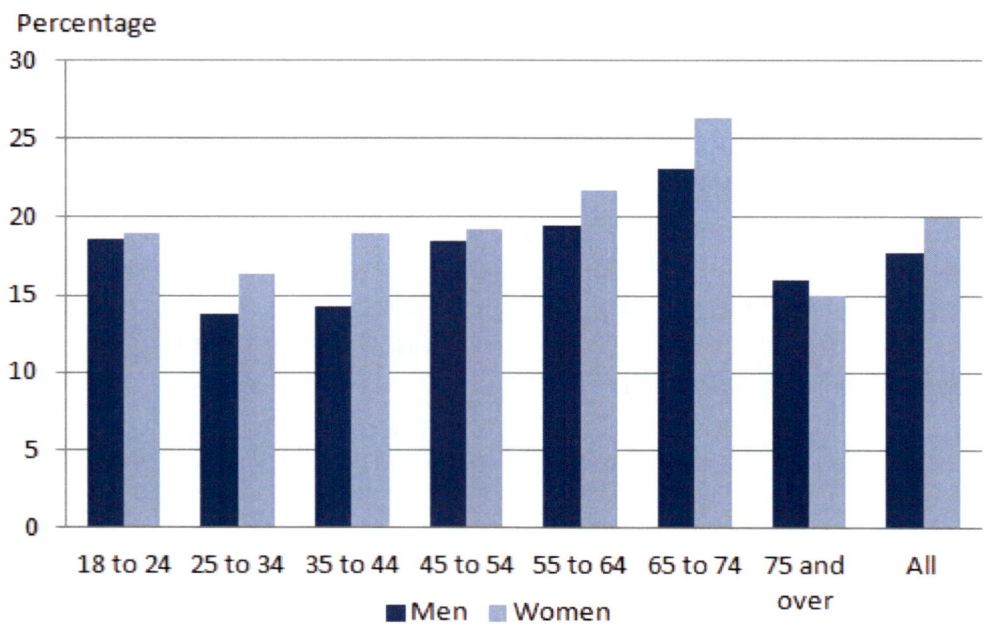

Source: Understanding Society

Download chart

XLS XLS format
(39 Kb)

Gender gap in membership of organisations

Men (55%) were more likely to be members or organisation (whether political, voluntary, professional or recreational) than women (49%) in 2011 to 2012 (Figure 8). This gender gap in membership in organisations was significant for all ages, except at ages 35 to 44 and 75 and over. It was largely driven by differences in memberships in sports clubs. Around 42% of men of all ages reported being members of a sports club compared to 24% of women of all ages in 2011 to 2012. Conversely, around 26% of women belong to religious or church organisation, compared to 17% of men. A similar proportion of men (22%) and women (19%) reported being members of professional organisations.

The likelihood that people are members of organisations gradually increased with age and peaked at 45 to 54, staying relatively stable until age 75 and over, when the likelihood declined. Around 41% of those aged 18 to 24 reported being members of organisations, compared to 58% of those aged 45 to 54 (Figure 8).

People of different ages belonged to different types of organisations in 2011 to 2012. For example, around 33% of those aged 45 to 54 were members of a trade union, 32% were members of a sports club, but only 18% were members of a religious or church organisation. In comparison, among those aged 25 to 34, 41% are members were members of a sports club, 26% were members of a trade union and 15% were members of a religious or church organisation. Among those aged 75 and over, 39% were members of a religious group or church organisation and 16% of a sports club.

Figure 8: Proportion of people who are members of organisations, whether political, voluntary, professional or recreational by sex and age, 2011 to 2012

United Kingdom

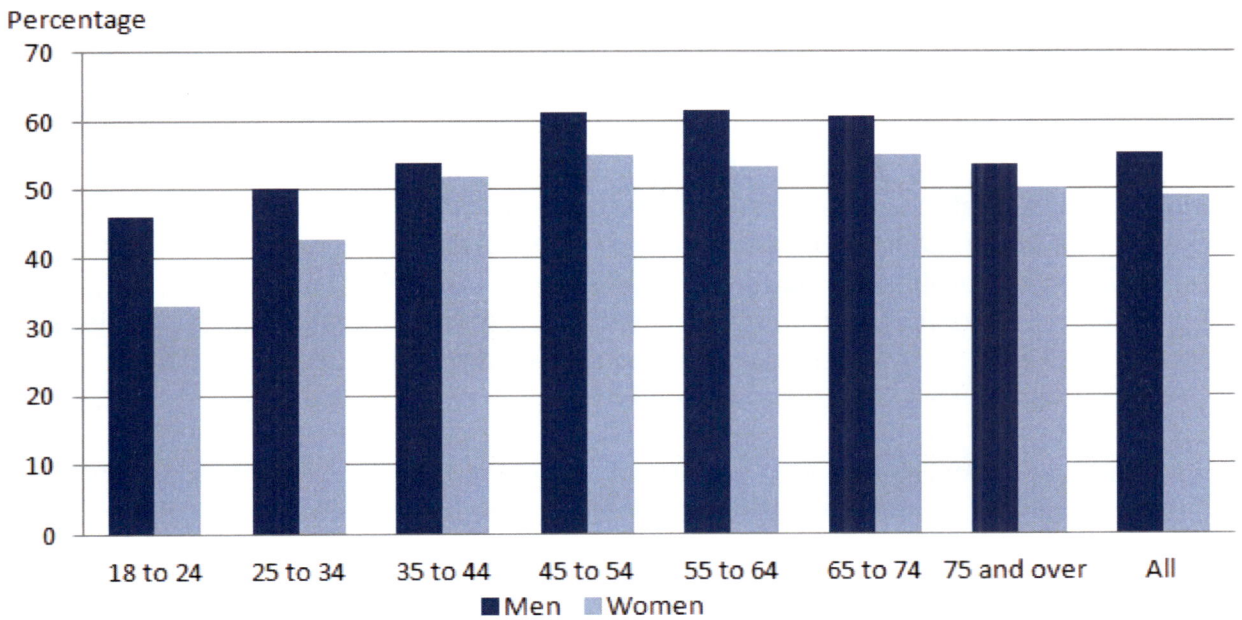

Source: Understanding Society

Download chart

XLS XLS format
(34.5 Kb)

Age gap in community engagement in local area

Social action can be described as "people getting together to cover a community project in their local area" (Cabinet Office, 2014). It includes activities such as setting up a new service or amenity to help local residents or trying to collectively stop something happening in a local area. Previous research has shown that most people get involved because they are asked by someone they know, while one of the main barriers is not being asked (Cabinet Office, 2013).

Men and women were equally likely to get involved in social action (18%) and equally likely to feel they can influence decisions affecting their local area (34%) (Community Life Survey, 2013/14).

The level of involvement in social action was lower amongst the under 35s and the over 75s, with 11% of those aged 25 to 34 and 12% of those over 75 reporting having been involved in social action in the previous 12 months. In comparison, nearly a quarter (22%) of those aged 35 to 74 reported having been involved in social action in the preceding 12 months.

The older age groups (65 to 74 and 75 and over) were the least likely to feel that they were influential, with only 29% and 27% respectively feeling that they definitely or somewhat feel able to influence decisions affecting their local area in 2013 to 2014, compared to 36% of those aged 18 to 64.

Younger people are less likely to vote

Voter turnout is a good indicator of the degree of civic engagement. Voter turnout is low among young people compared to older age groups, and whilst voting has declined for all, the decline between 1964 and 2005 has been sharpest amongst voters aged 18 to 24. (Table 1). The lowest proportion in 40 years was observed in 2005, when only 38% of 18 to 24 year olds voted in the General Election. However, the proportion increased in 2010, with over half (52%) of people aged 18 to 24 voting in the General Election, indicating a possible new engagement of young people in politics. This proportion remains low compared compared to that of people aged 65 and over: three-quarters (75%) of them voted in the 2010 General Election.

Previous ONS research has shown that in 2011 to 2012, just under 4 in 10 (39%) of those aged 18 to 24 agreed or strongly agreed that they would seriously be neglecting their duty as a citizen if they did not vote, compared with over 8 in 10 (80%) of those aged 65 and over.

Table 1: Estimated percentage turnout by age at General Elections 1964 to 2010

United Kingdom

	1964	1966	1970	1974[2]	1974[3]	1979	1983	1987	1992	1997	2001	2005	2010
18 to 24	76.4	60.5	64.9	70.2	62.5	62.5	63.9	66.6	67.3	54.1	40.4	38.2	51.8
25 to 34	70.7	70.8	66.5	77.2	69.0	72.4	67.6	74.0	77.3	62.2	45.0	47.7	57.3
35 to 44	79.5	80.0	72.8	78.7	73.9	76.3	76.2	74.9	78.3	70.2	55.7	61.6	64.4
45 to 54	79.1	79.8	74.9	73.1	76.6	81.2	77.6	79.9	81.8	76.4	63.2	65.5	67.5
55 to 64	78.4	78.0	74.1	82.2	76.6	81.4	77.2	78.9	78.1	79.9	64.0	72.6	69.8
65 and over	76.7	75.9	77.2	79.2	76.0	77.7	73.1	76.0	79.2	77.7	70.1	74.3	74.7
All	77.1	75.8	72.0	78.8	72.8	76.0	72.7	75.3	77.7	71.4	59.4	61.3	65.0

Table notes:

1. Source: The international Institute for Democracy and Electoral Assistance
2. February 1974
3. October 1974

Download table

XLS XLS format
(27.5 Kb)

Younger people and those over 75 are less likely to be involved in political action

Political actions include attending a demonstration, contacting an official or signing a petition. A similar proportion of men (33%) and women (34%) in the UK reported having been involved in at least 1 political action during the previous 12 months, according to the European Quality of Life Survey, 2011 to 2012.

The proportion of having been involved in a political action was the lowest amongst the younger people and for those aged over 75 and the highest for people in the middle-aged groups. Around 28% of those aged 18 to 24 reported having been involved in a political action in the previous 12 months, compared to 41% of those aged 45 to 54 and only 18% of those aged 75 and over.

Women and younger people less interested in politics

Women (43%) were less likely than men (55%) to be very or quite interested in politics in 2012 to 2013 (Figure 10). This is despite the previous finding that a similar proportion of men and women were engaged in political actions.

Interest also differed across age bands (Figure 9). The youngest age group was the least likely to be interested in politics, which reflects the voter turnout results; around 39% of those aged 18 to 24 and 42% of those aged 25 to 34 reported being very or quite interested in politics in 2012 to 2013 . People in the 65 to 74 age group were the most likely to be very or quite interested in politics (64%), which is in line with our previous findings (2014). Whether people are more or less likely to feel they have any say over how governments run the country may be an important factor to their continued political interest (ONS, 2014b).

The low levels of political interest have been well documented and could have several possible implications. It could be that younger age groups are more disillusioned with politics than older generations. Some people have suggested that younger people reject conventional politics in favour of single issues such as the environment, human and animal rights (Wilkinson and Mulgan, 1995), or using new ways of political engagement such as boycotting for political, ethical or environmental reasons (Yates, 2011). Other possible reasons are that young people perceive politics as boring and irrelevant to their present life and lack trust in politicians to keep promises and be responsive to their needs (White et al., 2000).

Figure 9: Proportion of people who are very or quite interested in politics by age, 2012 to 2013

United Kingdom

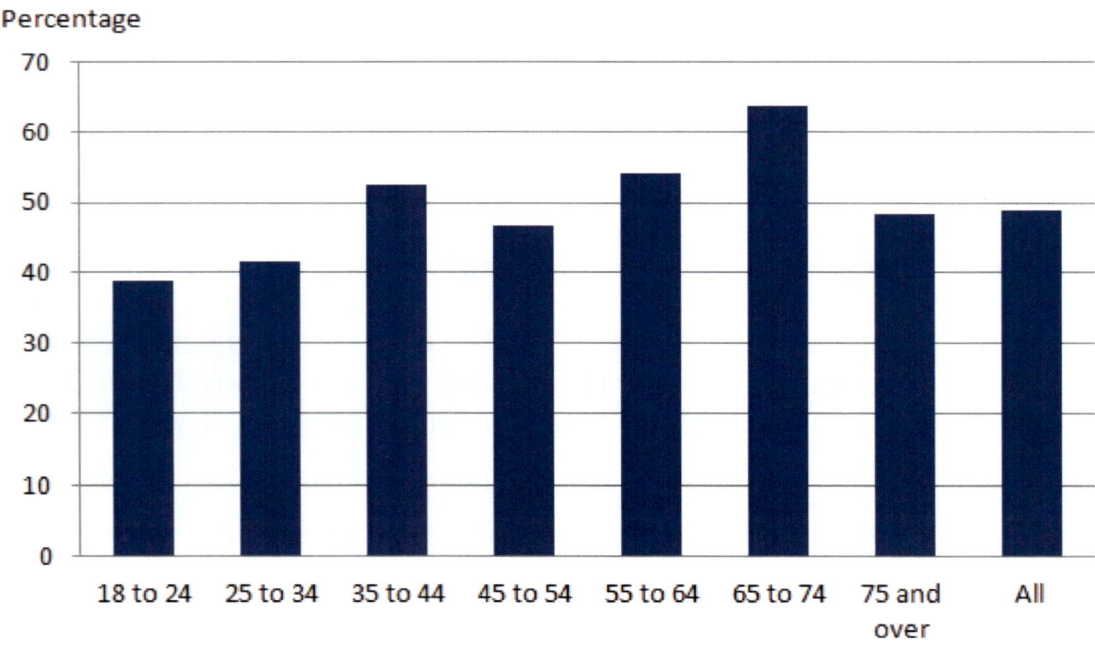

Source: European Social Survey

Download chart

XLS XLS format
(26 Kb)

Trust and cooperative norms

This section looks at differences in trust in national government, trust in others and measures of local community and neighbourhood, by age and sex.

People over 35 were less likely to trust the National Government in 2014

Nearly a third of men (32%) and women (31%) trusted the National Government in the UK in November 2014 (Source: Eurobarometer). The proportion of people who tended to trust the National Government was lower amongst those over the age of 35 than those under 35 (Table 2). For example, only a quarter (23%) of those aged 45 to 54 tended to trust their National Government compared to 38% of those aged 25 to 34.

Table 2: Proportion of people who tend to trust the National Government by age and sex, November 2014

United Kingdom

	Tend to trust	Tend not to trust	Don't know
18 to 24	39.0	50.0	11.0
25 to 34	38.0	53.0	9.0
35 to 44	28.0	67.0	5.0
45 to 54	23.0	72.0	5.0
55 to 64	30.0	64.0	6.0
65 to 74	28.0	67.0	5.0
75 and over	33.0	59.0	8.0
Men	32.0	62.0	6.0
Women	31.0	61.0	8.0
All	**31.0**	**62.0**	**7.0**

Table notes:
1. Source: Eurobarometer

Download table

Younger people less likely to trust others

Men were more likely than women to trust others, with 37% of men reporting that most people can be trusted compared to 34% of women in the UK in 2009 to 2010 (Figure 10), although these differences were not statistically significant across all ages. Around 44% of women and 39% of men reported that "you can't be too careful" when asked whether they trust others.

The proportion of people who reported that most people can be trusted increased with age until ages 65 to 74 for both men and women (Figure 10). The lowest proportions of people trusting others were found amongst women (18%) and men (23%) aged 18 to 24. In comparison, 43% of women and 46% of men aged 65 to 74 reported that most people can be trusted.

In the European Social Survey, trust in others is measured on a scale of 0 to 10. On such a scale, 0 indicates that people think that you have to be careful in dealing with people, whereas 10 shows that they think most people can be trusted. Results show that the average score for trust in others in the UK increased steadily with age, from 5.1 for those aged 18 to 24 to 5.8 in those aged 75 and over in 2012 to 2013. Conversely, previous research has shown that overall in 27 European countries, younger age is associated with higher trust, and that trust of people aged 65 and over was affected more negatively during the years of financial crisis, 2009 to 2010 (Eurofound, 2012). This indicates that socio-demographics, such as age, are likely to have a different affect on trust across different countries.

More research is required to better understand what causes the lower trust in younger people, especially women. The difference in trust with age could be caused by a cohort effect, where younger people are less trusting because they have grown up in a society where they have access to a wider range of information, but can also connect to a wider range of different people through internet usage and social network websites. Younger people, especially women, might feel more vulnerable to others, which results in fear of negative experiences with strangers.

Figure 10: Proportion of people who feel that most people can be trusted by age and sex, 2009 to 2010

United Kingdom

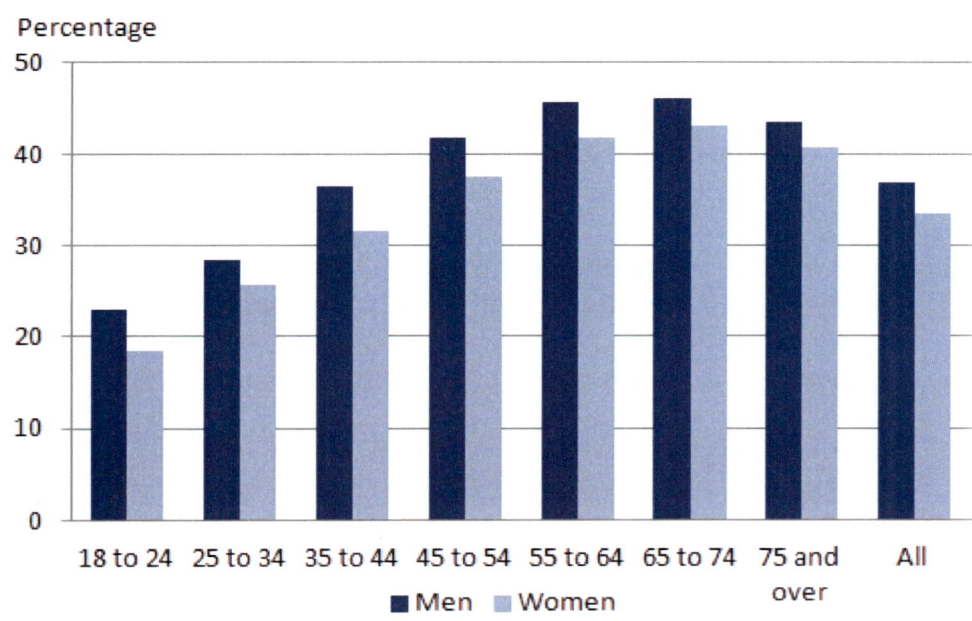

Source: Understanding Society

Download chart

XLS   XLS format
(26.5 Kb)

Wide gap between sexes at every age for feeling safe walking alone in the local area

Fear of walking alone at night is important because it can affect the decisions that people make, in terms of where to live and how they spend their time.

A large majority of men (85%) reported feeling very or fairly safe walking alone in their local area in England and Wales in 2013 to 2014, compared to 58% of women (Figure 11). This gap between men and women was the widest for ages 18 to 24 and 75 and over.

There was no statistically significant difference between age groups in the proportion of people feeling safe walking alone in their local area, with the exception of women aged 75 and over. In this group, less than half (41%) reporting feeling safe walking alone in their local area, the lowest proportion across all age bands and sexes (Figure 11).

Research shows that the gender gap in feeling of personal safety is universal, with women feeling less safe walking alone in the night in 2013 than in any point in the previous 8 years, and with the largest differences being observed in high-income and highly prosperous countries (Legatum Institute, 2014).

Women were also more likely than men to perceive that crime across the UK (68%) and in their local area (36%) have been rising in 2015, as described in chapter 2 of Crime Statistics, Focus on Public Perceptions of Crime and the Police, and the Personal Well-being of Victims, 2013 to 2014. Additionally, women were more likely to worry about being a victim of violent crime than men.

It has been previously shown that at a national level, there is a gap between the levels of crime (which has been falling since 1995) and subjective feelings of crimes. Conversely, at a local area level, there is a clear relationship between objective levels of crime and subjective perceptions of crime.

More research is needed to investigate how the feelings of feeling safe walking in local area, which is a subjective perception, relate to objective levels of crime for both men and women.

Figure 11: Percentage of people who feel safe walking alone in their local area after dark by sex and age, 2013 to 2014

England and Wales

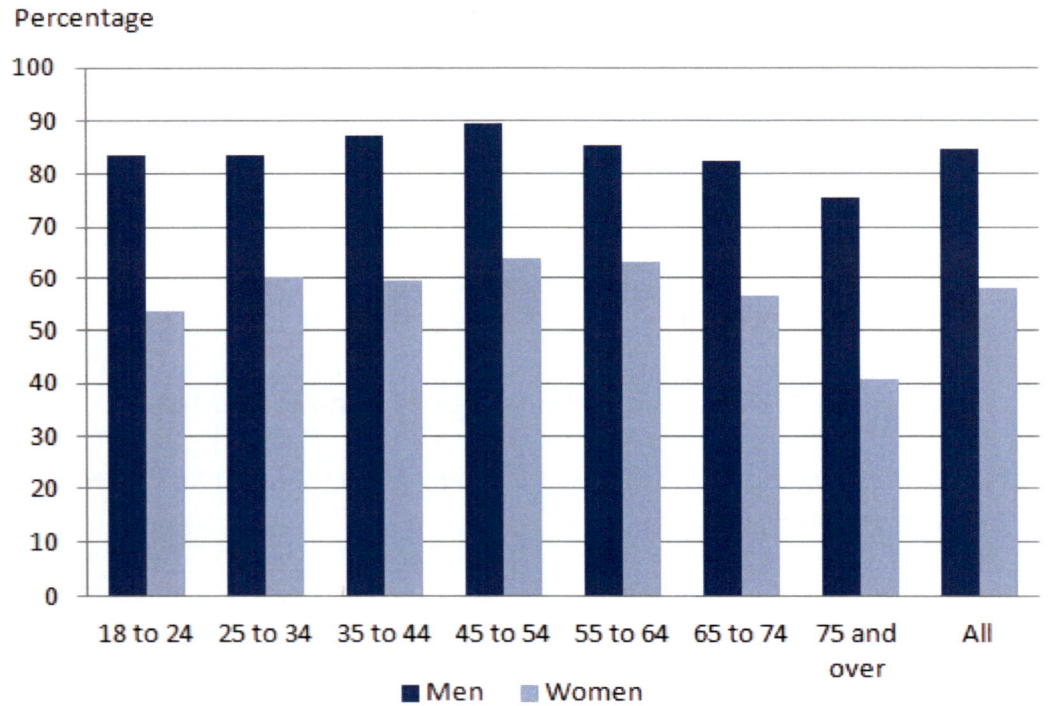

Source: Crime Survey for England and Wales - Office for National Statistics

Download chart

XLS XLS format
(27 Kb)

Younger people are less likely to trust people in their local area and to feel they belong to their local area

Although women were less likely than men to trust others in general, they were as likely as men to trust people in their local area (around 65% in 2011 to 2012). Women and men were also equally likely to feel that people in their local area are willing to help their neighbours (around 7 in 10 people in 2011 to 2012) and to agree that their local area is a place where people from different backgrounds get on well together (85% in 2013 to 2014).

Indicators of social capital in the local area were strongly associated with age. Those aged 18 to 24 were significantly less likely to report trusting others in their local area (47%) and feeling that people in their local area are willing to help their neighbours (60%) than any other age groups. In comparison, among those aged 75 and over, around 8 in 10 reported trusting people in their local area and feeling that people in their local area are willing to help their neighbours (82% and 79% respectively) (Figure 12).

Those aged 18 to 24 were also less likely to stop and talk with their neighbours and borrow things and exchange favours with their neighbours, as shown in this article. Less than half (47%) of those aged 18 to 24 reported feeling that they belong to their local area, compared with around 8 in 10 people (81%) of those aged 75 and over.

However, a high proportion of people reported that their local area was a place where people from different backgrounds got on well together in 2013 to 2014, across all age groups (80% of those aged 18 to 24 and 93% of those aged 75 and over).

More research is needed to investigate the drivers of this age gap in interaction with neighbours, and how this relates to trust in others in the local area and sense of belonging in the local area. We also need to look at why these indicators of social capital are low for young people, yet most people, including the young, feel that people from different backgrounds get on well in the local area.

Our previous research has shown that the 2 peak ages for internal migration from one local authority to another was 19 and 22, with nearly a quarter (23%) of 19-year olds and 15% of 22 year-olds living in England and Wales moving between local authorities in mid-2012. It can reasonably be assumed that time is needed to build trust and relationships in local communities. If younger people are more likely to be new residents in an area, they are also less likely to know and trust their neighbours, and to feel they belong to where they live.

More longitudinal research is required to investigate whether people change attitudes to their neighbours as they get older and as they have higher residential stability, and the differences between rural and urban areas. We need to look at whether this is a generational effect, where younger people today are less likely to be involved with their neighbours and their community, which would lead in a decline in social capital in the long-term. In any case, young people have an important role in building social capital. Their involvement in local area is important for building safe, cohesive and engaged communities.

Figure 12: Proportion of people who feel people in their local area, can be trusted, are willing to help their neighbours and feel they belong to their local area by age, 2011 to 2012

United Kingdom

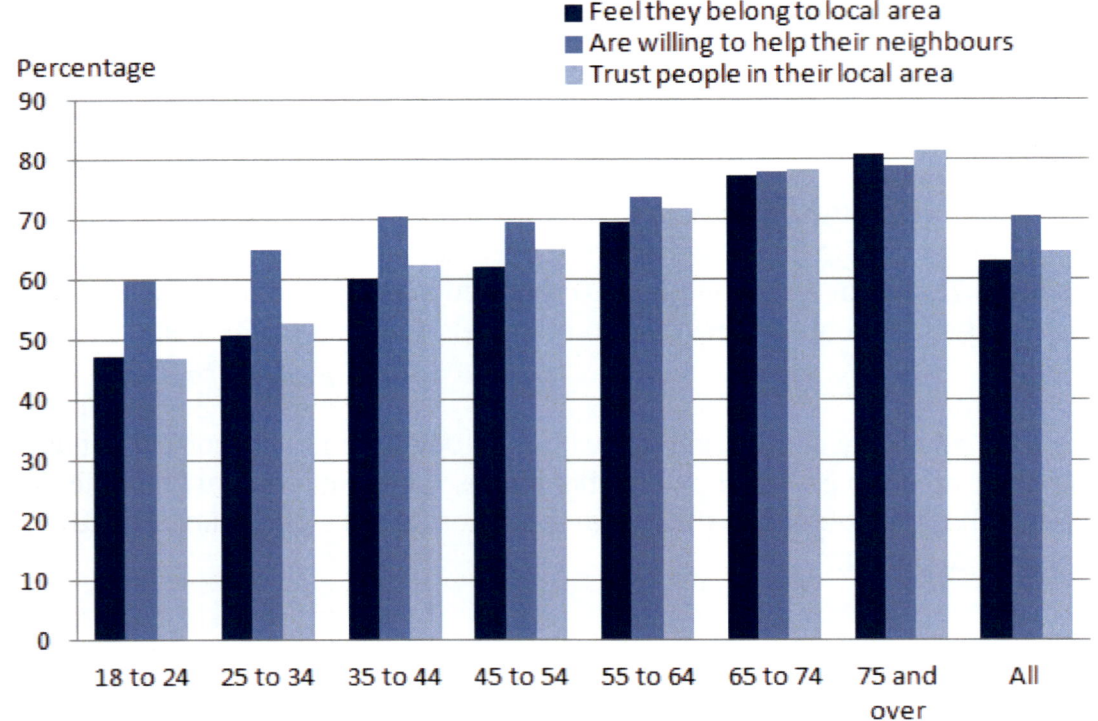

Source: Understanding Society

Download chart

XLS XLS format
(27 Kb)

References

Blanchflower D. G and Oswald A .J. (2008). Social Science & Medicine vol. 66 , 1733-49.

Blanchflower,D.G and Oswald, A,J. (2011). Antidepressants and age. Discussion paper series // Forschungsinstitut zur Zukunft der Arbeit, No. 5785.

Cabinet Office. (2013). 'Giving of time and money. Findings from the 2012-13 Community Life Survey'

Cabinet Office (2014), Community Life Survey Statistical Bulletin 2013-14

Community Life Survey. (2014). Community Life Survey 2013 to 2014

Eurobarometer surveys. Public Opinion. European Commission

Eurofound. (2014). Social cohesion and well-being in the EU

Eurofound. (2012a). Third European Quality of Life Survey - Quality of life in Europe: Impacts of the crisis, Luxembourg: Publications Office of the European Union. Eurofound. (2012b). European Quality of Life Survey

Legatum Institute. (2014). The 2014 Legatum Prosperity Index

Lloyd, J. (2014). The Bigger Picture: Policy insights and recommendations. London, Strategic Society Centre and Independent Age.

Lloyd J and Ross A,. (2014). The Bigger Picture: Understanding disability and care in England's older population, . London: Strategic Society Centre and Independent Age.

Office for National Statistics: Measuring National Well being Programme. ONS.

Office for National Statistics (2013a). Personal Well-being in the UK.

Office for National Statistics, (2013b). Internal Migration by Local Authorities in England and Wales,Year Ending June 2012. Statistical Bulletin.

Office for National Statistics, Smith, C.W. (2014a). 2011 Census Analysis. Do the Demographic and Socio-Economic Characteristics of those Living Alone in England and Wales Differ from the General Population? ONS.

Office for National Statistics, Randall.C. (2014b). Measuring National Well-being, Governance, 2014. ONS.

Office for National Statistics, Siegler, V. (2015a). Measuring National Well-being - An Analysis of Social Capital in the UK Measuring Social Capital. ONS.

Office for National Statistics, (2015b). Overview of the UK Population. Population estimates:ONS.

Office for National Statistics. (2015c). Statistical bulletin: Suicides in the United Kingdom, 2013. ONS.

Office for National Statistics, (2015d). Internet Users, 2015. UK. ONS

Office for National Statistics, (2015e). Chapter 2: Public Perceptions of Crime. ONS

The International Institute for Democracy and Electoral Assistance. (1945 - 2015). Voter turnout data for United Kingdom.

White,C., Bruce and Ritchie, J. (2000). Political interest and engagement among young people . Joseph Rowntree Foundation.

Wilkinson and Mulgan. (1995). Freedoms Children: Work, Relationships and Politics for 18-34 year olds in Britain today. Demos.

Yates,L. (2011). Critical Consumption: Boycotting and Buycotting in Europe. European Societies;13:2 , 191-217.

Background notes

1. Details of the policy governing the release of new data are available by visiting www.statisticsauthority.gov.uk/assessment/code-of-practice/index.html or from the Media Relations Office email: media.relations@ons.gsi.gov.uk

Copyright

Office for National Statistics

Statistical Bulletin

Personal Well-being in the UK, 2014/15

Coverage: **UK**
Date: **23 September 2015**
Geographical Area: **Country**
Theme: **People and Places**

1. Main points

- Reported personal well-being has improved every year since financial year ending 2012 when data were first collected, suggesting that an increasing number of people in the UK are feeling positive about their lives.

- Proportions reporting the highest levels of personal well-being have increased since the financial year ending 2012 for each of the 4 measures considered. The greatest improvement has been for levels of anxiety.

- The proportion of people rating their well-being at the lowest levels for all 4 of the measures has reduced, but not as much as the proportion reporting high levels has grown.

- People in Northern Ireland gave higher average ratings for personal well-being for all measures except anxiety compared to the other 3 UK countries (based on figures before rounding). This has been the case in every year since data were first collected.

- People in London reported lower personal well-being on average for each of the measures than the equivalent UK averages, but London has seen improvements across all the average measures of personal well-being, particularly in reductions to anxiety since data were first collected.

- Since the financial year ending 2012, average ratings of personal well-being have improved significantly across all measures in the West Midlands. The region also had the lowest average anxiety rating of any English region in financial year ending 2015.

- Wales was the only UK country that did not have any significant positive improvements between the financial year ending 2014 and the latest estimates across any of the measures for average ratings.

- The North West of England reported increases in the rate of personal well-being for 3 out of 4 of the measures, compared with the financial year ending 2014.

- The North East and Yorkshire and The Humber were the only 2 English regions with no significant reductions in low levels of well-being across any of the personal well-being measures compared with the financial year ending 2014.

2. Summary

Reported personal well-being has been improving every year since financial year ending 2012, when we started to collect the data across all 4 measures.

Comparing the average ratings for the financial year ending 2015 with the previous year for each of the 4 measures of personal well-being:

- life satisfaction was 7.6 out of 10 (up 0.10 points)
- feeling that what one does in life is worthwhile was 7.8 out of 10 (up 0.08 points)
- happiness yesterday was 7.5 out of 10 (up 0.08 points)
- anxiety yesterday was 2.9 out of 10 (down 0.07 points)

The year-on-year differences are small but statistically significant in each case. The proportion of people giving the highest ratings (scores of 9 or 10 out of 10 for life satisfaction, worthwhile and happiness, and 0 to 1 out of 10 for anxiety) for each measure of personal well-being also increased significantly in financial year ending 2015.

Additionally, the proportions of people reporting personal well-being at the lowest levels (scores of 0 to 4 for life satisfaction, worthwhile and happiness and ratings of 6 to 10 for anxiety) reduced, although the decreases in low well-being were small compared with the improvements in the highest ratings.

This is important because it indicates that while improvements are widespread across the population, they are uneven. The proportion reporting very high personal well-being is growing faster than the proportion reporting low levels is falling. This indicates increasing inequality in personal well-being.

Also released today, 23 September 2015:

[Interactive maps](#) for exploring the personal well-being estimates in local areas of the UK

Picture of Interactive Maps

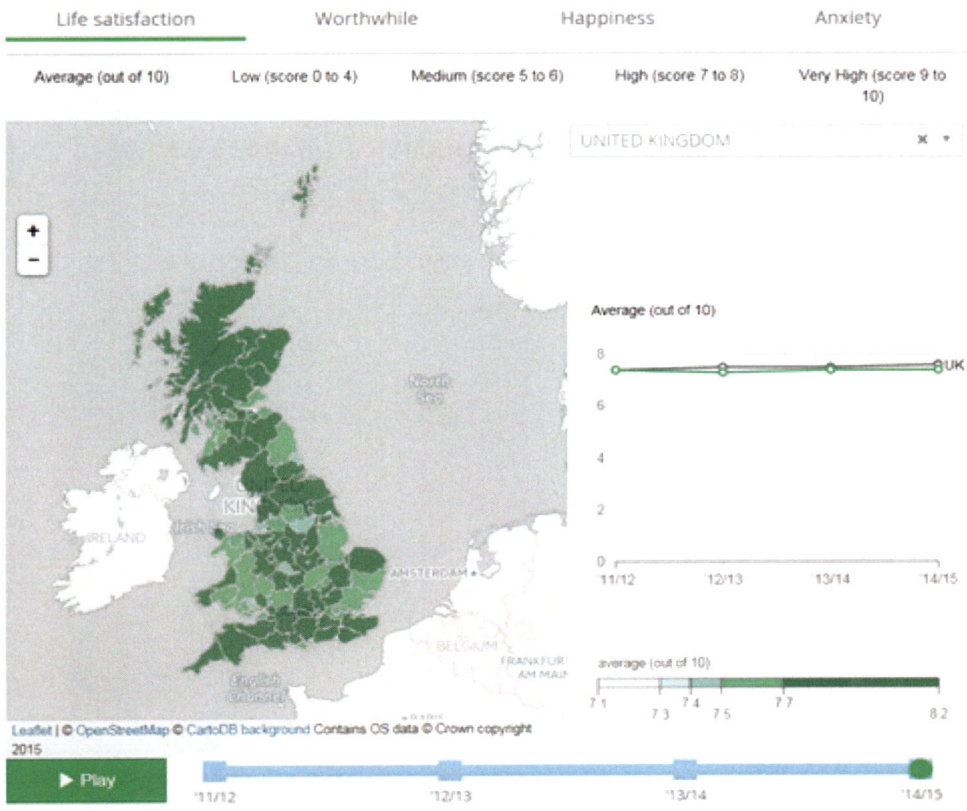

[Short story exploring personal well-being and tenure](#).

For more information on National Well-being please see [National Well-being Interactive Wheel](#) and [Measuring National Well-being - Domains and Measures - September 2015](#) - September 2015 due to be published on 29th September 2015.

3. Measuring personal well-being in the UK

This bulletin is published as part of our Measuring National Well-being programme. It presents annual estimates of personal well-being in different areas of the UK for the financial year ending 2015. It also compares the latest results to our previous personal well-being estimates covering the same periods in financial years ending 2014, 2013, and 2012 ([ONS 2014a](#); [ONS 2013a](#), [ONS 2012](#)). The latest estimates of personal well-being among people with different characteristics or circumstances are included in the [reference tables](#) with this release.

The personal well-being estimates in this bulletin are based on data from the Annual Population Survey (APS) with responses to the personal well-being questions from around 165,000 people. This provides a large representative sample of adults aged 16 and over living in residential households in the UK.

Personal well-being, people's thoughts and feelings about their own quality of life, is an important aspect of national well-being. It is part of a much wider initiative in the UK and internationally to look beyond Gross Domestic Product (GDP), and to measure what really matters to people. We regularly monitor 41 different headline measures in areas such as the natural environment, our relationships, health, what we do, where we live, personal finances, the economy, education and skills, governance and personal well-being to measure the progress and well-being of the nation. The latest updates to these headline measures will be available in Measuring National Wellbeing - Domains and Measures, released by the end of September 2015. Section 7 provides further information about how the well-being data are used.

The UK Statistics Authority has designated our personal well-being statistics as National Statistics, signifying compliance with the Code of Practice for Official Statistics.

This means that these statistics:

- meet identified user needs
- are well explained and readily accessible
- are produced according to sound methods
- are managed impartially and objectively in the public interest

It is a statutory requirement that the Code of Practice shall continue to be observed.

3.1 How personal well-being is measured

We began measuring personal well-being in April 2011. Since then, the Annual Population Survey (APS) has included 4 questions which are used to monitor personal well-being in the UK:

1. Overall, how satisfied are you with your life nowadays?
2. Overall, to what extent do you feel the things you do in your life are worthwhile?
3. Overall, how happy did you feel yesterday?
4. Overall, how anxious did you feel yesterday?

People are asked to give their answers on a scale of 0 to 10, where 0 is "not at all" and 10 is "completely". These questions allow people to make an assessment of their life overall, as well as providing an indication of their day-to-day emotions. Although "yesterday" may not be a typical day for an individual, the large sample means that these differences "average out" and provide a reliable assessment of the self-reported anxiety and happiness of the adult population in the UK over the year.

Since the introduction of these 4 questions they have been introduced in over 20 other surveys across government and numerous surveys in the academic, private and third sector.

It is important to remember that the findings presented are based on survey estimates and are subject to a degree of uncertainty. Therefore, they should be interpreted as providing a good estimate, rather than an exact measure of personal well-being in the UK. For more information about how the statistics are produced and implications for the accuracy of the estimates, see the Methodology section (section 8).

Differences in the personal well-being estimates over time are described only where they are statistically significant. That is where the change is not likely to be only due to variations in sampling, but to a real change over time. A 5% standard is used, which means that there is no more than a 5% chance that a difference will be classified as significant when in fact there is no underlying change. The country and regional estimates for financial year ending 2015 are compared to the equivalent estimates for the UK and discussed only where a statistically significant difference is found.

3.2 How people in the UK rated their personal well-being in financial year ending 2015

Figure 1 shows how people rated each aspect of their personal well-being based on the 0 to 10 scale in each of the 4 years.

Figure 1: Distribution of personal well-being ratings, financial years ending 2012 to 2015 (1)

United Kingdom

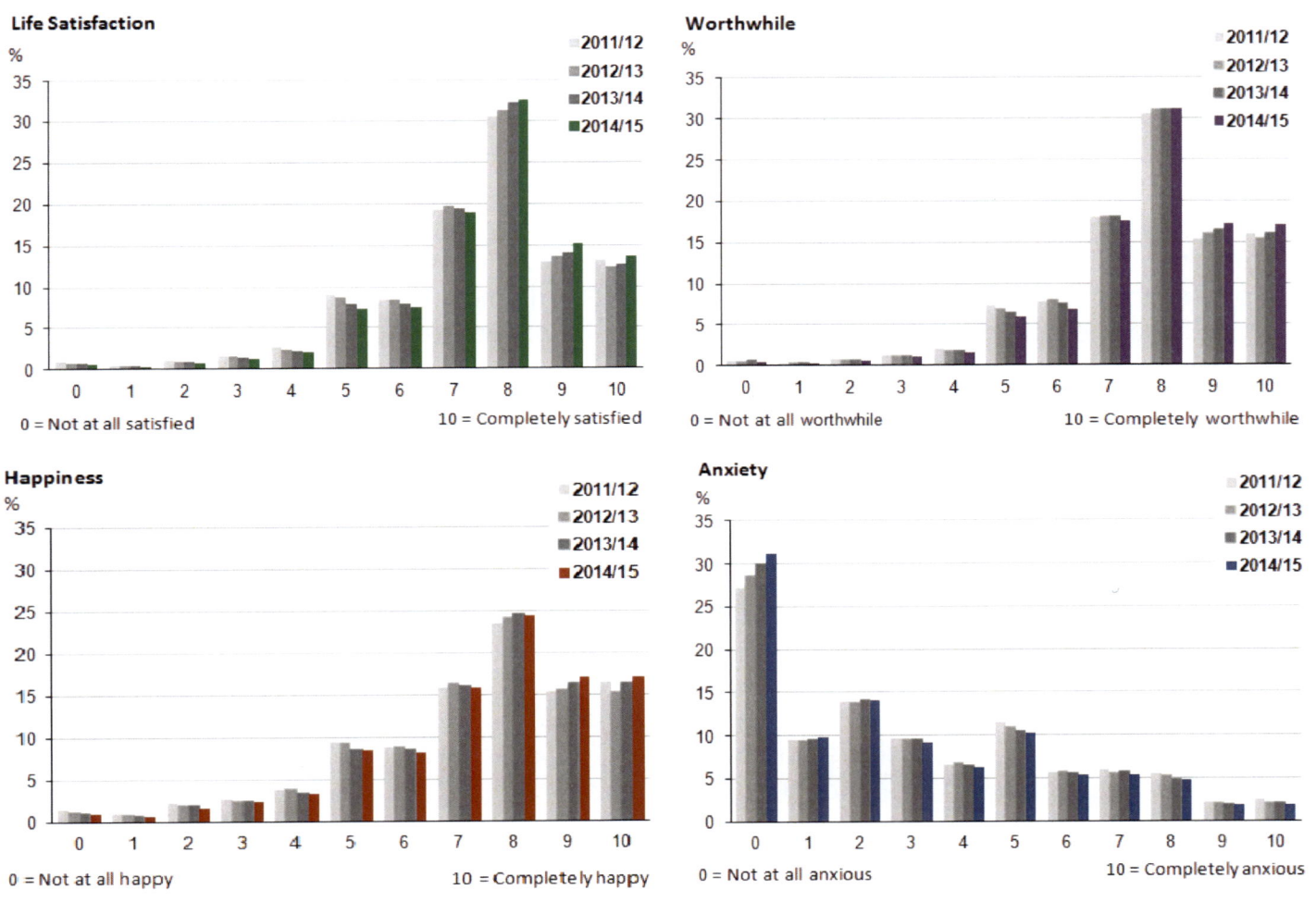

Source: Annual Population Survey (APS) - Office for National Statistics

Notes:

1. Adults aged 16 and over were asked: "Overall, how satisfied are you with your life nowadays?" "Overall, to what extent do you feel the things you do in your life are worthwhile?" "Overall, how happy did you feel yesterday?" "Overall, how anxious did you feel yesterday?" Where 0 is "not at all" and 10 is "completely"
2. Please click on the image to view a larger version

Download chart

XLS XLS format
(32 Kb)

People in the UK tend to rate their life satisfaction, feeling that what they do in life is worthwhile and happiness at the high end of the scale. This indicates that people tend to answer towards the end of the 0-10 scale for these measures. People most commonly rated each of these questions at 8 out of 10. A higher proportion rated their life satisfaction and feelings that what they do in life are worthwhile at 8 out of 10 (just over 30% in each case) than rated their happiness levels this way (just under 25%).

The pattern for how people rate their anxiety is different to the other questions. For the anxiety question the scale is reversed as a score of 10 out of 10 indicates the highest possible anxiety, and a score of 0 out of 10 indicates the lowest possible anxiety. Compared to the other 3 measures, a much higher proportion of people rate their anxiety at the lower end of the scale (as 0 or 1), but more also rate their anxiety levels in the middle of the scale (as 5 out of 10). In each year, the majority of people rated their anxiety at a low level between 0 and 3. The most common response was 0 out of 10, which indicates that they felt "not at all anxious" on the previous day.

This pattern of personal well-being ratings in the UK has been fairly consistent for each of the 4 years with small (but statistically significant) increases emerging year-on-year.

3.3 Average ratings of personal well-being in the UK

Average ratings of personal well-being are a simple way to make comparisons over time. The average ratings for each of the 4 measures of personal well-being in the financial year ending 2015 compared with the previous year:

*   life satisfaction was 7.6 points out of 10 (up 0.10 points)
*   feeling that what one does in life is worthwhile was 7.8 out of 10 for (up 0.08 points)
*   happiness yesterday was 7.5 out of 10 (up 0.08 points)
*   anxiety yesterday was 2.9 out of 10 (down 0.07 points)

The latest estimates suggest improvement in the past year in the average ratings of personal well-being in the UK across all of the measures. The year-on-year differences are small but statistically significant in each case.

Comparing the latest average estimates with those from financial year ending 2012, there have also been small but significant improvements in personal well-being across all 4 measures (as shown in Figure 2).

Figure 2: Change in average annual UK personal well-being ratings between the financial year ending 2012 and 2015

United Kingdom

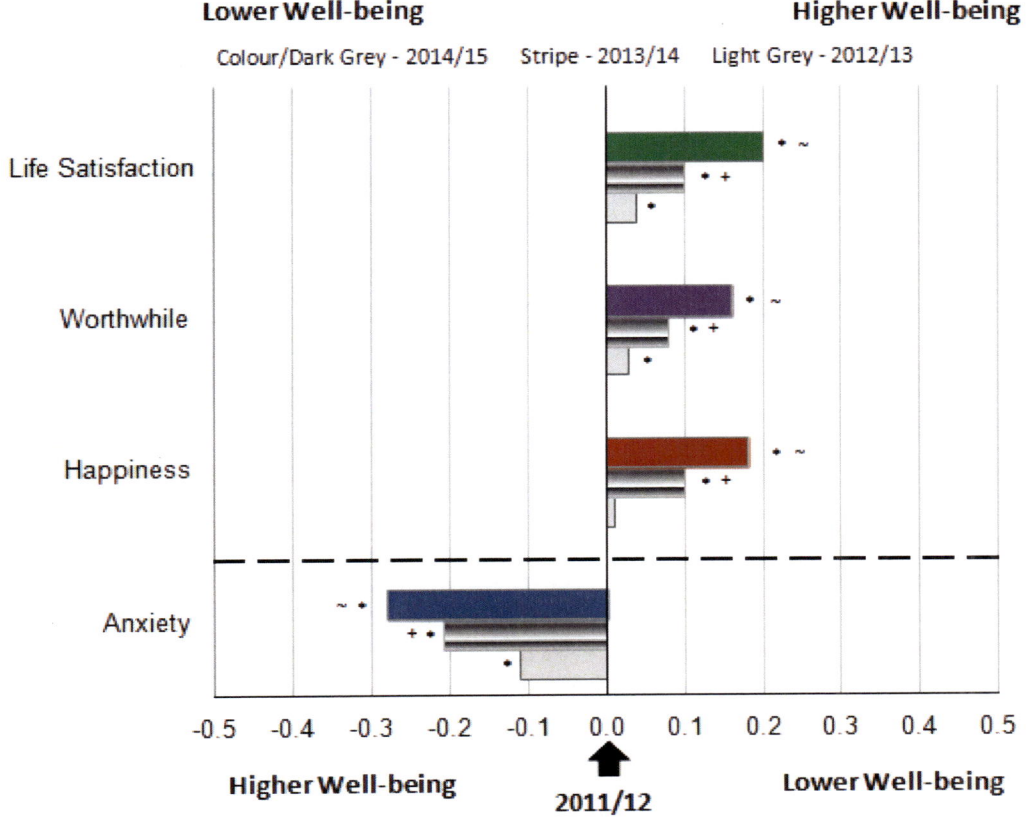

Source: Annual Population Survey (APS) - Office for National Statistics

Notes:

1.   * Indicates a statistically significant difference from 2011/12 at the 0.05 level.
2.   + Indicates a statistically significant difference from 2012/13 at the 0.05 level.
3.   ~ Indicates a statistically significant difference from 2013/14 at the 0.05 level.

Download chart

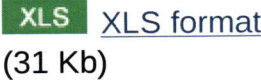 XLS format
(31 Kb)

The continued significant improvements in the UK are interesting, especially when viewed in the context of Eurobarometer estimates for the UK for life satisfaction which have shown proportions with high life satisfaction to be broadly stable over 35 years but with similar increases in recent years (Cabinet Office, 2014).

3.4 Highest and lowest personal well-being in the UK

Average ratings of personal well-being provide a useful summary, but do not tell the whole story. An important consideration is whether the proportions of people in the UK who rated their personal well-being at the highest and lowest levels in financial year ending 2015, compared to financial year ending 2014, and financial year ending 2012 has changed over time. This helps us to see whether the overall improvement in average personal well-being has resulted from increases in people reporting personal well-being at the highest levels, and/or reductions in the proportions of people reporting personal well-being at the lowest levels. In other words, this helps us to understand if improvements in personal well-being are a result of raising the ceiling and or lifting the floor. This is important as it has implications for how equal the distribution of personal well-being is in society.

3.4.1 Measuring "highest" and "lowest" personal well-being

The highest levels of personal well-being for life satisfaction, worthwhile and happiness are defined as ratings of 9 or 10. For reported anxiety, ratings of 0 or 1 are used, because lower levels of anxiety suggest better personal well-being. On the other hand, lowest levels of personal well-being are defined as ratings of 0 to 4 for life satisfaction, worthwhile and happiness. For reported anxiety, ratings of 6 to 10 are used, because higher levels of anxiety suggest lower personal well-being. It is particularly important to look at concentrations of low levels of personal well-being over time so that policy makers can target and measure interventions designed to reduce the proportions of people with low levels of personal well-being.

3.4.2 Highest and lowest personal well-being in the UK, financial year ending 2015

Figure 3 shows the percentages of people in the UK reporting the highest and lowest levels of well-being in financial year ending 2015 and how this has changed since financial year ending 2012.

The reported highest and lowest well-being for financial year ending 2015:

- 28.8% rated their life satisfaction at the highest levels compared to 4.8% at the lowest
- 34.4% rated their sense that what they do in life is worthwhile at the highest levels, compared to 3.8% at the lowest
- 34.1% rated their happiness at the highest levels, while 8.9% rated their happiness at the lowest
- 40.9% rated their anxiety at the lowest levels, while 19.4% rated it at the highest levels

Figure 3: Percentages rating personal well-being at highest and lowest levels, financial years ending 2012 to 2015

United Kingdom

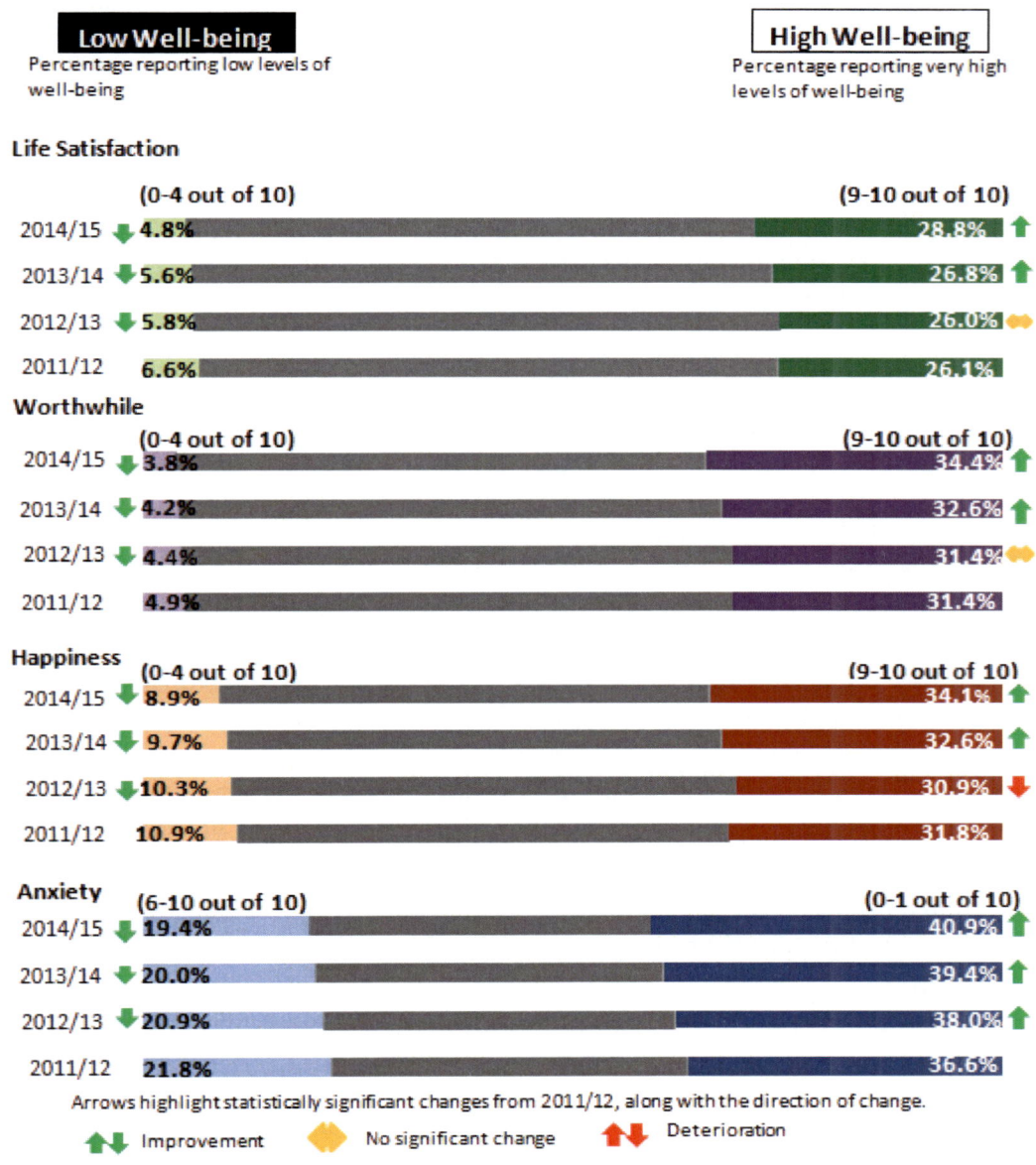

Source: Annual Population Survey (APS) - Office for National Statistics

Download chart

XLS XLS format
(30 Kb)

3.4.3 Changes over time in highest and lowest personal well-being in the UK

The proportion of people giving the highest ratings for each aspect of personal well-being increased significantly in financial year ending 2015 compared to the previous year. The biggest changes in percentage points were for life satisfaction (up 2.0) and worthwhile (up 1.9) .This suggests that more people in the UK are feeling positive about their lives, and is consistent with the higher average ratings of personal well-being noted in the previous section.

This positive picture is also reflected in significant decreases in the proportions of people reporting low well-being across all 4 measures between financial year ending 2015 and the previous year, although the changes are smaller than for the increases in the proportions of people giving the highest ratings.

Looking at how ratings have changed over the 4 year period, there have been statistically significant gains in the proportions of people reporting very high personal well-being for each of the 4 measures in financial year ending 2015 compared to financial year ending 2012, particularly for improvements in low levels of anxiety.

3.5 Possible reasons for the personal well-being patterns observed in the UK

The latest picture of personal well-being, similar to findings last year, is of more positive well-being across all of the 4 measures in financial year ending 2015 compared to both financial year ending 2014 and financial year ending 2012, when we started to collect personal well-being data. This improvement appears to have resulted more from the proportions of people reporting the highest levels of personal well-being growing, than by reductions in people reporting low levels of personal well-being. This is important as it has implications for how equal the distribution of personal well-being in society is, and suggests growing inequality in reported personal well-being.

This is only the fourth year we have collected personal well-being data, so it is too early to identify definite trends over time. However, one reason for the overall small improvement in personal well-being over the past year may be the economic outlook in financial year ending 2015 compared with financial year ending 2014. ONS economic data shows that unemployment has been on a downwards trend since the beginning of 2013 and fell to 5.5% in the 3 months to March 2015 (ONS 2015a). Our research (ONS 2013b) and academic sources (Blanchflower et al, 2013) has shown that unemployment has a negative effect on personal well-being, therefore this finding is to be expected.

Additionally, research into personal well-being has found that "periods of rapid change...are often associated with drops in happiness" (Graham et al., 2015). It could be that the rapid changes that occurred with the economic downturn in 2008 - 2009 were being felt more strongly in financial year ending 2012, and the greater stability in financial year ending 2015 could be one of the reasons for an improvement in personal well-being over this period. Looking at the 4 measures since financial year ending 2012, the biggest improvement has been for anxiety. However, as personal well-being data was not collected prior to the economic downturn it is not possible to determine with accuracy the effect of the downturn on personal well-being measures.

Looking at the 4 countries of the UK (see section 4) and English regions (see section 5), we can see that not all countries and regions are seeing the positive improvements to personal well-being at the same rate, and some areas have improved more than others. For example, Wales was the only

UK country that did not have any significant positive improvements in average personal well-being between financial years ending 2014 and 2015 across any of the measures.

In some English regions the proportion of people reporting very low well-being remained largely static between financial years ending 2014 and 2015. For example, the North East and Yorkshire and The Humber were the only 2 English regions with no significant improvement in low levels of well-being across 2 out of the 4 measures (see section 5.4).

One possible reason for the slower improvement in personal well-being for some areas could be differing economic situations, for example, from February to April 2015 unemployment in the UK was highest in the North East at 7.4%, and second highest in Yorkshire and The Humber at 6.9% (ONS, 2015b).

The North West was the English region that had the largest average improvements for life satisfaction, worthwhile and happiness when comparing financial year ending 2015 and financial year ending 2014. During the financial year ending 2015 there has been discussion about the 'Northern Powerhouse' proposal to boost economic growth in the North of England. It could be that this proposal has contributed to a feeling of optimism in the North West.

The West Midlands had the largest average improvements in average life satisfaction, worthwhile and happiness between financial year ending 2012 and financial year ending 2015. The West Midlands had the third largest percentage point decrease in the unemployment rate (those aged 16 and over) between financial years ending 2012 and 2015 compared to the other English regions (ONS 2015c). HMRC data shows that the West Midlands was the region with the largest increase in the value of exports between the first quarter of 2012 and the first quarter of 2015 (HMRC 2015) which as well as potentially contributing to reducing unemployment, may have contributed to improved feelings of optimism.

Between the financial years ending 2012 and 2015 average reported anxiety levels have decreased the most in London, although London, jointly with the North East, still has the highest reported average anxiety of all the English regions and countries of the UK.

4. Personal well-being across UK countries

This section examines the latest findings on personal well-being across UK countries.

4.1 Average reported personal well-being in UK countries

Figure 4 shows the latest average ratings of personal well-being across the UK countries and how they compare to the UK averages.

In financial year ending 2015:

- Northern Ireland had the highest average reported rating for life satisfaction in the UK (7.9 out of 10), and was the only country to be significantly higher than the UK average
- Wales was the only country to have reported significantly lower life satisfaction than the UK as a whole (7.55 compared with 7.61)[1]

- Northern Ireland was the only country where reported average ratings for worthwhile (8.1), were significantly above the UK average; Wales was the only country where average reporting ratings for worthwhile were significantly below UK average (UK 7.82, Wales 7.77)[1]
- Northern Ireland had highest average reported happiness (7.8), and again, was the only country where this measure was significantly higher than the UK average
- Average reported anxiety in England and Wales was the same as the UK average at 2.9, both Scotland and Northern Ireland had slightly lower average anxiety at 2.8; although none of the 4 countries had a significantly different average anxiety compared to the UK as a whole
- Northern Ireland had the highest reported personal well-being for 3 out of the 4 measures; Wales had the lowest reported average for 3 out of the 4 measures

Figure 4: Average personal well-being ratings compared to UK averages: by country, financial year ending 2015

United Kingdom

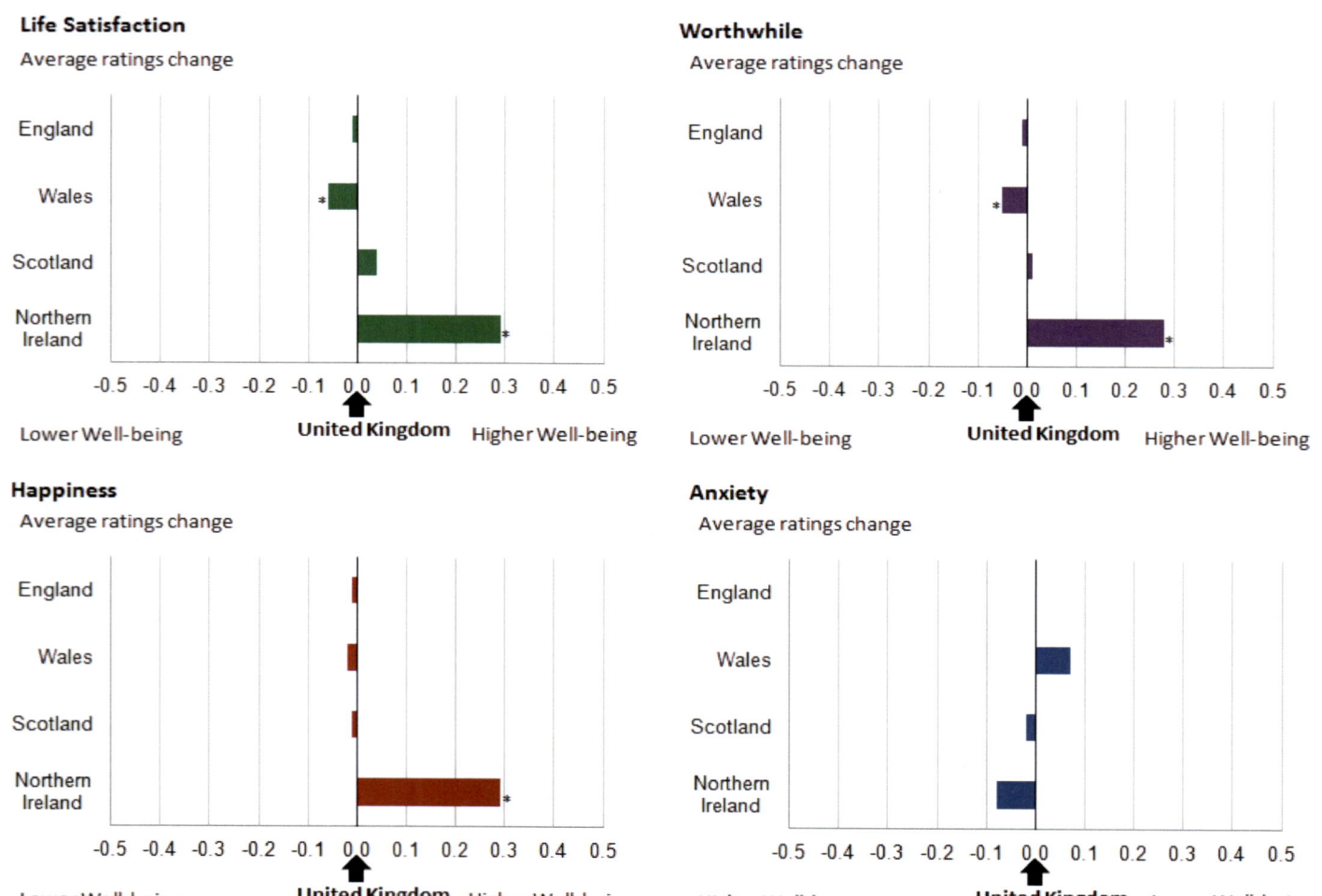

Source: Annual Population Survey (APS) - Office for National Statistics

Notes:
1. * Indicates a statistically significant difference determined on the basis of non-overlapping confidence intervals.
2. Please click on the image to view a larger version

Download chart

4.2 Changes over time in average reported personal well-being in the UK countries

When comparing the latest average estimates for each country to the previous year's estimates, as shown in Figure 5, important points include:

- England, Scotland and Northern Ireland all had significant improvements in the average estimates for life satisfaction
- England and Scotland had significant improvements in ratings for the things that we do in life being worthwhile and for happiness
- England was the only country with significant reductions in anxiety levels
- Wales was the only country that did not have any significant positive improvements between financial year ending 2015 and the previous year across any of the measures

The average ratings of personal well-being in Wales did not improve between financial year ending 2014 and financial year ending 2015. However, Wales reported the greatest improvements across the UK in the preceding period, financial year ending 2013 to financial year ending 2014, for all personal well-being measures except anxiety.

Since financial year ending 2012, when we first collected the personal well-being data, there have been statistically significant improvements across all of the measures and in each of the UK countries. This is to be expected given the overall improvement in personal well-being for the UK as a whole during this period.

Figure 5: Annual change in average UK personal well-being ratings compared from the financial year ending 2012, by country

United Kingdom

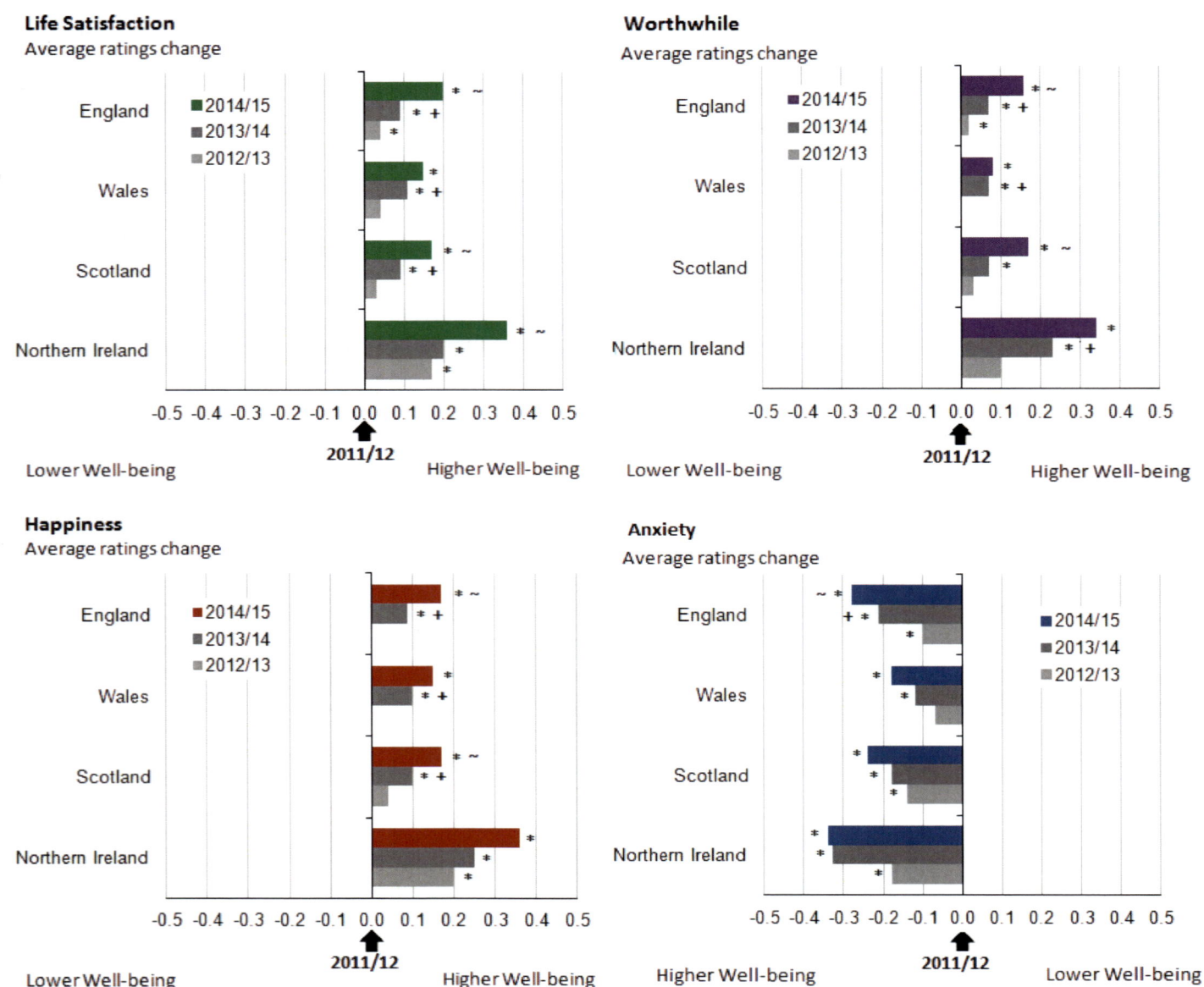

Source: Annual Population Survey (APS) - Office for National Statistics

Notes:

1.   * Indicates a statistically significant difference from 2011/12 at the 0.05 level.
2.   + Indicates a statistically significant difference from 2012/13 at the 0.05 level.
3.   ~ Indicates a statistically significant difference from 2013/14 at the 0.05 level.
4.   Please click on the image to view a larger version

Download chart

XLS XLS format
(36.5 Kb)

4.3 Highest and lowest ratings of personal well-being across UK countries

This section provides the latest estimates of the proportions of people in each country reporting the highest and lowest levels of personal well-being.

Concentrations of highest well-being across the UK countries in the financial year ending 2015:

- In financial year ending 2015, England, Scotland and Wales all had similar proportions of people reporting the highest levels of life satisfaction, and happiness
- England and Wales had similar proportions of people reporting a very high sense that the things that they do in their lives are worthwhile, while Scotland had a significantly lower score than the equivalent proportion for the UK as a whole
- Northern Ireland had the highest percentages of people rating their life satisfaction, sense that the things they do in their lives are worthwhile and happiness as very high; it was the only country that had significantly higher proportions to the equivalent proportion for the UK for life satisfaction, worthwhile and happiness, for example, 45.0% of people in Northern Ireland rated the things they do in life as worthwhile as a 9 or 10, compared to 34.4% in the UK as a whole

Concentrations of lowest well-being across the UK countries in the financial year ending 2015:

- Wales was the only country with significantly higher proportions of people with lower life satisfaction, lower sense that the things they do in their lives are worthwhile as well as higher proportions of people reporting high levels of anxiety compared to the UK average

4.4 Changes over time in highest and lowest personal well-being across the UK countries

Comparing the latest estimates of highest well-being for each country to the financial year ending 2014 estimates:

- all countries, except Scotland, had significant increases in the proportions of people reporting very high life satisfaction
- England and Scotland had significant increases in the proportions of people reporting a very high sense that the things that they do in life are worthwhile
- England and Scotland had significant increases in the proportions of people reporting very high happiness
- England was the only country that had an increase in the proportions of people reporting very low anxiety compared with financial year ending 2014

Comparing the latest estimates of lowest well-being for each country to the financial year ending 2014 estimates:

- For England and Northern Ireland the proportions of people reporting very low life satisfaction between financial year ending 2014 and financial year ending 2015 had significantly reduced
- England was the only country which had a significant reduction in the lowest ratings for people's sense that the things we do in life are worthwhile, happiness, and anxiety

This is interesting as it suggests that the improvements in average scores, particularly for Scotland and Wales, have resulted more from an increase in people reporting very high personal well-being, than by a decrease in people reporting low well-being.

Since financial year ending 2012, when we first collected well-being data, there have been changes in the lowest and highest personal well-being ratings in each UK country (as shown in Figure 6). These changes include:

- England, Wales and Northern Ireland all had significant improvements in the proportions of people reporting very high life satisfaction
- all countries, except Wales, had a significant improvement in the proportions of people rating the things that they do in life are worthwhile as very high
- all countries had significant improvements in the proportions of people reporting very high happiness and very low anxiety

Changes in the proportions of people reporting lowest well-being since the financial year ending in 2012:

- the proportions of people rating life satisfaction and happiness as very low had significantly reduced in all 4 countries
- the proportions of people reporting that their sense that the things they do in life are worthwhile at the lowest levels significantly reduced for all countries except Wales
- the proportions of people reporting very high anxiety significantly reduced for all countries except Northern Ireland, however, it should be noted that Northern Ireland has had the lowest proportions of people reporting high anxiety for each year since financial year ending 2012 compared to England, Scotland and Wales

Figure 6: Percentages rating personal well-being at highest and lowest levels, by country

Comparing the financial year ending 2012 and the financial year ending 2015, United Kingdom

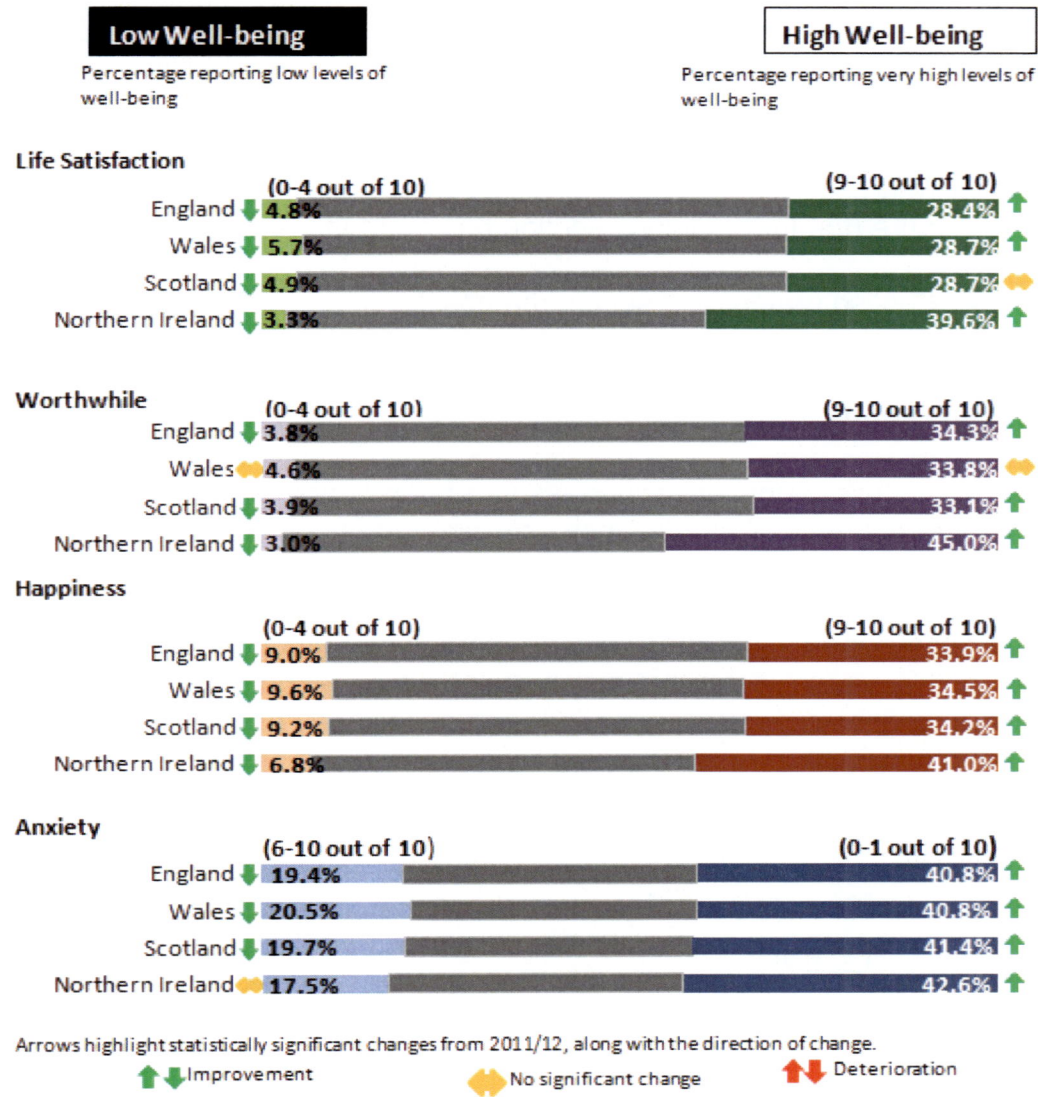

Source: Annual Population Survey (APS) - Office for National Statistics

Download chart

 XLS format
(35 Kb)

Notes for 4. Personal well-being across UK countries

1. Displayed to 2 decimal places to show difference.

5. Personal well-being in the English regions

This section focuses on personal well-being across the English regions in financial year ending 2015 and changes over time. Our previous analysis (ONS 2013c) found that a range of characteristics relating to individuals and where they live, the region where they live in, and whether they live in an urban or rural area are related to personal well-being. However, the effect is not as strong as other aspects of life, such as employment situation or health, for example. As the differences between regions may not be statistically significant, comparisons are made between each region and the equivalent UK figure. They are commented on only where there is a statistically significant difference between the regional and the UK figure (the Methodology section has more information).

As discussed in section 3.5 not all English regions are seeing the positive improvements to personal well-being at the same rate, and some areas have improved more than others.

5.1 Average personal well-being ratings in the English regions

The average reported ratings across the regions for each measure of personal well-being in financial year ending 2015 are shown in Figure 7, as well as how they compare to the UK averages. Regions where reported average ratings were significantly above the UK averages include:

- the South West and South East reported significantly higher average ratings of life satisfaction (both 7.7), additionally the South East was the only English region which reported significantly higher sense that things they do in life are worthwhile (7.9) and happiness (7.5)
- the West Midlands was the region with the lowest levels of reported average anxiety (2.6)

Regions where average ratings were significantly below the UK averages include:

- London and Yorkshire and The Humber had the lowest reported life satisfaction (7.5), London was among the lowest for people reporting a low sense that things we do in life are worthwhile, along with the North East (7.7)
- the North East, North West and London reported significantly lower happiness ratings than the UK average
- the North East, London, and Yorkshire and The Humber reported significantly higher anxiety levels

Figure 7: Average personal well-being ratings compared to UK averages: by English region, financial year ending 2015

United Kingdom

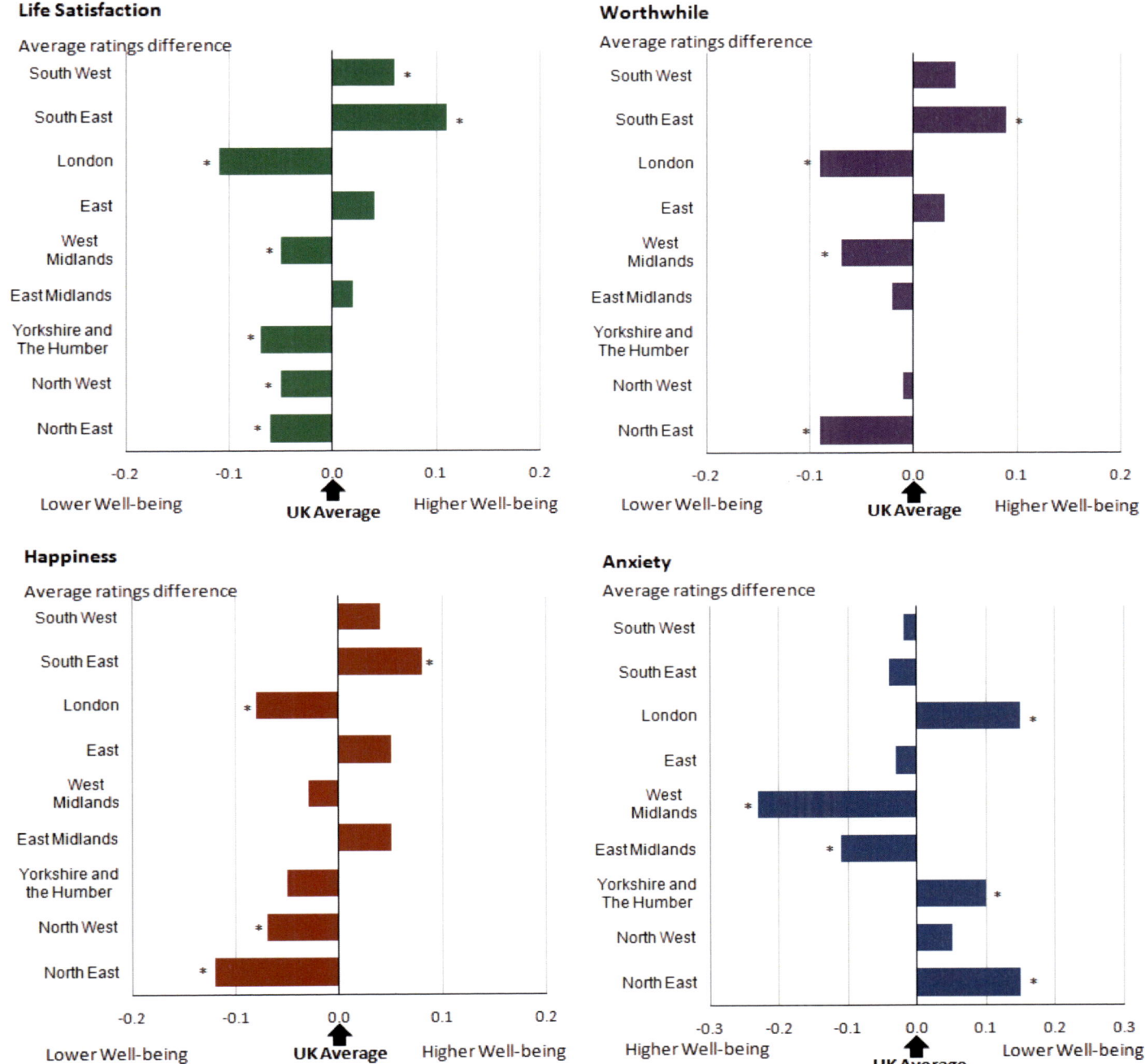

Source: Annual Population Survey (APS) - Office for National Statistics

Notes:

1. * Indicates a statistically significant difference determined on the basis of non-overlapping confidence intervals.

2. Please click on the image to view a larger version

Download chart

XLS XLS format
(100 Kb)

5.2 Changes over time in average personal well-being ratings in the English regions

Comparing the latest average estimates for each region to the financial year ending 2014 estimates:

- the North West had the biggest reported improvement for average life satisfaction, worthwhile and happiness
- all regions except Yorkshire and The Humber had a significant improvement in average life satisfaction ratings
- all regions except the North East, East Midlands and the West Midlands had significantly improved average ratings for the things we do in life being worthwhile
- for average happiness the picture was more mixed with 5 out of the 9 English regions reported a significant improvement in happiness levels including: the North West, East Midlands, East of England, South East and South West; there was no significant improvements for London, the West Midlands, Yorkshire and The Humber and the North East
- only the East of England and London reported significant reductions in average ratings for anxiety; London had the largest reduction, although it has one of the highest average anxiety levels overall

The only 4 regions where positive changes were not seen for at least 2 out of the 4 measures were the North East, West Midlands, East Midlands and Yorkshire and The Humber.

Since financial year ending 2012, when we first collected these data, all of the English regions have reported significant increases in life satisfaction, happiness and worthwhile, and reductions in average anxiety. This is to be expected given the overall improvement in personal well-being in the UK as a whole. The region which has seen the biggest average improvement for life satisfaction, worthwhile and happiness was the West Midlands. People in London reported the biggest reduction in average anxiety levels over this period.

Figure 8: Annual change in annual average personal well-being ratings, by region, between the financial years ending 2012 and 2015

United Kingdom

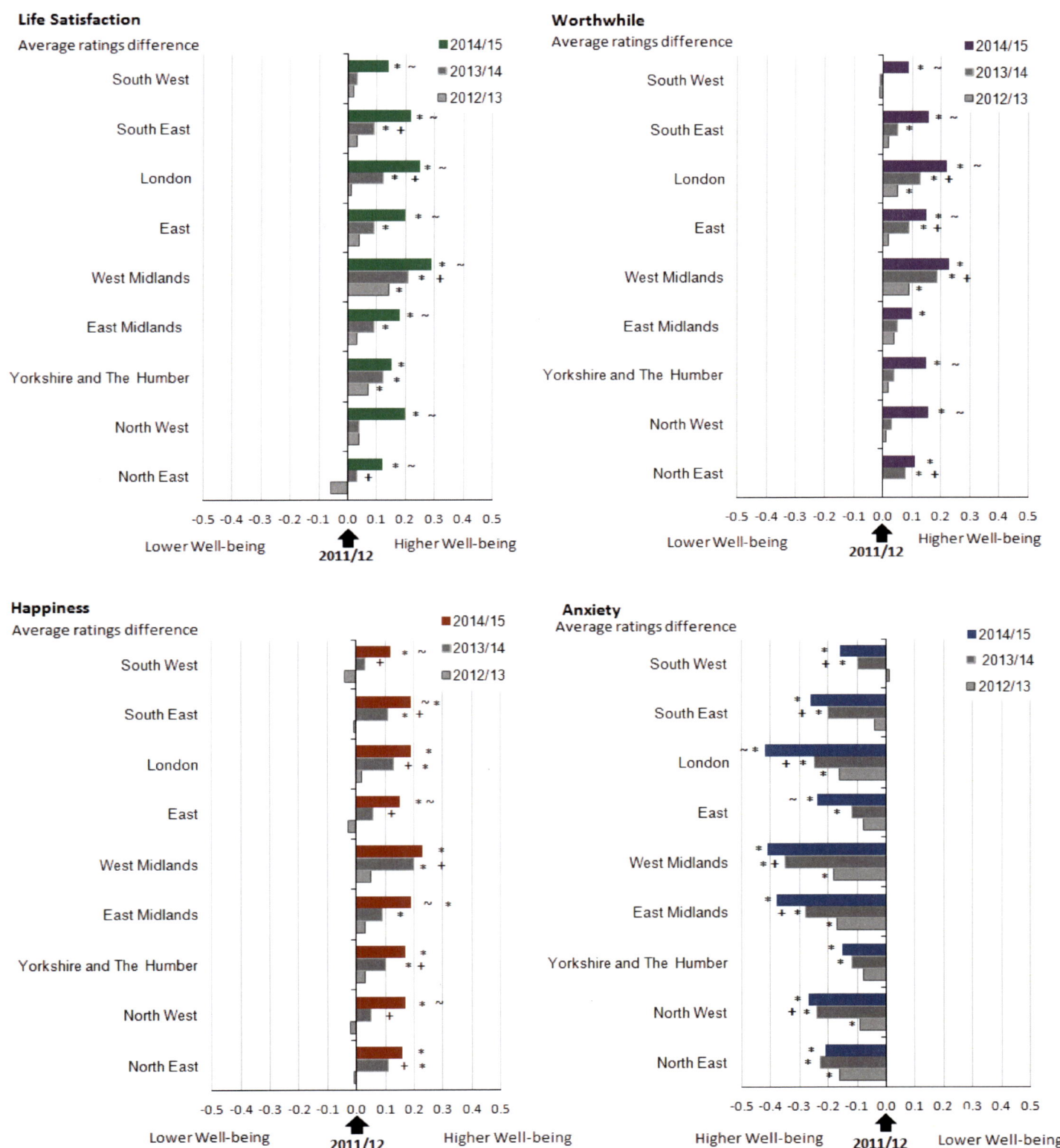

Source: Annual Population Survey (APS) - Office for National Statistics

Notes:

1. * Indicates a statistically significant difference from 2011/12 at the 0.05 level.
2. + Indicates a statistically significant difference from 2012/13 at the 0.05 level.
3. ~ Indicates a statistically significant difference from 2013/14 at the 0.05 level.
4. Please click on the image to view a larger version

Download chart

XLS XLS format
(39.5 Kb)

5.3 Highest and lowest personal well-being in the English regions in the financial year ending 2015

This section considers whether the highest and lowest reported personal well-being is spread evenly across the regions or whether highest and lowest well-being are concentrated in certain areas.

The percentages of people in each region reporting the highest well-being in financial year ending 2015 is shown in Map 1 and the lowest reported well-being shown in Map 2. These maps also show the direction of changes in the estimates since financial year ending 2012.

The concentrations of highest levels of reported personal well-being across the English regions, compared the UK as a whole, are:

*   the South East was the only region with a significantly higher proportion of people reporting very high life satisfaction compared to the UK
*   the North West and Yorkshire and The Humber had a significantly higher proportion of people reporting a very high sense that the things that they do in their lives are worthwhile compared to the UK as a whole
*   only the East Midlands had a significantly higher proportion of people reporting very high happiness compared to the UK as a whole
*   the East Midlands and West Midlands were the only 2 regions that reported statistically significantly higher proportions of people reporting low anxiety

This also shows that the patterns of high well-being across the UK differ for each of the 4 measures.

Map 1: Percentages rating personal well-being at highest levels: by English region for financial year ending 2015 and change since financial year ending 2012

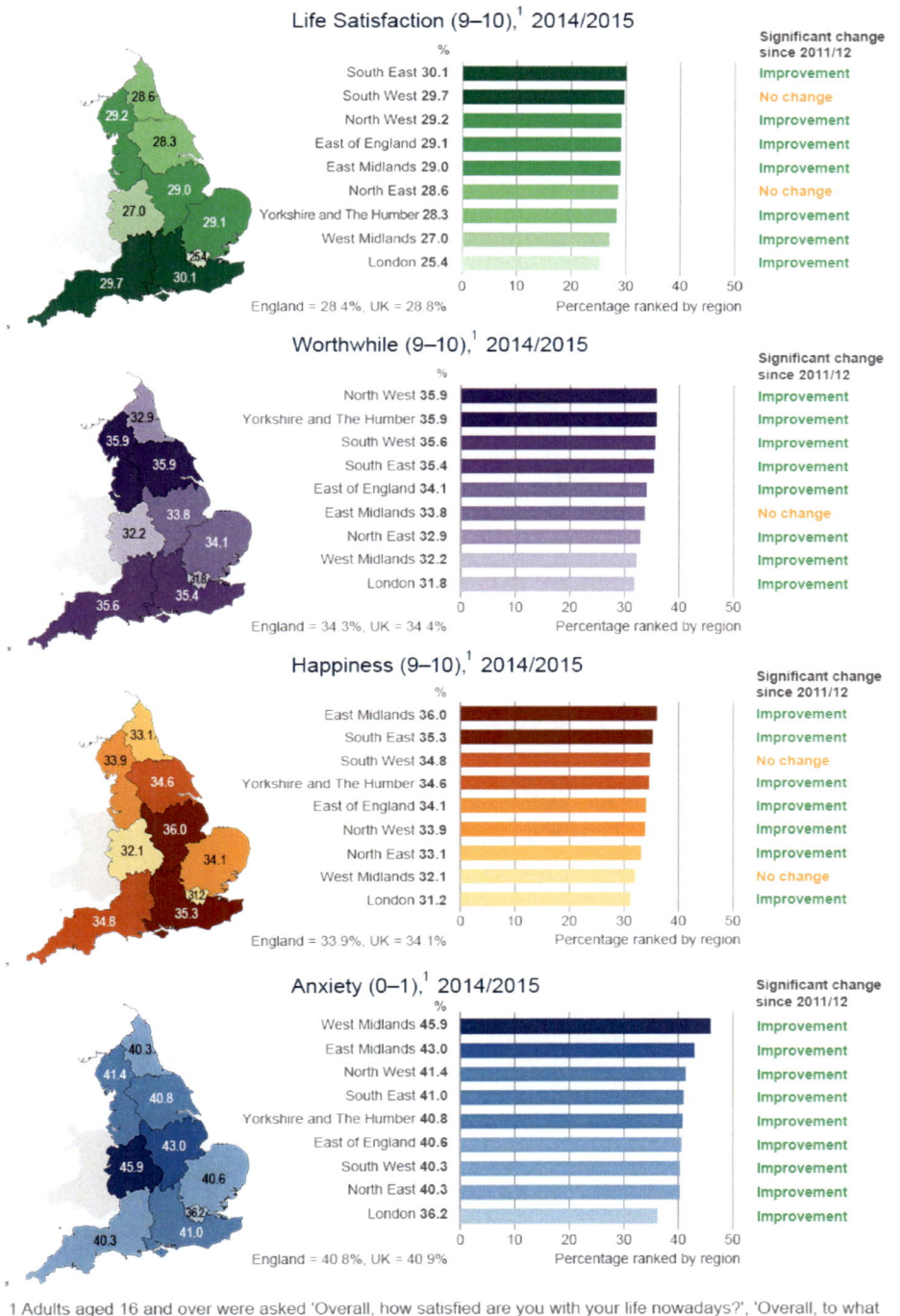

1 Adults aged 16 and over were asked 'Overall, how satisfied are you with your life nowadays?', 'Overall, to what extent do you feel the things you do in your life are worthwhile?', 'Overall, how happy did you feel yesterday?' and 'Overall, how anxious did you feel yesterday?' where 0 is 'not at all' and 10 is 'completely'.

Source: Office for National Statistics licensed under the Open Government Licence v.3.0.
Contains OS data © Crown copyright and database right 2015

Source: Annual Population Survey (APS) - Office for National Statistics

Notes:

1. Adults aged 16 and over were asked:

    "Overall, how satisfied are you with your life nowadays?"

"Overall, to what extent do you feel the things you do in your life are worthwhile?"

"Overall, how happy did you feel yesterday?"

"Overall, how anxious did you feel yesterday?"

Where 0 is "not at all" and 10 is "completely"

2.   Please click on the image to view a larger version

Download map

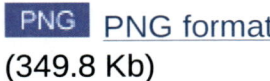 PNG format
(349.8 Kb)

The concentrations of the lowest levels of reported personal well-being across the English regions, compared to the UK as a whole, are:

*   the North East, North West and Yorkshire and The Humber all had significantly greater proportions of people reporting very low life satisfaction, happiness and high anxiety, only the South East had a significantly lower proportion of people reporting very low life satisfaction and happiness
*   the North East and North West also had greater proportions of people reporting low ratings for sense that what they do in life is worthwhile, while again the South East and also the East of England had lower proportions of people reporting low worthwhile compared to the UK as a whole
*   only the West Midlands had a significantly lower proportion of people reporting high anxiety compared to the UK figure

Map 2: Percentages rating personal well-being at lowest levels: by English region financial year ending 2015 and change since financial year ending 2012

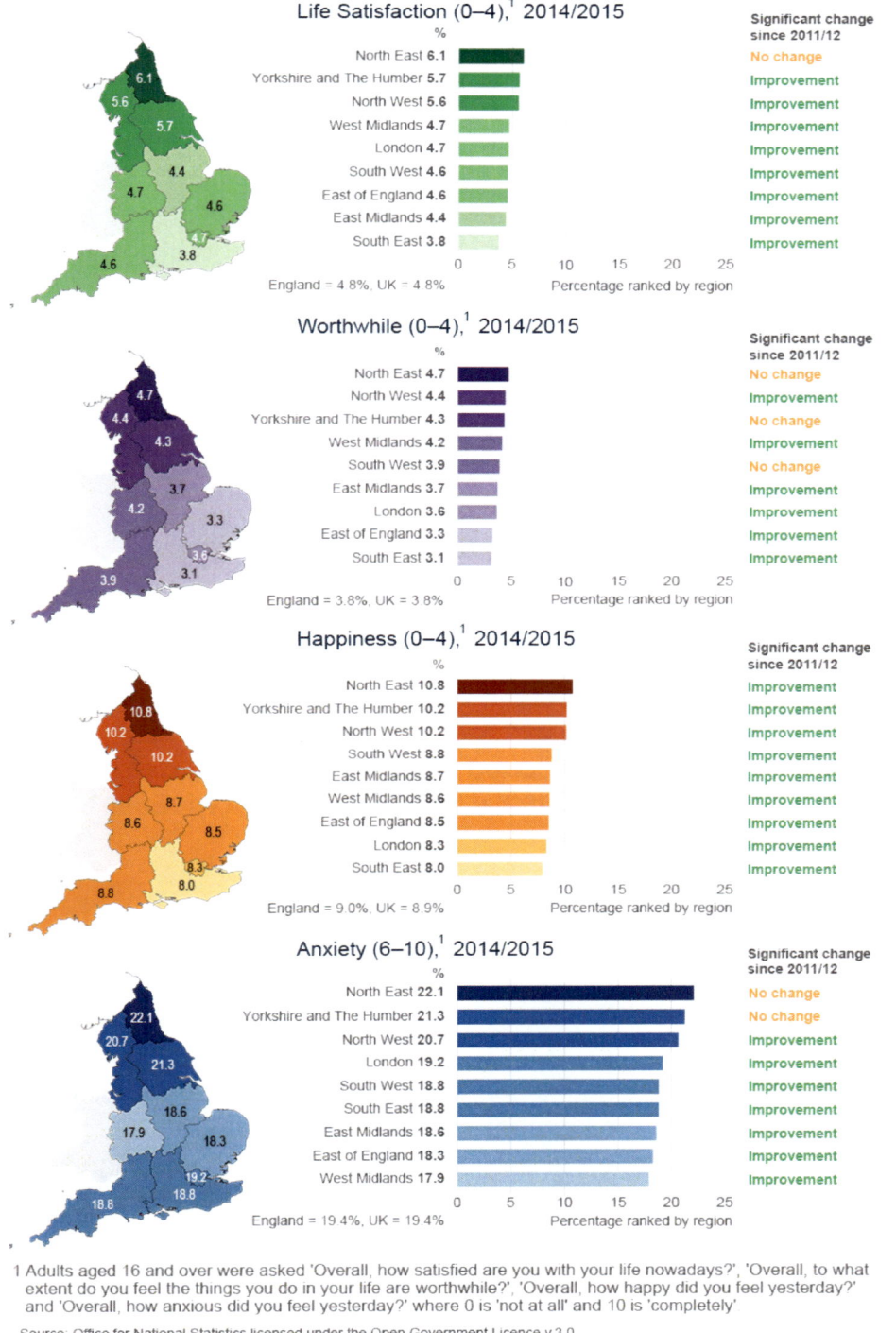

Life Satisfaction (0–4),[1] 2014/2015

%

Region	%	Significant change since 2011/12
North East	6.1	No change
Yorkshire and The Humber	5.7	Improvement
North West	5.6	Improvement
West Midlands	4.7	Improvement
London	4.7	Improvement
South West	4.6	Improvement
East of England	4.6	Improvement
East Midlands	4.4	Improvement
South East	3.8	Improvement

England = 4.8%, UK = 4.8%   Percentage ranked by region

Worthwhile (0–4),[1] 2014/2015

%

Region	%	Significant change since 2011/12
North East	4.7	No change
North West	4.4	Improvement
Yorkshire and The Humber	4.3	No change
West Midlands	4.2	Improvement
South West	3.9	No change
East Midlands	3.7	Improvement
London	3.6	Improvement
East of England	3.3	Improvement
South East	3.1	Improvement

England = 3.8%, UK = 3.8%   Percentage ranked by region

Happiness (0–4),[1] 2014/2015

%

Region	%	Significant change since 2011/12
North East	10.8	Improvement
Yorkshire and The Humber	10.2	Improvement
North West	10.2	Improvement
South West	8.8	Improvement
East Midlands	8.7	Improvement
West Midlands	8.6	Improvement
East of England	8.5	Improvement
London	8.3	Improvement
South East	8.0	Improvement

England = 9.0%, UK = 8.9%   Percentage ranked by region

Anxiety (6–10),[1] 2014/2015

%

Region	%	Significant change since 2011/12
North East	22.1	No change
Yorkshire and The Humber	21.3	No change
North West	20.7	Improvement
London	19.2	Improvement
South West	18.8	Improvement
South East	18.8	Improvement
East Midlands	18.6	Improvement
East of England	18.3	Improvement
West Midlands	17.9	Improvement

England = 19.4%, UK = 19.4%   Percentage ranked by region

1 Adults aged 16 and over were asked 'Overall, how satisfied are you with your life nowadays?', 'Overall, to what extent do you feel the things you do in your life are worthwhile?', 'Overall, how happy did you feel yesterday?' and 'Overall, how anxious did you feel yesterday?' where 0 is 'not at all' and 10 is 'completely'

Source: Office for National Statistics licensed under the Open Government Licence v 3.0
Contains OS data © Crown copyright and database right 2015

Source: Annual Population Survey (APS) - Office for National Statistics

Notes:

1. Adults aged 16 and over were asked:

    "Overall, how satisfied are you with your life nowadays?"

"Overall, to what extent do you feel the things you do in your life are worthwhile?"

"Overall, how happy did you feel yesterday?"

"Overall, how anxious did you feel yesterday?"

Where 0 is "not at all" and 10 is "completely"

2.   Please click on the image to view a larger version

Download map

 PNG format
(325.8 Kb)

5.4 Changes over time in highest and lowest personal well-being in the regions

Comparing the concentrations of highest reported personal well-being in the regions compared to financial year ending 2014:

- the regions with the largest growth in the proportion of people reporting well-being at the highest levels were: the East of England and the South East for life satisfaction, the North West, Yorkshire and The Humber and the South East for worthwhile
- for high levels of happiness the regions with the largest growth in the proportion of people reporting high levels of happiness since financial year ending 2014 were the North West and the East Midlands
- the regions that reported the biggest improvements in reported low levels of anxiety were the East Midlands and London; note that London is the region that, jointly with the North East, reported the highest average anxiety in the financial year ending 2015

Comparing the concentrations of lowest reported personal well-being to those of financial year ending 2014:

- the proportions of people reporting low levels of life satisfaction significantly reduced for all regions except for the North East, Yorkshire and The Humber and the East of England
- for the other measures of personal well-being there were only a few regions which had significant reductions in the proportions of people reporting very low well-being: for worthwhile the only region that had a significant reduction was the North West
- for happiness, the only 2 regions with significant reported reductions were the West Midlands and London
- for anxiety, the only significant reported reductions in the proportions of people reporting high anxiety were the East of England and London
- the North East and Yorkshire and The Humber were the only 2 English regions with no significant reported improvement in low levels of well-being across all 4 of the measures

It is important to look at concentrations of low levels of personal well-being over time so that policy makers can target and measure interventions designed to improve personal well-being for these groups.

There has been a greater improvement in the proportions of people reporting high well-being than reductions in people reporting well-being at the lowest levels. This reflects the pattern for the UK as a whole, as well as for the 4 UK countries.

Since financial year ending 2012, when we first collected these data, changes in concentrations of highest reported personal well-being across the regions, as shown in Map 1, include:

- significant increases in the proportions of people reporting very high life satisfaction for all regions apart from the North East and the South West
- significant increases in the proportions of people reporting very high sense that the things they do in life are worthwhile across all regions except for the East Midlands
- significant increases in the proportions of people reporting low anxiety for all regions

Of the 4 measures, anxiety is the one that has seen the most positive improvement. This could be due to greater stability in the UK economy compared to financial year ending 2012, which may have affected people's anxiety levels more than the other measures of personal well-being.

Since financial year ending 2012, when we first collected the data, changes in concentrations of lowest reported personal well-being across the regions, as shown in Map 2 include:

- significant reductions in the proportions of people reporting low life satisfaction in all English regions except the North East
- significant reductions in the proportions of people reporting a low sense that the things they do in life are worthwhile except in the North East, Yorkshire and The Humber and the South West
- significant reductions in the proportions of people reporting low levels of happiness in all regions
- significant reductions in the proportions of people reporting high anxiety in all regions except the North East and Yorkshire and The Humber

This is to be expected given the general improvements in personal well-being in the UK as a whole during this period; however, as was found in for the 4 countries of the UK, the gains in personal well-being are greater in some areas than others.

5.5 Summary of Personal Well-being in English Regions

5.5.1 Summary of Personal Well-being in the English Regions in financial year ending 2015

The South East was one of the regions with highest personal well-being, including the highest average reported life satisfaction and worthwhile, but also for the proportions of people reporting life satisfaction at the highest levels, and was the region with the highest average reported happiness.

In terms of reported anxiety, the pattern of reporting was different in the English regions compared to the other 3 measures. For example, the West Midlands was the region with the lowest average anxiety and the lowest proportions of people reporting high anxiety, but was not among the regions with the highest reported life satisfaction, sense that the things we do in life are worthwhile or happiness. This shows that it is important to capture personal well-being for all 4 measures as they capture different aspects of personal well-being.

Regions that reported 2 or more below average/low levels personal well-being across all the measures were the North East, North West, London, and Yorkshire and The Humber.

5.5.2 Summary comparison of Personal Well-being change in the English Regions between financial years ending 2014 and 2015

For change in average ratings, only the North East, West Midlands, East Midlands and Yorkshire and The Humber did not report significant improvements for at least 2 out of the 4 measures. The North East and Yorkshire and The Humber were the only 2 English regions with no significant improvement in low levels of well-being across all 4 of the measures.

The regions with the largest growth in the proportions of people reporting well-being at the highest levels were: the East of England and South East for life satisfaction, the North West, Yorkshire and The Humber and South East for worthwhile. For high levels of happiness the biggest growth in proportions were the North West and East Midlands. For anxiety the regions that reported the biggest improvements in those reporting low levels of anxiety were the East Midlands and London. This is interesting as London was one of the regions which had the highest average anxiety reported for the financial year ending 2015, and with the lowest proportions of people reporting low levels of anxiety.

Both average levels in reported personal well-being and proportions of people reporting low levels of personal well-being have remained static in some regions, despite overall improvements for the UK as a whole.

6. Personal well-being in local areas of the UK

For more local areas of the UK, the personal well-being estimates are available as interactive maps, which can be explored in a variety of ways, and in the reference tables accompanying this bulletin. The personal well-being estimates have been published for the following administrative areas in England, Scotland, Wales and Northern Ireland in the reference tables:

- unitary authorities or counties in England
- local authority districts in England
- unitary authorities in Wales
- local authorities in Scotland
- local government districts in Northern Ireland

We have also published further analysis looking at how personal well-being differs according to the characteristics of areas and the people living there (ONS, 2013b; ONS, 2014b). In 2014 we released the first combined 3 years of personal well-being data (ONS, 2015d). We will publish a rolling combined 3 year personal well-being dataset annually. This is designed to provide larger sample sizes and more robust analysis of personal well-being in local areas and among smaller population subgroups.

We would welcome feedback on this bulletin, particularly how the data are used.

Please contact us via email at: personal.well-being@ons.gsi.gov.uk or telephone Lucy Tinkler 01633 455713.

7. Uses of the data

The personal well-being statistics are used to inform decision making among policy-makers, individuals, communities, businesses and civil society. They complement other traditional measures of progress and quality of life, such as unemployment and household income. We use the personal well-being estimates as part of a wider programme to monitor and understand UK national well-being over time and in comparison to other countries.

One of the main benefits of collecting personal well-being data is that people are able to give their views about each aspect of their well-being. Without it, assumptions must be made about how objective conditions, such as people's health and income, might influence their individual well-being. However, personal well-being measures are grounded in individuals' preferences and take account of what matters most to them by allowing them to decide what is important when providing an assessment of their own quality of life.

The uses of personal well-being data are varied, but the 4 main uses are:

- overall monitoring of national well-being
- use in the policy making process
- international comparisons
- public decision making

7.1 Overall monitoring of national well-being

Collected regularly, personal well-being data can provide an indication of how the well-being of a nation is changing. To get a full picture of national well-being we believe it is important to use this information to supplement existing objective information. After extensive public consultation we have identified different aspects (or domains) of well-being that sit alongside the personal well-being domain. These include:

- health
- our relationships
- what we do
- where we live
- personal finance
- education and skills
- the economy
- the environment
- governance

The [National Well-being wheel of measures](#) includes indicators for all these.

7.2 Use in policy making

Personal well-being data, within the framework of wider measures of national well-being, focuses on how people think and feel about their lives. This is an important addition to official statistics, helping policy makers understand how their decisions may affect people's quality of life. Personal well-being data is increasingly being used both in the UK and internationally in the development and evaluation of policies and services. These include:

- in 2015 the airports commission assessed personal well-being around airports to inform it's recommendations on airport expansion;
- the Cabinet Office has recently released results analysing personal well-being in areas where social action projects have been running.
- the What Works Centre for Well-being released personal well-being results by occupation and this is being used to develop a new careers application for young people.
- the Behavioral Insights Team recently evaluated the personal well-being of young people participating in Youth Social Action trials compared to control groups.

The What Works Centre for Well-being was launched in October 2014. They aim to encourage greater use of well-being data among decision makers by making it easy to understand and use in practical ways.

7.2.1 Identifying need and targeting policies

The large sample size of the Annual Population Survey (APS) Personal Well-being dataset allows for comparisons between different groups of the population (for example, different age groups or different ethnic groups) and between different areas in the UK (for example, countries, regions and local authority districts). This can help policy-makers target policy at the groups or areas with highest need in terms of personal well-being.

Analysis can also be carried out to look at how different circumstances relate to personal well-being and which are most strongly associated with it. This can help to identify which policies could be most effective in improving personal well-being. In May 2013 we published analysis looking at What matters most to personal well-being? ([ONS, 2013b](#)) which identified health, relationship status and employment status as the factors most highly associated with personal well-being in the APS. Our recent publications have also looked at relationships between commuting and personal well-being ([ONS, 2014c](#)), household income and expenditure ([ONS, 2014d](#)), and aspects of where we live ([ONS, 2014b](#)).

7.2.2 Policy appraisal

Another use is in cost-benefit analysis for policy appraisal. Personal well-being estimates can provide an alternative method to value the costs and benefits of different policies. This process could also help inform decisions about what forms of spending will lead to the largest increases in personal well-being ([Dolan et al, 2011 (99.8 Kb Pdf)](#)).

The Green Book is HM Treasury's guide for government departments on the appraisal of the costs and benefits of projects through social cost-benefit analysis. A Green Book discussion paper (Fujiwara and Campbell, 2011), produced jointly by HM Treasury and the Department for Work and Pensions, looks at the potential uses of personal well-being measures in social cost-benefit analysis. Another recent example of the use of personal well-being data in this area has been to produce a method for the monetary valuation of volunteering (Fujiwara et al, 2013).

7.2.3 Examples of use of personal well-being data for policy evaluation and monitoring

Personal well-being data are increasingly being used to evaluate and monitor the effectiveness of policy interventions in the UK. A recent example is the National Citizen Service, the reported personal well-being of young people before and after their participation in the service was evaluated. The results compared people's reported personal well-being before and after participation in the programme and found statistically significant increases. The well-being of participants' also improved compared to a control group of similar people who had not participated in the programme. As well as government interventions, other civil society and third sector interventions could be evaluated in a similar way. Added to this, looking at policies through a "well-being lens" and using data to inform, not only the formulation of policy, but also how policy could be better implemented with people's well-being in mind is also important. The Social Impacts Taskforce (SITF), comprising of senior analysts from across government, has been working to make use of personal well-being data and share approaches and findings across government. The Cabinet Office has also convened a cross-Whitehall steering group of senior policy makers to encourage the consideration of well-being in policy.

Separate initiatives to investigate well-being are being undertaken by the devolved governments. These include: the National Performance Framework, which forms part of the "Scotland performs" initiative and the recently published Analysis of subjective well-being in Wales: Evidence from the Annual Population Survey. These initiatives reflect the specific needs of the countries they represent.

Most UK government departments are actively engaged in well-being research in some way, particularly analysis of personal well-being data. This explores how people's ratings of their personal well-being are associated with particular policy areas including housing, crime, adult learning, sport, culture, volunteering and health.

Further information, including examples of how personal well-being data are being used in the policy process, is available in recent government evidence submitted by the Cabinet Office to the UK Parliament's Environmental Audit Committee as part of their inquiry on well-being,

Well-being Policy and Analysis is also available; this report provides updated information about well-being work across Whitehall (including use of our personal well-being questions and data in evaluations, surveys and specialised data exploration tools).

7.3 International developments to monitor well-being

The benefit of understanding where the UK is placed compared to other nations is another important reason for the collection of personal well-being data. There are increasing calls from international organisations, such as Eurostat (the Statistical Office of the European Union) and the Organisation for Economic Cooperation and Development (OECD), to develop national personal well-being estimates and increasing recognition internationally that this should be included in official data collection. Eurostat (the Statistical Office of the European Union) have started to collect personal well-being statistics from member states as part of the European Statistics on Income and Living Conditions (EU-SILC) in an ad-hoc well-being module in 2013. Eurostat's Quality of Life Indicators, currently being developed, will also include personal well-being information to supplement objective information already collected across Europe.

The OECD has also published guidance on the measurement of subjective well-being, which we have contributed to (OECD, 2013).

8. Methodology

8.1 The APS Personal Well-being dataset

The data analysed in this bulletin are from the Annual Population Survey (APS) Personal Well-being dataset, covering the period April 2014 to March 2015. ONS will release a new annual APS Personal Well-being dataset every year, soon after the publication of the latest Personal Well-being in the UK statistical bulletin in September. The dataset includes responses to the four ONS personal well-being questions as well as a range of other variables useful for the analysis of personal well-being. Also, special weighting is included in the dataset to make the data representative of the UK population. The weighting also adjusts for the fact that each respondent must answer the questions for themselves, with no one else in the household allowed to answer on their behalf. Estimates for 2014/15 have been weighted using population totals from the 2011 census. Estimates from previous years were weighted to population totals from the 2001 census. This difference may impact estimates but it is impossible to quantify and is likely to be small.

Since 2012, the annual version of the APS Personal Well-being dataset has been archived so that approved researchers can use the data for their own analysis. Further details of how researchers can access the data are available from our Frequently Asked Questions page or by contacting the Personal Well-being Team: personal.well-being@ons.gsi.gov.uk.

8.2 The ONS personal well-being questions and their development

The ONS personal well-being questions were developed as part of the Measuring National Well-being Programme. ONS sought advice from experts working in the field of subjective well-being (see Dolan et al, 2011 (99.8 Kb Pdf)) and consulted with specialists on the National Statistician's Measuring National Well-being Advisory Forum and Technical Advisory Group. Based on this, as well as extensive question testing, four questions were designed. They provide a concise and balanced approach to the measurement of subjective well-being, drawing on three main theoretical approaches (Dolan et al, 2011 (99.8 Kb Pdf), ONS, 2011a (240.8 Kb Pdf)). These include:

- The 'evaluative' approach which asks people to reflect on their life and assess how it is going overall in terms of their satisfaction with life;
- The 'eudemonic' approach which asks people to consider the extent to which they feel a sense of meaning and purpose in life;

- The 'experience' approach which ask about people's positive and negative experiences and emotions over a short period of time to assess these aspects of personal well-being on a day-to-day basis.

ONS conducted focus groups with members of the public in 2013, and found that 'personal well-being' is clearer and simpler for people to understand than 'subjective well-being'. Since then, both the questions and estimates have been referred to as 'personal well-being'.

The following are the ONS personal well-being questions that have been included on the Annual Population Survey each year since 2011:

- Overall, how satisfied are you with your life nowadays? (evaluative approach)
- Overall, to what extent do you feel the things you do in your life are worthwhile? (eudemonic approach)
- Overall, how happy did you feel yesterday? (experience approach)
- Overall, how anxious did you feel yesterday? (experience approach)

All are answered using a 0 to 10 scale where 0 is 'not at all' and 10 is 'completely'.

Further information on the ONS approach to measuring personal well-being can be found in the paper 'Measuring Subjective Well-being' (240.8 Kb Pdf) (ONS, 2011a).

8.3 APS design and its implications for the personal well-being statistics

Early in the Measuring National Well-being Programme, ONS selected the Annual Population Survey (APS) as the key survey on which to include the personal well-being questions for the national estimates of personal well-being. The APS is one of the largest household surveys run by ONS and offers a very cost-effective means of measuring personal well-being in a representative way across the UK and for each UK country. Also, because of its very large sample size, it provides opportunities for analysis of the personal well-being estimates of smaller groups, such as minority ethnic groups, and across regional and local areas. These are important considerations in deciding how best to monitor the personal well-being of the nation.

Whenever including new questions on a survey originally designed for another purpose, there are some aspects of the design and coverage of the survey which present challenges. These are highlighted in this section wherever they are relevant.

8.3.1 How the APS is constructed

The APS is an annual version of the quarterly Labour Force Survey (LFS). It is constructed by combining data collected on the LFS (waves 1 and 5), and also includes data from LFS 'boost' samples in England, Wales and Scotland (all 4 waves). The APS is comprised of data collected over a 12 month period, and includes a panel element where a household, once selected for interview, is retained in the sample for a set period of time (known as 'waves'). The way the APS is constructed makes sure that no person appears more than once in the dataset. **Table 1** shows this, with all the bold text highlighting the waves contributing to the APS data between April 2014 and March 2015:

Table 1: Data structure of the APS Personal Well-being dataset, 2014/15 (1, 2)

	APS Personal Well-being dataset: April 2014 to March 2015			
	April - June 2014	July - Sept 2014	Oct - Dec 2014	Jan - March 2015
LFS cohort 1 (first sampled April - June 2013)	**Wave 5**			
LFS cohort 2 (first sampled July - Sept 2013)	Wave 4	**Wave 5**		
LFS cohort 3 (first sampled Oct - Dec 2013)	Wave 3	Wave 4	**Wave 5**	
LFS cohort 4 (First sampled Jan - March 2014)	Wave 2	Wave 3	Wave 4	**Wave 5**
LFS cohort 5 (First sampled April - June 2014)	**Wave 1**	Wave 2	Wave 3	Wave 4
LFS cohort 6 (first sampled July - Sept 2014)		**Wave 1**	Wave 2	Wave 3
LFS cohort 7 (first sampled Oct - Dec 2014)			**Wave 1**	Wave 2
LFS cohort 8 (First sampled Jan - March 2015)				**Wave 1**
LFS boost cohort 1 (first sampled April 2011 - March 2012)		**Wave 4**		
LFS boost cohort 2 (first sampled April 2012 - March 2013)		**Wave 3**		

	APS Personal Well-being dataset: April 2014 to March 2015			
	April - June 2014	July - Sept 2014	Oct - Dec 2014	Jan - March 2015
LFS boost cohort 3 (first sampled April 2013 - March 2014)		Wave 2		
LFS boost cohort 4 (first sampled April 2014 - March 2015)		Wave 1		

Table source: Office for National Statistics

Table notes:

1. LFS households are interviewed over a 5-wave period, with 3 months between interviews.
2. LFS boost households are interviewed over a 4-wave period, with 1 year between interviews.

Download table

XLS XLS format
(28.5 Kb)

8.3.2 Sample sizes and representativeness

In total, the APS personal well-being file includes responses from over 300,000 people per year, based in around 135,000 households. Unlike other questions on the APS, people are only asked the personal well-being questions directly and no one else in the household is allowed to respond on their behalf. For this reason the sample size for the APS Personal Well-being dataset is smaller than the normal APS dataset, at around 165,000 people per year. This still makes it the largest dataset in the UK to include the personal well-being questions.

The APS is a household survey, and after weighting, the APS Personal Well-being dataset provides a representative sample of adults (aged 16 and over) living in residential households in the UK. It is not representative of young people under the age of 16 nor people living in institutional settings such as nursing homes, care homes, prisons or hostels. It also does not include homeless people. It is important to acknowledge that the personal well-being of people living in these circumstances might differ substantially from that of adults living in household settings. As a result, the estimates of personal well-being from the APS can only be seen as representative of the adult population of the UK living in household settings and any generalisations should be made on this basis.

8.3.3 Data collection methods and their implications

The APS uses both face-to-face and telephone interviewing methods. These different data collection methods appear to affect how people respond to the personal well-being questions. In general, people rate each aspect of their well-being more positively when interviewed by telephone than when interviewed face-to-face by an interviewer. For example, in 2014/15, higher ratings were given on average for the life satisfaction, worthwhile, and happy yesterday questions during telephone interviews compared to face-to-face (see **Table 2**).

Table 2: Average personal well-being, by mode of interview, 2014/15

United Kingdom

		Average
	Telephone	**Face-to-face**
Life satisfaction	7.7	7.5
Worthwhile	7.9	7.8
Happy yesterday	7.6	7.4
Anxious yesterday	3.0	2.8

Table source: Office for National Statistics

Download table

XLS XLS format
(28.5 Kb)

The relationship between the mode of interview and average responses to the personal well-being questions has been examined using regression analysis to hold other possible influences on personal well-being constant. This shows the same pattern found in descriptive statistics: on average, people give more positive responses when interviewed by telephone than when interviewed face-to-face. These findings, first published by ONS in May 2013 (ONS, 2013a), are reproduced in **Table 3**.

Table 3: Effects of interview mode on ratings of personal well-being (1,2,3) after controlling for individual characteristics

Great Britain

				Coefficients
	Life satisfaction	**Worthwhile**	**Happy yesterday**	**Anxious yesterday**
Reference group: Telephone Interview[4]				
Face to Face Interview	-0.171*	-0.165*	-0.132*	0.054*

Table source: Office for National Statistics

Table notes:

1. Adults aged 16 and over were asked 'Overall, how satisfied are you with your life nowadays?', 'Overall, to what extent do you feel the things you do in your life are worthwhile?', 'Overall, how happy did you feel yesterday?' and 'Overall, how anxious did you feel yesterday?' where nought is 'not at all' and 10 is 'completely'.
2. Data from April 2011 to March 2012.
3. All data weighted.
4. The reference group for interview mode is 'telephone interviews'.
5. * shows that the relationship is statistically significant at the 5% level.

Download table

 XLS format

(28 Kb)

The findings in Table 3 indicate the size and statistical significance of the mode effects, or the extent to which people rate their well-being differently by telephone or in person. The effect is smallest for the question about anxiety yesterday which people rate 0.05 points higher on average on the 0-10 scale when interviewed face-to-face compared to telephone. The effect is greatest on ratings of life satisfaction which people rate 0.17 points lower on average when interviewed face-to-face compared to telephone. These differences are statistically significant for all four questions, implying that they are likely to be due to factors other than sampling variation.

Table 4 shows proportions of people interviewed via each method in each of the three years for which the personal well-being data are available.

Table 4: Proportions of respondents: by mode of interview, 2011/12 to 2014/15 (1)

United Kingdom

Percentage

Type of Interview	2014/15[2]	2013/14	2012/13	2011/12
Telephone	37.6	44.2	41.7	42.2
Face-to-face	62.4	55.8	58.3	57.8
Total	100.0	100.0	100.0	100.0

Table source: Office for National Statistics

Table notes:

1. Data is weighted.
2. Proportions differ from previous years due to a movement from telephone to face to face interviewing, and the greater weight given to face to face interviews.

Download table

8.3.4 Implications of mode effects for personal well-being estimates

It is challenging to account for mode effects when using statistics. As regression analysis has found mode of interview to be significant to all personal well-being measures, it is advisable to include mode of interview in any planned regression analysis using the APS Personal Well-being dataset.

In the ONS national estimates of personal well-being, the impact of mode is statistically significant. It has been roughly consistent over the period for which the data are available, suggesting that mode effects are unlikely to affect any substantive conclusions drawn.

There may be more of an impact of mode effects on comparisons between personal well-being for lower level geographical estimates. This is for two reasons: different groups may have different balances of telephone and face-to-face response; and the impact of mode may differ by area.

In general, most wave 1 interviews will be conducted face-to-face and subsequent wave interviews will be by telephone. This should lead to a roughly equal balance of face-to-face and telephone respondents for most geographic regions south of the Caledonian Canal. North of the Caledonian Canal all APS interviews are conducted by telephone. Care should therefore be taken when comparing geographies north of the Caledonian Canal to those which are south of the Caledonian Canal, and users may wish to disregard any differences between such areas which are only marginally statistically significant.

There is some preliminary evidence that the impact of mode may vary between areas, potentially introducing bias into geographical comparisons. However, this impact tends to be smaller than the standard error, implying that a difference which is statistically significant according to the published standard errors would be likely to remain if it were possible to account for the variation in mode effects (although it may no longer be significant). ONS plan to investigate this further and to make the results of further analysis available to users.

8.3.5 Topic coverage of the APS

As the APS is based on a labour market survey, it includes an extensive range of questions which are important for understanding labour market participation, many of which are also useful for the analysis of personal well-being. For example, it includes a wide range of social and demographic questions as well as items about housing, employment and education. For full details of the variables included in the APS Personal Well-being dataset, please see the survey user guide (1.01 Mb Pdf).

As interest in personal well-being data extends to the full spectrum of policy areas, ONS has also included the questions on other major surveys that it runs. It has worked collaboratively with other UK government departments and with the European statistical institute, Eurostat, to encourage wide use of the questions. A list of the surveys that currently include the questions, their broad topic coverage and how to get further information is available on our [Frequently Asked Questions](#) page or from the [Cabinet Office website](#).

8.4 How to access the APS personal well-being data

There is a range of ways in which the data are made available. A regular set of key estimates from the data are available in Excel spreadsheets published alongside the Personal Well-being in the UK statistical bulletin:

[Reference Table 1: Personal Well-being estimates geographical breakdown, 2014/15 (664.5 Kb Excel sheet)](#)

[Reference Table 2: Personal Well-being estimates change over time, 2011/12 to 2014/15 (118.5 Kb Excel sheet)](#)

[Reference Table 3: Personal Well-being estimates personal characteristics, 2014/15 (575 Kb Excel sheet)](#)

The APS Personal Well-being data are deposited with the UK Data Service (UKDS) about six weeks after the publication of the Personal Well-being in the UK statistical bulletin. It is available from UKDS in two formats:

- End User License (a fully anonymised non-disclosive set of data containing basic demographic information, available to UK and overseas academics),
- Special License versions (a more disclosive set of data, containing more detailed variables such as Unitary Authority / Local Authority, however Unitary Authority / Local Authority level data is only available for Great Britain but not for Northern Ireland. Access to this data requires Approved Researcher accreditation, and is only available to UK-based researchers).

Further information about these options and how to access the data is available from the [UK Data Service](#).

Data can also be accessed through the ONS Virtual Microdata Laboratory (VML) or through the Secure Data Service of UKDS. This is usually the way to access more detailed data with smaller sample sizes or lower levels of geography, which require access through a more secure route. Users accessing data in this format will require Approved Researcher accreditation. Overseas academics interested in this can also apply through this route but they must travel to the UK to use these facilities. Please contact either [UKDS](#) or [socialsurveys@ons.gov.uk](#) for further details.

ONS also provide the data directly to UK Civil Service statisticians and government researchers. Government analysts interested in this option should please contact ONS at: [socialsurveys@ons.gov.uk](#).

8.5 Interpreting the personal well-being estimates

8.5.1 Using average ratings versus grouped ratings

When comparing differences between average ratings of groups or areas, it must be remembered that this does not account for variability within the groups. Just because the average of sample respondents has a certain rating of personal well-being does not necessarily mean that all people with that characteristic will have that particular outcome. For example, even though women on average have higher life satisfaction than men, it is important not to infer that all women are more satisfied with their lives than men. Recent research suggests that women may tend to rate their life satisfaction as either very high or very low. This pattern of responses may be masked when using averages alone. Looking at the percentage who rate their well-being at different levels can add further insight into patterns of well-being and this is why both methods are used in this bulletin. It also helps to make clear that what is true for part of the sample with a certain characteristic is unlikely to be true for all people with that characteristic.

8.5.2 Association versus causation

The APS personal well-being data have been analysed by different personal characteristics and circumstances in the online reference tables accompanying this bulletin, but any relationships observed should not necessarily be taken to imply causation. It can only be asserted that a specific characteristic or circumstance is associated with higher or lower well-being, not that it has caused this outcome. Although some groups are more likely to give higher life satisfaction ratings on average, it may not be the particular characteristic that is causing them to rate their well-being at a higher level. There are other factors that could also influence their ratings which would need to be controlled for in a regression model, and even then causation is often difficult to infer. For example, although married people on average rate their happiness at higher levels, it is difficult to say with certainty whether marriage increases reported happiness or whether happier people are more likely to marry. Longitudinal data which tracks people's characteristics, experiences and views over time is needed to establish whether the well-being or the circumstance came first.

8.5.3 The meaning of small differences

The size of differences between ratings of personal well-being between groups of people with certain characteristics or in specific areas of the UK can appear fairly small. This is also the case for the size of year-on-year changes in the national personal well-being estimates. The personal well-being estimates in this bulletin are generally presented to one decimal place, but the estimates relating to change over time are presented to two decimal places. This is to present more clearly the direction of change over time for these estimates.

A key challenge is to determine the relevance of these changes. One theory suggests that people may have a personal set-point for well-being to which they naturally return after a positive or negative life event. This would suggest that levels of well-being may only vary within a fairly small range over time, particularly in the aggregate (Cummins, 1998; Allin and Hand, 2014, p.13).

Other research suggests that there may be some shocks from which people do not necessarily regain their previous set-point such as the death of a spouse (Dolan, Peasgood and White, 2008; Lucas et al, 2004) or that policy initiatives can affect levels of personal well-being in a sustained way (Helliwell, Layard, Sachs, 2012).

Although the size of the changes reported in this bulletin may appear small in the aggregate, they may mask larger changes in the well-being of particular groups within society or within particular areas of the UK. This is why ONS look not only at changes in average levels of personal well-being, but also in the proportions of people who rate their personal well-being as very high or very low and how this changes over time and between groups. Both are required to get a rounded picture of personal well-being in the UK and regular monitoring will help to uncover any important patterns.

8.5.4 Approaches to statistical significance

In this bulletin, when describing changes over time the term 'significant' refers to statistical significance (at the 95% level). Unless otherwise stated, the changes over time mentioned in the text have been found to be statistically significant at the 95% confidence level. Standard errors have been calculated and used in tests of statistical significance and are available in the reference tables published alongside this bulletin.

The statistical significance of differences in the estimates for a specific area of the UK and the equivalent UK estimate are approximate, and determined on the basis of non-overlapping confidence intervals. This method provides a conservative estimate of statistical significance but may result in estimates which are statistically significantly different to one another being assessed as not. The result is that some estimates which may be significantly different to the UK estimates may not be identified as such. This would tend to underestimate the differences observed in personal well-being between a country or English region, and the equivalent UK estimates.

As the personal well-being data have only been collected for three years, it is not yet possible to know how volatile the data will be over time. This makes it difficult to put the seemingly small changes reported here into a wider context which would help to shed light on how important they are. This is also a key reason why ONS do not plan to change the questions in the near future as building up a consistent time series will help interpretations.

8.6 Personal well-being question testing

A number of other methodological issues have been/ are being tested as part of a programme of work looking at how the questions perform in different circumstances (see ONS, 2011b). This involves both quantitative testing of question variations using the Opinions and Lifestyle (OPN) Survey, and qualitative testing methods in which people are asked to explain more about the way they answered the questions and why. It is important to note that, although ONS continue to test the questions they have not been changed on the APS since they were first introduced in 2011. This is to make sure a consistent time series is developed.

The Personal Well-being Team are also in contact with researchers who have used the questions in a range of different settings. Their feedback provides valuable information for ONS and other prospective users. If you have used the questions or have done analysis which could benefit others, please let us know by contacting the Personal Well-being Team at personal.well-being@ons.gsi.gov.uk. One way we intend to share the results of our question testing is via the Measuring National Well-being group of StatsUserNet. We would encourage other researchers to share their findings there as well.

The following section summarises some of the key issues looked at by ONS in the question testing to date.

8.6.1 Contextual effects

The respondent's mood and the immediate context of the interview can affect responses to evaluative questions. In a household survey context, responses to the personal well-being questions could be affected by other household members being present during face-to-face interviews. ONS have explored this issue in cognitive testing conducted in 2013 among OPN respondents. The results suggested that people may give both more positive and more negative responses to the questions depending on which other member of the household is present. In order to test this more fully, a 'flag' has been added to the OPN survey to indicate if someone else is present when a respondent is interviewed. This work is ongoing and results are expected later in the year.

Another effect of context that appears to influence responses is the day of the week on which the respondent is interviewed. Interviewing on the APS is conducted every day of the week throughout the year, but many fewer interviews are conducted on Sundays and certain public holidays. As two of the questions refer to 'yesterday', there are inevitably fewer responses relating to Saturdays, when personal well-being ratings may be different to other days of the week.

The process for identifying the day of the week on which a respondent has been interviewed is complicated. ONS are currently working on a simpler means of identifying day of the week when the interview took place so this can be added to the dataset.

The month of the year in which a respondent is interviewed may also affect responses. Preliminary evidence suggests that there may be a seasonal effect, but with only three years of data available, it is too early to be sure. This is something that ONS will continue to monitor as the time series builds.

8.6.2 Question order

Responses to personal well-being questions have been shown to be affected by earlier questions in the survey (for example, questions about health or labour market status). Prior to the introduction of the questions on the APS in April 2011, ONS carried out cognitive testing of the placement of the personal well-being questions (see: Measuring Subjective Well-being (240.8 Kb Pdf)). This suggested that the questions should be asked early in the interview, immediately after the questions on household and individual demographics. This allows time for rapport to be built up between the interviewer and respondent but does not allow questions on other topics, such as health or employment, to influence responses to the personal well-being questions. ONS advise researchers to follow this approach whenever the questions are included on surveys in order to avoid potential bias from earlier questions.

Quantitative question testing found that the order in which the personal well-being questions are asked does not significantly affect responses (Summary of results from testing of experimental subjective well-being questions). Qualitative testing showed that respondents preferred the positive questions first as they were easier to answer. ONS always include the four questions in the same order on every survey to be sure that the findings are as consistent and comparable as possible. The recommended order is:

- life satisfaction
- worthwhile
- happy yesterday
- anxious yesterday

8.6.3 Response scales

For all APS personal well-being questions, an 11 point scale is used. This ranges from 0–10 where 0 is 'not at all' and 10 is 'completely'. This means that the scales are consistent between the questions, which helps respondents to answer the questions more easily and also aids subsequent analysis. Additionally, 11 point scales are commonly used across other similar surveys, particularly internationally. The use of this type of scale will also aid comparisons with other survey findings.

Cognitive testing has suggested that people may misinterpret the scale for the anxiety question as this is the only question where a higher score suggests worse well-being. The use of show cards (which provide a visual aid of response options for respondents) has been tested on the OPN survey to see whether this helps to remind people of how the scale works for each question. The results of this work showed that while higher scores were given for the life satisfaction, happiness and anxiety questions when show cards were used, the differences were only significant for the life satisfaction and happiness questions. These results were not as expected but the sample used for this test was small. Further details are available in the paper: Summary of results from testing of experimental subjective well-being questions.

Show cards are not used on the APS and it is not feasible to use them due to interviews being conducted both face-to-face and by telephone. For this reason, we have not done any further testing of the effects of show cards on responses.

8.6.4 Question wording

ONS have used both cognitive testing techniques and split trial testing of data collected on the Opinions Survey to look at whether asking the questions in different ways may affect responses to the questions. For example, cognitive testing has suggested that the word 'anxious' may be interpreted by some people as representing severe mental distress, while 'stress' or 'worry' are more commonly used to describe daily emotions. These differences are also being tested using the OPN to see how people respond to each way of asking the question.

9. The Measuring National Well-being programme

NWB logo 2

This bulletin is published as part of the ONS Measuring National Well-being programme.

The programme aims to produce accepted and trusted measures of the well-being of the nation - how the UK as a whole is doing. It is about looking at 'GDP and beyond' and includes:

- Greater analysis of the national economic accounts, especially to understand household income, expenditure and wealth.
- Further accounts linked to the national accounts, including the UK Environmental Accounts and valuing household production and 'human capital'.
- Quality of life measures, looking at different areas of national well-being such as health, relationships, job satisfaction, economic security, education environmental conditions.
- Working with others to include the measurement of the well-being of children and young people as part of national well-being.
- Measures of 'personal well-being' - individuals' assessment of their own well-being.
- Headline indicators to summarise national well-being and the progress we are making as a society.

The programme is underpinned by a communication and engagement workstream, providing links with Cabinet Office and policy departments, international developments, the public and other stakeholders. The programme is working closely with Defra on the measurement of 'sustainable development' to provide a complete picture of national well-being, progress and sustainable development.

ONS published the third 'Life in the UK' report in March 2015, giving the latest snapshot of the nation's well-being. The next update of the National Well-being Measures data is released 29 September 2015. A summary of all the work completed during the first three years of the Measuring National Well-being Programme is available here. A full list of outputs from the Measuring National Well-being programme is available here.

Find out more on the Measuring National Well-being website pages.

Name	Phone	Department	Email
Lucy Tinkler	+44 (0)1633 455713	Measuring National Well-being	personal.well-being@ons.gsi.gov.uk

10. Further Information

Further information and guidance can be found in the various downloads available on the Personal Well-being survey user guide page. Additionally, the Personal Well-being Frequently Asked Questions page provides answers to common questions about the ONS personal well-being questions and data.

Name	Phone	Department	Email
Lucy Tinkler	+44 (0)1633 455713	Measuring National Well-being	personal.well-being@ons.gsi.gov.uk

11. References

Blackaby, D, Drinkwater, S, Jones, M, Murphy,P, Parhi, M and Robinson, C. (WISERD) (2012) An Analysis of Subjective Wellbeing in Wales: Evidence from the Annual Population Survey.

Blanchflower D.G, Bell D.N.F, Montagnoli A and Moro M. (2013) "The effects of macroeconomic shocks on well-being".

Cabinet Office (2013) Evidence to the Environmental Audit Committee.

Cabinet Office (2014) Wellbeing - Measuring 'What Matters'

Dolan P, Layard R and Metcalfe R, Office for National Statistics (2011) Measuring Subjective Well-being for Public Policy.

Eurostat (2013) Quality of Life Indicators.

Fujiwara D, Oroyemi P & McKinnon E (2013) Well-being and Civil Society; Estimating the value of volunteering using subjective wellbeing data Cabinet Office and Department for Work and Pensionsa

Fujiwara D and Campbell R, HM Treasury and Department for Work and Pensions (2011) Valuation Techniques for Social Cost-Benefit Analysis: Stated Preference, Revealed Preference and Subjective Well-Being Approaches.

Graham C, Shaojie Z and Zhang, J (2015) Happiness and Health in China: The Paradox of Progress. Global Economy and Development. Working Paper 89.

HMRC (2015) Regional Trade Statistics Second Quarter 2015.

Office for National Statistics (2011a) Measuring Subjective Well-being.

Office for National Statistics (2012) First Annual ONS Experimental Subjective Well-being Results.

Office for National Statistics (2013a) Measuring National Well-being – Personal well-being in the UK, 2012/13.

Office for National Statistics (2013b) Measuring National Well-being – What matters most to Personal Well-being?

Office for National Statistics (2013c) Personal Well-being across the UK, 2012/13.

Office for National Statistics (2014a) Personal Well-being in the UK, 2013/14.

Office for National Statistics (2014b) Measuring National Well-being – Exploring Personal Well-being and place in the UK.

Office for National Statistics (2014c) Measuring National Well-being – Commuting and Personal Well-being.

Office for National Statistics (2014d) Income, Expenditure and Personal Well-being, 2011/12.

Office for National Statistics (2015a) The Economic Review August 2015.

Office for National Statistics (2015b) Regional Labour Market, June 2015.

Office for National Statistics (2015c) Regional Labour Market, July 2015.

Office for National Statistics (2015d) Measuring National Well-being, Personal Well-being in the UK, Three Year Data 2011/2014.

Organisation for Economic Cooperation and Development (2013) Guidelines on measuring subjective well-being.

The What Works Centre for Well-being (2015) Personal wellbeing for major and sub-major Standard Occupation Codes.

Background notes

1. If you have comments on the ONS approach to measuring personal well-being and/ or the presentation of the personal well-being data, please email us at personal.wellbeing@ons.gsi.gov.uk.

2. The data analysed in this report was collected from the Annual Population Survey (APS) which is the largest constituent survey of the Integrated Household Survey. The sample size of the 12 month APS dataset is approximately 165,000 adults aged 16 and over and living in residential accommodation in the UK (England, Scotland, Wales and Northern Ireland). Data used are weighted to be representative of the population and to take account of the fact that responses made on behalf of other household members are not accepted.

3. The UK Statistics Authority has designated these statistics as National Statistics, in accordance with the Statistics and Registration Service Act 2007 and signifying compliance with the Code of Practice for Official Statistics.

    Designation can be broadly interpreted to mean that the statistics:

    *   meet identified user needs;
    *   are well explained and readily accessible;
    *   are produced according to sound methods; and
    *   are managed impartially and objectively in the public interest.

    Once statistics have been designated as National Statistics it is a statutory requirement that the Code of Practice shall continue to be observed.

4. Details of the policy governing the release of new data are available by visiting www.statisticsauthority.gov.uk/assessment/code-of-practice/index.html or from the Media Relations Office email: media.relations@ons.gsi.gov.uk

Copyright

Statistical contacts

Name	Phone	Department	Email
Lucy Tinkler	+44 (0)1633 455713	Measuring National Well-being	personal.well-being@ons.gsi.gov.uk

Issuing Body:
Office for National Statistics

Media Contact Details:
Telephone: 0845 604 1858
(8.30am-5.30pm Weekdays)

Emergency out of hours (limited service): 07867 906553

Email:
media.relations@ons.gsi.gov.uk

Office for National Statistics

4 insights into Personal Well-being

Estimates of Life Satisfaction, Worthwhile, Happiness and Anxiety from the Annual Population Survey for 2014/2015

Personal well-being measures: life satisfaction, feelings that the things we do in life are worthwhile, happiness and anxiety.

On average people in the UK rated their Life Satisfaction as 7.6 in financial year ending 2015 when measured on a scale from 0- 10. This is up 0.2 from financial year ending 2012.

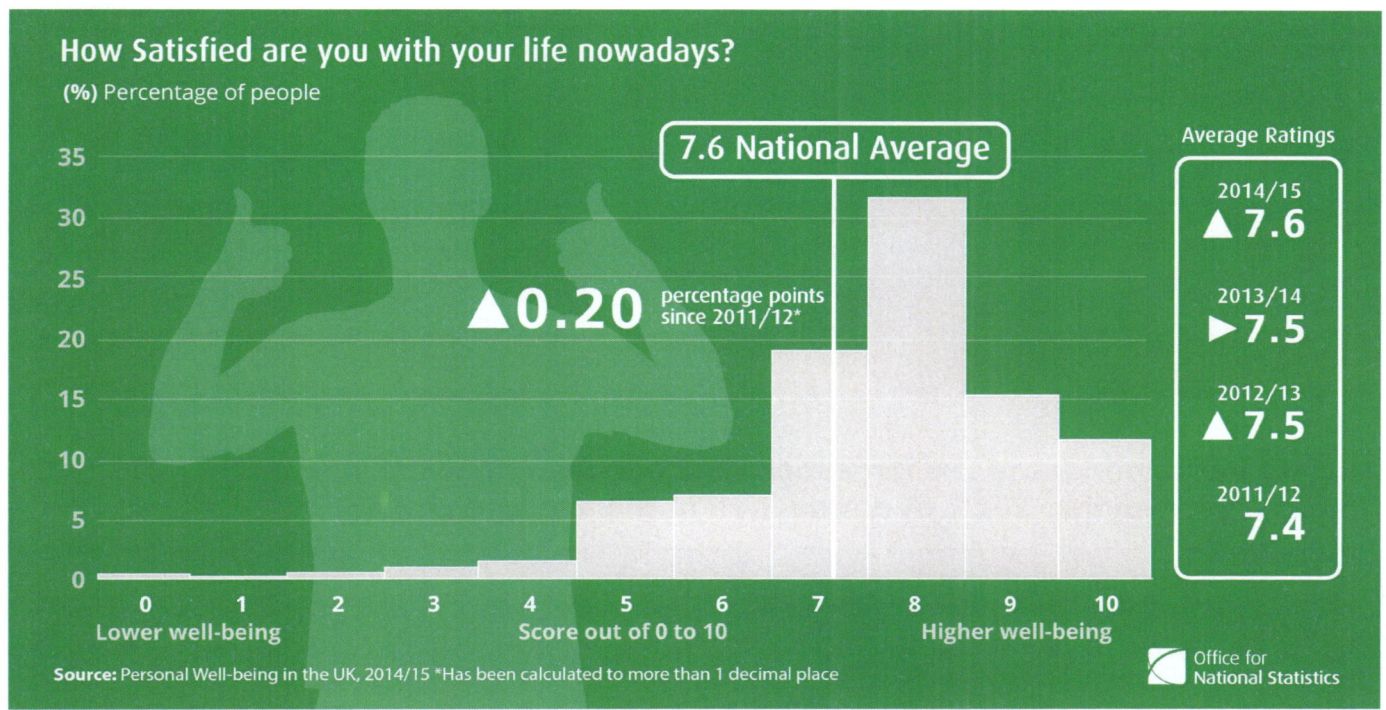

In financial year ending 2015 for the first time, the UK average rating of worthwhile has significantly increased from financial year 2012, to 7.8.

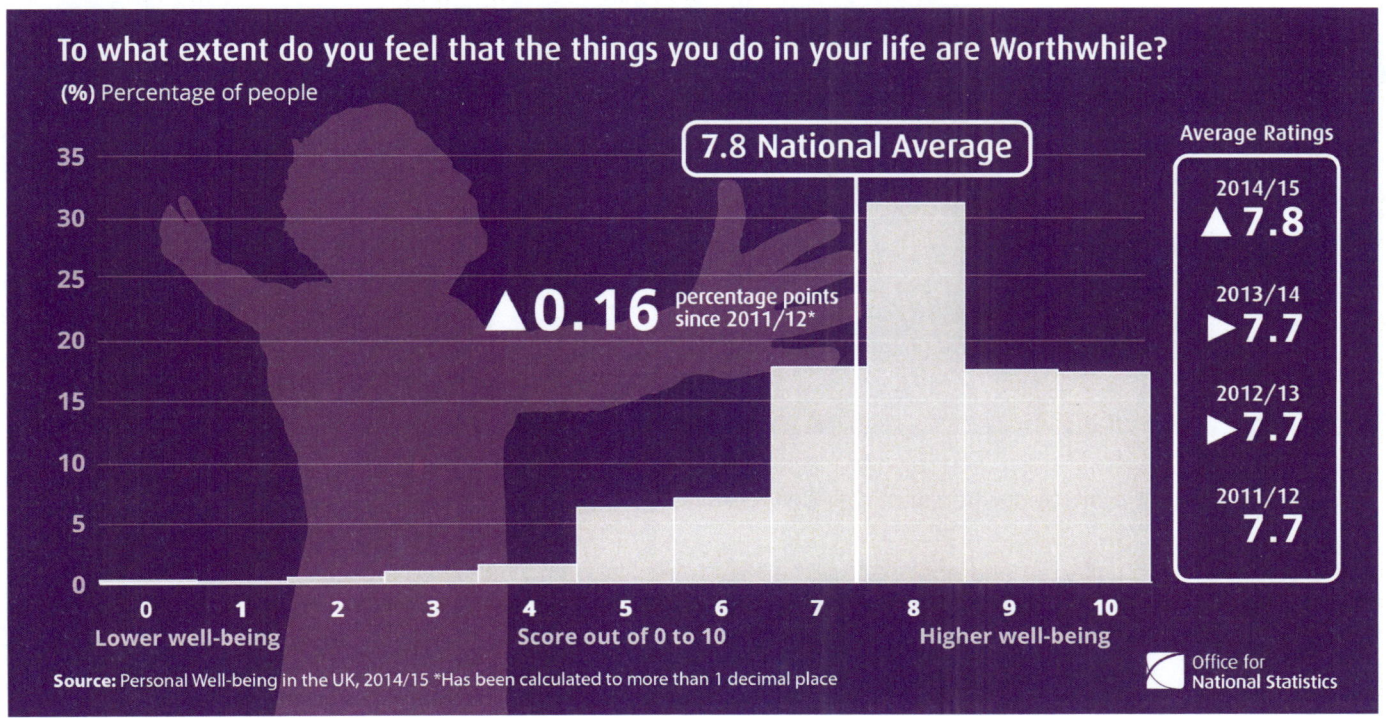

Average UK Happiness has increased by 0.18 between financial year ending 2012 and financial year ending 2015 to reach 7.5 out of 10.

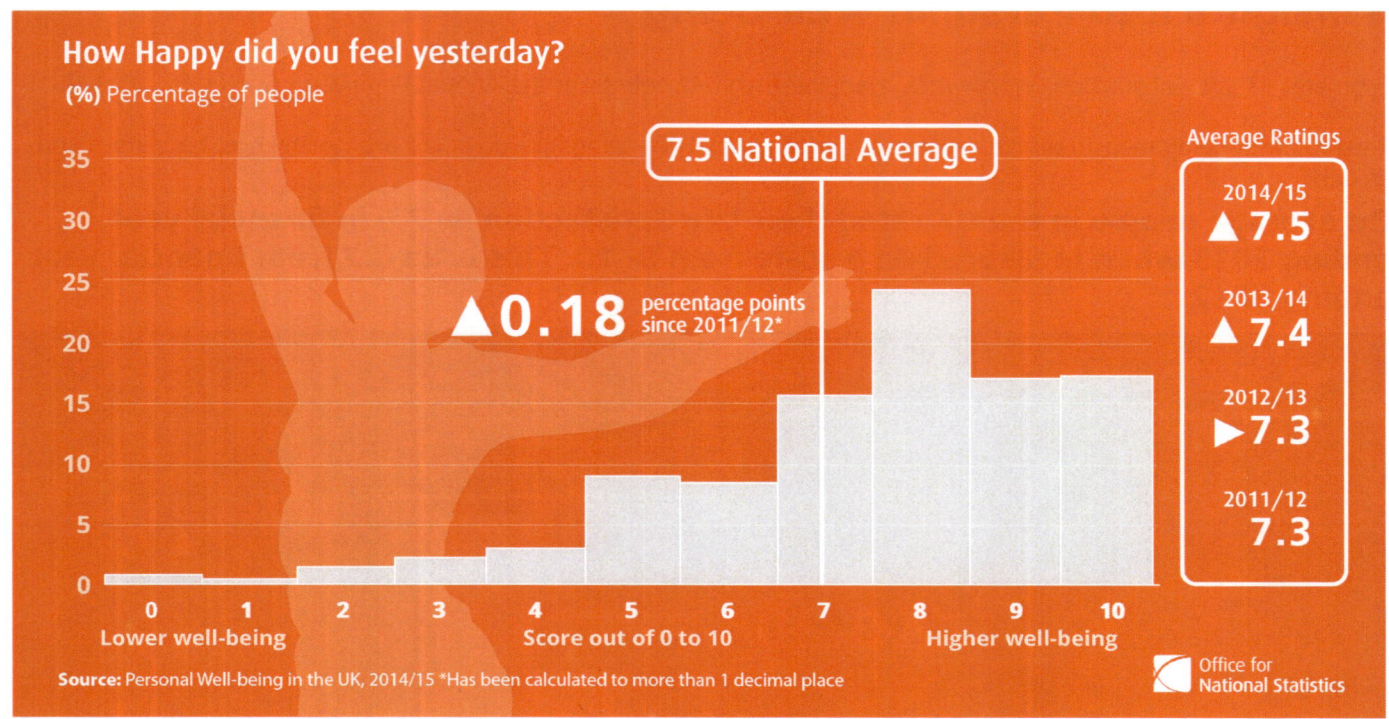

Anxiety has experienced the largest change between financial year ending 2012 and financial year ending 2015, at a reduction in the average of 0.28.

Where can I find out more about personal well-being?

These statistics were collected and analysed by the Measuring National Well-being programme at ONS. If you'd like to find out more about the latest personal well-being statistics, read Personal well-being in the UK, 2014/15 or explore the data for yourself using our interactive maps.

Office for
National Statistics

Personal Well-being and Housing Tenure

Estimates of Personal Well-being from the Annual Population Survey by housing tenure 2014/2015.

How do personal well-being ratings differ among people with different housing tenure?

The latest personal well-being estimates suggest year-on-year improvements in reported well-being in the UK since 2011/12[1], when we started to collect the data. This analysis looks at the latest data from the Annual Population Survey and focuses on UK personal well-being estimates and housing tenure[2], and changes between 2011/12 and 2014/15. The findings show that personal well-being is higher amongst those who live in owned outright households or those being bought with a mortgage or loan than those living in rented or part rent/part mortgage households and has increased significantly across all tenures except for part rent/part mortgage and rent free households since 2011/12. The findings also show significant differences in personal well-being between individuals living in private and individuals living in social renting households with social renters having the lowest well-being across all 4 measures.

Why analyse personal well-being and housing tenure?

The most common forms of housing tenure in the UK are home-ownership and renting. Home-ownership is often looked at in a positive way in the UK. It may give us more independence and financial benefits along with more security and stability. However, over the last decade there has been a fall in owner occupancy and a rise in the rented sector (ONS, 2013).

A report from the English Housing Survey 2013/14 (DCLG, 2015) showed that life satisfaction was highest among those owning a home outright and lowest amongst social renters. According to a report published by the ONS based on the Wealth and Assets survey (ONS, 2015a), there is no significant relationship between net property wealth and personal well-being of individuals living in those households. Other factors relating to housing tenure may therefore have a stronger influence on personal well-being. A study by Flakarti and Fox (1995) found poorer health and quality of life among those who rent compared with home owners. The differences in personal well-being across 5 different tenure types – 'owned outright', 'being bought with mortgage or loan', 'part rent, part mortgage', 'rented' and 'rent free' - provide the focus for below.

Personal well-being and housing tenure in 2014/15

Figure 1 shows the average ratings for personal well-being by housing tenure using the latest estimates for 2014/15. People who lived in households owned outright or being bought with a mortgage or loan had significantly higher well-being than those who lived in rented or paid part rent/part mortgage households across the 4 measures of personal well-being. There could be many reasons for this. For example, owning a home is usually cheaper over time and the opportunity for independence, greater control over living environment and financial benefits are usually associated with owning a home. Conversely, private tenants may have a short or insecure tenancy, which could make their life and finances unpredictable, while social tenants may face uncertainty from various reforms to housing benefits.

Figure 1: Average Personal Well-being ratings (1) by housing tenure, 2014/15

United Kingdom

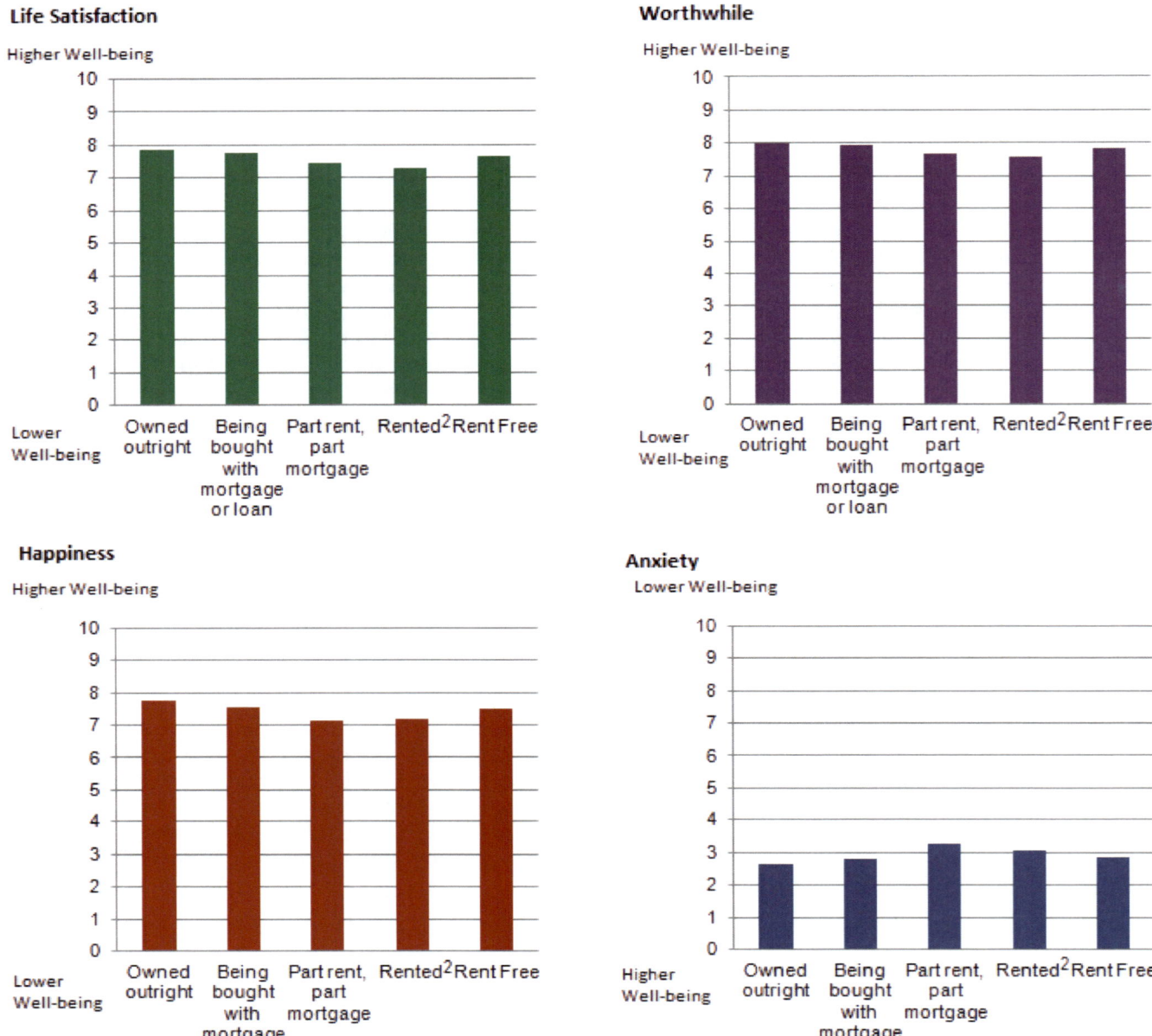

Source: Annual Population Survey (APS) - Office for National Statistics

Notes:

1. Adults aged 16 and over were asked 'Overall, how satisfied are you with your life nowadays?', 'Overall, to what extent do you feel the things you do in your life are worthwhile?', 'Overall, how happy did you feel yesterday?' and 'Overall, how anxious did you feel yesterday?' where 0 is 'not at all' and 10 is 'completely'.

2. Rented includes both private and social rented.

3. Please click on the image to view a larger version

Renting can be divided into private and social where social includes renting from:

- local authorities or council or Scottish homes

- housing association or charitable trusts or local housing company

and private includes renting from:

- an employer (employing organisation or individual employer)

- another organisation

- a relative of household member

- other individual private landlord

Individuals living in private rental households had significantly higher well-being in 3 of the personal well-being measures (life satisfaction, worthwhile and happiness) in 2014/15 than those living in social renting households. They also rated their anxiety significantly lower than social renters.

For individuals living in private rental households:

- the average rating of life satisfaction was 7.5 out of 10 compared to 7.0 out of 10 for social rental

- the average rating of worthwhile was 7.7 out of 10 compared to 7.4 out of 10 for social rental

- the average rating of happiness was 7.4 out of 10 compared to 7.0 out of 10 for social rental

- the average rating of anxiety was 2.9 out of 10 compared to 3.2 out of 10 for social rental

Changes over time

Personal well-being estimates showed small but significant improvements overall for 3 out of the 5 tenure types between 2011/12 (when data was first collected as part of the Annual Population Survey) and 2014/15. For example, the average rating of life satisfaction for individuals living in households owned outright (7.9 out of 10 in 2014/15) or being bought by a mortgage or loan (7.7 out of 10) or those who rented (either private or social) (7.3 out of 10) had increased significantly between 2011/12 and 2014/15.

However, there was no significant change for those living in part rented/part mortgaged households and those who lived rent free over the same period. This was also the case for the 3 other measures of personal well-being (worthwhile, happiness and anxiety) which are shown in Figure 2.

Reasons for these differences may be down to those in a part rent/part mortgage household finding it difficult to move to a point in time where they are no longer renting due to stagnant wage growth (ONS, 2014) which was shown until mid-2014 (ONS, 2015b) and increased rental payments (ONS, 2015c).

Figure 2: Change in average personal well-being ratings (1) by housing tenure, 2014/15

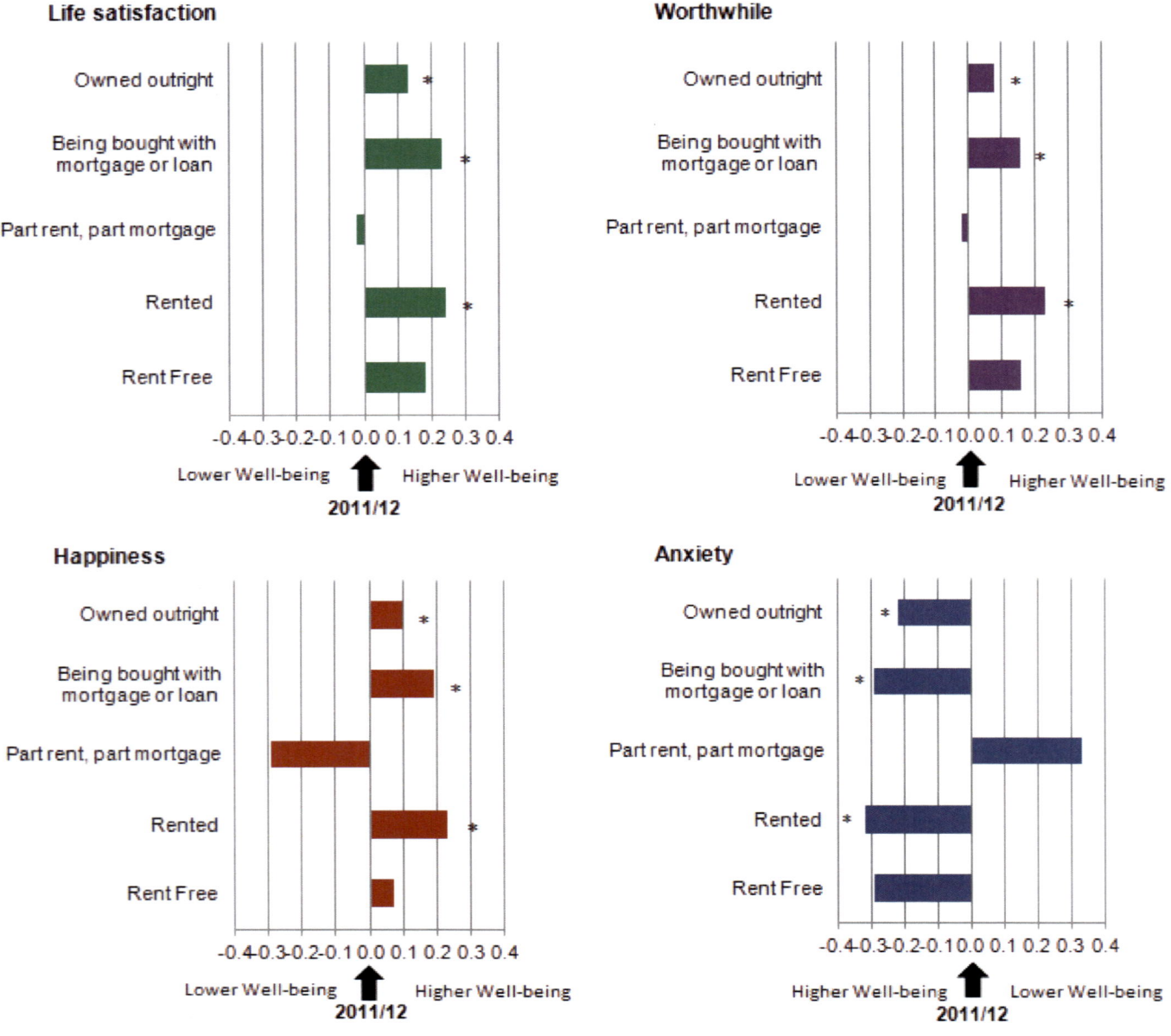

Source: Annual Population Survey (APS) - Office for National Statistics

Notes:

1. Adults aged 16 and over were asked 'Overall, how satisfied are you with your life nowadays?', 'Overall, to what extent do you feel the things you do in your life are worthwhile?', 'Overall, how happy did you feel yesterday?' and 'Overall, how anxious did you feel yesterday?' where 0 is 'not at all' and 10 is 'completely'.

2. * indicates that change was statistically significant at the 0.05 level.

It should be noted that we have not controlled for the different characteristics of each sub-group, for example, age, income or employment status. There are also likely to be different demographics for each category, for example those who owned outright are likely to be older and the current personal well-being data published alongside this report shows that those aged over 65 generally have a higher rate of well-being when compared to the UK average.

Notes for Personal Well-being and Housing Tenure

1. Throughout this story financial years are written as 2011/12. This refers to the financial year ending 2012. This convention is applied for all years.

2. Housing Tenure is a household variable and as such the tenure type of the household representative person is applied to all those that live in the household. For example should a family with children over the age of 16 live in a property owned outright by the parents, the tenure type for the children will be set as owned outright to reflect the household status, so does not reflect the fact that they personally do not own the house.

References

1. Department for Communities and Local Government (2015) English Housing Survey

2. Filakti and Fox (1995) - Differences in mortality by housing tenure and by car access. Population Trends, 81, pp.27–30

3. Office for National Statistics (2013) 2011 Census Analysis, A Century of Home Ownership and Renting in England and Wales

4. Office for National Statistics (2014) An examination of falling real wages

5. Office for National Statistics (2015a) Wealth in Great Britain Wave 3, Wealth, income and personal well-being

6. Office for National Statistics (2015b) Supplementary analysis of average weekly earnings, September 2015

7. Office for National Statistics (2015c) Index of Private Housing Rental Prices, April to June 2015 results

Office for
National Statistics

National Well-being Measures, September 2015

Abstract

Measures of national well-being are published in spring and autumn each year. Since March 2015, updates have included assessments of change – overall, indicating whether national well-being is getting better or worse; and individually, to help signpost areas which may require attention in order to bring about improvements in national well-being. This release provides the autumn 2015 update.

Introduction

Measures of national well-being are designed to help us understand how we are doing, as individuals, as communities and as a nation, and how sustainable this is for the future. They include measures of personal well-being (latest figures were published 23 September 2015), which indicate how we feel about our lives overall, but it is only through examining changes in the other areas, or "domains", of national well-being, such as health, education, where we live and the economy, that we can impact on national well-being.

We look at overall change, and whether national well-being is improving or deteriorating, as well as individual assessments of change for each of the 41 measures. While it is acknowledged that the measures are headline measures and so do not represent the complete picture for each domain, they provide a useful signpost to areas that may need further attention to improve national well-being.

Comparisons have been made with the previous year's data, or – if year on year data are not available – with the previously published figure, as well as an assessment of change over a 3 year period. In future years, as more data become available, we will publish assessments of change over a longer time series.

For the majority of measures, change is assessed based on whether 95% confidence intervals overlap. For a small number, actual change is measured, for example, the proportion of registered voters who voted. In some cases, the assessment is based on progress towards a target, or the advice of the data provider.

Summary of changes in national well-being in September 2015

Figure 1 summarises the assessments of change in measures of national well-being. These include 43 measures in total; the headline measures of healthy life expectancy and feeling safe walking alone after dark are presented for both men and women.

Figure 1: Assessments of change - National Well-being measures

September 2015

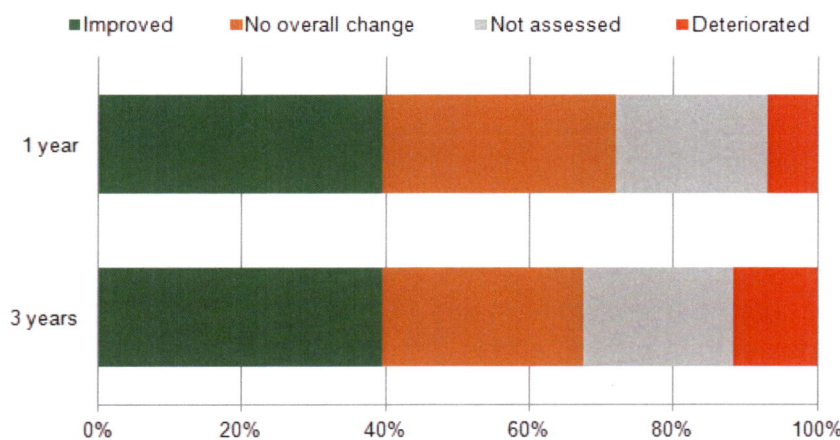

Source: Office for National Statistics

Download chart

XLS XLS format
(24.5 Kb)

Looking at the 1 year change[1]:

- 40% (17 measures) had improved
- 33% (14 measures) showed no overall change
- 21% (9 measures) were not assessed for this publication
- 7% (3 measures) had deteriorated

Over the 3 year period[1]:

- 40% (17 measures) had improved
- 28% (12 measures) showed no overall change
- 21% (9 measures) were not assessed for this publication
- 12% (5 measures) had deteriorated

Since the last assessment of change, published in March 2015:

- over both the short and long-term, 40% of measures showed an improvement
- the largest change has been in the 3 year assessment of those showing improvement, rising by 12 percentage points from 28% to 40%
- the number of measures that have deteriorated increased in the short term from 5% to 7%, but decreased in the long term from 19% to 12%
- the number of measures not assessed in the long term has fallen from 30% to 21%, this is mainly because long term assessments are now possible for the 4 personal well-being questions
- a number of measures have not been assessed, because data are not available for comparison, or where the direction of change is not a clear indication of improvement or deterioration

Notes

1. Figures may not add to 100% due to rounding.

What has changed?

A fuller picture of the changes that have occurred is available in Life in the UK, which is published in March. This publication looks at examples of change from two domains, "Governance" and "Where we live". Governance is the domain with the fewest measures, and is also the only domain where all measures have been assessed as improving over the 1 year and 3 year periods. In comparison, "Where we live" is one of two domains with 6 measures, which together are showing no clear direction of change over either the 1 year or 3 year period.

Where we live has a direct impact on our well-being. Housing costs are one of our biggest expenses – and for some, investments. However, according to a report published by the ONS based on the Wealth and Assets survey, there is no significant relationship between net property wealth and the personal well-being of individuals living in those households.

We spend a lot of time in our homes, and so how we feel about where we live is naturally important to our personal, and therefore national, well-being. In the financial year ending 2014, 89.2% of adults in England were very or fairly satisfied with their accommodation. This was a deterioration compared with the financial year ending 2013 (90.6%). Looking beyond the physical aspects of our accommodation to the area we live in, the proportion of people who feel a sense of belonging to their neighbourhood is an important factor, not only to personal well-being but also to the local community, because people are more inclined to live, work and invest in an area they have an affinity with. In the financial year ending 2012, 62.8% of adults in the UK reported that they strongly agreed or agreed that they felt that they belonged to their neighbourhood. Again, this was a deterioration compared with the previous period (financial year ending 2010, 66.0%).

High or increasing crime levels have a negative effect on local communities. This can result in residents increasing desire to move house and a weaker attachment and satisfaction with their neighbourhood. Although crime rates in England and Wales improved over the 1 year and 3 year periods, this was not reflected in measures of how safe people felt. The proportion of women who felt safe walking alone after dark improved over the 1 year period, but deteriorated over the 3 year period. The proportion of men who felt safe walking alone after dark showed no overall change. Almost 25% more males felt comfortable walking alone after dark than females (85.8% and 61.7%

respectively) in the financial year ending 2015 even though men were more likely to be victims of crime than women.

The proximity of housing to a range of services and facilities and green space could have a bearing on the satisfaction level with the area in which they live. The proportion of households with good transport access to key services in England, and the proportion of people accessing the natural environment in England at least once a week, show little or no overall change in the short term.

Governance is a contextual domain of well-being; it may not be immediately apparent how voter turnout or trust in government affects our personal well-being, but political engagement is important to our national well-being. It provides citizens with a voice and can help shape government activities, which in turn help build strong and resilient communities.

Voting is the most prominent form of political participation and, for many people, it is the only engagement with politics that they have. In the General Election of 2015, 66.2% of those aged 18 and over in the UK voted, an improvement on both the 2010 (65.1%) and 2005 (61.4%) elections. Trust in, and accountability of, the national government was one of the main concerns reported during the National Well-being debate. In the spring of 2015, 37% of adults in the UK reported that they trusted the government, a significant improvement over the 3 year period from spring 2012 (21%).

Why measure change?

The original aim of the Measuring National Well-being (MNW) programme was to, "develop and publish an accepted and trusted set of National Statistics which help people to monitor national well-being". To assist policy makers (and others) in their decision making and help them make sense of and monitor well-being, it is vital to be able to show how things have changed.

The measurement of national well-being

The measurement of national well-being is a long term process. We are already building increasing evidence by providing an overall indication of progress in national well-being and highlighting how individual measures are changing over time. This provides information for policy making and supporting further research. Examples include:

- Implementing policies that are focussed on well-being - the Department for Transport have used our well-being domains in a tool to help policy makers assess the social impacts of major transport investment decisions. The UK Airports Commission used our domains to conduct a quality of life impact assessment for a third London runway/alternative flight path scenario.
- Adding well-being to existing surveys to generate new evidence across a broad range of policy areas - our 4 personal well-being questions are now used in over 20 different government surveys, covering topics such as health, crime, housing and taking part in sport and culture.
- Valuing social goods and services using subjective well-being - the Cabinet Office and the Department for Work and Pensions released 'Well-being and civil society', in 2013, which estimated the value of volunteering using subjective well-being data. The analysis estimated that the value a frequent volunteer gives to volunteering is about £13,500 per year, at 2011 prices, and that not being able to volunteer equates to a 1.9% reduction in life satisfaction.

- Implementing staff well-being strategies to support productivity and performance – an example is the Boorman Review (2009) which undertook a review of NHS health and well-being; an important area identified in the associated report was taking action on health and well-being in the NHS workforce, including:

  - improving organisational behaviours and performance

  - achieving an exemplar service

  - embedding staff health and wellbeing into NHS systems and infrastructure

Where to find the latest national well-being measures data

The latest release of domains and measures is available in various formats:

- National Well-being Measures Excel (1.19 Mb Excel sheet) spreadsheet containing the latest and time series data, plus links to data sources; this spreadsheet has also been revised to include age, sex and regional breakdowns for some headline measures and confidence intervals have been included where possible
- interactive Wheel of Measures, which includes data for the latest and previous periods plus time series charts
- Wheel of Measures PDF (128.2 Kb Pdf) "print and keep" version showing the latest data
- interactive charts showing the latest data for selected measures by region and country

Background notes

1. Details of the policy governing the release of new data are available by visiting www.statisticsauthority.gov.uk/assessment/code-of-practice/index.html or from the Media Relations Office email: media.relations@ons.gsi.gov.uk

Copyright

This document is also available on our website at www.ons.gov.uk.

Insights into Loneliness, Older People and Well-being, 2015

Author Name(s): **Jennifer Thomas, Measuring National Well-being**

Abstract

This article focuses on older people's well-being, loneliness and some of the risk factors associated with loneliness such as living alone, housing tenure, marital status, ill health and support networks. The ONS Measuring National Well-being programme aims to produce accepted and trusted measures of the well-being of the nation - how the UK as a whole is doing.

Introduction

The average age of the UK population is expected to increase over the coming decades. We have projected (National Population 2012 based estimates) that the number of people aged 80 and above is expected to more than double by 2037 and the number of people aged over 90 is expected to triple. The number of centenarians show an expected increase of sevenfold in Estimates of the very old from 14,450 in mid 2014 to 111,000 in mid 2037.

Age UK identify loneliness as one of the major factors older people worry about. It defines it as a subjective sense of lacking desired affection, closeness and social interaction with others. Whilst it has a social aspect, it is defined by the individual's emotional state. As such, loneliness can be felt even when surrounded by other people. Loneliness has an impact on one's wellbeing and a range of personal circumstances such as poor health, living alone and lack of support network are factors contributing to feelings of loneliness (ONS, 2015a; ONS, 2013a, Age UK, 2015). This report uses the latest personal well-being dataset for financial year ending 2015 and new analysis from the Opinions and Lifestyle Survey financial year ending 2015 to explore some of these characteristics in regard to age, well-being and loneliness.

Notes

1. The ONS Opinions and Lifestyle Survey is an omnibus (random selection) survey that collects information on a range of topics from people living in private households in Great Britain. Questions are included on a monthly ad hoc schedule. This analysis used combined data, collected over 5 months (April 2014, July 2014, October 2014, April 2015 and May 2015), that included the question 'On a scale where 0 is not at all lonely and 10 is extremely lonely, how

lonely do you feel in your daily life?' The derived dataset had a sample size of 5159 and a response rate of 56%.

2. Unless otherwise stated, the differences mentioned in the text have been found to be statistically significant at the 95% confidence level. Standard errors have been calculated and used in tests of statistical significance, determined on the basis of non-overlapping confidence intervals. This method provides a conservative estimate of statistical significance but may result in estimates which are statistically significantly different to one another being assessed as not. This would tend to underestimate the differences observed.

Older people, well-being and loneliness

Figure 1 shows that those aged 65 to 79 are most likely to report high levels of life satisfaction, worthwhile activities and happiness and low levels of anxiety, than those of working age. However, these proportions are lower for the oldest old (80 and above).

Figure 1: Highest and lowest personal well-being ratings by age group, 2014 to 2015

UK

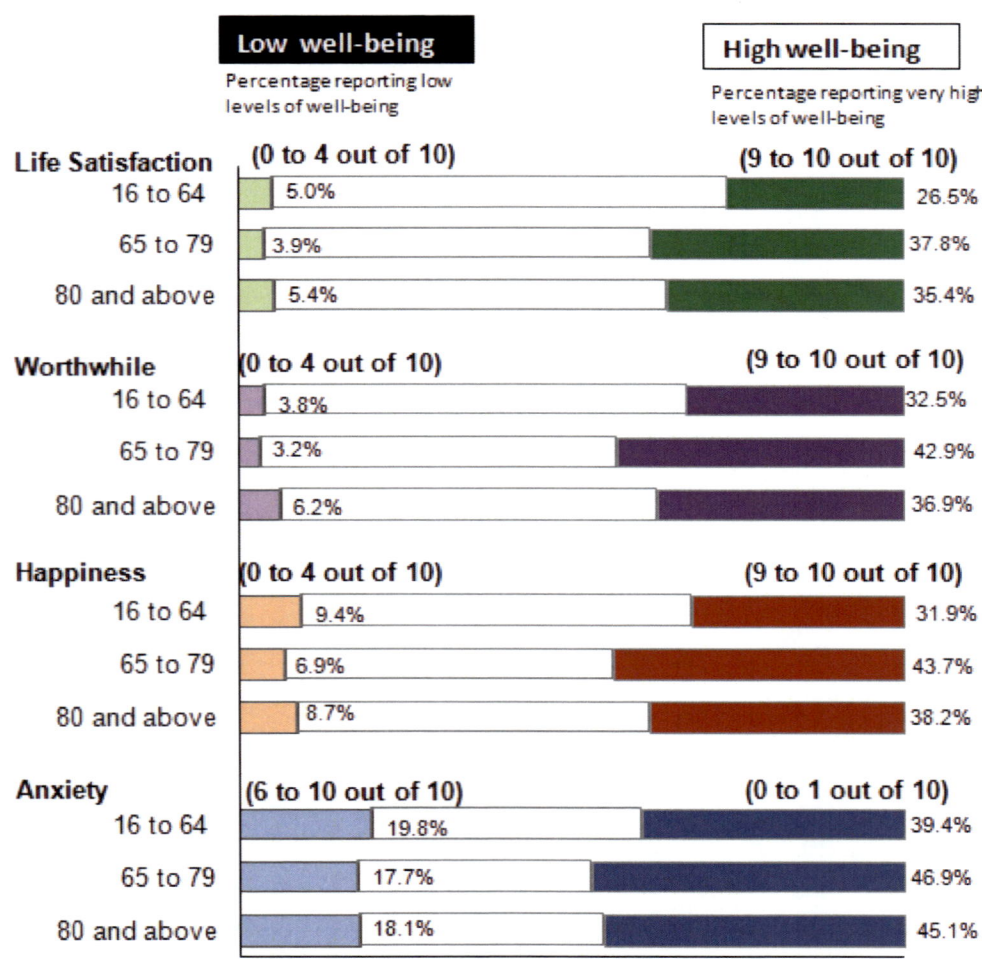

Source: Annual Population Survey (APS) - Office for National Statistics

Notes:

1. Adults aged 16 and over were asked 'Overall, how satisfied are you with your life nowadays?', 'Overall, to what extent do you feel the things you do in your life are worthwhile?', 'Overall, how happy did you feel yesterday?' and 'Overall, how anxious did you feel yesterday?' where 0 is 'not at all' and 10 is 'completely'.

2. The highest levels of personal well-being for life satisfaction, worthwhile and happiness are defined as ratings of 9 or 10. For reported anxiety, ratings of 0 or 1 are used because lower levels of anxiety suggest higher personal well-being.

3. On the other hand, the lowest levels of personal well-being are defined as ratings of 0 to 4 for life satisfaction, worthwhile and happiness. For reported anxiety, ratings of 6 to 10 are used because higher levels of anxiety suggest lower personal well-being.

Download chart

XLS XLS format
(28.5 Kb)

3 in 10 of those aged 80 and over report being lonely

Our recent analysis looked at factors associated with well-being among older people and one possible reason for lower personal well-being for those aged 80 and over, compared to the 65 to 79 age group, could be related to feeling lonely (ONS, 2013a).

Those aged 80 and over have a higher average loneliness rating (3.3 out of 10) than the working age population (2.1) and the 65 to 79 age group (1.9). Figure 2 shows that, those aged 80 and over are also twice as likely to report feeling lonely (a rating of 6 or more out of 10) than those in the working age and the 65 to 79 age group (29.2% compared to 14.8% and 14.5% respectively).

Figure 2: Proportion of people who report feeling lonely in their daily life by age group, 2014 to 2015

Great Britain

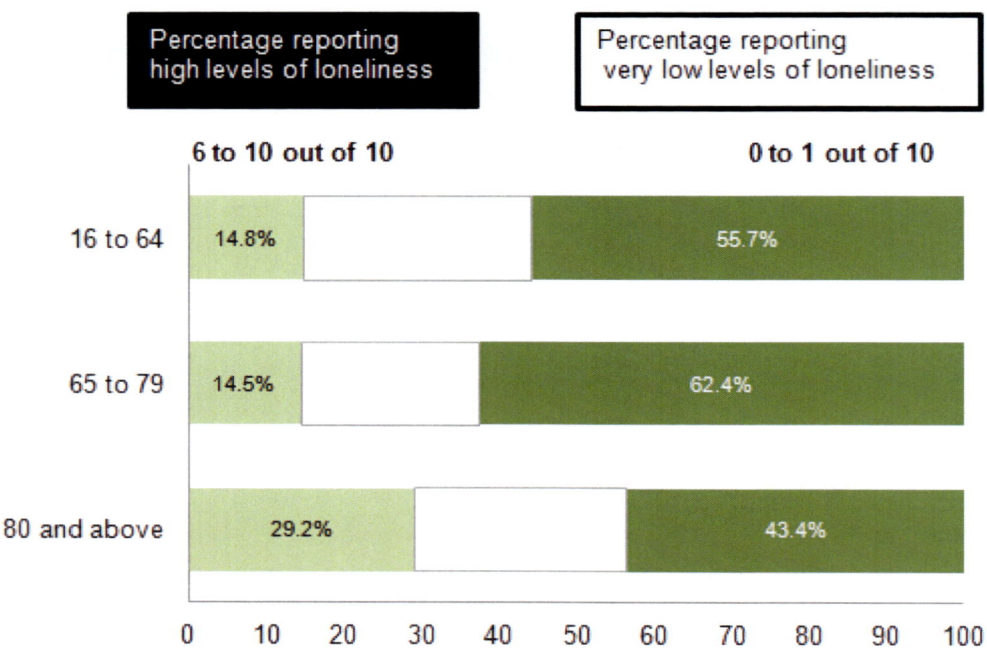

Source: Opinions and Lifestyle Survey - Office for National Statistics

Notes:

1. Adults aged 16 and over were asked "On a scale where 0 is not at all lonely and 10 is extremely lonely, how lonely do you feel in your daily life?".
2. Responses were grouped into those who reported high levels of loneliness (those who rated their loneliness between 6 and 10), those who reported low to medium levels of loneliness (those who rated their loneliness between 2 and 5) and those who reported very low levels of loneliness (those who rated their loneliness at 0 or 1). This is in-line with the grouping of the other personal well-being measures regularly published by the Office for National Statistics.

Download chart

XLS XLS format
(26 Kb)

Notes

1. Previous ONS research found that there is variation within the working age group; with those aged between 35 and 54 being the most lonely (ONS 2015a).

Loneliness and well-being

Those who report being lonely are 7 times more likely to have low life satisfaction

Loneliness has a strong relationship with low personal well-being ratings. Figure 3 shows that those who report feeling lonely are almost 10 times more likely to report low feelings of worth (10.5% compared with 1.1%), over 7 times more likely to report low life satisfaction (15.2% compared to 1.9%) and over 3 times more likely to report feeling unhappy (18.8% compared to 5.6%) than those who have low ratings of loneliness. They are also twice as likely to report feeling anxious (34.8% compared to 15.1%).

Figure 3: Personal well-being by loneliness, all adults aged 16 and over, 2014 to 2015

Great Britain

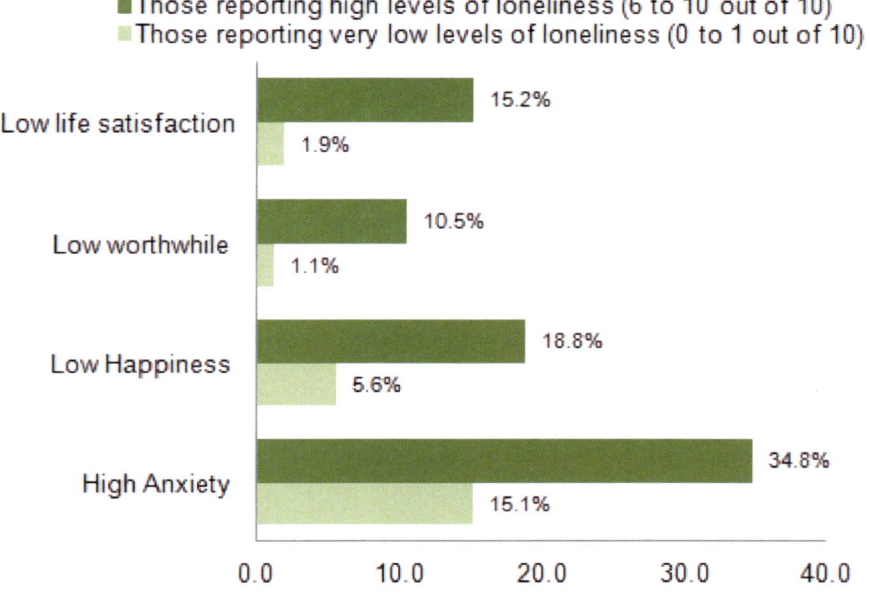

Source: Opinions and Lifestyle Survey - Office for National Statistics

Notes:

1. Adults aged 16 and over were asked 'Overall, how satisfied are you with your life nowadays?', 'Overall, to what extent do you feel the things you do in your life are worthwhile?', 'Overall, how happy did you feel yesterday?' and 'Overall, how anxious did you feel yesterday?' where 0 is 'not at all' and 10 is 'completely'.

2. The highest levels of personal well-being for life satisfaction, worthwhile and happiness are defined as ratings of 9 or 10. For reported anxiety, ratings of 0 or 1 are used because lower levels of anxiety suggest better personal well-being.

3. On the other hand, the lowest levels of personal well-being are defined as ratings of 0 to 4 for life satisfaction, worthwhile and happiness. For reported anxiety, ratings of 6 to 10 are used because higher levels of anxiety suggest lower personal well-being.

4. Adults aged 16 and over were asked "On a scale where 0 is not at all lonely and 10 is extremely lonely, how lonely do you feel in your daily life?".

5. Responses were grouped into those who reported high levels of loneliness (those who rated their loneliness between 6 and 10), those who reported low to medium levels of loneliness (those who rated their loneliness between 2 and 5) and those who reported very low levels of loneliness (those who rated their loneliness at 0 or 1). This is in-line with the grouping of the other personal well-being measures regularly published by the Office for National Statistics.

Download chart

XLS XLS format
(35 Kb)

Risk factors of loneliness

Personal characteristics such as living alone, housing tenure, going through relationship break up or loss and ill health can all be factors contributing to feelings of loneliness (ONS, 2013a; Age UK, 2015). The following section explores these relationships for the whole population. Older people are more susceptible to these risk factors and to experiencing multiple risk factors at the same time.

Those who live alone, rent or are widowed are most likely to report being lonely

16% (7.1 million) of us reported living alone in the 2011 Census. Figures show that older people are more likely to live alone, with 59% of those aged 85 and over and 38% of those aged 75 to 84 living alone (ONS, 2014a). Table 1 shows that people who live on their own are more than twice as likely to report feeling lonely (30.8% compared to 12.6%).

In 2011, 57% (5.3 million) of those aged 65 and over were married or in a civil partnership , 29% were widowed or a surviving partner, while those who were single constituted 5.5%. The remaining 8.7% were divorced (ONS, 2013b). Table 1 shows that those who are widowed or separated/divorced are approximately 3 times more likely to report feeling lonely than those who are married (34.7% and 27% respectively compared to 9.6%). In 2011, of those aged 85 and over, and living alone, 8 in 10 men and 9 in 10 women were widowed (ONS, 2013e).

Table 1 also shows that respondents who were renting in local authority or housing association accommodation were the most likely to feel lonely. ONS (2015b) found that those who rented had lower personal well-being scores than those who owned their property outright or with a mortgage. However, older people are more likely to own their homes. In 2011, the majority of households with a household reference person (HRP) aged 65 and over were owner occupied (75% or 4.6 million) compared to 64% of the general population (ONS, 2013b).

Those who report very bad or bad health are 2.5 times more likely to report feeling lonely

Older people are more likely to report poor health. In 2014 to 15, 14.8% of people over 80 reported very bad or bad health, compared to 4.2% of the working age population. Poor health conditions can lead to social isolation (Lloyd, J, 2014). Reduced mobility, cognitive impairment, and sensory impairment increase older people's chances of being lonely (ONS, 2013a). Consequently, those in poor health are more than 2.5 times more likely to report feeling lonely than those reporting good health (34.7% compared to 13%).

In turn, feeling lonely has been shown to increase blood pressure, elevate stress levels weakening the immune system, and heighten feelings of depression and anxiety. Age UK (2015) report that loneliness can be as harmful to our health as smoking 15 cigarettes a day, and people with a high degree of loneliness are twice as likely to develop Alzheimer's as people with a low degree of loneliness.

Table 1: Proportion of people who report feeling lonely in their daily life by risk factors, all adults aged 16 and over, 2014 to 2015

Great Britain

Percentages

	Those reporting		
	Very low levels of loneliness	Low to medium levels of loneliness	High levels of loneliness
Daily risk factors			
Tenure			
Owns outright	59.4	25.3	15.3
Owns mortgage	61.7	26.6	11.7
Rents LA/HA	44.7	33.5	21.8
Rents privately	50.5	32.6	16.9
Living alone			
Living alone	31.9	37.3	30.8
Not living alone	60.7	26.7	12.6
Marital status			
Married, remarried or in a legal partnership	67.4	23.0	9.6
Single	40.3	37.9	21.8
Separated or divorced	36.4	36.6	27.0
Widowed	30.8	34.5	34.7
Self reported health			
Very good or good health	59.9	27.1	13.0
Fair health	44.7	34.1	21.1
Very bad or bad health	34.4	30.8	34.7
Total	56.2	28.4	15.4

Table source: Office for National Statistics

Table notes:
1. LA - local authority; HA – housing association.
2. Adults aged 16 and over were asked "On a scale where 0 is not at all lonely and 10 is extremely lonely, how lonely do you feel in your daily life?".
3. Responses were grouped into those who reported high levels of loneliness (those who rated their loneliness between 6 and 10), those who reported low to medium levels of loneliness (those who rated their loneliness

between 2 and 5) and those who reported very low levels of loneliness (those who rated their loneliness at 0 or 1). This is in-line with the grouping of the other personal well-being measures regularly published by the Office for National Statistics.

Download table

XLS XLS format
(29 Kb)

Older people are more satisfied with their relationships with family and friends and are more likely to have someone they can ask for help.

As a result of poorer health, older people are likely to have higher social care needs and their ability to draw on their communities and relationships for support will influence how these are experienced, particularly at a time when the social care system is challenged.

Figure 4 shows that the oldest old are most satisfied that they have any relatives, friends or neighbours that they can ask for help with a rating of 8.6 out of 10. This compares to a rating of 8.2 out of 10 for the working age population. They are also most satisfied with the relationships that they have with family; rating their satisfaction at 8.9 out of 10 compared to 8.7 out of 10 for the working age population. This is consistent with the previous finding that the highest proportion of people who felt that they could rely on their family a lot, was found amongst those aged 75 and over for both men (73%) and women (82%) ONS (2015a). The 65 to 79 year olds are most satisfied with the relationships they have with friends, with a rating of 8.6 out of 10 compared to 8.3 out of 10 for the working age population.

That said, ONS (2015a) found that social participation decreased with age. People aged 75 and over were the least likely to have at least one close friend, 11% of them reported having no close friend at all, compared to 2% of those aged 18 to 24. In addition, only 1 in 4 (25%) people aged 75 and over reported meeting with friends, relatives and work colleagues less than once a week. This seemingly contradictory finding could be explained by different age groups having different expectations.

Figure 4: Average ratings of satisfaction with relationships with family, friends and the extent to which you have people you can ask for help by age, 2014 to 2015

Great Britain

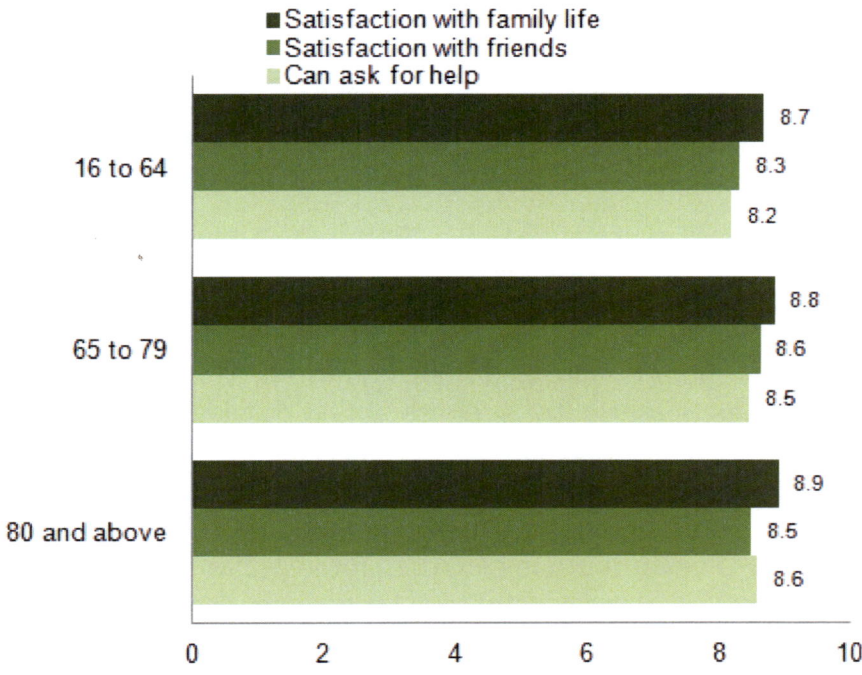

Source: Opinions and Lifestyle Survey - Office for National Statistics

Notes:

1. Adults aged 16 and over were asked "To what extent do you feel you have any relatives, friends or neighbours that you can ask for help?", "Overall, how satisfied are you with your relationships with friends?" and "Overall, how satisfied are you with your relationships with family, including spouse/partner?" where 0 is 'not at all' and 10 is 'completely'.

Download chart

 XLS format
(25.5 Kb)

Notes

1. A civil partnership includes those who are separated but still legally married or in a civil partnership.

2. The concept of a household reference person (HRP) was introduced in the 2001 Census (in common with other government surveys in 2001/2) to replace the traditional concept of the 'head of the household'. HRPs provide an individual person within a household to act as a reference point for producing further derived statistics and for characterising a whole household according to characteristics of the chosen reference person.

Conclusion

This analysis shows that older people are more satisfied with life generally and with their social networks and the support they provide. This may be due to having lower expectations due to a cohort effect or more mature perspectives (ONS 2013c) but ultimately they are more content than their younger counterparts. However, the impact of loneliness on well-being is considerable, especially for the oldest old who are most likely to feel lonely and are subject to a high number of risk factors. The UK is an ageing population, 1 in 12 of the population is projected to be aged 80 and over by 2037 (ONS, 2013d). Loneliness is going to become more of a problem over time.

An important target for the government is to help improve the quality of the ageing experience in the UK and make sure the impact of the ageing population is a positive one for citizens of all ages (GO-science 2015). The UK therefore needs to consider how to minimise some of the impact that risk factors of loneliness has particularly bereavement, poor health, and housing tenure. This support could be from public, private or community services. Importantly, support can be provided by family, friends and neighbours. Evidence suggests that we are conscious of our roles in supporting older people in our communities; almost half of us (46%) believe we need to keep in touch with elderly family members who may be lonely and 4 in 10 of us feel the need to keep in touch with elderly neighbours who may be lonely (YouGov, 2010). However there is still room for improvement in awareness of the scale of loneliness and its impact. In particular, that social participation decreases with age, along with the increasing likelihood of ill health, living alone and bereavement.

References

Lloyd, J (2014) The Bigger Picture: Policy Insights and recommendations. London, Strategic Society Centre and Independent Age.

Background notes

1. Details of the policy governing the release of new data are available by visiting www.statisticsauthority.gov.uk/assessment/code-of-practice/index.html or from the Media Relations Office email: media.relations@ons.gsi.gov.uk

Copyright

Office for
National Statistics

Children's Well-being overview: 2015

In 2015, there is a mixed picture of children's well-being in the UK

Children's well-being is an important part of the nation's well-being. In 2014, there were an estimated 12 million children aged 0 to 15, nearly a fifth of the UK population. This summary highlights some of the latest findings from the 2015 update to the children's well-being measures and builds on earlier analysis of the measures[1] (Exploring the Well-being of Children in the UK, 2014). It focuses on the latest data on children's views of their overall health and how children spend their time. Together they present a mixed picture of the well-being of children in the UK today. The full set of 31 measures can be found in the reference tables (428 Kb Excel sheet) .

Most children report high or very high personal well-being

In 2014, most children were happy with their lives with over three-quarters of children having high or very high personal well-being[2] scores for life satisfaction, happiness and sense of worth. However, 1 in 10 reported low levels of happiness.

Figure 1: Children's personal well-being proportions, 2014

Great Britain

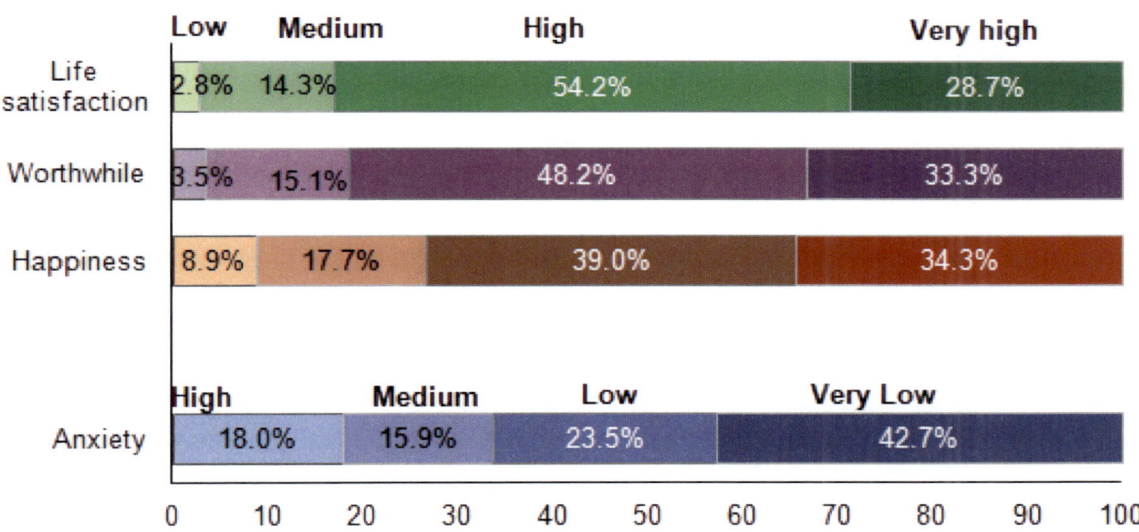

Notes:

1. Source: The Children's Society; Household Panel Survey.
2. Children aged 10 to 15 years.
3. Low is a score of 0-4 out of 10; medium, 5-6; high, 7-8; very high 9-10.

Most children participate in arts or cultural activities and sport

Leisure time is important for people's well-being for the direct satisfaction that it brings, in addition to the physical and mental health benefits (Measuring Leisure in OECD Countries).

Almost all children (96.7%) had engaged with or participated in arts or cultural activities at least 3 times in the last year. Most (75.7%) had done so at least once in the last week. In 2014 to 2015, 8 in 10 (78.2%) children had participated in sport in the last week. Almost 7 out of 10 (69.1%) children aged 5 to 10 years and 9 out of 10 (89.5%) children aged 11 to 15 years had participated in sport[3].

Children who are bullied are 4 times more likely to have symptoms of mental ill-health

In 2011 to 2012, 1 in 8 (12.0%) children reported they were bullied frequently[4]. The Good Childhood Report 2015 reported that children in England experienced the highest levels of emotional bullying out of the 15 countries that were surveyed. ONS has also found that children who have been bullied are more likely to have low personal well-being (Exploring the well-being of children in the UK, 2014).

The article, Insights into children's mental health and well-being, identifies that in the year ending March 2012, 1 in 8 (12.4%) of children had symptoms of mental ill-health[5]. This was similar for boys and girls (12.4%). Children who were bullied frequently were 4 times more likely to report a high or very high score for symptoms of mental ill-health, than those that were bullied less frequently or not at all (40.9% compared to 8.5%).

Notes:

1. Caution is advised when comparing the measures for children with those for young people and adults as data are collected in a different way.

2. The personal well-being data are derived from a customised weighted 12 month dataset from The Children's Society's household panel survey. This dataset was produced specifically for the analysis of subjective well-being data by ONS. Children aged 10 to 15 years were asked: "Overall, how satisfied are you with your life nowadays?", "Overall, to what extent do you feel the things you do in your life are worthwhile?", and "Overall, how happy did you feel yesterday?" 0 is "not at all" and 10 is "completely".

   The highest levels of personal well-being for life satisfaction, worthwhile and happiness are defined as ratings of 9 or 10. On the other hand, the lowest levels of personal well-being are defined as ratings of 0 to 4 for life satisfaction, worthwhile and happiness.

3. Data for 5–10 year olds relates to out of school activities only, whereas data for 11–15 years olds relates to activities undertaken both in and out of school.

4. This measure is constructed from 2 questions asked of children aged 10 to 15 years: "How often do you get physically bullied at school, for example getting hit, pushed around or threatened, or having belongings stolen?", "How often do you get bullied in other ways at school such as getting called names, getting left out of games, or having nasty stories spread about you on purpose?" Response categories were: never, not much (1 to 3 times in the last 6 months), quite a lot (more than 4 times in the last 6 months), a lot (a few times every week).

5. This measure uses the Strengths and Difficulties Questionnaire, a behavioural screening questionnaire for use with children aged 2 to 17. It measures a child's strengths and difficulties in 5 areas:

   1. emotional symptoms

   2. conduct problems

   3. hyperactivity or inattention

   4. peer relationship problems

   5. pro-social behaviour

The first 4 are combined to provide a "total difficulties score" out of 40. Scores are categorised as: 0 to 14 close to average; 15 to 17 slightly raised; 18 to 19 high; 20 or more very high. A high or very high score is considered an indication of mental ill-health.

Office for
National Statistics

Young People's Well-being overview: 2015

Latest data shows changes in young people's well-being

There were around 7.5 million young people aged 16 to 24 in the UK in 2014, according to ONS mid-year population estimates. This summary highlights some of the latest findings for young people's well-being, which builds on earlier analysis of the well-being measures (Exploring the well-being of young people in the UK, 2014). It focuses on young people's views of their health and income. The latest data for the full set of 28 measures can be found in our reference tables.

Young people's personal well-being has improved over time

In 2014 to 2015, most young people were happy with their lives, with approximately three-quarters of young people having high or very high personal well-being[1]. The proportion of young people reporting high or very high life satisfaction increased from 79.3% in 2011 to 2012 to 82.9% in 2014 to 2015, while the proportion reporting a high or very high sense that the things they do are worthwhile increased from 77.3% to 81.4% over the same period. Similarly, the proportion of young people who reported that their happiness yesterday was high or very high increased to 73.4% in 2014 to 2015, compared with 71.0% in 2011 to 2012. There were two-thirds (66.2%) of young people who reported low or very low levels of anxiety in 2014 to 2015, up from 63.3% in 2011 to 2012, but 18.0% reported high levels of anxiety.

Figure 1: Young people's personal well-being proportions, 2014 to 2015

United Kingdom

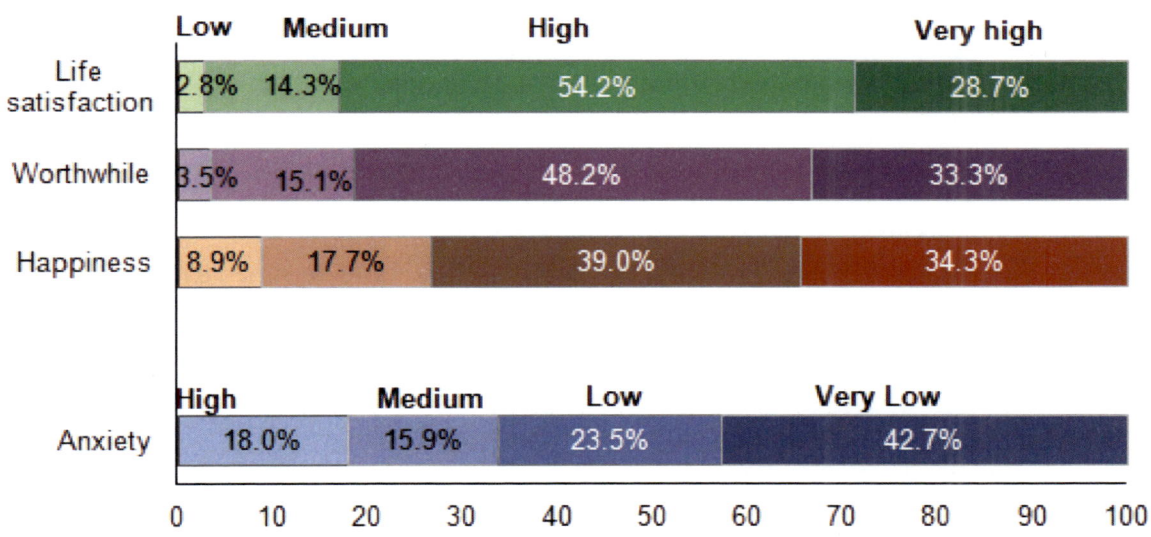

Source: Annual Population Survey (APS) - Office for National Statistics

Notes:

1. Young people aged 16 to 24 years.
2. For Life satisfaction, Worthwhile, and Happiness, low is a score of 0-4 out of 10; medium, 5-6; high, 7-8; very high 9-10.
3. For Anxiety, very low is a score of 0-1 out of 10; low, 2-3; medium, 4-5; high, 6-10.

The number of young people who are unemployed, NEET[2] and struggling to get by financially has decreased over time

Unemployment has been shown to be strongly associated with how people rate their personal well-being. (What matters most to personal well-being?). The unemployment rate[3] for young people has decreased from 19.6% in 2012 to 14.1% in 2015; over the same period, the proportion of young people who are not in employment, education or training (NEET) has decreased from around 16.2% to 12.7%. Similarly, the proportion of young people who were finding it quite or very difficult to manage financially[4] declined from around 15.4% in 2009 to 2010 to 9.7% in 2012 to 2013. These findings reflect national trends in labour market changes and personal well-being. (Has personal well-being improved for people in and out of work?)

Young people's satisfaction with their health has fallen over time

Self-reported health has been identified as the most important factor associated with subjective well-being (What matters most to personal well-being?).

In 2009 to 2010, three-quarters (74.6%) of 16 to 24 year olds were relatively satisfied with their overall health, whereas in 2012 to 2013, only around two-thirds (65.1%) reported being somewhat, mostly or completely satisfied with their health. Young men were more likely to be relatively satisfied with their health[5] than young women in 2012 to 2013, (6.0% report being satisfied compared to 61.0% of women).

Positive mental well-being can affect a person's emotional and psychological development in both the immediate and longer-term. It is measured using a 7 question survey[6], each with a score between 1 and 5, giving a total score of between 7 and 35. Overall, young people's mental well-being has worsened between 2009 to 2010 and 2012 to 2013 (from 25.0 out of 35 to 24.2 out of 35). Young men have higher mental well-being (24.6 out of 35) than young women (23.8 out of 35).

Notes:

1. Adults aged 16 to 24, were asked: "Overall, how satisfied are you with your life nowadays?", "Overall, to what extent do you feel the things you do in your life are worthwhile?", "Overall, how happy did you feel yesterday?" and "Overall, how anxious did you feel yesterday?" 0 is "not at all" and 10 is "completely".

2. Not in employment, education or training.

3. The unemployment rate is the number of unemployed people (aged 18 to 24) divided by the economically active population (aged 18 to 24).

4. Adults aged 16 to 24, were asked to rate how they were coping financially on a 5-point scale ranging from "finding it very difficult" to "living comfortably".

5. Adults aged between 16 and 24, were asked to rate their satisfaction with their general health on a 7-point scale from "completely dissatisfied" to "completely satisfied". Responses for somewhat, mostly and completely satisfied are used as the measure.

6. The population mental well-being (SWEMWBs) measure was developed to capture a broad concept of positive mental well-being, including psychological functioning and affective emotional aspects of well-being. Adults aged 16 to 24, were asked to complete a 7 question survey, each response is given a score of between 1 and 5, resulting in a total score of between 7 and 35.

Office for
National Statistics

Insights into children's mental health and well-being

Abstract

Mental health problems in children can affect their overall well-being in both the immediate and longer-term. The Children's Well-being 2015 publication includes a new measure of children's mental ill-health. This is in response to feedback from stakeholders who identified mental health as missing from the initial set of measures for children. The new measure uses the total difficulties score from the child self-completion aspect of the Strengths and Difficulties Questionnaire (SDQ) from the UK Household Longitudinal Survey (Understanding Society). This article provides an in-depth look at why mental health is an important aspect of children's well-being, outlines the reasons why the SDQ was chosen and looks at what the data tells us about the prevalence of mental ill-health and how it relates to other factors, such as bullying and family relationships.

Main points

- there were 1 in 8 children aged 10 to 15 who reported symptoms of mental ill-health in 2011 to 2012, as measured by a high or very high total difficulties score
- being bullied was strongly related to mental ill-health; children who were bullied frequently were 4 times more likely to report a high or very high score
- children who quarrelled with their mother more than once a week were 3 times more likely to report a high or very high score than children who quarrelled less frequently
- One third of children who were relatively unhappy with their appearance reported high or very high total difficulties score, compared with 1 in 12 children who were relatively happy with their appearance
- children who spent over 3 hours on social websites on a normal school night were more than twice as likely to report a high or very high score as children spending less time on social websites

What is mental health?

There are two aspects to mental health: mental illness or ill-health[1], and mental or psychological well-being.

Mental ill-health measures consider whether a person has a higher likelihood of a clinically diagnosable illness[2], from anxiety or depression to problems such as bi-polar disorder or schizophrenia. Mental ill-health in children can manifest in different ways to adults, often resulting in behavioural and conduct problems, such as Attention Deficit Hyperactivity Disorder (ADHD) or Oppositional Defiant Disorder (ODD), as well as emotional problems such as depression or anxiety. These conditions can also be symptoms of underlying problems, which may be environmental (for example, parental conflict) or developmental (for example, Autistic Spectrum Disorders). In this article we discuss the prevalence of mental ill-health, as shown by the total difficulties score from the SDQ.

Mental well-being is concerned with how people feel about their lives and whether their lives are worthwhile. It is not just the absence of mental health problems and can be described as "a dynamic state, in which the individual is able to develop their potential, work productively and creatively, build strong and positive relationships with others, and contribute to their community" (Foresight report, 2008). The 31 measures of children's well-being (428 Kb Excel sheet) capture many aspects of mental well-being using measures such as quarrelling with parents, talking to parents about things that matter, happiness with family and friends, satisfaction with time use, desire to go on to further education, and considering the things that one does are worthwhile. Furthermore, subjective measures of both life satisfaction and happiness are included.

Notes

1. This aspect may also be termed 'mental health problems' or 'mental disorders'.

2. For example as defined by the International Classification of Disease (ICD10) or the Diagnostic and Statistical Manual of Mental Disorders (DSM-V).

Why is mental ill-health important?

The World Happiness Report cites research that found over half of children who have a mental health problem will suffer from mental ill-health as adults. Furthermore, it explains that mental health problems such as depression can be more disabling than physical problems such as arthritis or asthma.

The Mental health of children and young people in Great Britain, 2004 (5.7 Mb Pdf) study found that 1 in 10 children aged 5 to 16 years had a clinically diagnosable mental disorder. Boys were more likely to have a problem than girls and prevalence increased with age. Girls were more likely to have emotional problems whereas boys were more likely to report conduct or hyperactivity problems. The study also found that children with mental disorders were more likely than children without mental disorders to have time off school, especially unauthorised absences, and were less likely to have a network of family and friends with whom they felt close.

More recently, Mental Health Difficulties in Early Adolescence compared mental ill-health prevalence from two different cross-sectional samples of children aged 11 to 13 years in 2009 and 2014 and found that there were similar levels of mental ill-health in both cohorts (19.7% compared with 19.0%). However, the study did identify a significant increase in emotional problems amongst girls and a decrease in the proportion of boys reporting "at-risk" levels of total difficulties scores. The authors suggest that an increased focus on interventions to tackle disruptive behaviour has helped boys, but there have been no similar interventions to tackle emotional problems, which are more likely to affect girls.

In March 2015 the government pledged £1.25 billion to improve children and young people's mental health services over the next 5 years. In tandem with this announcement the Department of Health and NHS England published 'Future in mind', detailing the work of the children and young people's mental health and well-being taskforce, which was set up to identify ways of improving mental health services and access to these services for children and young people. Proposals include:

- a hard hitting anti-stigma campaign which raises awareness and promotes improved attitudes to children and young people affected by mental health difficulties
- a five year programme to develop a comprehensive set of access and waiting times standards that bring the same rigour to mental health as is seen in physical health
- commissioning a new national prevalence survey of child and adolescent mental health
- encouraging schools to continue to develop whole school approaches to promoting mental health and wellbeing

More recently, local transformation plan guidance has been published to help local areas implement changes and ensure the momentum of improvement is maintained.

How is mental ill-health measured?

The national measures of well-being include the proportion of adults aged 16 and over reporting symptoms of mental ill-health using the General Health Questionnaire (GHQ12). However, this has not been validated for use in children; it is focused on symptoms experienced by adults and would not be appropriate or informative if used for children. To measure children's mental ill-health, a more "child-centric" measure had to be identified. The Strengths and Difficulties Questionnaire (SDQ) was designed by Professor Robert Goodman as a behavioural screening questionnaire for use with children aged 2 to 17[1]. It consists of questionnaires administered to the child, a parent and a teacher. As its name suggests, it measures a child's strengths and difficulties in a number of areas:

1. Emotional symptoms
2. Conduct problems
3. Hyperactivity or inattention
4. Peer relationship problems
5. Pro-social behaviour

The first four of these areas can be combined together to provide a "total difficulties" score, which can then be used as a predictor of mental ill-health. The SDQ has been extensively validated and was used as the screening tool for the Mental health of children and young people in Great Britain, 2004 (5.7 Mb Pdf) report[2]. It must be noted that only the child self-reported questionnaire (not those from the parent or teacher) is being used to provide the total difficulties score for use as a measure of mental ill-health in the children's well-being framework. The sensitivity of predicting clinical diagnosis is much higher using a multi-informant SDQ, and so the total difficulties score presented here should only be considered an indication of the prevalence of mental ill-health.

The self-completion SDQ is included in every other wave of the <u>Understanding Society Youth module</u>[3], providing regular and reliable estimates for a headline measure of children's mental ill-health. Furthermore, the longitudinal design of the Understanding Society survey will allow for further exploration of changes in total difficulties scores as the survey progresses.

The total difficulties score can be reported as an average (mean) score, or categorised into 4 groups:

1. Close to average or normal (score 0 to 14 out of 40)
2. Slightly raised (score 15 to 17 out of 40)
3. High (score 18 to 19 out of 40)
4. Very high (score 20 or more out of 40)

For the purposes of children's well-being, the headline measure for the prevalence of mental ill-health is the proportion of children reporting a high or very high total difficulties score, although the mean score will also be provided for completeness.

Notes

1. The standard SDQ can be used with children aged 4 to 17 years, and the early years SDQ is suitable for children aged 2 to 4 years.

2. The sensitivity of the SDQ varies according to the diagnoses. It is less sensitive for problems such as specific phobias, eating disorders and separation anxiety.

3. The SDQ was included in Wave 1 (2009-10) and Wave 3 (2011-12) of the Understanding Society survey.

What do the data tell us?

The latest data from Understanding Society (2011 to 2012) shows that around 12% of children aged 10 to 15 reported high or very high total difficulties scores. The proportion was the same for both boys and girls (12%) and did not significantly differ from the proportions reported in the 2009 to 2010 wave of Understanding Society. Similarly, the average score was 10.6 out of 40 in 2011 to 2012, broadly similar to the 2009 to 2010 average score of 11.0. There are, however, some interesting differences in the associations between the average total difficulties scores and other factors.

Of the <u>31 children's measures of well-being</u> (including the total difficulties score), 12 are sourced from the Understanding Society survey. Measures other than total difficulties score are:

- happiness with appearance
- quarrel with mother/father
- talk to mother/father about things that are important
- bullied at school (physically, in other ways or both)
- time spent on social websites
- feel safe walking in your neighbourhood after dark

- like your neighbourhood
- happiness with school
- want to go on to full-time education

In the 2011 to 2012 wave of the survey, all 12 measures were included so a more detailed analysis of the associations between the total difficulties scores and these other measures was possible. All of the variables shown in Table 1 (in Appendix A), including age and gender, were included in a regression analysis, which allows us to look at the relative importance of these different factors for children's mental health. It must be noted that these measures are not a definitive list of factors affecting children's mental health. Other factors may be as or more important, but have not been included as they are either not a measure of children's well-being, or not available in the Understanding Society dataset.

Bullying

Bullying has been found to be an important factor associated with children's mental health. One study – reported in "Peer victimisation during adolescence and its impact on depression in early adulthood" – found that children who had been bullied at age 13 were more than twice as likely to have depression at age 18. A meta-analysis (where several studies are combined) of longitudinal research on bullying and internalised problems (for example, depression and anxiety) reported a "symmetrical bi-directional relationship between peer victimization and internalizing problems". That is to say, after taking initial levels of depression and anxiety into account, children who were bullied were more likely to report an increase in depression and anxiety over time and conversely, after taking initial levels of being bullied into account, children who had depression or anxiety were more likely to be bullied over time.

In 2011 to 2012 around 1 in 8 children (12%) reported being bullied at school physically, in other ways, or both more than 4 times in the last 6 months. The proportions were similar for boys and girls (13% and 11% respectively) and there had been no change since 2009 to 2010 (11% of all children).

Figure 1: Total Difficulties difficulties score category by bullying status, 2011 to 2012

United Kingdom

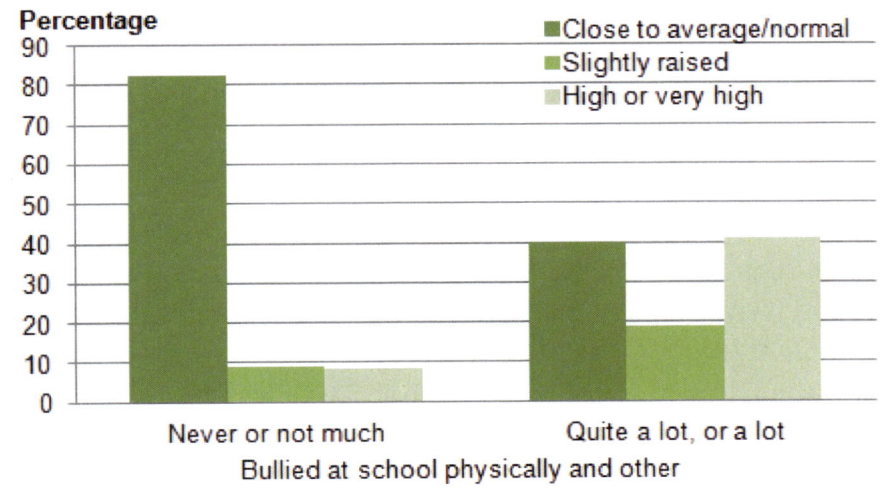

Notes:

1. Source: Understanding Society, the UK Household Longitudinal Study.
2. Children aged 10 to 15 years.

Download chart

XLS XLS format
(26.5 Kb)

In 2011 to 2012, children who were bullied more than 4 times in the last 6 months reported significantly higher average total difficulties scores (16.2) than those children who had never been bullied or had been bullied less frequently (9.8). Furthermore, Figure 1 shows that those who were bullied frequently in the last 6 months were over 4 times more likely to report high or very high total difficulties scores (41%) than those who were bullied less frequently or not at all (9%).

Frequency of being bullied was by far the strongest predictor of higher total difficulties scores of all the measures included in the regression analysis.

Parental relationships

In 2013, The Children's Society reported that a child's relationship with their parents is an important factor associated with overall well-being. Children's relationships with their parents are particularly prominent and powerful influences on children's mental health, and disruptions or tumultuous relationships can often lead to behavioural difficulties. Parents are often children's primary care givers and attachment figures, and quarrels between a child and their mother or father can disrupt children's lives. Indeed, closeness to mothers and closeness to fathers have both been shown to have independent contributions to children's happiness, life satisfaction, and psychological distress over and above demographic variables (Amato, 1994).

Just over a quarter (27%) of children reported quarrelling with their mother more than once a week in 2011 to 2012, a decrease from around 31% in 2009 to 2010. This compares with only 19% who reported quarrelling with their father in 2011 to 2012 – a similar proportion to 2009 to 2010. However, children were also more likely to talk to their mother about things that matter more than once a week. In 2011 to 2012, just over 63% reported talking to their mother about things that matter frequently, whereas only 40% reported talking to their father about things that matter frequently. While there is no difference between the proportions of boys and girls quarrelling frequently with either parent, boys are less likely to talk to their mothers than girls (60% compared with 67%) whereas girls are less likely to talk to their fathers than boys (36% compared with 44%).

There is no evidence to prove a causal link between poor child-parent relationships and mental ill-health; however, there is an association between them. A child with a mental health issue may not be able to articulate their needs and emotions as well as a child with good mental health, and thus they may be more argumentative and disruptive. A poor relationship with parents may exacerbate mental health issues and lead children to exhibit undesirable behaviour or inappropriate emotional responses. The data from Understanding Society shows how difficult child-parent relationships are associated with mental ill-health.

Figure 2: Proportion of children with high or very high total difficulties scores by parental relationship, 2011 to 2012

United Kingdom

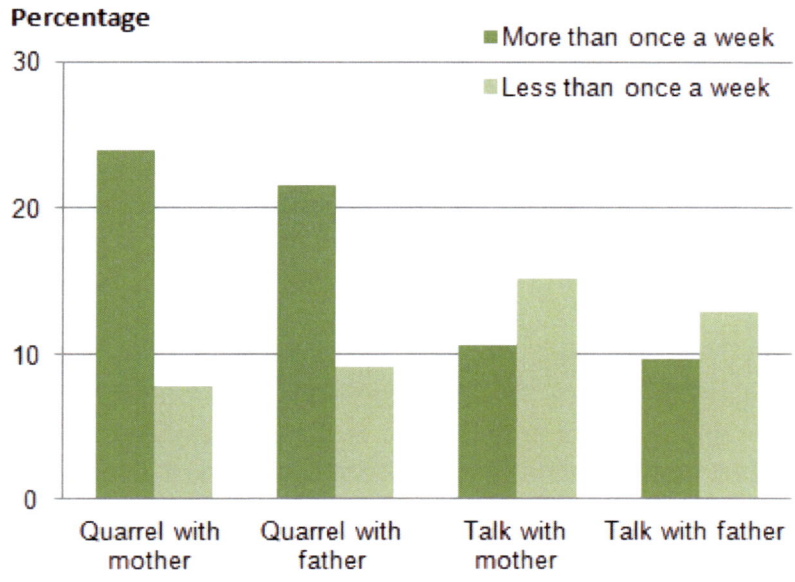

Notes:

1. Source: Understanding Society, the UK Household Longitudinal Study.
2. Children aged 10 to 15 years.

Download chart

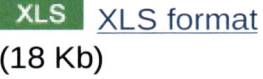 XLS format
(18 Kb)

The 4 parental relationship variables in the measurement are: quarrelling with mother, quarrelling with father, talking to mother about things that matter and talking to father about things that matter. Children who quarrelled with their mother or father more than once a week in 2011 to 2012 reported average total difficulties scores of 13.3 and 13.1 respectively. This compares with average scores of 9.5 and 9.8 for those children who reported quarrelling with their mother or their father less than once a week. Figure 2 illustrates the proportions of children with high or very high total difficulties scores according to how frequently they quarrelled with or talked to each of their parents. Children who quarrelled more than once a week with their mother were around 3 times more likely to report a high or very high score (24%) than those who quarrelled less than once a week (8%). Similarly, children who quarrelled with their father more than once a week were more than twice as likely to report a high or very high score (22%) than those who quarrelled less than once a week (9%).

Being able to talk to parents about things that matter may be a "protective" factor for children, helping to dampen any detrimental consequences associated with mental ill-health. In 2011 to 2012, those children who talked to their parents more than once a week reported lower average total difficulties scores (10.1 mother, 9.5 father) than children who talked to their parents about things that matter less than once a week (11.3 mother, 11.0 father). The proportion of children who had high or very high total difficulties scores was higher among those who talked to the mother less than once a week compared with those who talked to their mother more than once a week (15% compared with 11%). There was a similar difference in those reporting high or very high total difficulties scores between those who talked with their father less than once a week and those who talked to their father more than once a week (13% compared with 10%).

The regression analysis showed that quarrelling with either parent was more strongly related to total difficulties than talking with either parent, with a higher frequency of quarrelling associated with a higher score. Quarrelling with mother had the strongest relationship with total difficulties scores of the 4 parental relationship variables, and the second strongest of all the variables in the analysis. Quarrelling with father had the next strongest relationship with higher scores. However, talking more frequently with either parent was associated with a lower total difficulties score and talking frequently to father was more strongly related to lower scores than talking frequently to mother.

Research has suggested that children's relationships with their mother and fathers can vary according to the gender of the child (Russell & Saebel, 1997). We investigated if the 4 parental relationship variables interacted with sex of the child by running two more regression analyses; one analysis for the "talking to mother or father about things that matter" variables and one for the "quarrelling with mother or father" variables. These analyses revealed no differences between boys or girls in the association between quarrelling with either parent and total difficulties scores. However, there were differences between boys and girls for the associations between talking with parents and total difficulties scores. Talking frequently with fathers reduced total difficulties scores for both boys and girls, whereas talking frequently with mothers was only significantly related to lower total difficulties scores for girls.

Body image

Poor body image has been found to be negatively associated with self-esteem and depression, particularly amongst teenage girls. Siegel et al.'s study of American teenagers found that there was a difference between girls and boys body image, self-esteem and depression levels and the more positive a child's body image, the less depressed they were and the higher self-esteem they had. Furthermore, they found that poor body image accounted for the higher prevalence of depression and low self-esteem amongst girls.

Data from Understanding Society shows that around 1 in 10 children aged 10 to 15 years old are unhappy with their appearance (11% in 2011 to 2012 and 10% in 2012 to 2013). The proportion of girls reporting that they are unhappy with their appearance is around double that of boys (14% of girls compared with 7% of boys in 2012 to 2013).

Figure 3: Total difficulties score category by happiness with appearance, 2011 to 2012

United Kingdom

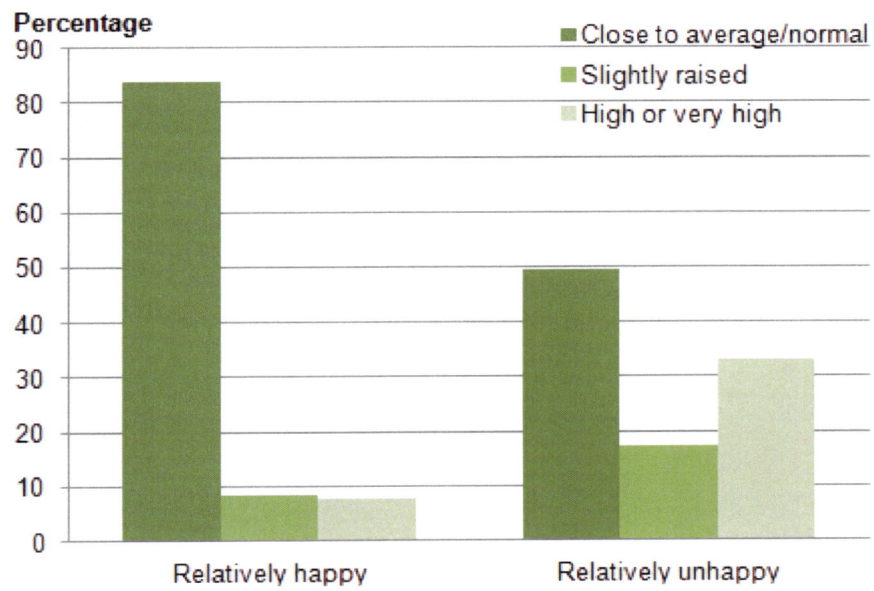

Notes:
1. Source: Understanding Society, the UK Household Longitudinal Study.
2. Children aged 10 to 15 years.

Download chart

 XLS format
(18 Kb)

Children who reported being relatively happy with their appearance in 2011 to 2012 had a lower average total difficulties score (9.5) than those children who were relatively unhappy with their appearance (15.1). Furthermore, those children who were relatively unhappy with their appearance were over 4 times as likely to report high or very high total difficulties scores than children who were relatively happy with their appearance (33% compared with 8%), as shown in Figure 3. The data from Understanding Society showed no significant differences between the average total difficulties scores of boys and girls who were relatively unhappy with their appearance. The regression analysis showed that greater happiness with appearance was associated with lower total difficulties scores, and had the third strongest relationship with total difficulties scores of all the variables analysed. Further analyses indicated that this association did not vary between boys and girls.

Happiness with school

Children spend a significant amount of time at school and their happiness within the school is an important part of their life. It reflects a range of determinants, including peer relationships, academic ability, socioeconomic status, and sporting ability. A study of the Avon Longitudinal Study of Parents and Children looked at pupil and school effects during primary school. It found that different children have different experiences even at the same school, and that for well-being, "child-school" fit is as important as attending a "good" school (Gutman and Feinstein, 2008).

Since 2009 to 2010, around 8 out of 10 children have reported being relatively happy with their school and 1 in 10 reported being relatively unhappy with their school[1]. There is no difference between the proportions of boys and girls reporting being happy or unhappy with their school.

Figure 4: Total difficulties score category by happiness with school, 2011 to 2012

United Kingdom

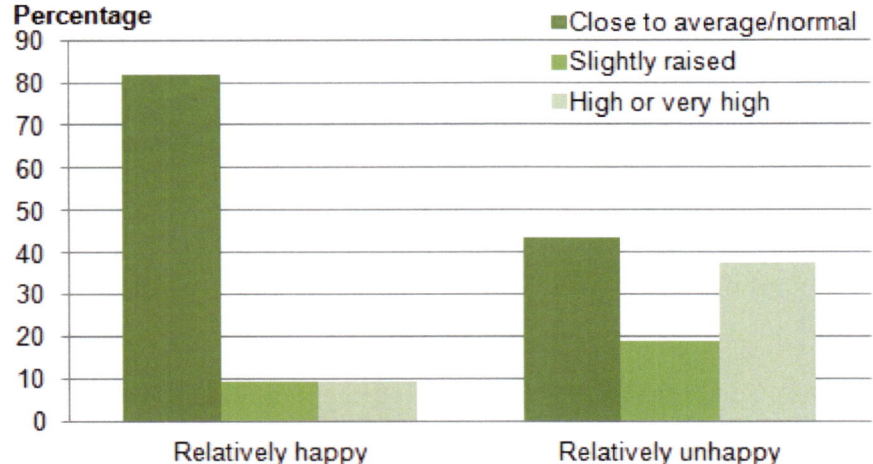

Notes:
1. Source: Understanding Society, the UK Household Longitudinal Study.
2. Children aged 10 to 15 years.

Download chart

 XLS format
(18 Kb)

Children who reported being relatively unhappy with school in the 2011 to 2012 Understanding Society Survey had an average total difficulties score over 50% higher than children who reported being relatively happy with school (16.0 compared with 9.8). Figure 4 illustrates that children who were relatively unhappy with school were over 4 times more likely to report high or very high total difficulties scores than those children who were relatively happy with school (38% compared with 9%). The regression analysis showed that happiness with school was significantly associated with lower total difficulties, and had the fourth strongest relationship with total difficulties scores of the variables tested.

Notes

1.   The remaining 10% reported being 'neither happy nor unhappy' with the school that they go to.

Social media

Social websites are ever-present features of social life, especially for the young. While they may provide an additional way to connect with others and form relationships and thus increase children's mental health, they could also be a source of social comparison, cyber bullying and isolation, reducing children's mental health (Best, Manktelow, & Taylor, 2014). The Public Health England report, How healthy behaviour supports children's well-being, identifies a large body of research that shows a negative association between screen time (including watching television, DVDs and videos) and mental well-being. It also reports that "children who spend more time on computers, watching TV and playing video games tend to experience higher levels of emotional distress, anxiety and depression" and that this is particularly the case for those children spending more than 4 hours a day engaged in those activities.

The Understanding Society survey asks children how much time they spend on social networking websites on a normal school day. Between 2009 to 2010 and 2011 to 2012, the proportion of children spending no time on social networking websites decreased from 38% to 32%. In the same period, the proportion spending up to 3 hours on social networking websites increased from 56% to 61%. However, in the latest wave of the survey (2012 to 2013), these proportions returned to 2009 to 2010 levels, with 37% of children spending no time on social networking websites and 56% spending up to 3 hours.

In 2012 to 2013, around 8% of children spent over 3 hours on social networking websites on a typical school day. Girls were far more likely than boys to spend over 3 hours on social networking websites. In 2012 to 2013, around 1 in 10 girls (11%) spent over 3 hours on social networking websites compared with just 5% of boys.

Figure 5: Total difficulties score category by time spent on social networking websites, 2011 to 2012

United Kingdom

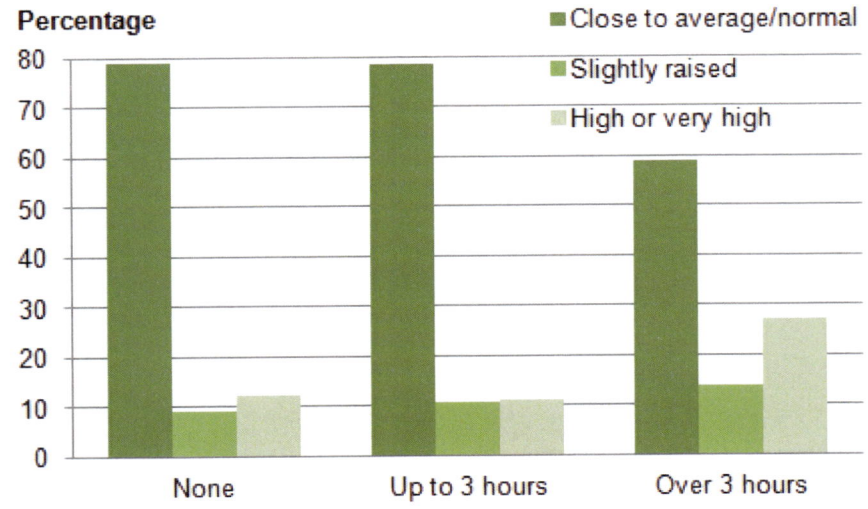

Notes:
1.   Source: Understanding Society, the UK Household Longitudinal Study.

2. Children aged 10 to 15 years.

Download chart

`XLS` XLS format
(18.5 Kb)

Analysis of the 2011 to 2012 total difficulties scores of children grouped by "time spent on social websites on a normal school day" also shows that there is a clear association between longer time on social websites and higher total difficulties scores. There was no difference in average scores for children who spent up to 3 hours on a social website compared with those who did not use them (10.5 compared with 10.2). However, those children who spent more than 3 hours on social websites on a normal school day reported significantly higher total difficulties scores (13.3) than either those who did not use social websites or who spent less time on them. Looking at the proportions of children in each category, shown in Figure 5, the association becomes even more apparent. Of those children who spent more than 3 hours on a social website on a normal school day, around 27% reported high or very high total difficulties scores. This is more than double the proportion of those children spending no time on social websites on a normal school day (12%) and the proportion spending up to 3 hours a day on a social website (11%). The regression analysis also showed that spending more time on social websites was associated with a higher total difficulties score.

Conclusion

Mental ill-health is an important area of children's well-being that is affected by a variety of factors. Of the well-being measures available from the Understanding Society survey, bullying and quarrelling with mothers had the strongest associations with mental ill-health. These results are consistent with findings from academic research and previous national surveys of children's mental ill-health. Future analysis could utilise the longitudinal aspect of the Understanding Society survey to see how total difficulties scores change as children move into and out of poor peer and familial relationships.

Appendix A

Table 1: Estimates from ordinary least squares regression analyses

Variable	β	t	p	b	SE of b	95% confidence interval	
Age	-0.03	-2.14	0.03	-0.11	0.05	-0.20	-0.01
Age squared	0.05	3.53	0.00	0.10	0.03	0.05	0.16
Gender	-0.04	-2.53	0.01	-0.39	0.15	-0.69	-0.09
Bullied, physical or other	0.31	21.51	0.00	2.85	0.13	2.59	3.11
Quarrels with mother	0.19	12.57	0.00	1.06	0.08	0.89	1.22
Quarrels with father	0.08	5.18	0.00	0.46	0.09	0.29	0.64
Time spent on social websites	0.06	4.42	0.00	0.37	0.08	0.21	0.53
Talks with mother	-0.04	-2.44	0.02	-0.20	0.08	-0.35	-0.04
Feel safe in neighbourhood	-0.04	-2.93	0.00	-0.71	0.24	-1.18	-0.23
Talks with father	-0.07	-4.53	0.00	-0.36	0.08	-0.51	-0.20
Feel safe walking alone in the dark	-0.08	-5.42	0.00	-0.48	0.09	-0.65	-0.30
Happiness with school	-0.18	-12.75	0.00	-0.72	0.06	-0.83	-0.61
Happiness with appearance	-0.19	-12.79	0.00	-0.71	0.06	-0.82	-0.60

Table source: Office for National Statistics

Table notes:

1. β Standardized coefficients.
2. *t* t-statistic.
3. *p* 2-tailed signficance.
4. *b* coefficients.
5. **SE of *b*** Standard Error of coefficients.

Download table

XLS **XLS format**
(28 Kb)

All of the variables together explain around 40% of the variation in total difficulties scores among the sample, and each is a statistically significant predictor.

Background notes

1. Author: Rachel Beardsmore.

2. ONS would like to thank Dr. Matthew Easterbrook of the University of Sussex for his work producing the regression analysis included within this report.

3. The Understanding Society survey is a unique and valuable academic study that captures important information every year about the social and economic circumstances and attitudes of people living in 40,000 UK households. It also collects additional health information from around 20,000 of the people who take part. Information from the longitudinal survey is primarily used by academics, researchers and policymakers in their work, but the findings are of interest to a much wider group of people. These include those working in the third sector, health practitioners, business, the media and the general public. The data in this analysis is from the youth self-completion questionnaire module of Waves 1-4 of the survey and has been weighted using the combined cross-sectional youth interview weight.

4. Throughout the bulletin, only statistically significant findings are commented on.

5. Details of the policy governing the release of new data are available by visiting www.statisticsauthority.gov.uk/assessment/code-of-practice/index.html or from the Media Relations Office email: media.relations@ons.gsi.gov.uk

Copyright

www.nationalarchives.gov.uk/doc/open-government-licence/ or write to the Information Policy Team, The National Archives, Kew, London TW9 4DU, or email: psi@nationalarchives.gsi.gov.uk.

This document is also available on our website at www.ons.gov.uk.

References

1. Arsenault, L., Bowes, L., and Shakoor, S., (2010) "Bullying victimization in youths and mental health problems: 'Much ado about nothing'? in Psychological Medicine, 40, 717-729, Cambridge University Press.

2. Hagell A., Coleman J., and Brooks F., (2015) Key Data on Adolescence 2015. London: Association for Young People's Health.

3. Layard, R., Hagell, A., (2015) "Healthy Young Minds: Transforming the mental health of children" in Helliwell, John F., Richard Layard, and Jeffrey Sachs, eds. 2015. World Happiness Report 2015. New York: Sustainable Development Solutions Network.

4. Parkinson, J., (2012) Establishing a core set of national, sustainable mental health indicators for children and young people in Scotland: Final Report, NHS Health Scotland, Edinburgh.

5. Parry-Langdon, N., et. al., (2008) Three years on: Survey of the development and emotional well-being of children and young people, Office for National Statistics.

6. Ryff, C. D., (1989) "Happiness is everything, or is it? Explorations on the meaning of psychological well-being" in Journal of Personality and Social Psychology, Vol 57, No. 6, 1069-1081.

7. Schucksmith, J., et. al., (2009) A critical review of the literature on children and young people's views of the factors that influence their mental health, NHS Health Scotland, Edinburgh.